The Communist Party of China

The Communist Party of China has ruled mainland China since 1949. From Marxist revolution and class struggle to market reforms and national rejuvenation, the Party has repeatedly reinvented itself and its justification for monopolizing political power. Bringing together experts from a range of disciplines around the globe, this collection serves as a guide to understanding the Party's unparalleled durability. They examine a range of themes including the mechanics and organization of one-party rule, the ideologies underpinning party rule, the Party's control of public discourse, technologies of social control, and adaptive policymaking. Read together, these essays provide a comprehensive understanding of the reasons for the Party's continued grip on political power in China today.

Ben Hillman is Director of the Australian Centre on China in the World at the Australian National University.

Fengyuan Ji is Associate Professor at the School of Culture, History and Language in the Australian National University's College of Asia and the Pacific.

The Communist Party of China
Understanding the Durability of the World's Most Powerful Political Organization

Edited by
Ben Hillman
Australian National University

Fengyuan Ji
Australian National University

CAMBRIDGE
UNIVERSITY PRESS

CAMBRIDGE
UNIVERSITY PRESS

Shaftesbury Road, Cambridge CB2 8EA, United Kingdom

One Liberty Plaza, 20th Floor, New York, NY 10006, USA

477 Williamstown Road, Port Melbourne, VIC 3207, Australia

314–321, 3rd Floor, Plot 3, Splendor Forum, Jasola District Centre, New Delhi – 110025, India

103 Penang Road, #05–06/07, Visioncrest Commercial, Singapore 238467

Cambridge University Press is part of Cambridge University Press & Assessment, a department of the University of Cambridge.

We share the University's mission to contribute to society through the pursuit of education, learning and research at the highest international levels of excellence.

www.cambridge.org
Information on this title: www.cambridge.org/9781009668439

DOI: 10.1017/9781009668385

© Cambridge University Press & Assessment 2026

This publication is in copyright. Subject to statutory exception and to the provisions of relevant collective licensing agreements, no reproduction of any part may take place without the written permission of Cambridge University Press & Assessment.

When citing this work, please include a reference to the
DOI 10.1017/9781009668385

First published 2026

Cover image: boonchai wedmakawand / Moment / Getty Images

A catalogue record for this publication is available from the British Library

A Cataloging-in-Publication data record for this book is available from the Library of Congress

ISBN 978-1-009-66843-9 Hardback
ISBN 978-1-009-66842-2 Paperback

Cambridge University Press & Assessment has no responsibility for the persistence or accuracy of URLs for external or third-party internet websites referred to in this publication and does not guarantee that any content on such websites is, or will remain, accurate or appropriate.

For EU product safety concerns, contact us at Calle de José Abascal, 56, 1°, 28003 Madrid, Spain, or email eugpsr@cambridge.org

Contents

List of Figures and Tables		*page* vii
List of Contributors		viii
Acknowledgments		xii
1	The Communist Party of China: Understanding its Durability BEN HILLMAN	1
2	The CPC's Metamorphosis from Class-Based Organization to Nationalist Party YINGJIE GUO	24
3	The Chairman's Long Shadow: Mao Zedong and Mao Zedong Thought in Post-Maoist China MATTHEW GALWAY	42
4	Language, Discourse, and Hegemony FENGYUAN JI	72
5	Patriotic Nationalism as Commodity DELIA LIN	95
6	Manufacturing Consent and "Correct Collective Memory" SHUYU ZHANG	115
7	Neo-Maoist Sticks and Nationalist Carrots: Maintaining Party Cohesion in the New Era FENGMING LU	140
8	Co-opting the Private Sector MINGLU CHEN	174
9	China's Adaptive State Capitalism and Its International Sources WENDY LEUTERT AND SARAH EATON	194

	10	Digital Power: Technological Leadership, Smart Governance, and Ideological Control JOHN LEE AND KATJA DRINHAUSEN	214
	11	Social Stability through Responsive Social Policy BINGQIN LI	242
	12	Dealing with Dissent ANNA HAYES	263
	13	The Party and the Army JI YOU	290
	14	After Xi RICHARD MCGREGOR AND JUDE BLANCHETTE	310
		Index	331

Figures and Tables

Figures

3.1 Poster reproduction of Luo Gongliu's 1951 oil painting *Chairman Mao Reports on the Rectification at the Cadre Meeting in Yan'an* (1985), Zhongyang wenxian chubanshe. Source: Image courtesy of the Stefan R. Landsberger collection, BG E13/108, https://chineseposters.net/posters/e13-108. *page* 62

3.2 Poster reproduction of Liu Chunhua's 1967 oil painting *Chairman Mao en route to Anyuan* (1968), Hebei renmin meishu chubanshe, Beijing. Source: Image courtesy of the International Institute of Social History (IISH) collection, BG E12/703. https://chineseposters.net/posters/e12-703. 63

6.1 Xinhua News Agency: Weibo matrix. 121

6.2 Wuheqilin Cheers on "Fighters in Shanghai." In the picture, he writes, "Shanghai Must Not Fall." 138

Tables

6.1 State-led memory-making through Weibo hot topics hosted by official accounts 135

9.1 Mechanisms through which international engagement can affect domestic policy-making 205

Contributors

Jude Blanchette is Distinguished Tang Chair in China Research and Director of the China Research Center at the RAND Corporation. Previously, he was Freeman Chair in China Studies at the Center for Strategic and International Studies (CSIS). His book, *China's New Red Guards: The Return of Radicalism and the Rebirth of Mao Zedong*, was published by Oxford University Press in 2019.

Minglu Chen is in the discipline of government and international relations and is a member of the Management Committee of the China Studies Centre at the University of Sydney, where she is also Director of the Local China Project. Her research concentrates on social and political change in China, especially the interaction between entrepreneurs and the state, and women's political participation. Her research has been published in *The China Quarterly*, *The China Journal*, *Journal of Contemporary China*, *Journal of East Asian Studies*, and *The Pacific Review*.

Katja Drinhausen heads the Politics & Society research program at the Mercator Institute of China Studies (MERICS). At MERICS, her research focuses on the development of China's legal and governance system, internal control mechanisms and state surveillance as well as political and public discourse in the PRC. Ms. Drinhausen is a co-founder and author of the *Decoding China Dictionary*, an online resource that explains China's official interpretation of key terms in international relations. She previously worked as a researcher and project manager in Beijing. Ms. Drinhausen studied Sinology in Leipzig and Erlangen, and received her LL.M. from China University of Political Science and Law.

Sarah Eaton is Professor of Transregional China Studies at Humboldt University Berlin and co-founder of the Berlin Contemporary China Network. She is interested in the study of contemporary Chinese politics and political economy from comparative and transregional perspectives. Her book, *Advance of the State in Contemporary China* (Cambridge University Press, 2016), analyzed the ideational roots of Chinese state capitalism and the results of her other research have appeared in political science and area studies journals, including *New Political Economy, Review of International Political Economy, Environmental Politics, The China Quarterly*, and the *The China Journal*.

Matthew Galway is Senior Lecturer in Chinese History at the Australian National University. An intellectual and Communist Party historian, he is the author of *The Emergence of Global Maoism: China's Red Evangelism and the Cambodian Communist Movement, 1949–1979* (Cornell University Press, 2022). He is also first editor and contributor to *Experiments with Marxism-Leninism in Cold War Southeast Asia* (ANU Press, 2022). His research has been published in several journals, notably *The Journal of Southeast Asian Studies, Modern Intellectual History*, and *China Information*, and he is a frequent contributor to the *Ear to Asia* podcast. Dr Galway is Editor-in-Chief of *East Asian History* and co-editor of *Asian Ethnicity*, and his current book project is entitled *Agents of Maoism: Overseas Chinese, Communist Spies, and Radicalism in Cambodia's Global Sixties*.

Yingjie Guo is Professor of Chinese Studies at the University of Sydney. His research focuses on China's cultural nationalism and cultural identities, and the discourse of class in the post-Mao era. His recent publications include *Jiaohua: Chinese Ideas and Practices of Moral Transformation*; *Class and the Communist Party of China, 1921–1978: Revolution and Social Change*; *Class and the Communist Party of China, since 1978: China in Reform*; *Unequal China: Political Economy and Culture Politics*; and *Handbook of Class and Stratification in the People's Republic of China*.

Anna Hayes is a senior lecturer in politics and international relations in the College of Arts, Society and Education at James Cook University. She teaches and supervises at undergraduate and postgraduate levels within the field of politics and international relations.

Ben Hillman is Director of the Australian Centre on China in the World (CIW) and Professor in Policy and Governance at the Australian National University. Ben is the author or editor of eight books on China, including *Patronage and Power* (Stanford University Press, 2014), *Conflict and Protest in Tibet and Xinjiang* (Columbia University Press, 2016), and *Political and Social Control in China* (ANU Press,

2024). Ben is Editor of *The China Journal*, a leading China studies journal that is published by the University of Chicago Press.

Fengyuan Ji is Associate Professor at the School of Culture, History and Language in the Australian National University's College of Asia and the Pacific. She has published on linguistic engineering, the relationship of language and thought, Western discourses on China, and the role of language in China from ancient times to the present.

Ji You (BA, Peking University and PhD, Australian National University) is Adjunct Professor in the Department of Government, University of Macau, China. He taught at the Australian National University and University of New South Wales for over two decades. He has authored four books, including *China's Military Transformation* (Polity Press, 2016); and numerous journal articles in leading China journals such as *The China Journal* and the *Journal of Contemporary China*.

John Lee is Director of consultancy East West Futures and a researcher at the Leiden Asia Centre. He is a visiting fellow at ISEAS–Yusof Ishak Institute, National University of Singapore, and was a senior analyst at the Mercator Institute for China Studies. John previously worked at the Australian Department of Foreign Affairs and Trade and Department of Defence. He focuses on China's advanced technology industries, including microelectronics, automotive, telecoms, and internet of things technologies. John's research areas also include China's cyberspace regulation and governance and military applications of artificial intelligence. John coleads the China Semiconductor Observatory project funded by the European Union.

Wendy Leutert is Associate Professor and GLP-Ming Z. Mei Chair of Chinese Economics and Trade at the Hamilton Lugar School of Global and International Studies at Indiana University. Her research focuses on China's politics and economy, specifically the historical evolution and global expansion of China's state-owned enterprises. Her book, *China's State-Owned Enterprises: Leadership, Reform, and Internationalization*, was published by Cambridge University Press in 2024. She holds a PhD in government from Cornell University.

Bingqin Li is Professor at the Social Policy Research Centre at The University of New South Wales and research affiliate with Sydney University Australia and the University of Johannesburg in South Africa. Her research is on social policy and governance with interests on implementing complex social programs, social inclusion and integration, urban governance, and social spending. She has conducted research on disability, aging, housing, volunteering, and public health in China and in Australia. She is now Member of the Executive Committee of Australian Social Policy Association. She is also an associate editor of the *Journal of Urban Governance*.

Delia Lin is Associate Professor in Chinese Studies at the Asia Institute, University of Melbourne. Her current research projects center on ideology, law, education, and social governance in contemporary China, where she draws on a broad range and large amounts of text to chart development of ideas and discourses that support institution building.

Fengming Lu is a lecturer (assistant professor) in the Department of Political and Social Change, Coral Bell School of Asia Pacific Affairs at the Australian National University. Between 2018 and 2020, he was a postdoctoral fellow of the Peking–Princeton Postdoctoral Program (PPPP). He received his PhD in political science at Duke University in 2018. Prior to his stay at Duke, he received his BA in political science from the University of Illinois, Urbana-Champaign.

Richard McGregor is Senior Fellow for North Asia at the Lowy Institute. McGregor is a former Beijing and Washington bureau chief for the *Financial Times* and the author of numerous books on East Asia. His book, *The Party* (Penguin Books, 2010), on the inner workings of the Chinese Communist Party, was translated into seven languages. His book on Sino-Japanese relations, *Asia's Reckoning: China, Japan and the Fate of U.S. Power in the Pacific Century* (Penguin Books, 2017), was called "shrewd and knowing" by the *Wall Street Journal* and the "best book of the year" by the *Literary Review* in the United Kingdom. His most recent book, *Xi Jinping: The Backlash*, was published by Penguin Australia in August 2019.

Shuyu Zhang has a PhD from the ANU School of Literature, Languages and Linguistics. Coming from a journalism and linguistics background, she writes on Chinese internet language, online discourse and censorship, and the media landscape in China.

Acknowledgments

We are indebted to the Australian Centre on China in the World in the College of Asia and the Pacific at the Australian National University for supporting this project from its inception through to fruition. We're also grateful to the Cambridge University Press team for their tremendous efforts in shepherding this volume into production, and to anonymous reviewers for their excellent suggestions. Special thanks are also due to the volume's expert contributors for sharing their expertise on such an important topic, and for their perseverance during the multiple rounds of review and editing.

1 The Communist Party of China
Understanding its Durability

Ben Hillman

The Communist Party of China (CPC) is arguably the strongest and most successful political party in the world today. The CPC has ruled China since 1949, which makes it the world's second-longest-ruling party. The length of its rule is surpassed – by only one year – by the Democratic People's Party of North Korea, which has much less to boast about. When the CPC won the civil war against the Nationalists and established the People's Republic of China (PRC) in 1949, China was an agrarian nation with a population of 540 million, only 12 percent of whom lived in urban areas, and a per capita gross domestic product (GDP) of just over US$600.[1] In the decades since, and notably after the party embraced economic reform and opening up to the world in the late 1970s, the party has steered the country's dramatic transformation from a peasant society into a modern, urbanized industrial powerhouse. China's population has more than doubled to 1.4 billion, of which nearly 65 percent now live in urban areas. Its per capita GDP in 2024 was above US$12,000, making China the second-largest economy in the world.[2] The country's remarkable economic development, particularly in the decades after Mao, has lifted hundreds of millions from poverty and propelled hundreds of millions more into the ranks of the middle classes. On the back of its economic might, the CPC is now overseeing China's rise as a global power and consequential actor in international affairs. That makes the story of the party's durability – its secrets and its challenges – essential reading for anyone interested in contemporary China and its role in the world.

There are many excellent books on the CPC, dealing with its structure and its governing strategies.[3] There are also volumes that

---

[1] www.nationmaster.com/country-info/stats/Economy/GDP-per-capita-in-1950.
[2] https://data.worldbank.org/indicator/NY.GDP.PCAP.CD?locations=CN. If adjusted for purchasing power parity (PPP) – i.e., taking into account the relative costs of goods, China's economy became the world's largest in 2013.
[3] Bruce Dickson, *The Party and the People: Chinese Politics in the 21st Century* (Princeton, NJ: Princeton University Press, 2021); Richard McGregor, *The Party: The Secretive World of China's Communist Rulers*, 2nd ed. (UK: Penguin, 2012).

examine the evolution of the party during the hundred years since its founding.[4] All of these works provide important insights into the history and contemporary operations of the world's most powerful political organization. This book complements such volumes by focusing systematically on two key questions: How has the CPC succeeded in monopolizing political power in China throughout multiple decades of profound social and economic change? And how did a revolutionary party of class struggle evolve to govern the world's largest economy (in purchasing-power terms) while maintaining popular legitimacy? The party's multidecade durability defies simple explanation. Each of the essays in this book examines a different dimension of the durability of CPC rule. Read together, the chapters provide a comprehensive understanding of the reasons for the CPC's unassailable monopoly on political power in China today. This introductory essay provides an overview of the sources of CPC strength and outlines the rich contents of this volume.

The book's chapters are organized around four aspects of party durability: (i) ideology and discourse, (ii) organization, (iii) co-optation and policy responsiveness, and (iv) coercion. The first chapters examine the ideological and discursive basis of the party's strength – that is, its formidable capacity to shape Chinese citizens' understanding of the party's historical role in leading the country from past humiliation to future glory. The second set of chapters analyzes the organizational strength of the party – how the CPC has built a modern and professional administrative apparatus to carry out its agenda and secure its grip on power. The third set of chapters explains how the party has won popular support by co-opting partners and by delivering policies that meet most people's evolving expectations, particularly those of the growing middle classes. The fourth set reviews the party's capacity to crush dissent and any shoots of political opposition, which is reinforced by an expansive domestic security apparatus and the party's direct control of the military. The final chapter examines an inherent weakness of one-party rule and a future threat to the party's durability – the problem of leadership succession.

---

[4] Tony Saich, *From Rebel to Ruler: One Hundred Years of the Chinese Communist Party* (Cambridge, MA: Harvard University Press, 2021); Timothy Cheek, Klaus Mühlhahn, and Hans van de Ven, *The Chinese Communist Party: A Century in Ten Lives* (Cambridge: Cambridge University Press, 2021). See also the special issue of the *China Quarterly* edited by Patricia Thornton, entitled *The CCP at 100: The Party's New Long March* (volume 248; November 2021).

Ideology and Discourse

A key feature of the party's endurance over more than seven decades of profound change, including radical changes in the party's governing strategies, has been its ability to adapt its ruling ideology to suit the times. According to official party history, CPC rule since 1949 can be divided into three distinct periods: the period of "socialist revolution and construction" (the Maoist period), the period of "reform and opening up" (the Dengist period), and the "new era of socialism with Chinese characteristics" (the Xi Jinping era). According to the party's 2021 Historical Resolution, an important document that harnesses the past to serve the present, the period of socialist revolution and construction began with the party's victory over nationalist forces and imperialists, allowing the Chinese people to "stand up." Following victory, the party's purpose was to "carry out socialist revolution, promote socialist construction, and lay down the fundamental political conditions and the institutional foundations necessary for national rejuvenation." The party acknowledges that mistakes were made during this period, notably the Great Leap Forward and the people's commune movement, which failed to bring about economic progress, and the Cultural Revolution (1966–1976), which "brought disaster to the country and the people." According to the official narrative, the party corrected course in the years following Mao Zedong's death in 1976, ushering in a new period that prioritized economic development over ideological dogma. According to the historical resolution, "the party came to recognize that the only way forward was to launch a program of reform and opening up; otherwise, our endeavors in pursuing modernization and building socialism would be doomed to failure." In the period of reform and opening, the party would build the national economy and bring moderate prosperity to the people by introducing market forces and retreating from centralized economic planning. The party packaged its ideological shift as "socialism with Chinese characteristics" (*you Zhongguo tese de shehuizhuyi*). This new mantra, which remains the party's bedrock principle to this day, allowed "socialism" to be infused with a variety of characteristics that suited the needs of the time, including the embrace of markets and private enterprise, which were once anathema to the party. China, according to party theorists, was still in the primary stage of socialism and needed to grow its industrial base before it could resume the journey toward communism. According to the party's constitution, "the highest ideal of communism pursued by Chinese Communists can be realized only when socialist society is fully developed and highly advanced." The transition to communism – a concept the party's constitution does not define – would be postponed, as the current period of socialist modernization would "take at least a century."[5]

As Yingjie Guo observes in his essay in this volume "Nationalism as a New Source of Strength" (Chapter 2), the party's ideological adaptability has been a key pillar of its durability. Most important, Guo notes, is the party's successful reorientation from a (Marxist) party prosecuting class struggle on behalf of workers and peasants into a (nationalist) party representing the interests of the entire population. Although nationalism was interwoven into the party's earliest doctrines and struggles, notably in the party's promise to rescue the nation from the humiliation wrought by foreign imperialism, Guo shows us how the party has transformed itself from "an exclusive class party to an inclusive national party that seeks to forge a common identification with a nation in the pursuit of national rejuvenation."

Although Guo argues that Marxism has been turned into an "empty signifier" that the party has sinicized out of existence, this should not be taken to mean that Marxist-Leninist ideology and Mao Zedong Thought are no longer relevant today. On the contrary, the CPC's interpretation of Marxism-Leninism serves to justify China's statist model of political economy, its interventions in Chinese social life, and its suppression of dissent. And the party still celebrates the achievements of Mao Zedong, chief protagonist of the Communist revolution and engineer-in-chief of the class struggles of the party's first era, because those achievements belong to the party and sustain its revolutionary legitimacy. This is why, despite the party's reversal of Maoist doctrine, the party leadership demands adherence to Xi Jinping's edict of the "two must not negates" (*liangge buneng fouding*). According to this edict, the Maoist period must not be criticized from the present standpoint since it laid the foundations for socialist modernization. And, in a warning to present-day leftists, the Mao era (of radical socialism) must not be harnessed to negate the present period (of recalibrated "socialism with Chinese characteristics"). Which is to say, no matter how much the party has changed course, never accuse it of forsaking its commitment to the revolutionary cause.

Just as his giant portrait towers over Tiananmen Square, Mao Zedong still looms large for the party because his contribution to its historical narrative is crucial. Mao is the spiritual progenitor of the party's original mission – a supreme ancestor in a nation of ancestor worshippers. Mao is to the party as the Yellow Emperor is to the Chinese people in popular historical mythology. In his essay "Mao's Long Shadow" (Chapter 3),

---

[5] For an English-language translation of the CPC's constitution see: http://english.www.gov.cn/news/topnews/202210/26/content_WS635921cdc6d0a757729e1cd4.html.

Matthew Galway offers a detailed explanation of Mao Zedong's significance for the continuation of CPC rule in China today. He also shows how Mao's ideas continue to serve as an "ideological system" (*sixiang tixi*) for party rule. This system consists of ideological principles, a framework for analyzing political threats, and a vocabulary for waging political struggle against enemies near and far. As today's party leaders reinterpret Mao and reprogram his thought into "socialism with Chinese characteristics for a New Era," Galway reminds us that the elasticity of "ever malleable" Maoism has always been a source of party power, including in Mao's own time. Malleable Maoism, helped by Mao's varied writings and his own changes in thinking over the decades, can be plundered and repurposed to suit the times.

The party's ability to legitimate its rule through ideological reinvention is made possible by its domination of public discourse in China. The party exercises creative control over the terminology used in China's public spaces, including online, to explain the party's role and policies and to discuss and interpret social, economic, and political phenomena. In her essay "Language, Discourse, and Hegemony" (Chapter 4), the linguist Fengyuan Ji explains how the party draws on practices of linguistic engineering that date back thousands of years to legitimate its rule. As she notes, Confucius advised that a ruler's first task is to regulate terminology. For Confucius, "correct" terminology supported a shared and correct perception of reality: "If the names are not correct, if they do not match realities, language has no object. If language is without an object, action becomes impossible – and therefore all human affairs disintegrate and their management becomes pointless and impossible."[6] Language was the basis for social harmony and good government. During the Mao era, the party introduced new terminology to motivate people to participate in class struggle. Specific language formulations were developed to glorify members of good (revolutionary) classes and vilify those from bad classes. The bad classes of "landlords" and "rich peasants" were joined by "Counterrevolutionaries," "Rightists," and "Bad Elements" in the "Five Black Categories" (*hei wulei*). As is common among enemy combatants in war, the party used language that dehumanized its political enemies, smoothing the path for it to mobilize others against them – they were "cow demons and snake spirits" (*niugui sheshen*), for example, a phrase borrowed from the ancient literary classic *Journey to the West*. Although the party today eschews the language of class struggle, it continues to weaponize language to target and eliminate threats. Such

---

[6] *The Analects of Confucius*, tr. Simon Leys (New York: Norton, 1997), xxvi; cited in Fengyuan Ji, "Language, Discourse, and Hegemony" (Chapter 4, this volume).

language appears in political campaigns such as in the "Campaign to Sweep Away Black and Eliminate Evil," a nationwide campaign from 2018 to 2020 against organized crime, corrupt local officials, and other "flies," or party-identified deviants.[7]

Fengyuan Ji reminds us how the party's ideological dexterity is underpinned by continual linguistic engineering – work carried out by armies of wordsmiths working within the party's Publicity (formerly Propaganda) Department, which oversees the media and other party agencies such as the Central Party School and the Party Research Office. Following Mao's death and the determination of the second generation of party leaders to dismantle the collectives and introduce market reforms, the party scoured Mao's sayings for words and phrases that could be used to legitimize the shift in policy directions. As noted earlier, Deng Xiaoping, for example, repurposed Mao's mantra to "seek truth from facts" to support more practical market-oriented reforms. Each successive leadership generation introduces new phraseology that is grounded in or connected to older terminology to maintain a semblance of ideological continuity (and thereby seamless historical legitimacy) even if the practical meanings represent a significant break with the past.

An important example of the party's linguistic inventiveness can be seen when the party decided in the late 1990s to recruit private entrepreneurs into its ranks (and thus become a truly nationalist party, as Guo notes in Chapter 4, rather than a party of workers and peasants). That step, inconceivable in Mao's day, was authorized and legitimized by Jiang Zemin's formulation of "the three represents" (*sange daibiao*), which states that the party must represent (i.e., incorporate) the nation's "advanced productive forces" (entrepreneurs and managers), "China's advanced culture" (intellectuals and creative industry workers), and "the overwhelming interests of the Chinese people" (others previously excluded from the party's ranks).[8] Importantly, linguistic engineering also helps the party to control its own narrative, including its role in history and destined leadership into the future. China's leaders and their theoreticians today believe that one of the reasons the Communist Party of the Soviet Union collapsed was that the Soviets lost control of the narrative, especially in the period of *glasnost* (transparency) under Gorbachev, when people were allowed to openly discuss the horrors of the Stalinist period. Party leaders do not want any such reevaluation of Maoist catastrophes such as the Great Famine and Cultural Revolution.

---

[7] Ben Hillman, "Law, Order and Social Control in Xi's China," *Issues and Studies* 57(2) (June 2021): https://doi.org/10.1142/S1013251121500065.

[8] CPC General Secretary Jiang Zemin first proposed the theory of the "three represents" in 2000. The party ratified the theory at its sixteenth national party congress in 2002.

The party has even coined a term to remind citizens of the correct way to think about the party-state. To engage in criticism of the party, especially its past mistakes, or even to discuss them openly, is to engage in "historical nihilism," which a leaked communiqué equated to denying the CPC's legitimacy as China's long-term rulers.[9]

The party now presents itself as the savior and custodian of Chinese civilization, even though the party repudiated traditional Chinese culture during its rise and in the first period of its rule. At the start of the Cultural Revolution in 1966, Mao Zedong called for the destruction of the "four olds" (old customs, old culture, old habits, old ideas), mobilizing red guards to destroy cultural artifacts, literature, and temples. Red guards even exhumed and mutilated the corpse of a descendant of Confucius in a symbolic act of denigration toward China's best-known philosopher.[10] The party now presents itself as the custodian of Chinese civilization and pays close attention to how China's past (and the party's role in it) is understood. By shaping the linguistic framework for talking and writing about, and therefore understanding, Chinese culture and history, the party retains control of the narrative. In July 2022, Xi Jinping published an essay in the party's flagship academic journal *Seeking Truth* (*Qiushi*) titled "Advancing research on the history of Chinese civilization, and developing a keener awareness of history while building up cultural confidence."[11] In the essay, which was a summary of a speech he gave to the Politburo in May that year, Xi expounded on ideas related to cultural nationalism and the party's role in guiding the country along its unique development path toward national rejuvenation. To consolidate correct thinking on the origins of China's civilization and the party's role as its savior, Xi called for a "discourse system" to sit alongside the nation's academic and "disciplinary" systems. Together, the systems would foster and promote historical and developmental narratives that countered Western social and political theories and discourse.

Xi tasked the discourse system with providing a comprehensive lexicon for such correct thinking. The academic system was to provide its evidentiary base: an increasing variety of academic centers (and not just Party

---

[9] See China File for an English-language translation of Document Number Nine (2012): www.chinafile.com/document-9-chinafile-translation.

[10] For further reading on the Cultural Revolution, see Joseph W. Esherick, Paul G. Pickowicz, and Andrew Walder (eds.), *The Cultural Revolution as History* (Palo Alto, CA: Stanford University Press, 2006); and Frank Dikköter, *The Cultural Revolution: A People's History 1962–1976* (London: Bloomsbury, 2016).

[11] Xi Jinping, "Ba Zhongguo wenmin lishi yanjiu yin xiang shenru, zengqiang lishi zijue jianding wenhua zixin" [Advancing research on the history of Chinese civilization and developing a keener awareness of history while building up cultural confidence], *Seeking Truth* (*Qiushi*) (July 2002). www.qstheory.cn/dukan/qs/2022–07/15/c_1128830256.htm.

Schools) have been mobilized to give scholarly credence to party dogma, including seventeen research centers dedicated to the study of Xi Jinping Thought, which represents the current ideological consensus. The discipline system, meanwhile, ensures that party officials and other thought leaders, including teachers, writers, and public intellectuals, maintain the correct line of thinking, forming a bulwark against the threats posed by Western liberal thought. According to Xi, if allowed to spread, Western liberal thought can corrupt minds and lead to "peaceful evolution" (demands for political liberalization). Xi and many among the party leadership believe that "peaceful evolution" contributed to the demise of the Soviet Union and facilitated the emergence of "colour revolutions" in post-Soviet Eurasia as well as the Middle East and Africa.[12]

In her essay "Patriotism as Commodity" (Chapter 5), Delia Lin notes that the party promotes a form of patriotism that embraces China's cultural heritage (narrowly interpreted) and the party's revolutionary history (carefully narrated) – fusing, as Yingjie Guo also points out, political and cultural nationalism into a "red nationalism." Delia Lin highlights the powerful reach of red nationalism in China today by showing how entrepreneurs, artists, filmmakers, and media commentators increasingly commodify and market such forms of patriotism in China's freewheeling market economy. Lin argues that they do so because it is politically safe and because "red-nationalist" products appeal to a growing appetite for narratives of China's return to glory. Lin notes that "loving China" is a huge industry involving websites and social media accounts as well as movies such as the *Wolf Warrior* franchise, in which a Rambo-like solider rescues Chinese citizens from dangerous international situations. Just as Mao Zedong was a master at connecting passion to politics, Delia Lin reminds us that the Communist Party continues to excel in manipulating feelings "as part of a conscious strategy of psychological engineering."[13] By commodifying red nationalism, party, nation, and profit become intertwined in people's everyday lives. Loving the country becomes synonymous with loving the party, which becomes synonymous with entrepreneurial possibility. In this way China's new entrepreneurial class has been mobilized to promote the party's interests across a wide range of popular media and consumer products.

---

[12] Titus C. Chen, "China's Reactions to the Color Revolutions: Adaptive Authoritarianism in Full Swing," *Asian Perspectives* 34(2) (2010): 5–51.

[13] See also Elizabeth Perry, "Moving the Masses: Emotion Work in the Chinese Revolution," *Mobilization* 7(2) (2002): 111–128 (122).

Organization

The party's ability to control discourse within China is underpinned by a strong party organization. The party's Publicity Department sets policies and guidelines for the media and oversees the internet. It sends out daily instructions to media outlets about which topics and terms are encouraged and which are *verboten*. It also licenses all media agencies and internet companies, including popular social media enterprises such as WeChat, Weibo, and Douyin (TikTok), and credentials, registers, and trains journalists. The Publicity Department has evolved from an organ of political propaganda into a formidable and sophisticated thought-policing machine. Its sophistication can be seen in its growing coordination of online discussion, where it acts not just as censor, but as an active player in shaping public opinion and popular narratives. Former journalist Shuyu Zhang explores the growing power of the CPC Publicity Department in her essay in this volume, "Manufacturing Consent and 'Correct Collective Memory': Digital Propaganda and Participatory Censorship" (Chapter 6). Zhang shows how the party shapes online debates by mobilizing media outlets, influencers, and key opinion leaders to sing from the party's song sheets. Zhang's case study focuses on Weibo (China's Twitter/X), where official accounts and patriotic individuals converge to tell a good China story (*jianghao Zhongguogushi*) that reflects the party's talking points. The party employs an army of online commentators, estimated to number as many as 500,000, to reinforce official positions and officially sanctioned perspectives and to promote unity and stability. Critics sometimes refer to the army as the "50 cent army" or the "50 cent party," which is a reference to the payments posters receive for their contributions.

Zhang reminds us that the party's domination of the online space is not just because of the paid "army," but because the party has been able to mobilize patriotic volunteers to boost approved content and crowd out competing voices. As Zhang explains, online patriots, affectionately known as "little pinks" (*xiao fenhong*), "are a burgeoning population of young Chinese netizens who voluntarily consume and promulgate fervent nationalist rhetoric, traditionally propelled by Chinese political elites to promote CPC legitimacy." Following Lin, Zhang highlights the party's capacity to harness youth passions to bolster its legitimacy and promote its political agenda to domestic and international audiences.

The Publicity Department is one of the party's three key departments. The other two are the Organization Department and the United Front Work Department.[14] The Organization Department oversees party-state

---

[14] In 2023, the party created a new Department of Social Work (*shehui gongzuobu*) to handle public petitions and manage public grievances. The department also oversees grassroots

personnel, including the appointment and promotion of party and government leaders, and the United Front Work Department oversees non-party social, cultural, religious, and economic associations and influential public figures to ensure such actors are aligned with and not antagonistic to the party's agenda. The role of each of these departments as key organizational weapons of the party will be discussed, in turn, but let us first review the overall structure of the party and its relationship to the state.

The party center (*dang zhongyang*) resembles a pyramid structure with the General Secretary and the seven-member Standing Committee of the Politburo at the top. The Standing Committee is a secretive body that meets regularly to discuss the top political issues of the day, but the content of its meetings is not publicized. The Standing Committee is part of a larger twenty-five-member Politburo, which meets monthly to discuss major policy concerns, and its meeting agendas are often made public. The Politburo sits within an even-larger Central Committee, which meets approximately once a year in a more publicly transparent plenum, and whose 205 full members and 171 alternate members represent the party's central and regional leaders as well as the military elite.[15] The Central Committee nominally elects the members of the Politburo, including the General Secretary, but the results of the elections are predetermined by the party's top leaders. During previous administrations, retired party elders would play a role in top appointments. However, such consultations have disappeared during Xi Jinping's tenure, as revolutionary party elders have died and as Xi concentrated decision-making authority in his own hands. At the twentieth party congress held in October 2022, Xi Jinping ensured that the Standing Committee and Politburo were stacked with people loyal to him.

The Central Committee and its senior executive offices, the Politburo and Politburo Standing Committee, constitute the party center where all high-level political and policy decisions are taken. The Committee operates according to the Leninist principle of "democratic centralism," which allows for internal debate but requires members to fall in line behind any decision taken by the party's leaders. The Central Committee rarely criticizes policy proposals from top leaders but will sometimes recommend minor adjustments. As the party's highest organ of authority, its primary function is to legitimize top-level decisions.

Since the Central Committee meets only once a year, its work is administered by a permanent General Office. Under the General Office

---

governance and party building in private enterprises. See Jane Cai, "China Seeks to Tighten Grip with New Social Work Department," *South China Morning Post*, March 17, 2023.

[15] Alternate members (*houbuweiyuan*) of the Central Committee do not have voting rights; they are considered full members-in-waiting.

sits the powerful Central Discipline Inspection Committee, which polices the integrity of Party and government officials, the Policy Research Office, which is responsible for developing the party's ideology and theories and drafting high-level policy proposals, and the Central Party School and Executive Leadership Academies, which train party leaders. The Central Committee also oversees the work of the party's permanent departments including the Publicity (Propaganda) Department, the Organization Department, and the United Front Work Department.

The party carries out much of its political work through its own departments, but it governs the state through its wider control of government agencies, the military, state-owned enterprises (SOEs) and other public institutions such as universities, and the media. The party sets strategy and policy priorities at the top in a system that has come to be known under Xi Jinping as "top-level design" (*dingceng sheji*). The party uses coordinating bodies known as leadership small groups (*lingdao xiaozu*) to develop guiding principles (*fangzhen*) for policy development. Implementing agencies then develop strategies and plans for putting policies into action. Party leaders have long used leading small groups as a vehicle of political power. Xi Jinping has expanded his personal influence by chairing the most important leading small groups, which are known as "commissions." These include the National Security Commission, which coordinates all aspects of domestic and international security (with military representation) and the Central Commission for Comprehensive Deepening of Reform, which Xi Jinping created as a mechanism for overseeing reforms across all areas of politics, economics, and social affairs.

Party policies will sometimes be codified in laws produced by the National People's Congress, but party policies set the bureaucracy in motion even without legislation. The party governs by managing the appointments and promotions of all leading cadres (*lingdao ganbu*), which includes all cadres serving at the level of county deputy and above (ranks one to nineteen out of twenty-nine civil service ranks). Leading cadres include not only party and government leaders, but also managers and administrators in SOEs) media organizations, universities, and other party-controlled agencies such as the Communist Youth League, the Women's Federation, and the All China Federation of Commerce and Industry. The party, through its village branches, now also determines the leaders (*cun zhuren*) of China's nearly 700,000 villages.[16] The party manages its estimated two million leading cadres through its Organization Department,

---

[16] Ben Hillman, "Shouldering the Burden: The Communist Party's Deepening Penetration into Village China," *China Quarterly* (2025), 1–15, https://doi.org/10.1017/S0305741025000232.

keeping detailed dossiers on all personnel and implementing a system of reward and punishment based on routine performance evaluations.[17] Evaluations routinely assess political loyalty and diligence in implementing the party's agenda.

Dossiers (*dang'an*) are kept on all personnel and contain a wide range of information, including physical attributes, school reports, supervisors' appraisals, membership of clubs and organizations, and "political history." Missteps follow people through their entire careers. The party also maintains control over officials through the powerful Central Discipline Inspection Commission (CDIC). The party's power to discipline and punish officials whose livelihoods depend on their careers has been a critical pillar of party durability. The CDIC investigates malfeasance and prescribes punishments ranging from expulsion from the party to criminal charges. Punishable infringements include failure to "conform with the party on major principles" (Article 44), "organizing secret groups within the party" (Article 48), "cultivating private power within the party" (Article 49), and "mocking the Party Central Committee's major directives and policies" (Article 46).[18]

Perhaps the most devastating weapon in the party's disciplinary arsenal is the extrajudicial detention system known as *liuzhi*, which means "retention in custody" but is still commonly referred to by the system's older, terror-inducing name, *shuanggui*. *Shuanggui* means "double designation": a person must report to a designated place at a designated time after which they will disappear into interrogation for an unspecified amount of time. The main purpose of *liuzhi*, which is undertaken outside of any judicial process, is to extract confessions and information that implicates other wrongdoers.

Despite the formidable capabilities of the discipline system, which have expanded during the Xi era, informal practices within the party-state have periodically constrained the party's centralized control of its officials. During the early reform era, the party decentralized its operations as part of its wider effort to stimulate growth and investment. The expansion of markets and private business created conditions in which party and government officials, who controlled land, licenses, and access to finance, could enrich themselves in collusion with the new class of entrepreneurs. Many officials became entrepreneurs themselves, setting up businesses in the names of family members to win government contracts or to invest in

---

[17] Nonleading cadres within government and other public agencies are managed by those agencies' human resource departments.

[18] For an English-language translation of the CPC Regulations on Party Disciplinary Action, see www.chinalawtranslate.com/en/2018-chinese-communist-party-disciplinary-regulations.

lucrative new opportunities that their access to internal information enabled them to identify.[19] Corruption became especially rampant during the 1990s and 2000s as China's economy boomed. As officials became more interested in lining their pockets than serving a higher cause, some in the party started to fret about the threat of corruption to party legitimacy and to the party's integrity as a governing organization. Throughout Chinese history, runaway corruption has been considered a portent of regime decay.[20]

By the time Xi Jinping came to power, it appeared the party elites had determined that something needed to be done to rein in corruption and rebuild dedication to the party's cause. Xi Jinping launched an expansive anticorruption campaign in his first term (2012–2017). This was accompanied by expanded party control over disciplinary agencies and increased training and testing requirements for party officials. As Fengming Lu explains in his essay in this volume, "Maoist Sticks and Nationalist Carrots: How the CPC Maintains Party Cohesion in the New Era" (Chapter 7), Xi came to power determined to ensure that party officials took the party organization seriously. Not being corrupt was not enough. Fengming Lu cites an unpublished speech Xi gave to the CPC Central Committee. In it he stated:

Some [party officials] go their own ways, overtly obeying but covertly disobeying, some are irresponsive to command and issue groundless criticism of the Party Central, etc. Some of them are extremely bold and reckless! Those problems often do not get the attention of regional and departmental Party organizations. Even if they pay attention to those problems, they do not punish those acts according to party regulations and state laws. That is wrong, and we must correct it.

The Xi administration has also sought to foster internal cohesion through positive incentives. Xi exhorts cadres to "not forget the [party's] original aspiration" (*buwang chuxin*). Cadres are encouraged to rally around the party's past achievements and harness the spirit of the revolution to achieve greater glories. Ahead of the party's centenary celebrations in 2021, the CPC promoted "the spiritual genealogy of the Chinese Communists" (*Zhongguo gongchandangren jingshen puxi*), which, as Fengming Lu notes, covers ninety-one different motivational "spirits" including the "Spirit of the Jiangxi Soviet,"[21] the "Spirit of fighting COVID-19," and the "Spirit of the women's volleyball team" – China's

---

[19] See Ben Hillman, *Patronage and Power: Local State Networks and Party-State Resilience in Rural China* (Palo Alto, CA, Stanford University Press, 2014).
[20] Minxin Pei, *China's Crony Capitalism: The Dynamics of Regime Decay* (Cambridge, MA: Harvard University Press, 2016).
[21] The Jiangxi Soviet was a large base area during the early years of the Communist revolution (1930s). It was the location of the first Chinese Soviet Republic (1930–1934) and the

most successful national sports team.[22] A related concept to "spirit" is "struggle" (*douzheng*), which, freed from its earlier class connotations, indicates the unified determination party members must possess to fulfill the party's historical mission. Fengming Lu observes that the "spirit of struggle" or "daring to struggle" is also identified as one of the ninety-one Communist "spirits."

As noted above, party members are required to speak, write and internalize the "party line." Although it is difficult to measure the extent to which this succeeds, during the Xi era party members are required to frequently demonstrate their knowledge of and fealty toward party values and priorities. Most of China's 4.8 million party branches hold meetings twice a week, and attendance is now mandatory. Party schools also provide regular and intensive training sessions for party officials at every level of government.[23] The party also fosters cohesion through continuous mobilization of its members via political campaigns in which party officials must work together to achieve political goals such as promoting "socialist core values," eliminating "black and evil forces," or struggling against "peaceful evolution." At a more granular level, party branches organize various activities that promote solidarity and shared purpose. These include "party theme days" (*zhuti dangri*) at which branch members discuss Xi Jinping's speeches or watch official documentaries before engaging in community service such as rubbish collection. Such activities are not new, but they have been reinvigorated under Xi Jinping, who has sought to strengthen the party organization and esprit de corps. Alibaba Group, one of China's largest tech companies, developed an app called "study to strengthen China" (*xuexi qiangguo*), but the app's name is a pun that can also be understood to mean "learn from Xi to strengthen China." The app offers courses on political ideology and access to documentaries on the history of the CPC. A key feature of the app is a weekly quiz on the party and Xi Jinping's life and thought for which study points can be earned. Party members and students are strongly encouraged to download and use the app.

Within every government agency is a party group or committee, which ensures that decisions, expenditure, and activities are in line

---

starting point of the Red Army's Long March (1934–1935) – both significant events in party history and folklore.

[22] "*Zhongguo gongchandangren jingshen puxi diyipi weida jingshen zhengshi fabu*" [The first batch of great spirits of the spiritual genealogy of the Chinese Communists is formally released], *Xinhua She* [Xinhua News Agency], September 29, 2021. www.gov.cn/xinwen/2021–09/29/content_5640143.htm.

[23] Gang Tian and Wen-Hsuan Tsai, "Ideological Education and Practical Training at a County Party School: Shaping Local Governance Contemporary China," *The China Journal* 85 (2021): 1–25.

with party priorities. In state-owned enterprises, all major business and investment decisions are screened by the enterprise's internal party branch. The party extends its control beyond the constitutional order by controlling appointments to all key public institutions – universities, trade unions, media enterprises – and party branches within those institutions provide constant oversight. Influenced by Vladimir Lenin's ideas, the party understands power to flow through social institutions as much as through the constitutional order. The party works to ensure that any person of standing in any organization of significance is either a party member or a reliable ally. Nonparty members with social standing are the responsibility of the United Front Work Department (UFWD), which sits alongside the Organization Department and the Propaganda Department as one of the three departments in the party's own bureaucracy. Following Mao, Xi Jinping has described the UFWD as one of the party's "magic weapons" (*fabao*). The UFWD was established to win the allegiance and cooperation of nonparty groups in society, including the private sector, faith groups, and ethnic minorities. It was instrumental in securing allies, including among minor democratic parties, during the Chinese civil war. Since then, the UFWD has grown to oversee a vast array of organizations and activities designed to promote CPC policies and perspectives.

The internal structure of the UFWD underscores the wide scope of its remit. There are nine bureaus. They cover party work (understanding and communicating party policies), ethnic and religious work, Hong Kong, Macau and overseas Chinese, nonparty cadres (officials), the (private) economic sector, independent (nonparty) intellectuals, and new social class representatives (e.g., entrepreneurs, artists, and celebrities). Tibet and Xinjiang each have their own department. Coordinating with the UFWD is the Chinese People's Political Consultative Committee, an advisory body that meets every year at the same time as the National People's Congress. Membership in this prestigious nonexecutive body is offered to nonparty elites such as ethnic and religious leaders, celebrities, entrepreneurs, and nonparty intellectuals to win their allegiance by providing them with recognition and a channel for influence. The UFWD also oversees the All-China Federation of Commerce and Industry, a nonindependent chamber of commerce for large private enterprises.

The UFWD is the party's agency of political co-optation. That is, the UFWD and its affiliate agencies work with groups (domestically and internationally) considered to be potential allies or sympathizers – people and groups who can be brought around to the party's way of thinking and aligned with the party's agenda. Arguably the most important target group for co-optation under China's business-friendly socialism with Chinese characteristics are entrepreneurs. Once persecuted as "capitalist running dogs" and counterrevolutionaries, private entrepreneurs are formally embraced by the party and allowed to join its ranks. The party encourages China's "advanced productive forces" to help achieve the party's nation-building goals, including the centennial goal of making China rich (high-income) and strong by 2049 – the party's mission in the Xi Jinping era. The party's relationship with private entrepreneurs is the subject of Minglu Chen's essay in this volume, "Co-opting the Private Sector" (Chapter 8). Chen's essay speaks to debates surrounding the "China model," which challenges the conventional wisdom that democracy is the only ticket to national wealth. The party has successfully overseen decades of economic growth by introducing economic reforms, including market liberalization, while resisting political liberalization. What's more, the authoritarian system has been strengthened by economic success, securing the approval of a populace that has enjoyed soaring incomes and standards of living. Economic opportunities have kept entrepreneurs on side. Minglu Chen explains that by successfully co-opting business owners, the party has prevented them from becoming a social force advocating for political change. A mutually beneficial and interdependent relationship has developed: business owners depend on the party-state for access to land and capital, and the party-state depends on the success of private business to generate jobs and wealth.

In recent years the Xi administration has shown preferential treatment of SOEs while cracking down on the activities (and profits) of some of the biggest private companies, including globally successful technology companies such as Alibaba, clearly wary of the potential challenge to its monopoly on power by rising tech giants and billionaires. The business community has complained that "the state advances and the private [sector] retreats" (*guojin mintui*). The party, in turn, has sent clear signals that the private sector is dependent on the country's political masters. It has demanded that wealthy individuals and firms contribute to "common prosperity," which is party-speak for reducing income inequality, by making significant donations to charities addressing economic inequality. Critics argue that such actions have populist appeal but do little to alter the structural causes of inequality.[24] In the meantime, business leaders can only strive to please the party, whose economic model is built on state ownership of land and control of the financial system.

---

[24] Andrew Walder, "China's Extreme Inequality: The Structural Legacies of State Socialism," *The China Journal* 90 (July 2023): 1–26.

Administrative Capabilities and Policy Responsiveness

The party's ability to steer the wider economy is the bedrock of its power. Over the decades, the party has shown a capacity to learn and adapt in its management of the economy and oversight of economic institutions, winning accolades, for example, for its handling of the 2008–2009 Global Financial Crisis. As Sarah Eaton and Wendy Leutert explain in their essay "China's Adaptive State Capitalism and Its International Sources" (Chapter 9), the party has successfully borrowed a great deal from other economic models and policies, notably those of the East Asian tiger economies. The learning and adaptation began in the late 1970s, when party leaders looked to Japan and the World Bank for reform ideas. As Beijing negotiated to join the World Trade Organization in the 1990s, "Chinese leaders' concerns about intensified competition with foreign firms motivated renewed efforts to build internationally competitive 'national champions' – large, central government-owned enterprises in strategic sectors." Since the 2000s, Chinese policymakers have looked to Singapore, notably its powerful government agency Temasek, as a model for managing state assets and effective corporate governance. The results have been nothing short of astounding. As Eaton and Leutert observe, in 2020 China surpassed the United States for the first time on the Fortune Global 500 annual ranking of the world's largest firms by revenue. Alongside the 121 American companies on this prestigious list were 124 Chinese firms – 92 of which were state-owned.[25]

Adaptation and learning can also be seen in the party's increasingly sophisticated approaches to governing. In their essay "Digital Power: Technological Leadership, Smart Governance, and Ideological Control" (Chapter 10), Katja Drinhausen and John Lee argue that the CPC "is building a digitally capable state that is globally competitive in every single aspect – from use of new technologies in domestic governance, to development of digital infrastructure, and fostering innovation and standard setting." The authors argue that the CPC "is advancing digitalization forcefully" to ensure the party "remain[s] at the vanguard of – and not just responding to – social and political development."

Successful economic policies have given the party an important new source of legitimacy in the postrevolutionary era. This performance legitimacy has been buttressed by the party's increasing capacity to develop and implement policies that respond to evolving public demands. As Bingqin Li explains in her essay in this volume, "Social Stability through Responsive Social Policy" (Chapter 11), a key pillar of the party's

---

[25] On the rise of global Chinese firms, see also Andrew Walder, "The Ascent of China's Corporate Giants," *The China Journal* 92 (July 2024).

strength lies in its capacity to respond to people's material, social, and environmental needs. Li notes that the "people's livelihoods policy" (*minsheng zhengce*) occupies the lion's share of each year's government work report by the State Council. Her chapter highlights the party's responsiveness to public opinion, noting that each General Secretary of the CPC since Mao has publicly cited the Confucian philosopher Xunzi's aphorism: "The ruler is like a boat and the people like water. Water can support a boat and also capsize it." This observation reminds us of party leaders' sensitivity to history, including the imperial concept of the mandate of heaven, which rulers lose if they fail to serve the people with sufficient benevolence.

Coercion

The party is concerned with public opinion and seeks approval. But it also cracks down harshly on dissent and on individuals and groups that cannot be easily co-opted or appeased because they seek policy change that the party is unwilling to make. In the spring of 1989, students began protesting against corruption and cost of living pressures that were by-products of the early years of market reforms. The protests began drawing in workers, intellectuals, artists, and other citizens who were equally anxious about the country's direction. Protests spread to hundreds of cities, morphing into large-scale prodemocracy protests that directly challenged the party's monopoly of political power for the first time since 1949. The party ultimately responded with force, declaring martial law on May 20 and infamously deploying the People's Liberation Army (PLA), which the party controls, to extinguish the protests in and around Beijing's Tiananmen Square on the night of June 3 and the morning of June 4. There are no accurate figures on the number of resulting deaths. Estimates ranging from several hundred to more than 2,000 are based on first-hand accounts by journalists and diplomats.[26]

The student protests of 1989 were arguably the only existential external threat the party has faced in its more than seven decades in power. Following the crackdown, the party tightened its domestic political security to ensure that future protests did not snowball into threats to the party's grip on power. The party now oversees an extensive domestic security apparatus, which includes the People's Armed Police, political security units within the police force, and agents within the Ministry of

---

[26] For closer reading on China during the first decade of reform, see Julian Gewirtz, *Never Turn Back: China and the Forbidden History of the 1980s* (Cambridge, MA: Harvard University Press, 2022). The book includes a detailed chapter on Tiananmen and its aftermath.

State Security. Other administrative structures further serve the party's goal of "stability maintenance" (*weiwen*) and maintaining its own political security. These include dedicated party committees at different levels of the system and grid management practices which task community members with monitoring and reporting on citizens' activities.[27]

In the decades since Tiananmen, the party has learned to accommodate localized protests that allow people to let off steam while ensuring that protests do not become a coordinated movement. In 1999, when adherents of the Falun Gong spiritual movement assembled en masse in Beijing to protest the group's treatment, authorities cracked down harshly, forming a dedicated security agency (Office 610) to identify, surveil, punish, and reeducate practitioners. When protesters emerged in multiple cities in the autumn of 2022 to oppose the harsh lockdowns under China's Zero-COVID policy, police initially allowed them to vent their frustrations. However, when protester demands turned political, with some calling for Xi Jinping to step down, the crackdown was swift. Some protesters quoted from the banners hung by Peng Lihua on Sitong Bridge in Beijing on October 13. One banner called for an end to lockdowns, and another called for elections and replacement of the current leadership.[28] Many protesters held aloft blank sheets of paper to signify their lack of voice and political censorship, lending the protests – the largest since 1989 – the popular moniker "A4 protests."

Despite their scale and intensity across multiple cities, the A4 or "white paper" protests were easily suppressed by the party's security apparatus, with many alleged ringleaders arrested.[29] Protesters or dissenters such as Peng Lihua who demand greater political, cultural, or religious freedom, or who promote narratives that contradict the party's, typically receive harsh sentences, which serve as a warning to others.

In Xinjiang and in Mongolian and Tibetan areas where local populations have sometimes opposed party rule, including violently in the case of some fringe groups in Xinjiang, the party has responded with some of its harshest measures of surveillance and control. Xinjiang became the focus of an increasingly intensive crackdown following street protests in 2009.

---

[27] Minxin Pei, "Grid Management: China's Latest Institutional Tool of Social Control," *China Leadership Monitor* 67 (Spring 2021).

[28] For a timeline of the protests, see Peter Lee, "Timeline: Key Dates in China's Blank Placard Zero-COVID Protests," *Hong Kong Free Press*, November 30, 2022. https://hongkongfp.com/2022/11/30/timeline-key-dates-in-chinas-blank-placard-zero-covid-protests/.

[29] For more on the A4 protests in the Spring of 2022, see Patricia Thornton, "The A4 Movement: Mapping its Background and Impacts." *China Leadership Monitor*, no. 75, Spring 2023; and Lynette H. Ong, "The CCP after the Zero-COVID Fail," *Journal of Democracy* 34(2) (April 2023): 32–46.

The crackdown was further intensified from 2014 following deadly terrorist attacks by Uyghur militants, including a bombing at Urumqi Railway Station while Xi Jinping was visiting the region and a knife attack at Kunming Railway Station.[30] From that time, the party pivoted from a counterterror approach targeting militants to a broad-based crackdown on what party leaders perceived to be the root of the problem: Islamic fundamentalism and ethnic nationalism.[31] Heeding Xi Jinping's call for more aggressive action, party bosses in Xinjiang began outlawing a wide range of Islamic practices including the wearing of headscarves and giving babies Islamic names. The policies were designed to extinguish ethnic consciousness (*minzu yishi*). Local authorities greatly expanded electronic and physical surveillance of the population. They also began rounding up Uyghurs deemed insufficiently loyal to the party's "socialist core values" and subjecting them to forced detention. By some estimates, between one and two million Uyghurs were sent to detention camps for varying periods to undertake "political (re)education" and various types of vocational training designed to raise levels of Uyghur participation in the Han-dominated socialist market economy, presumably to foster integration and conformity but under conditions some have described as slave labor.[32]

Reeducation camps are an old party tool used to discipline and punish. Until the practice was abandoned in 2013, "reeducation through labor" (*laogai*) was routinely used to punish a wide range of dissenters and "deviants" from Falun Gong practitioners to drug users. In their final year of operation, there were an estimated 350 such "camps" across China.[33] Those in Xinjiang were not formally classified as *laogai* camps, and, for a time, the party denied their existence.

In her chapter on "Dealing with Dissent" (Chapter 12), Anna Hayes notes that "a key source of CPC power has been its ability to manage or

---

[30] Ben Hillman and Gray Tuttle (eds.), *Ethnic Conflict and Protest in Tibet and Xinjiang: Unrest in China's West* (New York: Columbia University Press, 2016).

[31] Stefanie Kam, "Maintaining Stability and Authoritarian Rule: The Xi Era in Xinjiang," in *Political and Social Control in China: The Consolidation of Single-Party Rule*, ed. Ben Hillman and Chien-wen Kou (Canberra: ANU Press, 2024): 221–245; Adian Zenz, "Innovating Penal Labor: Re-education, Forced Labor and Coercive Social Integration in the Xinjiang Uyghur Autonomous Region," *The China Journal* 90 (July 2023): 27–53. See also Uradyn E. Bluag, "Minority Nationalities and Frankenstein's Monsters: Reshaping 'the Chinese Nation' and China's Quest to become a 'Normal Country,'" *The China Journal* 86 (July 2021): 46–67.

[32] James A. Millward, "(Identity) Politics in Command: Xi Jinping's July Visit to Xinjiang," *The China Story* (2022). www.thechinastory.org/identity-politics-in-command-xi-jinpings-july-visit-to-xinjiang/

[33] "Long Overdue: The Government Says It Will Reform Its System of Labour Camps," *The Economist*, January 12, 2013.

eliminate any form of dissent, and to weaken, co-opt, or destroy any organization or individual who does not express or demonstrate loyalty to the party above all else." Hayes notes the party's preference for co-option over coercion, though the party is ready to coerce whenever that's deemed necessary, whether dealing with human rights lawyers, feminists, or ethnic minorities. As Drinhausen and Lee note in their earlier chapter, the party-state has dramatically enhanced its surveillance and monitoring capabilities. Anna Hayes picks up on this discussion to explain how the party's digital surveillance capabilities empower it to identify and stifle potential dissent – what she calls "preemptive policing." Hayes situates the new technological capability within historical narratives and practices, including before the party came to power and in the early years of the People's Republic, to remind us that digital technology is a new tool deployed in the service of old practices and institutions. We are reminded that technologies merely augment the party's powerful ability to surveil, which still relies heavily on human labor, including domestic security agencies and networks of informants within communities, schools, universities, enterprises, and online.[34]

Although the PLA has been less involved in domestic affairs in recent decades, it remains a potent pillar supporting the party's monopoly of political power. As Mao Zedong famously said, "political power grows out of the barrel of a gun." In China, the army belongs to the party, not the state. Historically, many party leaders were also PLA leaders, and the organizations have been joined at the hip since the early revolutionary years. Every military unit has a party branch, and each level of command has a political commissar who is a trained party cadre. In his chapter in this volume, "The Party and the Army" (Chapter 13), Ji You explains the intricacies of the relationship between the CPC and the PLA, and how the PLA emerged as a powerful force, loyal to the party but immune to civilian oversight. The institutional arrangements are a result of Maoist design: the Politburo would manage the country's political affairs and the Central Military Commission (CMC) its military affairs. Since the CMC was comprised of professional soldiers and enjoyed an equal status to the Politburo, over time the PLA became a relatively autonomous institution. According to Ji You, PLA autonomy reached its zenith under the administration of Hu Jintao (2002–2012). Ji You notes that since coming to power, Xi Jinping has exerted more control over the CMC and PLA and has stacked the ranks of top brass with his loyalists. Significantly, for the first time in PRC history, senior military personnel have become the

---

[34] Minxin Pei, *The Sentinel State: Surveillance and the Survival of Dictatorship in China* (Cambridge, MA: Harvard University Press, 2024).

targets of anticorruption probes. The most famous case was CMC vice chairman and Politburo member General Xu Caihou, who was charged with corruption, court-martialed, and jailed in 2014. His crime was selling promotions – a widespread practice that reformers considered a major obstacle to the modernization of the military. Ji You asserts that Xi Jinping put the PLA under firmer control but asks to what extent this is a product of Xi's personalization of power rather than a solution to the fragmented nature of political and military power in China.

The Future of One-Party Rule

Xi Jinping's personalization of power has raised new questions about the future of one-party rule in China. From the 1980s through the 2000s, the party was led more collectively, with the party's top bosses serving as first among equals in the Standing Committee of the Politburo and sensitive to the views of retired party elders. This development was in part a response to the excesses of the Maoist era and the calamities that resulted from Mao Zedong's domination of the party. Xi Jinping has bolstered the role of the CPC within the state and across China's economy and society, but he has also used a stronger party organization to channel power toward him at the top of the party pyramid. He has methodically removed potential rivals and their supporters from within party ranks, including at lower levels. Such rivalry among the elite might have caused instability at different times (and the party formally forbids factionalism), but the existence of rival elite-linked networks served as a means of regulating political competition within the party and contributed to the consensual model of decision-making which underpinned political stability during more recent times.[35] Having eliminated rivals and persuaded the party to abandon term limits for the office of secretary-general, Xi has set himself to rule indefinitely, or at least until he decides to step down. As a result, personal loyalty to Xi has become the most important criterion for elevation to top party, government, and SOE posts, and the Chinese political system is orienting itself around the top leader's preferences. Xi's unsparing and interminable anticorruption campaign, which has targeted individuals and networks of suspect loyalty as well as straightforwardly venal officials, has caused widespread anxiety across the system. As local officials worry about the changing rules of the game, "bureaucratic slack" has set in: The dynamism which drove local officials to grow their local economies in recent decades has dissipated as they become more risk

---

[35] Ben Hillman, "Factions and Spoils: Examining Local State Behavior in China," *The China Journal* 62 (2010): 1–18.

averse.[36] A concentration of power risks limiting the information and feedback available to party leaders, as officials scramble to comply with directives and tell the boss what he wants to hear.[37] During the Great Leap Forward, the CPC leadership followed Mao off a cliff, after the brave General Peng Dehuai was purged for daring to voice concerns. With power concentrated in the hands of one man, such a calamity could happen again.

A major pitfall of a system which allows power to concentrate in the top leader, causing the entire system to orient itself around the top leader, is the risk of instability and conflict in the event the leader dies or becomes incapacitated. It is very often the failure to solve the problem of leadership succession that brings authoritarian regimes unstuck. As Jude Blanchette and Richard McGregor note in their essay in this volume, "After Xi" (Chapter 14), under Xi, the party has abandoned the consensus model for leadership succession. Blanchette and McGregor argue persuasively that although Xi has stacked party, government, military, and domestic security agencies with his loyalists, this is now such a large group of people that differences in interests and ideas are likely to coalesce into competing groups. It is far from clear that the party has the mechanisms in place to manage a smooth transition from Xi Jinping to his successor, whenever that should need to occur. Equally troubling, the party clearly lacks the mechanisms to constrain its leader and is unwilling to allow nonparty or even state institutions to provide such a check. As Xi Jinping approaches the end of his third five-year term (2022–2027), his party remains firmly in command and its monopoly on political power in the PRC appears unassailable. At the same time, the limits of one-party rule are becoming ever-more apparent.

---

[36] Wei Chen, Shu Keng, and Siyi Zhang, "China's Bureaucratic Slack: Material Inducements and Decision Risks among Chinese Local Cadres," *The China Journal* 86 (January 2023): 70–94.

[37] Susan L. Shirk, *Overreach: How China Derailed Its Peaceful Rise* (New York: Oxford University Press, 2022).

2 The CPC's Metamorphosis from Class-Based Organization to Nationalist Party

Yingjie Guo

Of all the reasons for the ability of the Communist Party of China (CPC) to stay in power in the post-Mao era, the most critical is its shift from Mao Zedong's "Chinese Revolution" to Deng Xiaoping's "reform and opening-up." The former, characterized by unpopular class struggle geared toward the achievement of socialism and communism, resulted in a subsistence economy, low living standards, political strife, and lasting trauma for millions of Chinese. The latter has led to what is commonly described in the international media as China's "economic miracle" and "China's rise." The success stories of the last century that the party singled out in its late 2021 "resolution" on history include the construction of a "moderately prosperous society," the eradication of absolute poverty, and unprecedented progress toward realizing "common prosperity" and the "China Dream."

It must be stressed, however, that "reform and opening-up" is not simply an economic project. It represents a paradigm shift with far-reaching political and cultural consequences that have received far less academic attention than its economic dimensions. This dramatic shift holds a key to understanding the CPC's legitimation and its firm grip on state power. Indeed, the shift has made China's "economic miracle" and "China's rise" possible in the first place. In political and cultural terms, it can be summed up as the CPC's metamorphosis from an exclusive class-based party to an inclusive nationalist party; it represents a switch from an unpopular and divisive Marxist obsession with class that privileges some "revolutionary" classes over others to a more inclusive and popular nationalism seeking to advance the national interest and enhance national unity, autonomy, and identity.[1] The switch bears upon the party's own

---

[1] This concept is based on Anthony Smith's definition of nationalism – "an ideological movement for attaining and maintaining autonomy, unity and identity on behalf of a population deemed by some of its members to constitute an actual or potential 'nation.'" Anthony Smith, *National Identity* (Reno: University of Nevada Press, 1991), 71. National interest has been brought to the fore here as an additional goal because of its prominence in Chinese discourses of nationalism.

identity, as well as its legitimacy and ability to win the hearts and minds of Chinese citizens.

Eager as the CPC may be to command the loyalty of all Chinese, it is ideologically committed to being a class party. This has created a major dilemma: How should the party position itself in relation to both the working classes and all Chinese citizens in a way that that enables it to win as much support as possible from both while also ensuring intraparty unity? Without both sufficient internal unity and popular support, the party would not be able to survive, let alone secure its grip on state power. The CPC's success in this regard depends on, among other things, the extent to which it reconciles class and nation in how it justifies its continued rule to the people of China in general and to its own members in particular.

Though the CPC still claims to represent both the working class and the nation, it is impossible conceptually and practically to represent both at the same time. So the general pattern that has emerged in the CPC's rearticulation of its own identity in relation to class and nation throughout its history can be compared to a pendulum swinging from left to right and back again. Every time the party leans toward the left, reaffirming its commitment to Mao's revolution, it focuses attention on "the people," made up of classes, or the "class-nation." It specifically stresses the proletariat and peasantry only when extreme leftism prevails – for example, during the Cultural Revolution. As the pendulum swings further to the right in response to national imperatives that require the contribution of all Chinese, the CPC evokes and mobilizes the pan-Chinese nation, including all Chinese nationals and overseas Chinese. This is what happened during World War II, when the party subordinated class struggle to the national struggle against the Japanese invasion. The People's Republic of China (PRC) citizenry, or the state-nation, was again brought to the fore, and the class-nation pushed to the background, following the party's abandonment of Mao's continuous revolution in favor of modernizing and market-based economic reforms.

Proreform leaders "nationalized" the party by expanding it into a more inclusive, legitimate "all-people party" (*quanmin dang*) or a "national party" (*minzu dang*).[2] It swung back to the discredited concept of class in the wake of June 4 1989 under Maoist influence, which resurged in response to the perceived plotting of Western "black hands" behind the student-led protests. The CPC leadership again eschewed the unpopular class concept when leftism receded following Deng Xiaoping's reform-boosting "southern

---

[2] Song Ping, quoted in Zhang Weiping (ed.), *Xinbian dangwu gongzuo quanshu* [A new manual for conducting party affairs] (Beijing: Zhongguo yanshi chubanshe, 1995), 1673.

tour" in 1992, during which he reiterated that socialism must liberate productive forces, while a market economy was not a capitalist economy. Jiang Zemin, who led the party from 1989 to 2002, rearticulated the CPC's identity as a representative of both class and nation. But nation is everywhere and class is nowhere in the national projects articulated by his successors, Hu Jintao and Xi Jinping. This pragmatic political strategy has served the party well for decades.

Tasks for the Post-Mao Age

Since 1978, when the CPC repudiated class struggle in favor of modernization and economic development, its top priority has been the construction of a "moderately prosperous society." In the Hu Jintao period, the party added the notion of a "harmonious society," and Xi Jinping later promoted the "Chinese Dream."[3] All of these goals entail the eradication of absolute poverty, the promotion of common prosperity, and satisfying the nation's material needs. Another pressing task for the party is to counter Western ideas and values which they consider subversive and believe to have fomented political dissent in China, threatening CPC rule and the country's political stability. A third major task is the unification with Taiwan, the integration of Hong Kong and Macau, and the prevention of national disintegration by quenching separatism.

Those tasks cannot be accomplished by relying either on selected groups and individuals or primarily on the "revolutionary classes" such as the proletariat and peasantry. Nothing short of an all-inclusive national community will do.

Party policies in the post-Mao era are not designed to only benefit selected classes either. The intended beneficiaries are the whole Chinese nation, all the people, irrespective of their class identities. In other words, the nation, not classes, is the new political subject of the PRC, whereas class and class struggle are not only undesirable but counterproductive as well. The CPC cannot renounce ideas of class and class struggle for ideological (and constitutional) reasons. If exploitation and exploiting classes have been eliminated in the PRC and the working class has become the masters of the country, socialism as defined in the Communist Manifesto will have been established, the PRC will have become a classless society, and class struggle will have ceased; yet the CPC formally hangs onto class struggle and insists that the country has only reached the "primary state of socialism." Theoreticians in the CPC

---

[3] Jane Golley, Linda Jaivin, Ben Hillman, and Sharon Strange (eds.), *China Dreams: China Story Yearbook 2019* (Canberra: ANU Press, 2020).

try to paper over the inconsistencies. But, clearly, its leaders have decided that it is logical and more advantageous to downplay this central aspect of its foundational ideology and embrace inclusive, popular nationalism over exclusive, unpopular classism.

Between Class and Nation: The CPC's Ideological Dilemma

The CPC has often shifted between claiming to represent class and claiming to represent nation regardless of its self-ascribed identity as a class organization. It usually does this by taking advantage of the slippery terms that are widely used in Chinese official discourses to refer to the "nation" in various contexts. Such terms include *renmin*, "the people" (a political category, as opposed to *ren*, just a "person" or "people" as in those you meet on the street); *qunzhong*, the "masses"; *renmin qunzhong*, the "masses of the people"; *renmin dazhong*, the "overwhelming majority of the people"; *laobaixing* or *baixing*, "common people" (literally the "old 100 surnames"); *Zhongguo renmin*, the "Chinese people"; *guomin* or *gongmin*, the "citizens of the PRC"; and *Zhonghua minzu*, the "Chinese nation" (a phrase that implies a single grouping).

Most pertinent to CPC discourses are the categories of "the people," the "Chinese people," and the "Chinese nation." Created mainly for domestic use, the first is essentially a political class-nation. Good classes like the proletariat and poor peasants were treated during the Mao era as revolutionary forces and motors of history driving societies forward from capitalism to socialism and communism, whereas bad classes like capitalists, landlords, rich peasants, and counterrevolutionary elements were excluded from "the people" and relegated to the bottom of society. It is usually replaced by the "Chinese people" in international communication and often used interchangeably with the latter in a domestic context. It has become largely indistinguishable from PRC citizens in general, or "all persons holding the nationality of the People's Republic of China," as clarified in the 1954 constitution and each amended version since 1988. However, it is worth noting that in the Mao era, the CPC considered the category of "citizens" to be inferior in status to "the people," as the former category accommodated those who were not entitled to the rights of "the people."[4] The citizenry and the "Chinese people" constitute an inclusive

---

[4] Zhou Enlai, "Report to the Chinese People's Political Consultative Conference," *China Digest*, October 5, 1949, 11; Standing Committee of the National People's Congress of the People's Republic of China, The Constitution of the People's Republic of China (adopted at the Fifth Session of the Fifth National People's Congress on December 4, 1982), Articles 52–56.

civil-political state-nation. The "Chinese nation" is a pan-Chinese nation in current PRC usage which comprises the citizens of mainland China, Hong Kong, Macau, and Taiwan, as well as overseas Chinese.

The nation that the CPC envisions thus looks like a three-tiered formation, with the class-nation at its core and the state-nation and pan-Chinese nation radiating from it. Each of these tiers has a distinct role to play in the party's general scheme of things and has been reconstituted time and time again, exclusively during the Mao era to purify the class-based people but inclusively in the post-Mao era to allow and encourage all Chinese citizens to participate in economic development and wealth creation. The discursive shifts can be seen most clearly from the amendments to the party and state constitutions over the past six decades.

Each party constitution between 1922 and 1997 defined the party as the "vanguard organization" or "vanguard" of the Chinese proletariat. The 1954 state constitution and all amended versions since 1988 have presented the PRC as a class-state, namely "a socialist state under the people's democratic dictatorship led by the working class and based on the alliance of workers and peasants." It became a "proletarian dictatorship" during the Cultural Revolution. The 1982 constitution reached an uneasy compromise between those definitions by redefining the PRC as a "people's democratic dictatorship, which is in essence a proletarian dictatorship." In other words, the two kinds of dictatorships are presented ambiguously as synonyms even though "people's" and "proletarian" denoted different entities.

The category of "the people" is central to the CPC's shifting discourses over the decades: The identities of both the party and the state are closely tied to it. Party leaders today rarely explain who is included in the category. The answer can be found in Mao Zedong's writings from the 1940s to 1956 and in the PRC's first constitution in 1954. The people were the industrial workers, the peasantry, the petite bourgeoisie, and the national bourgeoisie. The peasantry comprised those whom, before the Land Reform movement (1946–1952), the CPC classified as poor and middle peasants; it excluded landlords or rich peasants. The petite bourgeoisie included the intelligentsia, artisans, owners of small businesses, freelance professionals, and other urban residents. The national bourgeoisie consisted of the "progressive" elements of the bourgeoisie whose businesses did not employ foreign capital.

These classes occupied different positions in the PRC's status hierarchy. The state's constitutional function was as a political instrument by which the revolutionary ruling class suppressed the counterrevolutionary classes and reapportioned power, rights, opportunities, and so on. At the top of the country's pecking order was the proletariat, which the CPC portrayed as the most revolutionary class because it represented what

Marxists called "advanced productive forces." The peasantry was regarded as the proletariat's most trusted and reliable ally, although the CPC did not believe that the peasants were equipped to play a leading role among the people because it saw them as conservative and less revolutionary by nature. Together, however, in Maoist China, the proletariat and the peasantry were considered the "masters of the country." They are the party's ideological "us," represented in the form of a hammer and a sickle on the CPC's banner. The petite bourgeoisie and national bourgeoisie were placed below them; they needed to be united and educated by the CPC to support its revolution against its enemies.

The party has not formally defined "the people" since 1954, except during the Cultural Revolution, when, under the influence of Maoist leftism, the party narrowed down the category to just the "working people": the industrial workers, peasants, and soldiers. Those who were excluded from the category were denied educational and other opportunities, treated with suspicion, might have their homes ransacked, and were even physically attacked, tortured, and, in some cases, killed. The national bourgeoisie had ceased to exist as a class in 1956, following the socialization of all means of production, while the CPC reclassified those of the petite bourgeoisie who did not own productive property into other classes, such as workers and *shimin* ("urban residents"). The intelligentsia, meanwhile, was elevated into the proletariat at the beginning of "reform and opening-up," when technical know-how and professional knowledge were badly needed. There are only two classes in the PRC's current official class scheme – the proletariat and the peasantry.

At the same time, the party's new historical mission of economic development requires wealth creators and consumers with ample purchasing power, as opposed to revolutionary forces ready to wage class struggle. So its primary concern has shifted from the working class to the principal creators of wealth, including the new rich and a well-off middle class. From a Marxist standpoint, it is politically incorrect for the party to side with the new rich, but the proletariat, detached from the Chinese Revolution, is no longer central to the party's current historical mission. There is voluminous academic literature by Chinese social scientists advocating an olive-shaped social structure, where the middle class constitutes the mainstream of society, optimal for ensuring social stability; this schema envisions the middle class as the preferred collective agent for social change. The Chinese- and English-language literature tends to define the middle class as white-collar workers and middle-income groups. The ascendancy of this class contrasts starkly with the decline in power and status of industrial workers and peasants. The former, in particular, have "lost their world"[5] and shifted from master in name and privilege to a new underclass.[6]

The CPC needs to justify such a drastic alteration of the PRC's class map and status order so that it retains a semblance of ideological consistency while accommodating the whole citizenry in its political projects. Such justification is crucial to the party's legitimacy and the amount of support it receives from the populace as a whole, as well as specifically from the industrial workers and peasantry. Yet it is not easy to do, thanks to irresolvable contradictions between the party's stated ideology and its pragmatic reforms. While state ownership and the planned economy under Mao had a systematic class-leveling effect, "reform and opening-up" has done the opposite, polarizing, dividing, and stratifying society as never before in the PRC. It has created a distinct class society where class interests are highly differentiated while the gap between the rich and poor has increased dramatically. It is now possible to find bourgeois and proletarian classes that meet the criteria of Marxist classification.

The party's response to the emergence of a bourgeois class is denial. Deng Xiaoping simply asserted that a bourgeoisie, or any other exploiting classes, had not emerged in the PRC; the implication was that it could not.[7] Jiang Zemin placed all the "new social groups," including billionaires who ranked among the richest people in the world, into a new category of "socialist builders," together with the proletariat and peasantry.[8] This concept has continued into the Hu Jintao and Xi Jinping eras. The party's response to the declining status of the proletariat and peasantry is two-pronged. On the one hand, it continues to tell these classes that they remain "masters of the country," whatever the reality. On the other hand, it provides them with tangible economic benefits in the form of subsistence allowances, housing subsidies, and taxation relief, and by alleviating poverty in the name of "common prosperity."

Still more important is the party's discursive response. It has taken pains to erase the class symbolism in the national flag and state insignia

---

[5] Marc Blecher, "Hegemony and Worker's Politics in China," *The China Quarterly* 170 (2002): 283–303, 283.

[6] Dorothy Solinger, "The New Crowd of the Dispossessed: The Shift of the Urban Proletariat from Master to Mendicant," in *State and Society in 21st-Century China: Crisis, Contention, and Legitimation*, ed. Peter Gries and Stanley Rosen (London: Routledge Curzon, 2004): 50–66.

[7] Deng Xiaoping, "*Yi kao lixiang er kao jilu caineng tuanji qilai*" [Solidarity only derives from ideals and discipline], in *Selected Works of Deng Xiaoping*, vol. 3 (Beijing: Renmin chubanshe, 1993): 110–112, 111.

[8] Jiang Zemin, "*Zai qingzhu Zhongguo gongchandang chengli bashi zhouniandahu shang de jianghua*" [Speech at the celebration of the eightieth anniversary of the founding of the CPC] (July 1, 2001), in *Selected Works of Jiang Zemin*, vol. 3 (Beijing: Renmin chubanshe, 2006): 169–172, 169.

and to give the symbols a new meaning. In the Mao era, the four smaller stars stood for the proletariat, the peasantry, the petite bourgeoisie, and the national bourgeoisie. The five stars are now said to stand for the CPC and the "whole Chinese people": Nationhood thus takes the place of class in state symbolism. The PRC's 1982 constitution and all the subsequent amendments, as well the National Flag Act of 1990 and the State Emblem Act of 1991, all evade defining what the five stars stand for, invariably referring to them as "symbols of the People's Republic of China." An official youth study guide interprets the five stars as the CPC and "the people of all nationalities around the country."[9] The erasure of the class symbolism coincides with the party's downplay of its own class identity.

From Class Organization to National Party: The CPC's New Identity

The most dramatic transformation of the CPC's identity since 1978 took place during the Jiang Zemin era. Jiang first affirmed the party's traditional identity in December 1989 as "the class organization of the Chinese proletariat" and "the vanguard of the proletariat."[10] He reiterated that "the universal transformation of all class societies into classless ones could only be led by the proletariat," and that "the working class needed the party and the party could not do without the working class."[11] However, in the year 2000, he began to obliterate class with his theory of the "three represents," which transforms the "vanguard of the proletariat" into a political party that represents "the requirements for developing China's advanced productive forces, the orientation of China's advanced culture and the fundamental interests of the overwhelming majority of the people in China."[12]

It is not clear what he meant by "advanced culture," but it is quite clear that the other two "represents" were both related to class. His foregrounding of productive forces rather than the relations of production pushed class further into the background, as Marx's class analysis had divided individuals into classes according to their relationship to the means of production. Jiang's emphasis on "the fundamental interests of

---

[9] Wang Zhankui (ed.), *Guoqi, guohui, guoge zhishi wenda* [The national flag, the state emblem, and the national anthem: questions and answers] (Beijing: Guojia xingzheng xueyuan chubanshe, 1997), 12.
[10] Jiang Zemin, cited in Zhang Weiping (ed.), *Xinbian dangwu gongzuo quanshu* [A new manual for conducting party affairs] (Beijing: Zhongguo yanshi chubanshe, 1995), 1673.
[11] Jiang Zemin, cited in Zhang Weiping (ed.), *Xinbian dangwu gongzuo quanshu*, 1673.
[12] Jiang Zemin, cited in *Renmin Ribao* [*The People's Daily*], May 16, 2000, 1.

the overwhelming majority of the people in China" was an even more obvious move to expand the party's constituency from one based on class. Equally significant is the fact that Jiang's "people" was not the same as Mao's "people." Rejecting both the four classes as represented on the national flag and state emblem in its original conception and the two officially recognized classes of post-Mao China, Jiang's "people" included all the citizens of the PRC. In other words, Jiang formally turned the CPC into the "national party" or "all-people party" that proreform leaders had called for in the 1980s and elevated the concept of nation above that of class.

Jiang's redefinition of the CPC and "the people" has had far-reaching ramifications for China's economy, politics, society, and culture. It makes the nation the source of state power and legitimacy. It obligates the party to treat all the members of the nation as equal instead of granting different civil–political rights, sociopolitical status, or opportunities according to class as in the former system. Furthermore, the "three represents" affirm the role of the nation's traditional value system and culture in regulating social practices and relations in the PRC alongside what the CPC calls "socialist core values."[13] It is thus necessary and desirable for the party to affirm, legitimatize, and promote the nation's cultural traditions – even if it is not entirely clear what's meant by "advanced culture."

Hu Jintao's "scientific outlook on development," first introduced in 2003, moves the party even further away from Marxist class theory. It calls for the party to "take the interests of the people as the starting and end points of all work," to meet their multifaceted needs and promote their overall development in the course of economic development. It gives top priority to the construction of a "harmonious society."

Hu's "scientific development outlook" was probably intended to kill two birds with one stone. On the one hand, it subtly revises the economic development strategy of his predecessors Deng and Jiang. They prioritized the creation of wealth and GDP growth. But that ended up leaving large numbers of individuals and social groups behind, widening the gap between rich and poor, and thus jeopardizing social justice, stability, and harmony. Hu saw it as imperative for the party to concentrate not just on things (*wu*), such as material production, commodity consumption, or GDP growth, but also on people – whether he called them "the people," "people," or "citizens."

---

[13] The core values include patriotism, collectivism, socialism, and communism in general, and love of country, love for the people, love of labor, love of science, and love for socialism in particular.

The discursive shift reoriented economic development toward benefiting the majority of the population. By not spelling out the nation's composition in terms of classes or strata, as Jiang Zemin did, Hu rendered class meaningless and irrelevant and created a stronger impression of national unity and equality. His vision of a "harmonious society" – harmony among individuals, between individuals and groups, and among social groups regardless of class identity – reinforced this impression.

Xi Jinping has made the notion of people as nation even more prominent and elevated the importance of traditional values more than any other party leader since 1949. He used the word *renmin* (the people) 203 times in his report to the CPC's nineteenth national congress in 2017 and 86 times in his short speech at the ceremony marking the centenary of the CPC on July 1, 2021. By contrast, he only mentioned *renmin* (the people) three times and *gongmin* (citizens) once in the report – in the collocation of *gongmin daode* (citizens' morality), where "citizens" cannot be replaced by "the people." He has pledged that the party "shall exercise power for the people," "exercise power in the interests of the people," and "give full expression to the will of the people, protect their rights and interests, spark their creativity, and provide systemic and institutional guarantees to ensure the people run the country."[14] He has gone further to stress repeatedly "the running of the country by the people" and the people's participation in "the management of state, economic, cultural, and social affairs."[15]

Xi's "people-centered philosophy of development" simultaneously puts more emphasis on party-building and nation-building. Central to his "Chinese Dream" is the creation of a common national purpose – the shared dream of people's happiness and the nation's rejuvenation, which unites the CPC, incentivizes and unites the nation, and binds the party and the nation together. It also requires the party to appeal to, mobilize, and benefit the nation.

As a result of these post-Mao ideological revisions, both the CPC and the PRC have lost their class identity and taken on a national character. The state is no longer conceived of as a political mechanism by which one class oppresses another but as a set of political institutions that advance the national interest and strengthen national unity, autonomy, and identity. The CPC's *raison d'être*, meanwhile, is no longer to eliminate class-based exploitation but to realize the Chinese Dream.

---

[14] Xi Jinping, *Secure a Decisive Victory in Building a Moderately Prosperous Society in All Respects and Strive for the Great Success of Socialism with Chinese Characteristics for a New Era* (Report delivered at the nineteenth national congress of the Communist Party of China, October 18, 2017), Xinhua, October 27, 2017.

[15] Xi Jinping, *Secure a Decisive Victory*.

Nationalism: The New Ideology

The goal of national rejuvenation makes the Chinese Dream a nationalist dream. In embracing nationalism, the CPC has broken with Marxism's central internationalist focus as well as its basis in class theory. Nationalism is logically irreconcilable with Marxism – so much so that it is possible to argue that CPC leaders cannot claim to be both nationalists and Marxists. Marxism has thus become largely an empty signifier today.

"Reform and opening-up" has been a trial-and-error process involving the gradual and cumulative improvement of productive forces and living standards. Thus, revolutionary change has given way to evolutionary change as the CPC's preferred modus operandi. The CPC has also tweaked the Marxist view of history, an incessant, linear, and forward march from feudalism and capitalism through to socialism and communism; whereas Mao once dreamed of pushing China straight through to communism, Deng wound back the clock to the "primary stage of socialism." Xi has introduced the notion of the "New Era," also taking the long view on the achievement of communism.

Xi's "road of socialism with Chinese characteristics" also looks back to the past: He has likened traditional culture to the "soul" of the nation. The new cultural–historical outlook and worldview articulated by Xi hold that the nation's past and tradition are to be cherished and serve both present and future as a basis for a national mode of communication and socialization.

The current CPC leaders' new "historical outlook" hinges on an idealistic (and not historically accurate) idea of cultural homogeneity, unity, and continuity. It envisions Chinese history as a constant flow comparable to a mighty river, a continuous process of national evolution and development, and the accumulation of national essence. In Xi's own words, "history is a continuous movement from yesterday to today and then tomorrow. It is impossible to sever the ties between the present and the past. It is always on the basis of inheriting the legacy of their forerunners that people move forward. There are no exceptions anywhere in the past or present."[16] History, he adds, can be divided into periods or stages which are closely interconnected and interrelated. He stresses that no matter how many twists and turns history might take as it moves forward, history itself is continuous. This idea of continuous history is consistent with the constructed view, pushed by the party but widely accepted among ordinary Chinese, that China is the world's "only continuous

---

[16] Xi Jinping, "*Lingdao ganbu yao duodu dian lishi*" [Xi Jinping: Leading cadres must read more history], *Renmin ribao* [*The People's Daily*], July 5, 2011, 1.

civilization," lasting five millennia. This nation-based conception of the past, tradition, and change is relatively new for the party, which in the Maoist era in particular was violently antitraditionalist and saw the destruction of an immense portion of the nation's tangible and intangible cultural heritage.

Xi and CPC officials have switched to a nationalist conception of culture, describing Chinese cultural traditions as "Chinese cultural genes," "the nation's soul," and the source of the "Chinese spirit."[17] For the first time in its century-long history, the party almost exclusively praises traditional Chinese culture instead of reviling it as "feudal dross," representative of all that was backward and benighted in "old China" and even responsible for the country's weakness and humiliation at the hands of Western powers. According to the party's "Guidelines on Preserving and Developing Excellent Traditional Chinese Culture," issued in 2017, cultural traditions are both the sources and signs of China's greatness, have given the nation a unique identity, and benefit China and the world:

> Culture is the lifeblood of the nation and the spiritual haven of the people. Cultural self-confidence is a more basic, deeper, and more lasting force. The unique concepts, wisdom, temperament, and charm of Chinese culture add to the confidence and pride of the Chinese nation ... Chinese culture has a long history of splendid glory. The outstanding Chinese traditional culture cultivated in the development of more than 5,000 years of civilization has accumulated the deepest spiritual pursuit of the Chinese nation and represents its unique spiritual identity. It is the Chinese nation's rich nourishment in its long evolution and development, the fertile soil for socialism with Chinese characteristics, and an invaluable asset to China's development today. It plays an important role in the continuation and development of Chinese civilization and the promotion of human civilization.[18]

The central leadership has instructed party committees and governments at all levels to be "more conscious and more proactive in promoting the inheritance and development of excellent Chinese traditional culture," and to "further enhance cultural self-awareness and cultural self-confidence" and "strengthen the national cultural soft power." It has also asked the nation to "cherish our cultural roots," "keep alive and develop the visions, concepts, values, and moral norms" of traditional Chinese culture, and "do more to foster a Chinese spirit, Chinese values and Chinese strength to provide a source of cultural and moral guidance for our people."[19] The result is the most comprehensive cultural project in Chinese history, which is so wide-ranging as to encompass most aspects of China's cultural life.

---

[17] Xi Jinping, *Secure a Decisive Victory*.   [18] Xi Jinping, *Secure a Decisive Victory*.
[19] Xi Jinping, *Secure a Decisive Victory*.

This involves the coordinated creation of cultural products for domestic and international consumption, inevitably further narrowing the space for heterogeneous individual creativity and exploration of alternative approaches to cultural production. It entails the promotion of traditional Chinese values and virtues as defined by the state. It also means the state-sponsored rejuvenation of Chinese festivals as well as nationwide protection and restoration of ancient books, artifacts, and archival materials. Added to these are the compilation of a classical cultural canon and the introduction of new courses in schools and universities that will propagate this hegemonic, homogenized, and sanitized view of Chinese culture. These ideas will also be integrated into other subjects including moral education, history, arts, and sports. Schools and media will also promote Chinese operas, calligraphy, approved traditions of music, dance, and painting, acrobatics, and traditional sports. The list goes on. In short, the CPC, like nationalists elsewhere, have assumed a traditionalist posture of "piety for what actually, allegedly, presumably has always existed."[20] It privileges specific aspects of traditional culture and uses contents of these to enhance its own legitimacy and strengthen its monopoly on state power.[21]

The CPC's nationalist cultural–historical outlook and worldview depart from orthodox Marxism. The latter proceeds from the assumption that both the past and tradition will and should be "negated" in the incessant forward march toward the ideal society. Maoists followed Friedrich Engels's theory of dialectical materialism, which was premised on the "three laws of dialectics": the law of the unity and conflict of opposites, the law of the passage of quantitative changes into qualitative changes, and the law of the negation of the negation.[22]

The first law holds that the struggle between antagonistic forces – including the contradictions inherent in everything in nature – cause motion, change, and development. By breaking up unity and continuity, these struggles are key to the destruction of the old and its replacement by the new – to forward leaps.

According to the second law, the process of development begins with quantitative change – change in dimensions or magnitude. Once change

---

[20] Max Weber, "The Social Psychology of World Religions," in *From Max Weber*, ed. H. H. Gerth and C. Wright Mills (London: Routledge and Kegan Paul, 1948): 267–301, 296.
[21] Craig Calhoun, *Nationals Matter: Culture, History, and the Cosmopolitan Dream* (London: Routledge, 2007), 23.
[22] Friedrich Engels, "Dialectics of Nature," in *Marx–Engels Collected Works*, trans. Clemence Dutt, Vol. 25 (Moscow: Progress Publishers, 1987): 17–383. See also Vladimir Ilyich Lenin, "On the Question of Dialectics," trans. Clemence Dutt and ed. Stewart Smith, in *Collected Works*, Vol. 38 (Moscow: Progress Publishers, 1976): 357–361.

moves beyond a certain point, there is transformation of the identity of the thing that is changing – a qualitative change, following which a thing ceases to be its original self. National identity, for example, can be transformed completely in the process of revolutionary change.

The third law, the "negation of the negation," can be seen as a restatement of the second, except it represents progression. So, for example, progressive New China replaces backward Old China, and a socialist Chinese identity supersedes "feudal" Chinese identity.

This idea of change and negation underpins the related theory of historical materialism, which posits that the root cause of social change is contradictions between forces of production (labor, for example) and relations of production (exploitation, for example). As the productive forces advance, existing modes of production become obstacles to progress, eventually inducing a crisis that precipitates revolutionary transformation via class struggle.

This conception of change is profoundly unacceptable to cultural nationalists, who do not see change as the negation of the old by the new but as a gradual process. The process itself is more important than the end, so that identity can be maintained rather than negated. In Marxist terms, Chinese cultural nationalists want quantitative but not qualitative change. From their viewpoint, the national community has been formed over the course of history, in relation to the Chinese natural environment and on the basis of common myths and legends, values, and institutions that evolved over generations. Cultural nationalists envision the nation as a living organism comprising interrelated and interdependent members.

Nationalists also reject Marxist ideas of the conflict of opposites and class struggle, which disrupt the continuity of tradition and damage national unity and identity. In the nationalist ideal of harmony, dualisms, or component elements, in the natural and human worlds are not hostile or incompatible but coexist peacefully in mutual and harmonious interdependence. They reference the ancient cosmic notion of *yin* and *yang*, complementary (as opposed to conflicting) opposites. In such a cooperative and harmonious world, modes and relations of material production are completely irrelevant to moral relations, while antagonism is entirely unnecessary and undesirable.

The CPC has endorsed Confucianism, but as with history and culture, the party reserves the right to define it in the current context. Confucians traditionally regard opposites as "cosmic partners without whose joint activities the universal process would be impossible" and human society as an ordered hierarchy whose components complement and cooperate with each other to fulfill their respective functions.[23] Hierarchy is not just incidental to Confucian society, which privileges certain groups over others (scholars over soldiers, for example, and peasants over artisans, in traditional times). Crucial to the maintenance of hierarchy is the importance of individuals "knowing their place" within it.

The welfare and unity of the national community, in the Confucian view, depends on adherence to cultural and moral values including loyalty to one's superior (whether patriarchal family head or state ruler), as well as benevolence, faithfulness, and righteousness. This leads to social harmony and common good.

Cultural nationalists in the PRC began to argue in the 1980s that China's unity and identity had been badly damaged by the CPC's embrace of the theory of historical materialism, a better fit for wars and revolutions than civil society.[24] Others held class struggle responsible for all the traumatic political movements since 1949, which had upset the traditional moral–cultural order and torn up the social fabric by setting sons against fathers, wives against husbands, siblings against siblings, and class against class.[25] Marxism and Maoism brought about social disorder and chaos, they argued, and jeopardized the moral health of society, national unity, identity, and social harmony. China had to go back to its own cultural roots, rediscover the Chineseness of China, or "Chinese essence," and return to its own path of evolutionary development. Xi Jinping and top CPC leaders now see eye to eye with China's cultural nationalists. Indeed, on the philosophical questions of revolution versus evolution, change versus continuity, and class conflict versus social harmony, they sound much more like nationalists than Marxists – even if the party still claims that Marxism is "the single guiding ideology, the very soul of the CPC, and the banner under which it strives."

Conclusion

The CPC has morphed from a class organization to a national party, with a matching shift in ideology, and the PRC has similarly evolved from a class-state to a nation-state. As a result, the party has broadened its constituency, orienting its policies and projects to benefit the majority of the Chinese people. This move is reminiscent of how political parties

---

[23] Derk Bodde, "Harmony and Conflict in Chinese Thought," in *Studies in Chinese Thought*, ed. Arthur Wright (Chicago: University of Chicago Press, 1967): 19–80, 46–47.

[24] Tang Changli, "*Shidai tezheng yu rujia gongneng*" [Characteristics of the times and the function of Confucianism], *Dongyue luncong* [Shandong Forum] 1 (1989): 14–16, 15.

[25] Luo Yijun and Chen Kejian (eds.), *Lixing yu shengming* [Rationality and Life], Vols. 1 and 2 (Shanghai: Shanghai shudian chubanshe, 1994).

elected to power in countries with liberal democratic systems promise to govern on behalf of the whole citizenry.

It remains a question to what extent the shift has enhanced the party's appeal and legitimacy, contributed to its success in staying in power, or strengthened its authority. That question cannot be answered conclusively without extensive and independently conducted empirical research of the sort that is virtually impossible to do in the PRC today. Still, it is self-evident that the party's promotion of national interests, unity, autonomy, and identity has the potential to win the hearts and minds of more Chinese than continued promotion of class difference and struggle. Yet the CPC's shift toward nationalism is far from complete, with implications for its effectiveness in enhancing the party's legitimacy. One reason is the conflict of interest between the party/state and the nation; the other is the remaining tensions between classism and nationalism.

What the CPC presents as "national interest" is often party/state interest, although there is considerable overlap. A case in point is its recent response to the Biden administration's rhetorical attack on autocracy: As the American president put it in March 2022: "In the battle between democracy and autocracy, democracies are rising to the moment." At the previous year's two-day Summit for Democracy, Biden had called saving democracy "the challenge of our time." Official Chinese state media has asserted that this offensive is a thinly veiled attempt, part of a broader strategy, to undermine Chinese national interest by "containing" China, slowing down its economic development and thus delaying its national rejuvenation. Official media highlights the party's role in China's rise, stressing that China would not have become a strong nation-state without the party's able leadership and will only continue from strength to strength if the party's "ideological security" (*yishi xingtai anquan*)[26] and authority are maintained.

Chinese citizens who accept that the party's interests are identical to those of the nation, or who have little faith in liberal democracy, are likely to support the party. The danger to the party's nationalist claim on legitimacy comes from those who contend that the party's "ideological security" and its monopoly on state power, its autocracy, are in fact detrimental to the national interest. Though such an argument is scarcely audible in the PRC's highly regulated public domain, that does not mean it does not exist.

---

[26] "Ideological security" is defined in the *Guojia anquan lanpishu* [Annual report on China's national security studies] as "the security of guiding ideology, political belief, moral order, national spirit, etc." of a state. See Su Juan, "*Zhongguo yishi xingtai anquan mianlin de weixie yu duice sikao*" [Reflections on China's ideological security and challenges], *Jiangnan shehui xueyuan xuebao* [Academic Journal of the Southern China Institute of Social Studies] 4 (2013): 10–15.

Propaganda designed to muddy the waters by lumping party and national interests together only works as long as citizens do not see through it. Its "ideological security" relies on keeping those waters muddy, especially with regard to the contradiction between the Marxism to which it still pledges allegiance and the promotion of a nationalism that inherently negates Marxist theory. Otherwise, its citizens might reasonably ask: If the ideology is indeed necessary, how can the party abandon its core tenets? The party's failures to give convincing answers to these questions undermines its credibility to the extent that this is apparent to the Chinese citizenry itself.

Yet as the party's constitution still defines it as a class organization, as well as a national party, a legitimate question to ask is whom it should side with in the event of an obvious conflict of interest between the two categories and between various social groups. For example, whose rights would the party protect if an industrial worker sued the owner of a privately owned factory for exploitation? What would it do if "common prosperity" or the "Chinese Dream" undermined "the people's (proletarian) dictatorship" of the PRC or the status of the proletariat as the PRC's ruling class? Similarly, the PRC constitution continues to define its polity as a dictatorship and insists that "class struggle will continue to exist within certain bounds for a long time to come." This raises the question of who the contending classes are in the struggle. Is the dictatorship still intended to perpetuate class oppression? If so, which classes are oppressed? If not, why does the party insist on defining the PRC as a dictatorship?

Unless it resolves these questions, there will continue to be doubts and reservations about the national project. For example, private entrepreneurs cannot rest assured that the party will never again crack down on private businesses or even nationalize private property, given that the elimination of private property is an inevitable link in Marx's vision of socialist transformation. And while the party has claimed to have eliminated "absolute poverty," there is enough ongoing disadvantage and a big enough wealth gap that those members of the proletarian and peasant classes who have sunk to the bottom of society, including the 200–300 million rural migrant workers, have good reason to ask in what way they remain "masters of the country."

It is dangerous for the CPC to make believe that there is no clash between class interest and national interest. In a Marxist framework, class conflicts are not reconcilable, nor is it possible or desirable for conflicting classes to make peace: class trumps nation. The party's conversion to nationalism will be more credible if it makes a clean break with classism in rhetoric as well as in practice. Yet should the CPC renounce

Marxism it would logically entail renaming both the party (no longer "communist" in its goals) and the state (no longer a "people's republic" in the Marxist sense) – and this would delegitimize its historical claim on its right to rule. But an open endorsement of class struggle is inconceivable, as the party's achievements in the post-Mao era have been built upon its negation of class and class struggle. Its preferred option for now is to sit on the fence, while an unequivocal stand is more likely to win the hearts and minds of the Chinese nation.

3 The Chairman's Long Shadow
Mao Zedong and Mao Zedong Thought in Post-Maoist China

Matthew Galway

> If a people want to succeed (that is, achieve anticipated results), they must bring their ideas into correspondence with the laws of the objective external world; if these do not correspond, people will fail in their practice. After they fail, they draw a lesson from their failure, correct their ideas to make them correspond to the laws of the external world, and can thus turn failure into success; this is what is meant by "failure is the mother of success" and "a fall into the pit, a gain in your wit."
>
> Mao Zedong, Shijianlun (On Practice), July 1937[1]

In his December 26, 2013 speech, "Carry on the Enduring Spirit of Mao Zedong Thought" (*Jianchi he yunyong hao Mao Zedong sixiang huode linghun*), delivered at the symposium to commemorate the 120th anniversary of Mao's birth, Xi Jinping defined Mao Zedong Thought (*Mao Zedong sixiang*) as comprising three "basic aspects" (*jiben fangmian*).[2] He listed them: seeking truth from facts (*shishi qiushi*), the mass line (*qunzhong luxian*), and national independence and autonomy (*duli zizhu*). Xi invoked the first, a saying from the ancient *Book of Han* (*Hanshu*), to encourage Communist Party of China (CPC) members to "clearly understand" that despite marketization, China was still in the first stage of socialism, and so they should resolutely "uphold the truth and correct mistakes for the sake of the people's interest ... [and] promote theoretical innovation based on practice."[3] On the mass line, which he characterized as "the Party's lifeline and fundamental work principle," Xi called on the CPC to serve the people "wholeheartedly" and acknowledge that the people are "the fundamental force in deciding our future and destiny."

---

[1] Mao Zedong, "*Shijianlun*" [On Practice], in *Mao Zedongji bujuan* [Supplements to collected writings of Mao Zedong], Vol. 5, ed. Takeuchi Minoru (Tokyo: Sososha, [1937] 1984), 220–34.

[2] Xi Jinping, "*Jianchi he yunyong hao Mao Zedong sixiang huode linghun*" [Carry on the enduring spirit of Mao Zedong Thought], *Gongchandang yuan wang* [Communist party member network], December 26, 2013. https://syss.12371.cn/2015/05/18/ART I14319274099967168.shtml.

[3] Xi Jinping, *The Governance of China* (Beijing: Foreign Languages Press, 2014), 28.

As for the third, Xi referred not to Mao, but to Deng Xiaoping's "socialism with Chinese characteristics" (*Zhongguo tese shehuizhuyi*) and the PRC's vast territories, large population, and the importance of defending national sovereignty.[4]

Although Xi quoted Mao effusively, it is not always clear that the *substance*, rather than the *form*, of Mao and Mao Zedong Thought matters to him. There is no mention, for instance, of how the CPC's mass line emerged in 1943 as CPC methodology to encourage cadres to "listen to the masses and implement policies in accordance with popular will."[5] Xi also did not clarify or expand upon what "truth" and "facts" stand for in the context of the mass line.

Another instance when Xi invoked Mao was during the 2016 New Year's holiday. Xi went on a highly publicized trip to Jinggangshan, a remote mountainous region on Jiangxi's western border. The choice of location had a clear significance: It was where in 1927 Mao and a ragtag assembly of surviving Communists established the first Chinese Soviet Republic. Television footage, Klaus Mühlhahn recounts, captured Xi "paternalistically 'united with the masses,' sharing a meal with peasants in front of a poster of Chairman Mao." The CPC's aim for this televised trip, and more broadly, Mühlhahn elaborates, was to emphasize the "continued relevance of revolutionary legacy and rhetoric to contemporary politics ... [that there] would be an ongoing rediscovery and redeployment of the power of 'red culture.'"[6]

From these two examples, it is clear that Xi invokes Mao and Mao Zedong Thought to indicate his revolutionary *continuity* with the "rebel founding Emperor," with Xi as the inheritor of Mao's legacy.[7] If Mao and Mao Zedong Thought still matter, not solely as mere rhetorical devices for CPC figures to invoke when convenient, but as signposts of revolutionary

---

[4] Xi, *Governance of China*, 27–31; Deng Xiaoping, "*Dui qicao 'Guanyu jianguo yilai dangde ruogan lishi wentide jueyi' de yijian*" [Some views on the drafting of "Resolution on certain questions in the history of our party since the founding of the PRC"], in *Deng Xiaoping wenxuan, 1975–1982* [Selected writings of Deng Xiaoping, 1975–1982], ed. Deng Xiaoping (Beijing: Renmin chubanshe, [1981] 1983), 255–74.

[5] Aminda Smith, *Thought Reform and China's Dangerous Classes: Reeducation, Resistance, and the People* (Lanham, MD: Rowman & Littlefield, 2012), 18, 98–99; Qi Xiaolin, "Huabei geming genjudi nongmin canjia Zhonggong jundui dongji zhi kaocha" [An investigation of peasants' motives in North China revolutionary base areas for joining the Chinese Communist Party army], *Zhonggong dangshi yanjiu* [Research on the history of the Chinese Communist Party] 1 (2014): 77–89; John Fitzgerald, *Cadre Country: How China Became the Chinese Communist Party* (Sydney: University of New South Wales Press, 2022), 116.

[6] Klaus Mühlhahn, *Making China Modern: From the Great Qing to Xi Jinping* (Cambridge, MA: Harvard University Press, 2019), 564.

[7] Anita Andrew and John Rapp, *Autocracy and China's Rebel Founding Emperors* (Lanham, MD: Rowman & Littlefield, 2000).

continuity and legitimacy, then it is important to shed light on how Mao and his Thought became such multipurpose symbols.

Mao and his brain trust invested Mao Zedong Thought with Mao's personal charisma and idiosyncrasies yet established the CPC as a charismatic-impersonal Leninist organization, a Leninist innovation whereby Communist Parties recast heroism in organizational rather than individual terms.[8] Mao Zedong Thought nonetheless cycled back to Mao, the charismatic individual, in "faith Maoism," which elevated Mao Zedong Thought into unquestionable faith in Mao's wisdom and authority.[9] Mao Zedong Thought has remained ever-adaptable to suit whatever Mao and his lieutenants, and later, other leaders of the CPC, regarded as necessary for the party and PRC in the moment.[10] This is the secret of its enduring success, and with it, the resilience of CPC rule. For this reason, an "orthodox" (strictly defined) Mao Zedong Thought, or "Maoism" does not exist.[11] Nevertheless, certain features of it have enjoyed afterlives decades after Mao's death.[12] Xi Jinping himself, referring to its legitimizing role among the "four cardinal principles" (*si xiang jiben yuanze*) that Deng Xiaoping laid out, declared: "We [the CPC] should not abandon Marxism-Leninism and Mao Zedong Thought or we would be deprived of our foundation."[13]

In their book *Revolutionary Discourse in Mao's Republic*, David Apter and Tony Saich broke new ground by applying Pierre Bourdieu's concept of symbolic capital – the resources available to someone on the basis of prestige and recognition – to the relationship between the power of Mao's radical ideas and the CPC-led revolution and how Mao derived and dispersed this capital.[14] I explore the origins of Mao Zedong Thought

---

[8] Kenneth Jowitt, *New World Disorder: The Leninist Extinction* (Berkeley: University of California Press, 1993), 4.

[9] Timothy Cheek, *Propaganda and Culture in Mao's China: Deng Tuo and the Intelligentsia* (Oxford: Clarendon Press, 1997), 69–70.

[10] Matthew Galway, *The Emergence of Global Maoism: China's Red Evangelism and the Cambodian Communist Movement, 1949–1979* (Ithaca, NY: Cornell University Press, 2022), 33–34.

[11] Nick Knight, *Rethinking Mao: Explorations in Mao Zedong Thought* (Lanham, MD: Rowman & Littlefield, 2007), 48–49; Christophe Bourseiller, *Les Maoïstes: La folle histoire des gardes rouges français* [The Maoists: The crazy story of the French Red Guards] (Paris: Plon, 1996), 300.

[12] Christian Sorace, Ivan Franceschini, and Nicholas Loubere, "Introduction," in *Afterlives of Chinese Communism: Political Concepts from Mao to Xi*, ed. Christian Sorace, Ivan Franceschini, and Nicholas Loubere (Canberra: ANU Press and Verso Books, 2019), 1–7.

[13] Xi, *Governance of China*, 362; see also Martin Wagner, "Excoriating Stalin, Criticizing Mao: Entangled Reevaluations of the Past in the 1950s Soviet Union and 1970s/80s China," *The American Historical Review* 18(3) (September 2023): 1134–1135.

[14] David Apter and Tony Saich, *Revolutionary Discourse in Mao's Republic* (Cambridge, MA: Harvard University Press, 1998), 33–34, 107, 311, 338n15, citing Pierre Bourdieu, *Outline of a Theory of Practice* (Cambridge: Cambridge University Press, 1977).

with a view to accounting for its enduring importance today. I contend that its magnitude in contemporary times stems from its depersonalized, *revolutionary* symbolic capital, which Mao's successors in the CPC leadership have successfully mobilized to justify their one-party rule. They invoke Mao Zedong Thought to exhibit revolutionary continuity despite their various shifts away from the ideology and practice of the Mao era. Mao Zedong Thought thus fulfills what I call a legitimizing need rather than purely a social one.[15] CPC leaders must acknowledge, and frequently reference, Mao Zedong Thought to project continuity with the party's revolutionary origins and maintain a monopoly on power, whatever non-Maoist policies they are putting in place.

The Sandal Shaped in the Making: Mao Zedong Thought and the Centrality of Praxis to CPC Rule

Mao's emphasis on "seeking truth from facts," "uniting knowing with doing" (*zhixing heyi*), and creative ideological adaptation contributed to the CPC's revolutionary success and set the stage for the stability of its rule. Even in the years after his death, when CPC leaders critically reappraised the Mao era, they reaffirmed and lionized Mao's stress on praxis. The post-Mao CPC did so by invoking the slogan "to seek truth from facts," which formed the basis for CPC policies and the legitimation processes that stabilized the party's rule in the more than four decades since Mao's death.

Mao's development of his Thought laid the foundation for prolonged one-party rule in the PRC. In his January 1958 speech at the Supreme State Conference, which was attended by party-state leaders, Mao reflected on the importance of "permanent revolution" (*buduan geming*) and adaptability in struggle. "The Hunanese often say, 'Straw sandals have no form – they shape themselves in the making'" (*Hunanren chang shuo: "caoxie wu yang, bian da bian xiang"*). Much like the straw sandals metaphor in Mao's speech, the official PRC state ideology, Marxism–Leninism–Mao Zedong Thought, which has recently incorporated Xi Jinping Thought, was itself the product of creative adaptation of Marxism–Leninism in theory and later in praxis in Maoist China as Sinified Marxism–Leninism and beyond as Maoism. ("Maoism" is an English term coined by Benjamin Schwartz to stand for Mao Zedong Thought.[16]) Xi defines Mao Zedong Thought as "the fundamental guiding Thought of the CPC ... a series of theoretical

---

[15] Clifford Geertz, *The Interpretation of Cultures* (London: Basic Books, 1973), 220.
[16] Elizabeth Perry, "Debating Maoism in Contemporary China: Reflections on Benjamin I. Schwartz, Chinese Communism and the Rise of Mao" (Working Paper, Harvard-Yenching Institute Working Paper Series, Cambridge, MA, 2020), 1; Benjamin

summarizations and conclusions that Chinese Communists represented by Mao Zedong drew from their unique experience in China's revolution and development in accordance with the basic tenets of Marxism ... It is the crystallization of the collective wisdom of the CPC."[17]

Mao Zedong Thought is not merely a "guiding Thought," but an "ideological system" (*sixiang tixi*) that comprises a praxis-oriented ideological discourse, a critical interpretive paradigm (a Marxist-based system for explaining history), radical language for waging political struggle, and diverse strategies for engaging in protracted warfare and socialist development.[18] It represents the basis for governance in China.[19] Mao Zedong Thought is not purely of Mao's sole design, but the invention of a cast of characters, a brain trust, who helped to manufacture Mao Zedong into a charismatic "cosmocrat" (one who claims to be, or is elevated by others to be, the representative of higher truths) and position Mao Zedong Thought as irrefutable.[20] The CPC could then call upon either Mao or his Thought to legitimate, and ensure the stability of, continued CPC rule.

Any examination of the origins of Mao Zedong Thought must begin with the primacy that Mao placed on praxis and creative adaptation. "From the beginning," writes Brantly Womack, "Mao combined theory and practice, with the heavier emphasis on practice. And even before he became a Marxist, he was convinced that the ultimate political strength [lay in] mobilized popular support."[21] Later leaders rallied popular support by mobilizing Mao's image and revolutionary legacy.

In the first decades of the twentieth century in China, Mao inclined toward a "practical-political" approach to foreign ideas, with an initial interest in the anarchism of Kropotkin and the liberalism of Dewey, before he shifted to a "theoretical-organizational" approach.[22] The latter

---

I. Schwartz, *Chinese Communism and the Rise of Mao* (Cambridge, MA: Harvard University Press, 1951).

[17] Xi, *Governance of China*, 20n13.

[18] Galway, *The Emergence of Global Maoism*, 6–7; Fabio Lanza, "Global Maoism," in *Afterlives of Chinese Communism: Political Concepts from Mao to Xi*, ed. Christian Sorace, Ivan Franceschini, and Nicholas Loubere (Canberra: ANU Press and Verso Books, 2019), 85.

[19] Roderick MacFarquhar, "Does Mao Still Matter?" in *The China Questions: Critical Insights into a Rising Power*, ed. Jennifer Rudolph and Michael Szonyi (Cambridge, MA: Harvard University Press, 2018), 26–32, 27.

[20] Apter and Saich, *Revolutionary Discourse*, xvi.

[21] Brantly Womack, "From Urban Radical to Rural Revolutionary: Mao from the 1920s to 1937," in *A Critical Introduction to Mao*, ed. Timothy Cheek (Cambridge: Cambridge University Press, 2010), 61.

[22] Brantly Womack, *The Foundations of Mao Zedong's Political Thought, 1917–1935* (Honolulu: University of Hawaii Press, 1982), 81; Womack, "From Urban Radical to Rural Revolutionary"; Galway, *The Emergence of Global Maoism*, 23–25.

embraced the Marxist stress on revolutionary struggle over liberal democratic notions, such as popular elections. Mao gained fluency in Marxism only in the 1930s when Chinese translations of Marxist texts were more accessible. Yet Bolshevism, the centralized, cohesive, and disciplined doctrine and program of the Bolsheviks in Russia that advocated for the violent overthrow of capitalism and establishing a dictatorship of the proletariat, appealed most strongly to him. In the mid 1920s, Mao "declared his support for the 'total solution' and common ideology embodied in Bolshevist Communism."[23]

Several years earlier, in 1921, Mao was among a small group of men who founded the Communist Party of China. Chief of the Far Eastern Bureau of the Comintern (Soviet-run Communist International) Grigori Voitinsky and functionary Henk Sneevliet (alias Maring) had already introduced Leninist organization to Chinese leftists.[24] Tony Saich identifies four other "pushes," or factors that led to the CPC's establishment as: (1) recognition by many Chinese intellectuals that Marxism offered novel solutions to China's ills, (2) Chinese Marxists went from "ivory tower" theorists to becoming on-the-ground activists, (3) the strong interpersonal connections among participants in Marxist study groups, and (4) consensus within these circles that Leninist-style organization was necessary for cohesiveness and "resist [ance to] external pressures."[25]

A clear pathway to power was not in sight for the fledgling organization or for Mao. An opportunity arose to spread Communism, at Moscow's suggestion, via a "bloc-within strategy" in the form of the First United Front with the ruling Nationalist Party, the Kuomintang (KMT, or GMD in *pinyin* shorthand), which the Communists joined. But the anti-Communist KMT military commander Chiang Kai-shek turned on the Communists during the joint Northern Expedition against renegade powerbrokers (1926–1928) who had carved China into personal fiefdoms and by 1927 had established himself as head of the KMT and government. On April 12, 1927, Chiang loyalists, with the help of gangsters, violently attacked unionists and suspected Communist sympathizers (the "Shanghai Massacre") and purged Communists from the KMT. The resultant chaos forced 90 percent of the CPC's surviving members (roughly between 15 and 25,000) to flee to the countryside.[26]

---

[23] Rebecca Karl, *Mao Zedong and China in the Twentieth Century World* (Durham, NC: Duke University Press, 2010), 18.
[24] Tony Saich, *From Rebel to Ruler: One Hundred Years of the Chinese Communist Party* (Cambridge, MA: Harvard University Press, 2021), 46–51.
[25] Saich, *From Rebel to Ruler*, 44.
[26] Womack, *Foundations of Mao Zedong's Political Thought*, 49–53.

After the Shanghai Massacre, even the most diehard Communists struggled to imagine the CPC in state power. The nearly destroyed party, now divorced from its vanguard urban working-class base, had to adapt – an enduring feature of the party and a hallmark of Maoism. It did so by widening its membership, which allowed it not only to survive, but also to resuscitate in China's rural south and southwest.[27] There, in the years before establishing the Jiangxi Soviet from 1927 to 1930, the party shifted from Bolshevism, which focused on urban class-based revolution, to rural revolution. This presented Mao with the opportunity to build a reputation as a military leader and peasant organizer.[28] Mao distinguished himself as a shrewd tactician and military general whose personal charisma in interactions with local power-brokers and potential foes in Jinggangshan allowed him considerable room to maneuver. By winning over local leaders, the CPC continued to develop an "integrated" strategy that embedded Red Armies within local communities.[29]

Already a respected organizer and military leader by the 1934–35 Long March that followed the Jiangxi Soviet's collapse, Mao rose to party leadership at a meeting during the Long March. Once the Long Marchers settled into Yan'an, the capital of the Shaan-Gan-Ning Border Region, he set his sights on becoming the CPC's supreme theorist as well. It was during the Yan'an years (1936–42) that Mao authored the canon that became the ideological foundation of his Thought.

He had already begun to formulate some of these ideas in pre-Yan'an texts: "Analysis of the Classes in Chinese Society" (March 1926) and the arguably more important "Xingguo Investigation" (October 1930) were highly detailed rural investigations that shed light on wealth inequality and unequal landownership in the rural sector.[30] Mao's famous "Report

---

[27] Yung-fa Chen, *Making Revolution: The Communist Movement in Eastern and Central China, 1937–1945* (Berkeley: University of California Press, 1986), 121–222, 259–295.

[28] Alexander Vatlin and Stephen Smith, "The Comintern," in *The Oxford Handbook of the History of Communism*, ed. Stephen Smith (Oxford: Oxford University Press, 2014), 187–202; Huang Daoxuan, *Zhangli yu xianjie: Zhongyang suqude geming (1933–1934)* [Tensions and limits: Revolution in the Central Soviet base area (1933–1934)] (Beijing: Shehui kexue chubanshe, 2011).

[29] Ying Xing, "Cong 'difang junshihua' dao 'junshi difanghua': Yi Hongsijun 'banzhe fazhan' zhanlüede yuanyuan liubian wei zhongxin" [From "Local militarization" to "military localization": A focus on the origins and development of the Fourth Red Army's "integrated development" strategy], *Kaifang shidai* [Open Times] 5 (2018): 11–42.

[30] Mao Zedong, "*Zhongguo shehui ge jiejide fenxi*" [Analysis of the various classes in Chinese society], in *Mao Zedongji* [Collected writings of Mao Zedong], vol. 1, 2nd ed., ed. Takeuchi Minoru (Tokyo: Hokubosha, [1926] 1970), 161–174; Mao Zedong, "*Xingguo kaocha*" [Xingguo investigation], in *Mao Zedongji*, vol. 2, ed. Takeuchi Minoru (Tokyo: Hokubosha, [1930] 1971), 185–252.

on an Investigation of the Peasant Movement in Hunan" (February–March 1927)[31] highlighted the power of peasant organizations and contended that the Chinese proletariat had the potential to form a truly national revolutionary base only if it harnessed the peasantry's revolutionary zeal.

In Yan'an, Mao expanded on these earlier formative works to develop ideas into ideology, ideology into praxis, and ultimately, ideology *and* praxis into a cohesive, praxis-oriented ideological system. One of Mao's most famous essays, "On Practice" (July 1937), stresses the primacy of direct experience to knowledge and perception of the objective external world. Mao argues that *a priori* knowledge is dogmatism because only *a posteriori* knowledge, or knowledge derived from practice, refers to objective reality.[32] "On Contradiction" (August 1937) and "On Protracted War" (May–June 1938), respectively, articulate a locally relevant strategy for waging revolution, namely, how to approach the contradiction of the universal versus the particular and how to win a war against a numerically and technologically advantaged opponent.[33] The essay that historian Arif Dirlik describes as Mao's "classic formulation of the premises of Chinese Marxism,"[34] "On New Democracy" (January 1940), contends that the Chinese revolution comprises a democratic and a socialist revolution, with the former representing "New Democracy." Democracy, for Mao, was possible in China under terms and conditions that were distinct from those in the "Two Worlds" of Euro-America and the Soviet Union, with state and governmental structures emerging under the joint dictatorship of the anti-imperialist classes.[35] The essay's lasting power, argues Timothy Cheek, is that it "made sense of China's history and, more important, gave Chinese readers a sense of purpose, hope, and

---

[31] Mao Zedong, "*Hunan nongmin yundong kaocha baogao*" [Report on an investigation of the peasant movement in Hunan], in *Mao Zedongji* [Collected writings of Mao Zedong], vol. 1, 2nd ed., ed. Takeuchi Minoru (Tokyo: Hokubosha, [1927] 1970), 111–142.

[32] Mao Zedong, "On Practice: On the Relation between Knowledge and Practice, between Theory and Reality, between Knowing and Doing," in *Mao Zedong on Dialectical Materialism*, ed. and trans. Nick Knight (Armonk, NY: M.E. Sharpe, [1937] 1990), 132–153; Galway, *The Emergence of Global Maoism*, 30.

[33] Mao Zedong, "*Maodun lun*" [On Contradiction], in *Mao Zedongji bujuan* [Supplements to Collected Writings of Mao Zedong], vol. 5, ed. Takeuchi Minoru (Tokyo: Sososha, [1937] 1984), 240–278; Mao Zedong, "On Protracted War," in *Mao's Road to Power: Revolutionary Writings, 1912–1949. Volume 6: The New Stage, August 1937–1938*, ed. Stuart Schram (Armonk, NY: M. E. Sharpe, [1938] 2004), 319–389; Galway, *The Emergence of Global Maoism*, 30–31.

[34] Arif Dirlik, *Marxism in the Chinese Revolution* (Lanham, MD: Rowman & Littlefield, 2005), 79.

[35] Mao Zedong, "*Xinminzhuzhuyi lun*" [On New Democracy], in *Mao Zedongji* [Collected Writings of Mao Zedong], vol. 7, 2nd ed., ed. Takeuchi Minoru (Tokyo: Hokubosha, [1940] 1971), 143–202; Galway, *The Emergence of Global Maoism*, 31–32.

meaning."³⁶ Yet the most important of all these parts above is the sum: Mao's "Sinification of Marxism" into Mao Zedong Thought.

Mao's Sinification of Marxism, a strategy that he first introduced in a 1938 long report to the CPC Central Committee's Sixth Enlarged Plenum ("On the New Stage"), entrenched creative adaptation through praxis as a fundamental pillar of Mao Zedong Thought.³⁷ Lauded by Stuart Schram in *Mao Tse-tung* as Mao's "greatest theoretical and practical achievement," the Sinification of Marxism entailed applying the universal theory, or ideological discourse *cum* organizational structure of Marxism–Leninism, to the concrete practice of the Chinese revolution.³⁸ "[In] applying Marxism to China," Mao urged, "Chinese communists must fully and properly integrate the universal truth of Marxism with the concrete practice of the Chinese revolution, that is to say, the universal truth of Marxism must have a national form before it can be useful, and in no circumstances can it be applied subjectively and formulaically as a mere formula."³⁹ At first glance, Sinification implies mere "application" (*yunyong*) of Marxism to Chinese realities without theoretical development, or the sublimation of purportedly universal Marxism to national peculiarities. But as Dirlik notes, Sinification actually "left Marxism untouched in its basics [and] brought to Marxism a Chinese 'air' or 'style' . . . Sinification was the articulation of Marxism to a historical situation of which Chinese society was the terrain, but a terrain in the process of transformation by global forces."⁴⁰

This description is reminiscent of Dirlik's later argument that Mao's Marxism is at once locally Chinese and Marxist-universalist. "Mao did not reduce Marxism to a Chinese version or view China merely as another illustration of universal Marxist principles," Dirlik contends, but at once reduces the Chinese revolution to an aspect of a more general Marxism and elevates it to a relationship with it that highlights shared qualities.⁴¹ The result was a conception of the relationship that insisted on China's *difference* and yet represented Chinese Marxism as an embodiment of Marxism. Knight similarly regards Sinification as Mao's search for

---

[36] Timothy Cheek, "Mao, Revolution and Memory," in *A Critical Introduction to Mao*, ed. Timothy Cheek (Cambridge: Cambridge University Press, 2010), 3–30, 10.

[37] Galway, *The Emergence of Global Maoism*, 32–36, 78–79; Matthew Galway, "From Revolutionary Culture to Original Culture and Back: 'On New Democracy' and the Kampucheanization of Marxism-Leninism, 1940–1965," *Cross Currents: East Asian History and Culture Review* 24 (September 2017): 133, 138–139.

[38] Stuart Schram, *Mao Tse-tung* (Harmondsworth: Penguin, 1966), 68.

[39] Mao Zedong, "*Xinminzhuzhuyi lun*," 198.

[40] Arif Dirlik, "Modernism and Antimodernism in Mao Zedong's Marxism," in *Critical Perspectives on Mao Zedong's Thought*, ed. Arif Dirlik, Paul Healy, and Nick Knight (Atlantic Heights, NJ: Humanities Press, 1997), 59–83, 68–69.

[41] Dirlik, *Marxism in the Chinese Revolution*, 97.

a method for applying the universal theory of Marxism to the Chinese national context without abandoning its universality.[42] Here lies the core of Mao Zedong Thought: its emphasis on the primacy of practice and adaptability while maintaining the "laws" that Marx and Lenin made central to their purportedly universal and global ideological discourses.

Before Yan'an Rectification elevated Mao to CPC *primus inter pares* and "cosmocrat," he relied heavily on many others to disseminate his ideas and what he thought the CPC ought to do going forward.[43] Ai Siqi (Li Shengxuan), Chen Boda (Chen Jianxiang), Zhang Wentian, and Kang Sheng all played important roles, but Ai, a Hong Kong-educated philosopher, and Chen, a political theorist, grounded Marxist theory in practice. In the 1930s, Ai wrote extensively on Marxist concepts, including dialectical materialism, and encouraged Chinese intellectuals to apply and develop New Philosophy (*xin zhexue*), a competing Soviet current of Marxist philosophy; afterward, many flocked to the CPC.[44] Chen insisted that cadres perform a "systematic critique" of traditional philosophy (such as Confucianism), the "'enrichment' of dialectical materialism by 'concretizing' it in Chinese problems," and the synthesis of Chinese nationalism with proletarian internationalism.[45] The last represented a somewhat-imprecise precursor to Mao's Sinification, though Chen's calls for a concretized dialectical materialism in practice led him to coin the term "Sinification of Marxism" in May 1938 before Mao deployed it at the Sixth Plenum.[46] Mao nevertheless defined the Sinification of Marxism as the synthesis of Marxist universal laws that alone did not constitute Marxism as an ideological system with the specific laws that featured in China's historical situation and in the CPC's practice of waging revolution.[47]

Mao's stress on praxis is a fundamental reason for the enduring success of Mao Zedong Thought and the party long after his death in 1976. Deng Xiaoping invoked the slogan "to seek truth from facts," which he held as the "true spirit" of Mao Zedong Thought, throughout the Reform and Opening Up era. The concept of "socialism with Chinese characteristics" is another kind of pragmatic "Sinification" with emphases on praxis and creative adaptation. As Deng argued, the "correct way to hold high the banner of Mao Zedong Thought [is] to

---

[42] Knight, *Rethinking Mao*, 199.   [43] Apter and Saich, *Revolutionary Discourse*, 89.
[44] Nick Knight, *Marxist Philosophy in China: From Qu Qiubai to Mao Zedong, 1923–1945* (Dordrecht: Springer, 2005), 93–94, 103; Ai Siqi, *Sixiangfangfalun* [Methodology of Thought], 4th ed. (Shanghai: Shenghuo shudian, 1939), 160.
[45] Raymond Wylie, *The Emergence of Maoism: Mao Tse-tung, Chen Po-ta, and the Search for Chinese Theory* (Stanford, CA: Stanford University Press, 1980), 28–29.
[46] Wylie, *The Emergence of Maoism*, 36.   [47] Knight, *Rethinking Mao*, 199–213.

adapt to such changes [conditions favorable to economic relations with foreign countries] and promote foreign trade."[48]

Subsequent CPC leaders, most notably Xi Jinping in the 2013 speech discussed previously (p. 42), invoked "to seek truth from facts" in reference to Mao and as a continuance of a praxis-oriented approach to socialist development in China. In so doing, party leaders legitimize the continuation in power of the CPC, which since the late 1970s has opened China up to marketization (anathema to Mao's socialist vision), uncontested and unquestioned. The party represents both continuity *and* rupture, with its leaders strategically invoking those legitimating links to Mao to justify and maintain rule as they shift the PRC away from the high socialism of the Mao era.

Protecting Yan'an: Mao Zedong and Manufacturing Revolutionary Symbolic Capital

If Sinification was a type of adaptation that Mao and his brain trust invested with his idiosyncrasies and charisma, then Yan'an Rectification (1942–1945) consolidated Mao at the center of the CPC. Mao and his loyalists marshaled Sinification to draw in, then mobilize, rank-and-filers and green recruits from the party's aggressive recruitment efforts. Rigorous and relentless study of Mao's texts in Yan'an transformed new recruits into hardened Maoist disciples who held aloft Sinification and Mao as the supreme theory and supreme theorist, respectively.[49]

Mao's rise to CPC leadership was also facilitated by a fortuitous combination of the poor leadership of the early Long March leaders and his reputation as a successful military strategist and leader. Mao's political predecessors Chen Duxiu, Qu Qiubai, Li Lisan, and Wang Ming were, as I have written elsewhere, "messengers who knew how best to explain the ideology, rather than the organizers who had developed [the Chinese revolution]."[50] By stressing his individual contributions to party history, Mao and his lieutenants systematically outmaneuvered and sidelined Mao's challengers for party leadership, like the Moscow-backed Wang Ming. All who remained professed allegiance to Mao and Mao Zedong Thought. "The new orthodoxy," Saich writes, "situated Mao as the central player in the Chinese revolution, which in turn put him in an unchallengeable position of leadership."[51] As this section shows, the Yan'an Rectification Movement transformed Mao the successful military

---

[48] Ezra F. Vogel, *Deng Xiaoping and the Transformation of China* (Cambridge, MA: Harvard University Press, 2011), 228.
[49] Galway, *The Emergence of Global Maoism*, 34.
[50] Galway, *The Emergence of Global Maoism*, 29.   [51] Saich, *From Rebel to Ruler*, 130.

leader and theoretician into a symbol which the people in Yan'an, now energized with a sense of revolutionary purpose, raised alongside his writings as inextricable from the party.

The Yan'an Rectification's process of what Apter and Saich call "exegetical bonding," the common rigorous study of certain texts and collective self-transformation of those engaging with them, is especially important in explaining Mao's rise to CPC ideological stewardship. Mao's personal charisma was one aspect of this exegetic bonding. As Apter and Saich note, in Yan'an Mao appeared "a Socratic Mao, the philosopher-king, the teacher cum cosmocrat."[52] The second aspect involved rewriting party history to foreground Mao's contributions. Mao delivered two speeches in early February 1942 that signaled that Rectification sought to stamp out "intellectual diversity within the Party," particularly among new arrivals and loyalists to the Comintern-backed Soviet line of Wang Ming. The job of intellectuals, Saich notes, was not to offer independent critiques, but to "serve as cheerleaders for the Party, faithfully proselytizing its views."[53]

Intellectuals and higher-ranked cadres in Yan'an were to study Mao's "correct" interpretation of CPC history as represented by two volumes of party documents from the Sixth Congress that Mao had edited personally: *Since the Sixth Party Congress* (*Liuda yilai*) of December 1941 and *Before the Sixth Party Congress* (*Liuda yiqian*).[54] According to Mao's editions, *he* possessed the correct political line whereas Wang Ming and other rivals were "rightists" who had made no positive contribution to CPC history.[55] The purge of Mao critics during Rectification further consolidated Mao at the center of the party and its history by codifying his telling of the CPC's past, present, and future lines as "correct."[56] In eliminating those opposing lines of thinking that might challenge ideological harmony, Mao and his loyalists ensured that Mao arose as the CPC's supreme theorist. Thereafter, any questioning of Mao was "tantamount to committing a mistake in 'line.'"[57] The CPC purged party

---

[52] Apter and Saich, *Revolutionary Discourse*, 16, 264–265.
[53] Saich, *From Rebel to Ruler*, 132.
[54] Tony Saich, ed., *The Rise to Power of the Chinese Communist Party: Documents and Analysis* (Armonk, NY: M. E. Sharpe, 1996), 972.
[55] Gao Hua, *Hong taiyang shi zenyang shengqide: Yan'an zhengfeng de lailongqumai* [How the red sun rose: The origins and development of the Yan'an rectification movement] (Hong Kong: Xianggang Zhongwen daxue chubanshe, 2000), 241–248; Saich, *From Rebel to Ruler*, 130; Tony Saich, "Writing or Rewriting History? The Construction of the Maoist Resolution on Party History," in *New Perspectives on the Chinese Communist Revolution*, ed. Tony Saich and Hans van de Ven (New York: Routledge, 1995), 299–328, 305–306.
[56] Gao, *Hong taiyang shi zenyang shengqide*, 380–381.
[57] Saich, *The Rise to Power of the Chinese Communist Party*, lxi.

stalwarts like Wang Shiwei (born Wang Sidao) in 1947 (branded as an "internal traitor" and executed) and Ding Ling (pseudonym of Jiang Bingzhi) in 1957 (criticized and exiled).[58] The reason was, fascinatingly enough, not their criticism of Maoist revolutionary principles, but for identifying how the party ignored such principles in praxis. Violence and the persecution were indeed features of the CPC's consolidation of Maoist thought during Yan'an Rectification and in subsequent CPC campaigns in its first decade in power.[59]

As Apter and Saich observe, though, during Yan'an Rectification, Mao "appear[ed] as an agent, the spokesman for Marxist truths. But there was also a real Mao, always a palpable presence, who touched everyone's life. In front of large audiences, he always appeared modest, yet authoritative. But when the words faded, away, the texts remained, and with them, a hermetic language punctuated by earthy examples and classical allusions." As the site where revolutionaries "exegetically bonded" over Mao's works, Yan'an itself became a place of "symbolic revolutionary capital." Yan'an, Apter and Saich continue, is "a good story ... that people told themselves while they lived it and provides an uncommonly interesting example of beliefs becoming so powerful that they changed the way people acted, thought of themselves, and responded to others, at least for a time."[60]

In Yan'an, as Timothy Cheek describes, "an élan, an *esprit de corps*, a sense of heroic mission" developed within cadres as they studied Mao's works.[61] Yan'an, he continues, was host to its own distinct "discourse community" that was "revolutionary in object and inversionary in goal [and which] embodied a radical, disjunctive, and transformational nationalism." Yan'anite cadres, Huang Daoxuan observes, forged themselves into "transparent people" whose devotion to the party was absolute.[62] This was so because, at the end of the Rectification Movement, Yan'an's "redemptive" and "transformational character" metamorphosed Mao into a "cosmocratic figure who, although secular, might easily have been theocratic."[63]

---

[58] Apter and Saich, *Revolutionary Discourse*, 66; Christina Kelley Gilmartin, *Engendering the Chinese Revolution: Radical Women, Communist Politics, and Mass Movements in the 1920s* (Berkeley: University of California Press, 1995), 222; Lydia H. Liu, "Invention and Intervention: The Making of a Female Tradition in Modern Chinese Literature," in *Chinese Femininities, Chinese Masculinities: A Reader*, ed. Susan Brownell and Jeffrey N. Wasserstrom (Berkeley: University of California Press, 2002), 154–155.

[59] Galway, *The Emergence of Global Maoism*, 38–46.

[60] Apter and Saich, *Revolutionary Discourse*, 9, 16.

[61] Cheek, *Propaganda and Culture in Mao's China*, 13.

[62] Huang Daoxuan, "*Zhengfeng yundongde xinlingshi*" [An emotional history of the Rectification Campaign], *Jindaishi yanjiu* [Modern Chinese History Studies] 2 (2020): 5.

[63] Apter and Saich, *Revolutionary Discourse*, 2, 4.

The violence of the Rectification Movement, too, left many all too aware of what might happen to those who dissented or criticized this new cosmocratic figure. Nevertheless, Mao's charismatic leadership inspired spirited revolutionary action because of his personal charismatic authority, and he infused his idiosyncrasies into revolutionary theory in the name of Sinification. Once in power, Mao's "necessary charismatic authority could then justify CPC policies," no matter how ambitious.[64]

Exegetical bonding helped stabilize CPC rule even through the Cultural Revolution and after Mao's death. Party leaders from Deng onward often quoted from Mao's texts, namely ones that they had memorized during the Mao-centric frenzy of the Cultural Revolution, as if to lend credence to their own revolutionary bona fides. Reform and Opening Up could have undermined party rule, but despite reappraising Mao's reign, CPC leaders reiterated Mao Zedong Thought as their ideological *raison d'être*. Part of the reason for immediate CPC leaders' invocations of Mao is that party history is intrinsic to its very claim to legitimacy. Mao's successors, Martin Wagner intimates, "did not opt to suppress memories and maintain silence. Rather, they ended terror, reinvented regime legitimacy and tackled the historical burden," mainly because it was an "imminent historical" regime in nature. Wagner concludes, though, that Mao's heirs – in particular Deng – did so "within limits – confronting the horrors of dictatorship with the means of dictatorship."[65] The CPC did not de-Maoize but instead reassessed his legacy and reanimated his Thought with emphasis on positive contributions while acknowledging Mao's mistakes. It did so to ensure that his Thought remained important and a wellspring of experiential knowledge from which the CPC could draw lessons and guidance.

Exegetical bonding in Yan'an also gave the CPC an unprecedented sense of unity and discipline that was essential to its revolutionary success and has since underpinned the stability of its rule. Even amid the tumultuous Socialist Education Movement and Cultural Revolution, both of which were CPC programs to crush corruption and capitalist tendencies within the party and without and were marked by Mao's personal vendettas to eliminate CPC rivals, many Chinese still professed devotion to Mao and his Thought.[66] They did so for a host of reasons, not the least of which was a genuine fear of harsh reprisal, whether imprisonment, hard labor sentences, or execution, for doing otherwise.

---

[64] Galway, *The Emergence of Global Maoism*, 35.
[65] Wagner, "Excoriating Stalin, Criticizing Mao," 1142–1143.
[66] Galway, *The Emergence of Global Maoism*, 49–50.

CPC leaders have held the party together by limiting criticism in a starkly similar way to what Mao did in Yan'an. Party leaders, Gloria Davies notes, often frame their ideas as "guiding thought" (*zhidao sixiang*), or those ideas that guide the nation, while claiming simultaneously that they served at the forefront of "Chinese thought" (*Zhongguo sixiang*), those central ideas and debates that constitute "intellectual inquiry" in theory and practice in the Sinophone intellectual world.[67] This, she says, allows such leaders to "justify censorship in terms of protecting the nation from the harm of dangerous and subversive ideas that are at odds with their own."[68] A recent example, Roderick MacFarquhar observes, is Xi Jinping's effort to "reemphasize Deng's delineation of Marxism-Leninism and Mao Zedong Thought as components of the nation's four cardinal principles that cannot be questioned ... [with] ideology as a vibrant bulwark of China's exceptionalism, to inoculate its [China's] citizens against [Euro-American] democratic ideas."[69]

In his book *From Rebel to Ruler*, Saich identifies mastery of "correct" history, alongside the CPC's dominance of state and society, clandestine work, and military struggle, and emphasis on the indigenous nature of the Chinese revolution, among others, as a key feature of the Xi era that represents a holdover from the Mao years, particularly from Yan'an Rectification.[70] "Xi's campaign against historical nihilism," Saich notes, "sought to eliminate all writing that challenges official party history ... [as] control over narrative has been an essential element of the [CPC's] claims to be China's legitimate ruler." This campaign comprised CPC efforts to censor parts of its history and remove unsavory parts entirely, most notably "alternative views" of the CPC's past in magazines such as *Annals of the Yellow Emperor* (*Yanhuang chunqiu*). As Saich recounts, Xi loyalists seized control of its editorial board and deleted mention of more controversial programs in the CPC's history, particularly the Cultural Revolution. Xi's narrative today of "the China Dream" also bears a striking resemblance to Mao's emphasis on the CPC's leading role in resisting imperialism. "Xi Jinping's narrative," Saich observes, "follows a similar theme intended to complete the unfinished objective of fulfilling the China Dream of rejuvenating the Chinese nation ... [and] forms a crucial element in his claims to legitimate rule."[71]

---

[67] Gloria Davies, "Translator's Introduction to 'A China Bereft of Thought' by Rong Jian," in *Voices from the Chinese Century: Public Intellectual Debate from Contemporary China*, ed. Timothy Cheek, David Ownby, and Joshua A. Fogel (New York: Columbia University Press, 2020), 73.
[68] Davies, "Translator's Introduction," 73.
[69] MacFarquhar, "Does Mao Still Matter?" 30.
[70] Saich, *From Rebel to Ruler*, 435–466.   [71] Saich, *From Rebel to Ruler*, 438.

Xi's crackdown on corruption and party discipline, not to mention the rectification of the security forces that is underway at present, also have direct links in style, substance, and praxis to Mao-era rectifications that preceded them. As with Yan'an Rectification, "correct" interpretations of CPC history and matters of legitimacy underpin Xi's pushes to root out those members who have lost their way ideologically. The Xi administration identified "a network of entrenched interest groups made up of businesses and officials [which] had started to capture many institutions, such as state enterprises and government agencies," that the CPC regarded as forces that undermined party legitimacy and governance. In taking down these "tigers" (the most powerful senior officials) and "flies" (thousands of lower-ranking cadres), the Xi administration committed itself to ousting Xi's political rivals and consolidating the CPC around Xi and his loyalists.[72] The objective, MacFarquhar elaborates, is also "to restore the Party's reputation, reclaim popular support, and fend off any potential threats to its continued unfettered rule," all of which mirror Mao-era rectification efforts in Yan'an and the consolidation of the CPC's political power in the 1950s.[73] The trend of removing rivals in the post-Mao years has also carried on since Mao's death. Deng's 1987 removal of reformist CPC General Secretary Hu Yaobang (and his death two years later), himself twice-purged by Mao years earlier;[74] recently, the mysterious exit of former CPC General Secretary Hu Jintao from the Twentieth National Congress and the death of Xi's one-time rival Li Keqiang in late October 2023 are two events that are eerily reminiscent of Mao-era tactics to isolate and eliminate potential players for CPC power.[75]

Correct consciousness, lastly, remains ever important to the CPC under Xi, as it did in Yan'an. As the vanguard of the PRC's working class, CPC cadres distinguish themselves in Leninist fashion from the populace by holding what John Fitzgerald describes as a "heightened level of

---

[72] Mühlhahn, *Making China Modern*, 562; see also Barry Naughton, "Is China Socialist?" *Journal of Economic Perspectives* 31(1) (2017): 3–24.

[73] MacFarquhar, "Does Mao Still Matter?" 29; see also Galway, *The Emergence of Global Maoism*, 38–46; Mühlhahn, *Making China Modern*, 359–407.

[74] Jeremy Brown, *June Fourth: The Tiananmen Protests and Beijing Massacre of 1989* (Cambridge: Cambridge University Press, 2021), 24, 42.

[75] Helen Davidson, "Was Hu Jintao's Removal from China's 20th Party Congress Suspicious or Not?" *The Guardian* (October 28, 2022), www.theguardian.com/world/2022/oct/28/china-hu-jintao-removal-20th-party-congress-suspicious-or-not; James T. Areddy, "Hu Jintao's Exit from China's Communist Party Congress Causes a Stir," *The Wall Street Journal* (October 23, 2022), www.wsj.com/articles/hu-jintaos-exit-from-chinas-party-congress-causes-a-stir-11666450539; Stephen McDonell, "Why Li Keqiang's Death Is Dangerous for Xi Jinping," *BBC News* (October 28, 2023), www.bbc.com/news/world-asia-china-67236049.

'consciousness' ... [that] binds them through party discipline to the will and vision of the general secretary."[76] As the CPC Constitution dictates, CPC members "are vanguard fighters of the Chinese working class who possess Communist consciousness."[77] The "Four Consciousnesses" of the Xi years expand on this further by referring to the "consciousnesses of ideology, the whole, the core, and the line," all of which concern party members rather than the general populace. "From Mao," Fitzgerald says, Chinese communists today "learn that the conscious vanguard in the party must submit itself to constant re-education to remain loyal to the party leadership and, where possible, educate the people to the point where they concede that they want what the party wants for them."[78]

From Cosmocrat to Autocrat, Revolutionary Symbolic Capital to Revolutionary Cultural Capital

After the founding of the PRC on October 1, 1949, the party that had endured nearly two decades of civil and other wars had risen to state power. "By mid-1945," Saich notes, "the CPC had built the foundations for a strong, centralized, unified party focused around the ideas and persona of Mao Zedong."[79] But the party, which had some experience governing over large populations in rural base areas (*genjudi*) but no prior experience governing people in cities, had to consolidate its rule over a still politically disunited country. The CPC consolidated its power by carrying forward its movement of sweeping land reform (1947–1950), initiating a brutal campaign to suppress suspected counterrevolutionaries and others posing a problem for the new government such as corrupt bureaucrats (1950–1952), and launching a major campaign to punish intellectual criticism of, and within, the party (the 1957–1959 Anti-Rightist Campaign that followed the 1956 Hundred Flowers Campaign which expressly called for such criticism).[80] While violently crushing its opposition, the Maoist party-state initiated two industrial and agricultural development programs to reconfigure China economically, which capped off a decade of increasing collectivization. The latter of the two "Leaps," the 1958–1962 Great Leap Forward, aimed to "surpass Great Britain and catch up with the US" (*chao-Ying gan-Mei*) in steel output

---

[76] Fitzgerald, *Cadre Country*, 117. See also John Fitzgerald, "Cadre Nation: Territorial Government and the Lessons of Imperial Statecraft in Xi's China," *The China Journal* 85 (January 2021): 26–48.
[77] "Constitution of the Communist Party of China," Nineteenth Party Congress, October 24, 2017, quoted in Fitzgerald, *Cadre Country*, 117.
[78] Fitzgerald, *Cadre Country*, 117–118.   [79] Saich, *From Rebel to Ruler*, 144.
[80] Galway, *The Emergence of Global Maoism*, 38–46.

and to "dash into Communism" (*paobu jinru gongchanzhuyi*).[81] Instead, it ended in economic disaster along with an unprecedented famine with a death toll in the tens of millions, forcing Mao into semiretirement in 1959.[82]

How Mao recovered, and indeed surged, in popularity by the onset of the Cultural Revolution and how the CPC reestablished the stability of its rule in the aftermath of these disasters was no easy feat. CPC efforts during this period to lionize Mao and Mao Zedong Thought as icon and irrefutable wisdom, respectively, set the foundation for centralized and unquestioned party rule for decades thereafter. But they were hardly straightforward.

After the famine, President Liu Shaoqi, Deng Xiaoping, and other CPC leaders handled damage control. Liu criticized Mao at the early 1962 "7000 Cadres Conference" (*Qiqianren dahui*) for "China's dire situation" after the Great Leap.[83] Mao was furious with Liu and policy changes (such as the partial restoration of farmers' markets) that he regarded as a restoration of capitalism and a betrayal of the principles of the Great Leap Forward.[84] Mao's "close comrade-in-arms" (*qinmi zhanyou*) Lin Biao, whom the CPC had installed as Minister of Defense after purging his predecessor Peng Dehuai, who had dared to criticize the Great Leap back in 1958, was instrumental to organizing the personality cult around Mao. He delivered a bellicose speech at the same conference, blatantly ignoring the economic consequences and praising Mao Zedong Thought as a guiding light for a successful future.[85]

As Lin Biao and other Maoist devotees discovered, it was quite easy to attach symbolic capital to Mao and his Thought. By the end of the famine years, the CPC had lost a significant amount of rural support. Rural people, acutely aware of the local cadres' mistakes, blamed them for the disaster – an interpretation that state media encouraged as well. The same rural people knew Mao solely through propaganda which portrayed him

---

[81] Tian Zhu, *Catching Up to America: Culture, Institutions, and the Rise of China* (Cambridge: Cambridge University Press, 2021), 1–2; Galway, *The Emergence of Global Maoism*, 46.

[82] Galway, *The Emergence of Global Maoism*, 46–48; Yang Kuisong, "Reconsidering the Campaign to Suppress Counterrevolutionaries," *China Quarterly* 93 (March 2008): 102–121; Dali Yang, *Calamity and Reform in China: State, Rural Society, and Industrial Change since the Great Leap Famine* (Stanford, CA: Stanford University Press, 1996), 43–44; Cheek, *Propaganda and Culture*, 215–278; James Chieh Hsiung, *Ideology and Practice: The Evolution of Chinese Communism* (New York: Praeger, 1970), 191–199.

[83] Galway, *The Emergence of Global Maoism*, 50.

[84] Frederick Teiwes, *Politics and Purges in China: Rectification and the Decline of Party Norms, 1950–1965* (Armonk, NY: M. E. Sharpe, 1993), xxxix, xli.

[85] Galway, *The Emergence of Global Maoism*, 50; see also Frederick Teiwes and Warren Sun, *The Tragedy of Lin Biao: Riding the Tiger during the Cultural Revolution* (Honolulu: University of Hawaii Press, 1996), 196.

as the nation's great savior and wise leader. People's Liberation Army (PLA) soldiers also credited Mao with sending them out when they distributed food relief.[86] Although he was principally responsible for the cataclysm, Mao's image took less of a hit than that of the CPC more broadly. Thanks to his popularity and devotion to his Thought, the CPC retained legitimacy.[87]

The "Maoist resurgence" in the first half of the 1960s was due to a new brain trust of Maoist zealots like Lin who transformed the revolutionary symbolic capital that had eroded gradually during the CPC's first decade-plus in power into a revolutionary *cultural* capital. This presented Mao as an autocrat, august and supreme, the revolutionary genius who was singularly responsible for all the positive gains in the PRC and whose Thought represented unquestionable wisdom. Cheek says that the prevailing atmosphere within the CPC became one in which the supreme leader ruled as an "alcoholic father (drunk with supreme power)."[88] Yet, amid the turmoil, Mao continued to command enormous popular support to the extent that, with the help of fervent supporters within the CPC and the populace at large, the party was able to use his image as cultural capital to help maintain party legitimacy. One reason was what Cheek refers to as "faith Maoism," which "turned ideology into faith in the charismatic authority of the leader," bestowed upon cadres "the role of 'cog and screw' to carry out the leader's wishes," and elevated propaganda to "a chiliastic bonding ritual."[89] The chief proponent of faith Maoism was Lin Biao. As Cheek describes, Lin's faith-based Maoism, the "dominant version of Maoism during the Cultural Revolution," held that "politics is everything and correct politics stem from a nearly literal, and certainly ahistorical, reading of Mao's utterances." Lin's approach was "less a method than a way of pandering to Mao's current hobby-horses," he writes. The heart of Lin's version of Maoism is that "the atom bomb of the spirit is much more powerful and more useful than the material atom bomb. Only we can possess this."[90] The charismatic power of the party is thus indivisibly linked to (and analytically inseparable from) Mao the person and his utterances.

Other prominent "faith Maoism" hard-liners included the notorious "Gang of Four" (*Sirenbang*) – Mao's wife Jiang Qing, Zhang Chunqiao, Yao Wenyuan, and Wang Hongwen. But Lin's militant pronouncements

---

[86] Fengyuan Ji, *Linguistic Engineering: Language and Politics in Mao's China* (Honolulu: University of Hawaii Press, 2004), 95; Jasper Becker, *Hungry Ghosts: China's Secret Famine* (London: John Murray, 1996), 5.
[87] Ji, *Linguistic Engineering*, 95–97, 103–106, 150–152.
[88] Cheek, *Propaganda and Culture*, 219. [89] Cheek, *Propaganda and Culture*, 69.
[90] Cheek, *Propaganda and Culture*, 219–220.

represent most vividly the "faith Maoist" position of lionizing Mao as icon and symbol in blatant disregard of the human cost of policies such as the Great Leap.

Then there was the elevation of Mao to a symbol that could embed itself into daily life. The most radical faction of the CPC further transformed Mao into cultural symbolic capital in four important ways that helped their version of the party hold onto power: (1) the compilation and mass dissemination of Mao's writings, notably the "bible of the Red Guards," *Quotations from Chairman Mao* (*Mao zhuxi yulu*), or "Little Red Book";[91] (2) the promotion of *Quotations* such that people were encouraged by the CPC to own the book, carry it, wave it, hold it over their hearts, study it, and quote it to show their loyalty to Mao (and ensure their own survival); (3) the Red Guards, whose own style, pomposity, wearing of Mao badges, and almost-religious devotion to *Quotations* popularized Mao as cultural symbolic icon in form and substance; and (4) propaganda art that mythologized Mao, symbolized by the oil paintings *Chairman Mao Reports on the Rectification at the Cadre Meeting in Yan'an* (*Mao zhuxi zai Yan'an ganbu huiyishang zuo zhengfeng baogao*) by Luo Gongliu (1951, Figure 3.1) and *Chairman Mao en route to Anyuan* (*Mao zhuxi qu Anyuan*) by Liu Chunhua (1967, Figure 3.2).

The Little Red Book

The "Little Red Book" was originally to provide PLA soldiers with "a set of moral guidelines to act upon in military drill."[92] Over time, it became one of the most widely disseminated and mass-translated pieces of literature of the twentieth century. Daniel Leese lists five reasons for its popularity and spread in China: first, it was the latest example in a long tradition of "collected sayings" compilations that stretch back to the Confucian *Analects* of the fifth century BCE; second, the CPC presented it as part of the Marxist–Leninist canon; third, its durable red vinyl cover and compact size made it easy to carry; fourth, the CPC propounded that its mass production and dissemination symbolized the unshakable loyalty of the people to Mao both within China and globally; and fifth, Mao's quotations, removed from historical context, were malleable enough to suit whatever situation and interpretation any "skillful orators" saw fit.

---

[91] Roderick MacFarquhar and Michael Schoenhals, *Mao's Last Revolution* (Cambridge, MA: Harvard University Press, 2006), 107.

[92] Daniel Leese, "A Single Spark: Origins and Spread of the Little Red Book in China," in *Mao's Little Red Book: A Global History*, ed. Alexander C. Cook (Cambridge: Cambridge University Press, 2014), 40.

Figure 3.1 Poster reproduction of Luo Gongliu's 1951 oil painting *Chairman Mao Reports on the Rectification at the Cadre Meeting in Yan'an* (1985), Zhongyang wenxian chubanshe. Source: Image courtesy of the Stefan R. Landsberger collection, BG E13/108, https://chineseposters.net/posters/e13-108.

Despite Lin Biao's association with the *Quotations*, the genesis of which was a state secret for many years, the *Liberation Army Daily* (*Jiefang junbao*) editorial staff were the first to propose publishing a collection of Mao quotes "in book form for internal use."[93] A few weeks later, "a first issue of 200 quotations was distributed to the conference participants," and in mid May 1964, "the first regular print edition appeared, classified as 'internal' military reading, its size adjusted to neatly fit into the pockets of military uniforms."[94]

Performative Loyalty

Lin Biao promoted loyalty to Mao in the PLA and beyond through education programs that stressed that all policy failures had been the

---

[93] Barbara Mittler, *A Continuous Revolution: Making Sense of Cultural Revolution Culture* (Cambridge, MA: Harvard University Press, 2012), 195; Leese, "A Single Spark," 23, 29, 34–35.
[94] Mittler, *A Continuous Revolution*, 195.

The Chairman's Long Shadow

Figure 3.2 Poster reproduction of Liu Chunhua's 1967 oil painting *Chairman Mao en route to Anyuan* (1968), Hebei renmin meishu chubanshe, Beijing. Source: Image courtesy of the International Institute of Social History (IISH) collection, BG E12/703. https://chineseposters.net/posters/e12-703.

result not of following Mao's ideas, but of deviating from them. Lin urged "the 'lively study, lively application' of Mao Zedong Thought" to all tasks.[95] The CPC leadership pressured the Liberation Army Publishing House to pump out volumes in increasingly large quantities until by February 1966, as Barbara Mittler notes, "workers were working nonstop shifts," and "some 75 million copies had been printed, but all the same, demand far exceeded supply." "Some printing houses," Mittler continues, "disrupt[ed] their work on other publications [to] meet the quota of production for the *Little Red Book* and other works by Mao."[96]

---

[95] Leese, "A Single Spark," 28–29.   [96] Mittler, *A Continuous Revolution*, 195.

The elevation of *Quotations* to the level of Holy Scripture signaled the ascendance of Mao-as-symbolic-capital to new heights. *Quotations* provided a model to replicate whereas the symbol of Mao as genius provided successors with a reference point to legitimize their own ideological contributions. Xi's 2014 *The Governance of China* and subsequent volumes in 2017, 2020, and 2022 articulate Xi Jinping Thought through the compilation of his most important speeches and represent a literary and spiritual successor to Mao's *Quotations*. Much like with *Quotations*, *The Governance of China* has been translated into several languages.

Upon returning from his 1967 visit to the PRC, Italian novelist Alberto Moravia wrote *The Red Book and the Great Wall: An Impression of Mao's China* (*La rivoluzione culturale in Cina: Ovvero il Convitato di pietra*). Little Red Books were so pervasive, he noted, it was as if it was the *only* book in circulation. "Every Chinese carries [*Quotations*] about with him, to which he refers in all circumstances, which he knows almost by heart and where he looks, never doubting that he will find it, for the answer to every question which is not immediately obvious to him." This was because *Quotations*, Moravia elaborates, was

a substitute for conscience and at the same time the axis of a system of ritual behavior ... It is waved in the air at meetings, parades, and gatherings, thus we have exultation of the book, or threat and challenge by means of the book. It is opened and glanced at, and thus we have consultation. It is read aloud in answer to someone, and thus we have citation, communication. Closed it is caressed with the hand or pressed to the heart, and thus we have affection. It is held in the hand during dances, songs, propaganda, recitals, and thus we have symbolization.[97]

Red Guard Style and Substance

The Red Guards (*hong weibing*) represented radical forces from below that lionized Mao as iconic cultural symbol. Mao's appearance at a Red Guard rally served as the spark that set a prairie of Mao-centric iconoclasm ablaze. Mao's call "To rebel is justified!" spurred Red Guards to take violent action against authority figures, with his enthusiastic endorsement.[98] In the words of one former Red Guard: "if Chairman Mao is our Red-Commander-in-Chief and we are his Red Guards, who can stop us? First we will make China Maoist from inside out and then we will help the working people of other

---

[97] Alberto Moravia, *The Red Book and the Great Wall: An Impression of Mao's China* (London: Secker and Warburg, 1968), 36–37; Matthew Galway, "Who Are Our Friends? Maoist Cultural Diplomacy and the Origins of the People's Republic of China's Global Turn," *Made in China Journal* 6(2) (2021): 110–125.

[98] Yiching Wu, *The Cultural Revolution at the Margins: Chinese Socialism in Crisis* (Cambridge, MA: Harvard University Press, 2014), 17.

countries make the world red ... and then the whole universe."[99] Red Guards dressed like PLA soldiers, and Mao himself, in olive-green military uniforms complete with red-starred caps and fatigues, red armbands, and Mao badges.[100] "The sartorial symbols of the Red Guards' affiliation," Li Li contends, "certainly contributed to their sense of commonality in their utopian revolutionary goals, their loyalty to Mao, and similarity of self to other social groups."[101] Red Guards' ways of dressing, he elaborates, expressed their "evolving social identity" and gave them "a privileged status among other teenagers."

Red Guards also emulated Mao by fostering authoritarian personalities in themselves.[102] In donning PLA uniforms, proselytizing the brilliance of Mao and his Thought, and in their frenzied attacks on authority, Red Guards established Mao as material expression *and* cultural symbol of faith Maoism, personified and performed. More recently, the style of presentation and interpersonal power struggles among student leaders of the 1989 protests resembled those of the Red Guards: the strident form of address and grand gestures ("wash the square with our blood," for instance) stand out as especially noteworthy examples. The rhetorical style of Wolf Warriors and Neo-Maoists under Xi Jinping also bears a striking resemblance to that of the Red Guards and represents yet another example of how this feature of the Mao era has enjoyed a long and important afterlife in the PRC.[103]

Mythologizing Mao

Luo Gongliu was a woodcut artist trained in Hangzhou, Yan'an, and Leningrad and eventually became a professor at the Central Academy of Fine Arts (*Zhongyang meishu xueyuan*). In the early years of the People's Republic, the CPC commissioned him to commemorate Mao's leadership

---

[99] Woei Lien Chong, *China's Great Proletarian Cultural Revolution: Master Narratives and Post-Mao Counternarratives* (Lanham, MD: Rowman & Littlefield, 2002), 105.

[100] Li Li, "Revolutionary Culture, Girl Power, and the Red Guard Uniform during the Chinese Cultural Revolution," in *Uniform: Clothing and Discipline in the Modern World*, ed. Jane Tynan and Lisa Godson (London: Bloomsbury, 2019), 49–64; Emily Williams, "Red Collections in Contemporary China: Towards a New Research Agenda," *British Journal of Chinese Studies* 11 (July 2021): 71–90.

[101] Li Li, "Uniformed Rebellion, Fabricated Identity: A Study of Social History of Red Guards in Military Uniforms during the Chinese Cultural Revolution and Beyond," *Fashion Theory* 14(4) (2015): 441.

[102] Anita Chan, *Children of Mao: Personality Development and Political Activism in the Red Guard Generation* (Seattle: University of Washington Press, 1985), 220–221.

[103] Stephen N. Smith, "China's 'Major Country Diplomacy': Legitimation and Foreign Policy Change," *Foreign Policy Analysis* 17(2) (2021): 1–18; Jude Blanchette, *China's New Red Guards: The Return of Radicalism and the Rebirth of Mao Zedong* (Oxford: Oxford University Press, 2019), 127–147.

during the Yan'an Rectification in painting.[104] Luo was both well versed in Soviet-style painting and a Yan'an veteran, an ideal choice. As Luo recalled, the Museum of the Chinese Revolution handled the commission and assigned him to the topic of The Rectification Report (*Zhengfeng baogao*). They "insisted that it had to be done in oil."[105] *Chairman Mao Reports on the Rectification at the Cadre Meeting in Yan'an* (Figure 3.1) is one of many oil paintings that Luo produced during his career and is arguably one of his most iconic works.

In the painting, Luo depicts Mao standing at a podium at the CPC Central Committee headquarters in Yan'an with his hand outstretched, and with the exception of some people diligently taking notes, every person is sitting straight-backed and attentive. Behind him are portraits of Lenin and Marx. The padded, heavy clothes of the attendees indicate that it is winter, and the bare hills of Yan'an are visible outside the window. This famous painting also reemerged in a 1985 calendar. But what is most stark is its romanticization of Yan'an Rectification. In the painting, the cadres are all writing and paying close attention to Mao's oration as if he had *already* been ordained the supreme theorist. Mao's placement in front of portraits of Marx and Lenin signifies that his wisdom is the next evolutionary step of Marxism-Leninism. Most glaring is the total absence of peasants and lumpenproletarians, who, despite illiteracy or semiliteracy, were vital to the CPC's survival. Luo's painting thus reflects a party that in power had become, truly, Mao's own, with his contributions to revolutionary success almost singularly at the forefront.

Another rich example of art mythologizing Mao was by oil painter Liu Chunhua. Mao's wife Jiang Qing promoted Liu's Cultural Revolution-era painting *Chairman Mao Goes to Anyuan*, Elizabeth Perry writes, "as a 'revolutionary masterpiece' on a par with her eight model operas."[106] Liu studied at the Lu Xun Academy of Fine Arts in Shenyang and drew heavily on the inspiration of the Italian Renaissance painter Raphael for this, his first oil painting commission, 2.2 meters high and 1.8 meters wide.[107] *Chairman Mao Goes to Anyuan* (Figure 3.2) portrays what Perry describes as an "idealized image" of Mao as a twenty-seven-year-old intellectual in a scholar's gown and holding a Hunan oiled-paper

---

[104] Chang-Tai Hung, "Oil Paintings and Politics: Weaving a Heroic Tale of the Chinese Communist Revolution," *Comparative Studies in Society and History* 49(4) (October 2007): 791.

[105] Hung, "Oil Paintings and Politics," 787.

[106] Elizabeth Perry, "Reclaiming the Chinese Revolution," *The Journal of Asian Studies* 67(4) (November 2008): 1153.

[107] Julia Andrews, *Painters and Politics in the People's Republic of China, 1949–1979* (Berkeley: University of California Press, 1994), 338–339; Elizabeth Perry, *Anyuan: Mining China's Revolutionary Tradition* (Berkeley: University of California Press, 2012), 217.

umbrella, en route to Anyuan in 1921. He is marching heroically forward, eyes fixed on the horizon. His destination, Anyuan, has a coal mine where he will rally miners and rail workers in the 1922 Anyuan Miners' Strike.[108]

Although the painting "stood out for its simplicity and grandeur," Mao disapproved of it because it does not depict any workers.[109] Yet as Perry contends, the "romantic image" that Liu presents of Mao "epitomizes the efforts of later generations to rework the Anyuan story for their own purposes."[110] As such, it served many functions for the CPC party-state, symbolically and practically. As Liu reflected some years later on the painting:

I painted this work in 1967, the second year of the Great Cultural Revolution. The political background of that time was largely defined by the campaign to criticize Liu Shaoqi. Many people were aware that in the past Liu Shaoqi had led workers' strikes in Anyuan. But a group of young teachers and students at universities in the capital who had conducted in-depth research on party history had a more complete understanding of that period, and in their opinion the true leader of the Anyuan workers movement was Chairman Mao – prior to the Cultural Revolution, most reports mentioned only Liu Shaoqi. This group felt that Chairman Mao's [role] in the revolutionary movements at Anyuan should be positively portrayed and disseminated, with the ultimate aim of criticizing Liu Shaoqi. They planned to organize an exhibition [entitled] "Mao Zedong's Thought Illuminates the Anyuan Workers' Movement."[111]

Indeed, like Luo's earlier work, Liu's painting occludes other important actors in the story, notably the workers themselves and Liu Shaoqi. And as with Luo's painting, Liu Chunhua's depiction enjoyed a long afterlife. Reproductions of *Chairman Mao Goes to Anyuan* were, according to Perry, widely available in forms that ranged "from Mao buttons and postage stamps to embroidery and pottery renditions ... with more than 900 million poster copies in circulation at one time."[112] Its pervasiveness placed a young, heroic, self-sacrificing Mao in the spotlight as a moral and revolutionary exemplar for all Red Guards and ordinary Chinese alike to emulate. This image of Mao concretized in people's collective memories a Mao that never truly existed, but whose revolutionary bona fides were far-reaching and unquestionable.

---

[108] Perry, "Reclaiming the Chinese Revolution," 1153; Perry, *Anyuan*, 217.
[109] Perry, *Anyuan*, 217.   [110] Perry, "Reclaiming the Chinese Revolution," 1155.
[111] Zheng Shengtian, "Chairman Mao Goes to Anyuan: A Conversation with the Artist Liu Chunhua," in *Art and China's Revolution*, ed. Melissa Chiu and Zheng Shengtian (New York: Asia Society/Yale University Press, 2008), 119; Perry, *Anyuan*, 217–218.
[112] Perry, "Reclaiming the Chinese Revolution," 1155.

Nowadays, it is easy to spot Mao's visage on any manner of cheaply made commercial products: T-shirts, coffee mugs, clocks, watches, and a whole range of kitsch made in China (generally for the tourist market) and abroad. In commoditized form, it has shifted for many Chinese and non-Chinese from a revolutionary symbol to a "post-socialist thing," the value and meaning of which have become almost completely detached from revolutionary politics.[113] In whatever form, Mao and his Thought have endured in the collective conscience. His elevation to supreme theorist in Yan'an, the cultist devotion to him by "faith Maoist" zealot Lin Biao (before his demise in a plane crash while allegedly fleeing the country after a failed assassination attempt on Mao), and his global omnipresence in material form have kept his long shadow in sight.

The CPC leadership since Mao's death has invested a substantial amount of symbolic capital in the figure of Mao, which made it impossible to repudiate him during the Reform Era even as it was dismantling his policies and disowning the most radical and violent part of his legacy to justify post-Cultural Revolution CPC legitimacy. Deng reappraised Mao's positive contributions rather favorably as 70 percent good and noted that Mao's errors "were secondary to his achievements," namely Mao Zedong Thought, which he held "still provided important guidelines."[114] Although he admitted that Mao had made mistakes during his time as CPC leader and purged many of his most fanatical followers in his own "rectification" campaign that began in 1983, Deng could not more fully disown Mao without endangering his own legitimacy. In the 1980s, the CPC began to compartmentalize Maoism and disown the Cultural Revolution, notably with the 1981 "Resolution on Certain Questions in the History of Our Party since the Founding of the Nation" (*Guanyu jiandang yilai dangshi ruogan wentide jueyi*). The "Resolution" did not provide an assessment of Mao's contributions as 70 percent good, 30 percent bad, which were the exact same figures as Mao's 1963 assessment of Joseph Stalin and his own evaluation of the disastrous Cultural Revolution.[115] But as Cheek notes, in fact, "the interpretation has evolved that this was its point."[116]

In the late 1980s and early 1990s, a new version of faith Maoism manifested in a resurgent "Mao cult" of Chinese who held what Geremie

---

[113] Matthew Galway and Christian Sorace, "Newborn Socialist Things: A Conversation with Laurence Coderre," *Made in China Journal* 7(1) (2022): 72; Laurence Coderre, *Newborn Socialist Things: Materiality in Maoist China* (Durham, NC: Duke University Press, 2021).
[114] Vogel, *Deng Xiaoping*, 196, 368–369.
[115] Frederick Teiwes and Warren Sun, *The End of the Maoist Era: Chinese Politics during the Twilight of the Cultural Revolution* (Armonk, NY: M. E. Sharpe, 2007), 3–4.
[116] Cheek, "Mao, Revolution and Memory," 21n35.

Barmé calls "totalitarian nostalgia": an emotive, reflective, and often reflexive attachment to Maoist rhetoric and public discourse as a "language of denunciation that offered simple solutions to complex problems."[117] Amid mounting concerns over an uncertain future, a new "Mao cult," Barmé explains, "looked fondly on strong government, coherent national goals, authority, and power." To new Maoists, "Mao was, first and foremost, an unwavering patriot who led the nation against imperialism and expelled foreign capital." The massive failures of the Great Leap Forward, the chaos of the Cultural Revolution, and the violent excesses of rectification campaigns were of little import, for Mao was the champion of Chinese autonomy, an incorruptible force of stable government and sociopolitical harmony. The difficult questions became less complicated to answer when one applied Maoist formulas to them. As Barmé writes, Mao cultists found solutions in "direct collective action over painful individual decisions, reliance on the state rather than a grinding struggle for the self, national pride as opposed to self-doubt."[118]

More recently, aside from name-dropping Mao in his speech (p. 42), Xi Jinping has recast Mao as the CPC leader who is most responsible for laying the groundwork for China's reform and economic prosperity. "The first generation of the central collective leadership with Mao Zedong at the core," Xi claims, "provided invaluable experience as well as the theoretical and material basis for the great initiative of building socialism with Chinese characteristics in the new historic period."[119] It is irrelevant whether Mao would approve or disapprove of the degree of economic marketization, or that the CPC has members who are among China's wealthiest. These leaders have invested in, and drawn upon, Mao as symbol to highlight continuity with revolutionary ideals and history, even as they break from Maoist high socialism in almost every other aspect. Strategic use of Mao as symbolic capital is vital to the CPC's legitimation and continued justification for one-party rule.

Cultural Revolutionary Symbolic Capital Becomes Legitimizing Revolutionary Symbolic Capital

From Mao's death to today, CPC leaders have invoked Mao and his Thought not just for practical purposes (justifying their own policies), but also to satisfy those attached to the Maoist past and notions of radical egalitarianism, antibureaucratism, a fierce anti-imperialism, and perception

---

[117] Geremie R. Barmé, *In the Red: On Contemporary Chinese Culture* (New York: Columbia University Press, 1999), 317.
[118] Barmé, *In the Red*, 321.   [119] Xi, *Governance of China*, 40.

of China as a world-beating agricultural and industrial nation. Mao's revolutionary symbolic capital is important to a CPC whose current leadership lacks revolutionary bona fides in an increasingly unequal China. But importantly, in China, Cheek explains, "there exists a nearly endless set of personal Maos for those ... who experienced life under his rule ... These memories are vivid, powerful, and widely diverse."[120] They inspire a range of reactions "from respect and nostalgia to anger and disgust." All the more reason, then, for CPC leaders since Mao's death to mobilize Mao as symbol when it suits their needs: justifying one-party rule; bolstering the party's image as continuing Mao's legacy even as it distances itself ever further from it; and stirring up nationalist and statist fervor by referring to him as a symbol of anti-imperial resistance.

It is unlikely that the current CPC leadership will "make China Maoist again." As Fitzgerald reflects, "there was a time when the privileged status of cadres rested on their place in the command economy and their mastery of Marxism-Leninism-Mao Zedong Thought." But since Mao's death and especially in the years since Reform, cadre status "rests on the overwhelming wealth and power of the party and its determination to remain in command of a marketised economy through the cadre system."[121] Economic reform has indeed ushered in financial growth, an improvement in living standards, and an end to the widespread poverty and deprivation of the Maoist period. Problems such as a historic wealth inequality, however, have forced the CPC to redefine "the central contradiction" twice since the Maoist era. Xi addressed this matter with his promotion of "common prosperity." Instead of restoring Maoist radicalism and governance in the PRC, Xi has reemphasized that Deng's identification of Marxism–Leninism and Mao Zedong Thought are unquestionable components of the PRC's four cardinal principles. As MacFarquhar wrote, Xi's aim is to "revive communist ideology as a vibrant bulwark of China's exceptionalism [and] to inoculate its citizens against [Euro-American] democratic ideas."[122]

The current leadership's aim now is to appeal to a diverse populace whose understanding of Mao varies widely. Regardless of how many Maos may be remembered and mobilized for political capital – revolutionary, theorist, national father, and so on – his revolutionary symbolic capital remains important to a CPC leadership that wishes to maintain its iron grip on power without itself possessing the revolutionary

[120] Cheek, "Mao, Revolution and Memory," 25.
[121] Fitzgerald, *Cadre Country*, 124–125.
[122] MacFarquhar, "Does Mao Still Matter?" 30.

symbolic capital it needs to legitimize its one-party rule. Regardless of the degree to which Xi places primacy on his ideological vision and his most ardent firebrands personally enrich and empower themselves, Mao and Mao Zedong Thought do indeed "still matter" for the CPC's legitimation of its ongoing autocratic rule over the world's most populous nation.

4 Language, Discourse, and Hegemony

Fengyuan Ji

The stability of the Communist Party of China's (CPC's) rule is based partly on practices of linguistic engineering that have molded attitudes and beliefs for over 2,000 years. This chapter will explain how these practices contributed to the remarkable stability of the Chinese Empire; it will show how Mao and the party inherited them and transformed them into a lethal weapon of class struggle and totalitarian social control; and it will explain how, since 1978, the party has reverted to a nontotalitarian form of linguistic engineering compatible with the more open society of the Reform Era. Even in this looser form, linguistic engineering remains effective. In combination with the party's monopoly of armed force it gives the party an excellent chance of surviving crises, waiting out any loss of popularity, and rebuilding support.

Linguistic Engineering and Regime Persistence in Imperial Times

Long before the formation of a unified Chinese state, Chinese philosophers were arguing forcefully that governments had to mold people's attitudes and behavior by regulating language. Confucius (551–479 BCE), for example, said that the first task of a ruler should be to regulate terminology or "rectify names" (*zhengming*): "If the names are not correct, if they do not match realities, language has no object. If language is without an object, action becomes impossible – and therefore, all human affairs disintegrate and their management becomes pointless and impossible."[1] He believed that properly regulated terminology underpinned an agreed and correct perception of reality, and that this in turn created a basis for good government, a shared understanding of the law, and social harmony.

Chinese rulers agreed with this principle, whether or not they were Confucians. When the anti-Confucian King of Qin conquered his

---

[1] Simon Leys (trans.), *The Analects of Confucius* (New York: Norton, 1997), xxvi.

neighbors and created the first unified Chinese state in 221 BCE, for example, he immediately set about rectifying names. He elevated himself above everyone else as "Emperor" (*huangdi*), a title evoking China's mythical founders and the blessing of Heaven that had never before been claimed by a mortal ruler; he replaced the kings of the conquered states with a centralized bureaucracy and sometimes described them as having been mere "lords" (*zhuhou*); and he classified the commoners as simple "black heads" (*qianshou*).[2] These terms were the cornerstones of a discourse that legitimated the new hierarchy established by the Qin conquest. Later emperors followed precedent, consolidating their rule by issuing lists of banned characters and promoting "correct" terms that encouraged "correct" thought.[3] The Qing emperors, for example, were Manchus, and they banned characters expressing the ethnic slurs used to denigrate them and other ethnic minorities.[4]

Imperial control of the written language was far-reaching. The Qin dynasty began the transition to a standardized Chinese script, and the Han dynasty completed the process. The Han also made the characters less complicated and punished officials who wrote them incorrectly.[5] Moreover, this standardized system of writing was not tied to the phonetics of a particular Chinese language or dialect, which meant that literate people from different parts of the empire could read it. This was an enormous benefit in a society that even today, by one count, still has 299 mutually unintelligible languages including Mandarin, Cantonese, Shanghainese, and the languages of China's many ethnic minorities.[6] It also enabled imperial officials to communicate with each other, whether or not they were fluent in the spoken language of the court.

Even more important, as the historian Mark Edward Lewis has argued, is the way in which the character-based writing system underpinned "an education programme that embedded the vision of empire within the

---

[2] Charles Sanft, *Communication and Cooperation in Early Imperial China: Publicizing the Qin Dynasty* (Albany: State University of New York, 2014), 59, 175n9.

[3] Michael Schoenhals, *Doing Things with Words in Chinese Politics: Five Studies* (Berkeley: Institute of East Asian Studies, University of California, 1992), 2.

[4] P. Tangyenyong, "Banned Books as a State Apparatus in the Qing Dynasty: Ethnicity, Power and Concupiscence," *Thammasat Review* 20(1) (2017): 92–107, 100–101.

[5] Jerry Norman, *Chinese* (Cambridge: Cambridge University Press, 1988), 65–67; Imre Galambos, *Orthography of Early Chinese Writing: Evidence from Newly Excavated Manuscripts* (Budapest: Department of East Asian Studies, Eotvos Lorand University, 2006), 49–50; Imre Galambos, "The Myth of the Qin Unification of Writing in Han Sources," *Acta Orientalia Academiae Scientiarum Hung* 57(2) (2004): 181–203.

[6] Fengyuan Ji, "Language Planning and Policy in China: Unity, Diversity and Social Control," in Ernest Andrews (ed.), *Language Planning in the Post-Communist Era* (Cham: Palgrave MacMillan, 2018), 67, 87n1.

upper reaches of local communities."⁷ This vision, based on the Chinese classics, expressed the ideal of an imperial state based on Confucian principles and the example of the mythological Sage Kings. It was at the heart of the text-based culture that united the Emperor's court with literate people and local elites throughout the empire. Indeed, when dynasties collapsed, it was the vision's survival among local literate elites that "provided the mechanism by which the institution of the empire survived the collapse of each of its incarnations."⁸ Old dynasties were replaced by new ones that shared the same vision, and even the Mongol and Manchu conquerors found that the best way to run their empires was to rebuild the bureaucracy along traditional lines, work with local elites, and conform acceptably to the ideal of government enshrined in the Confucian classics.

Confucian texts, including later commentaries and elaborations, won friends among those who held power at every level of Chinese society in part because they "naturalized" and stabilized hierarchies of age and gender. These hierarchies were even reinforced by the written characters in the texts. The character for "filial piety" 孝, for example, was formed by placing the character for "old" 老 on top of the character for "child" 子, implying that the young must support the old and obey them. This underpinned the Confucian discourse on filial piety, in which an idealized father–son relationship was promoted as the model of all top-down relationships. This not only reinforced patriarchal dominance within the family but also cemented hierarchical structures within Chinese lineage groups and communities. Above all, because the Emperor was seen as the father of all the Chinese people, it reinforced imperial rule. It was therefore central to the ideology propping up the traditional sociopolitical order.

The Chinese writing system also underpinned the patriarchal discourse that subordinated women to men. The character for "woman" 女, for example, forms the radical or base component in ten characters representing different types of female attractiveness, as well as the radical for "slave," "prostitution," "jealousy," "witch," "adultery," and "concubine." This meant, as it does to this day, that when people learned to read and write they were also exposed to the implication that women merit intense scrutiny for their attractiveness and that they are also associated with servile status, jealousy, prostitution, adultery, and witchcraft.

---

[7] Mark Edward Lewis, *Writing and Authority in Early China* (Albany: State University of New York Press, 1999), 4.
[8] Lewis, *Writing and Authority*, 4.

From Han times, the government promoted the written language through state schools that were complemented by private academies and schools sponsored by lineage groups.[9] Communities valued these institutions because they held out the possibility that a local student might pass the imperial examination and enter the imperial bureaucracy, or at least advance local interests by working as a clerk in the county magistrate's office or by negotiating on the community's behalf in the language of an educated person. However, they also valued the schools because their curriculum was based on the Confucian classics, which prescribed an orderly and hierarchical society under the ruler, his officials, the senior males in the lineage groups that dominated local communities, and the husband and father who headed each individual family. In other words, the Confucian curriculum offered something to everyone with a position of authority in Chinese society.

With a limited supply of books, the schools placed great emphasis on rote learning, which of necessity employed a local variety of spoken Chinese. This enabled students and former students to display their accomplishments by reciting Confucian aphorisms and classical stories in local languages or dialects to nonliterate members of their communities, who in turn displayed their virtuosity by rote-learning them and passing them on to others. These chains of oral transmission taught ordinary people the "Five Relationships" that spelled out the Confucian social hierarchy, the "Three Obediences" that specified the subordination of women, and countless other linguistic formulae that gave "correct" linguistic form to "correct" thought.[10] The formulae were repeated endlessly, stabilizing Confucian discourses and extending their power over all levels of society. They transmitted the culture of China's literate few to the illiterate masses, transforming it into the culture of the whole society: into Chinese culture.

At multiple levels, then, the Chinese state, the schools, the local literate elites, and all who benefited from patriarchal hierarchies of age and gender actively promoted forms of linguistic engineering that stabilized the socio-political order of imperial China. The result of this cooperative effort was a truly hegemonic culture – a culture that linked the Emperor and his officials to all levels of society in patriarchal chains of authority and responsibility. This culture had an unchallenged pervasiveness that

---

[9] Thomas H. C. Lee, *Education in Traditional China: A History* (Leiden: Brill, 2000).
[10] The Five Relationships were between ruler and subject, father and son, husband and wife, older brother and younger brother, and friend and friend. The Three Obediences stated that a woman should obey her father before marriage, her husband after marriage, and her son after the death of her husband. These two linguistic formulae were cornerstones of imperial and patriarchal rule.

was never matched in the West, where there were always rival claims to authority linked to divisions between church and state or to divisions between state churches and dissenting ones. The hegemony of Confucian discourse in China lasted for over 2,000 years and was shattered only by China's humiliations at the hands of Western imperialist powers following the Opium Wars that began in 1840. In a divided and conflict-ridden society, it took more than a century for another discourse to become hegemonic, but then it did so with unparalleled force after the CPC took power in 1949.

Language, Coercion, and Revolutionary Consciousness in the Mao Era

Although traditional Confucian political discourse had largely been discredited in the early twentieth century by reformist and radical thinkers who saw it as antithetical to modernization and progress, political organizations still spread their message by getting people to learn by heart and pass on slogans and maxims. In a society that was still largely illiterate, this was by far the most effective way of starting and stabilizing a discourse that reached ordinary people. Chiang Kai-Shek's Nationalist Party used them extensively, but no party used them more effectively than the CPC. Not only had it inherited the Chinese tradition of linguistic engineering, but it also learned from the Soviet Union, where Lenin emphasized "the selection of language" because "people for the most part ... don't know how to *think*, they only *learn words* by heart."[11] By 1927, only six years after the party's foundation, the young Mao Zedong was celebrating the success of its slogans:

"Down with imperialism!" "Down with the warlords!" "Down with the corrupt officials!" "Down with the local tyrants and evil gentry!" – these political slogans have grown wings, they have found their way to the young, to the middle-aged and the old, to the women and the children in countless villages, they have penetrated into their minds and are on their lips.[12]

Mao then urged his comrades "to use every opportunity gradually to enrich the content and clarify the meaning of those simple slogans" – to elaborate them into more extended discourses.

---

[11] John Wesley Young, *Totalitarian Language: Orwell's Newspeak and Its Nazi and Communist Antecedents* (Charlottesville: University Press of Virginia, 1991), 126, 208, 211.

[12] Mao Zedong, "Report of an Investigation into the Peasant Movement in Hunan," in *Selected Readings from the Works of Mao Tsetung*, vol. 1 (London: Lawrence and Wishart, [1927] 1954), 47–48.

After Mao became the party's leader in 1935, he consolidated his power by turning the newly founded "Yan'an Soviet," where the party based itself from 1935 to 1947, into a revolutionary "discourse community" united by a special language, an associated body of theory, and the constant repetition of Maoist myths built around key words and phrases.[13] This meant that when the party won the civil war on mainland China in 1949, its cadres were perfectly equipped to undertake a nationwide program of linguistic engineering, teaching the whole population the basics of their own specialized vocabulary including the stock phrases and constantly repeated keywords that anchored its revolutionary discourses. This program was a key to the party's success.

The party's leaders controlled the process of linguistic engineering from the top down, mostly through directives from the Central Committee, the Central Propaganda Department, the New China News Agency, and other party organizations. The party's media monopoly implemented these directives to the letter. Meanwhile, local cadres held meetings in every workplace and neighborhood to explain party documents that used the new words and slogans, getting people to discuss them and introduce them into their own speech and writing. Many did this willingly, for after decades of warlordism, invasion, civil war, famine, inflation, corruption, and Nationalist Party misrule they welcomed the party's victory and were eager to help it create a new China. But learning the new language was not optional. Refusing to adopt it was a counter-revolutionary act, and people were expected to monitor their friends and colleagues, reminding them to use it in appropriate situations. The result, over time, was a revolutionary uniformity of expression achieved largely "by bureaucratic means."[14] The party used the new language as a core technology for creating new social realities and transforming people's worldview. Consider, for example, how it reworked the terminology of kinship to direct all forms of love, friendship, and filial piety to itself and the revolutionary cause. The term *xiongdi* (brother, brothers) now covered not just relatives but all revolutionary comrades (*tongzhi*); people with revolutionary-class backgrounds saw each other as *jieji xiongdi* (class brothers); the poor and lower-middle peasants became *nongmin xiongdi* (peasant brothers); friendly socialist countries were referred to as *xiongdi guojia* (fraternal nations); politically virtuous young people were called both "good children of Chairman Mao" (*Mao Zhuxi de hao haizi*) and "the party's good sons and daughters" (*dangde hao ernü*); and members of

---

[13] David E. Apter and Tony Saich, *Revolutionary Discourse in Mao's Republic* (Cambridge, MA: Harvard University Press, 1994).
[14] Schoenhals, *Doing Things with Words in Chinese Politics*, 51–52.

the armed forces became their Liberation Army uncles (*jiefangjun shushu*). Finally, the term *qin ren* (relatives), which had hitherto referred exclusively to blood relatives, now included the revolutionary masses as a whole.[15] This new language of kinship expressed the totalitarian turn in Chinese politics, subsuming family relationships, filial piety, and family loyalty within a totalizing discourse based on love for Mao, the party, and the "revolutionary masses." Whenever people used this language, they endorsed the ideal of revolutionary kinship and helped to make it part of lived social reality.

The most fundamental linguistic innovation, however, was a new language of class based on an analysis of people's occupations and political orientations before 1949. Its terminology turned China's traditional socio-economic order on its head. At the top were the "good classes" (*chengfen hao*), who comprised the party's "revolutionary cadres," "revolutionary soldiers," and "revolutionary martyrs," as well as the industrial workers and poor and lower-middle peasants. Next in rank were the "middle classes" (*yiban chengfen*), made up of groups of uncertain political allegiance such as the professions, white-collar workers, middle peasants, and petty bourgeoisie. At the very bottom were the "bad classes" (*chengfen buhao*), who consisted of landlords and rich peasants, along with all officials, party members, military officers, and capitalists associated with the former Nationalist government.[16] The party taught people to accompany references to the good classes with positive adjectives and references to the bad classes with negative ones, and to use prescribed words and slogans as the foundation of discourses glorifying the former and vilifying the latter. These discourses justified policies that favored the good classes and which dispossessed, impoverished, and discriminated against the bad classes.

The class system and the discourses attached to it were an effective means of isolating and punishing the bad classes. However, the party also needed a more flexible language that it could use to target people of any class. It achieved this with an array of political labels or "hats" that it could place on anyone, even revolutionary cadres. The main "hats" were "Counterrevolutionary," "Rightist," and the less serious "Bad Element." People tagged with these labels were lumped together with landlords and rich peasants as the Five Black Categories, which were named in contrast to the Five Red Categories – the collective term for the five "good" classes. The Black Categories were never trusted; they were shunned socially, and they were targeted with savage discourses.

---

[15] C. Li, *Studies in Chinese Communist Terminology*, no. 3 (Berkeley: East Asia Studies, Institute of International Studies, University of California, 1957), 17–22.

[16] Richard Curt Kraus, *Class Conflict in Chinese Socialism* (New York: Columbia University Press, 1981).

The language targeting the Black Categories was not simply intended to categorize and identify potential opponents, but also to *invent* them. During the campaign for the Suppression of Counterrevolutionaries in the early 1950s, for example, Mao imposed quotas that required local cadres to find the required number of counterrevolutionaries in their own areas, whether or not they existed.[17] Similarly, in rural areas with few or no landlords the party simply classified other politically vulnerable people as "landlords" until it had enough targets to attack as it taught the peasants to hate landlords, subject them to class struggle, and demand that they be punished.[18] Then, after it had eliminated the landlords and other classes as actual social entities by the mid 1950s, the party gave them an afterlife as linguistically sustained fictions by continuing to denounce them as "landlords," "rich peasants," and other class oppressors, even though their property had long since been confiscated. It even made class positions hereditary in the male line, so that by the later Mao era it was attacking members of the "bad classes" who had not been born when the last traces of actual classes were eliminated.[19]

The party perpetuated the existence of the Black Categories as a linguistic fiction so that it could continue to mobilize the "revolutionary masses" against them. Through this, it hoped to achieve three things:[20]

(i) Consolidate the collective identity of the revolutionary masses by getting them to engage in collective action under its leadership.
(ii) Implicate the revolutionary masses in the violence that it used to establish and sustain its rule.
(iii) Teach the whole country the most important lesson of all: that the party (or Mao acting in the name of the party) had the power to mobilize the masses to destroy anyone whom it targeted.

---

[17] Kuisong Yang, "Reconsidering the Campaign to Suppress Counterrevolutionaries," *The China Quarterly* 193 (2008): 102–121.

[18] Philip C. C. Huang, "Rural Class Struggle in the Chinese Revolution: Representational and Objective Realities from the Land Reform to the Cultural Revolution," *Modern China* 21(1) (1995): 105–143, 111–125; Yang Su, *Collective Killings in Rural China during the Cultural Revolution* (Cambridge: Cambridge University Press, 2011), 97–113; Brian DeMare, *Land Wars: The Story of China's Agrarian Revolution* (Stanford, CA: Stanford University Press, 2019); Edward Friedman, Paul G. Pickowicz, and Mark Selden, *Chinese Village, Socialist State* (New Haven, CT: Yale University Press, 1991), 92–98; Gao Wangling, and Liu Yang (2007). "On a slippery roof," *Études rurales* 179(1) (2007): 19–34.

[19] Fengyuan Ji, "The Power of Words: Labels and Their Consequences in Mao's China," in *Words of Power, the Power of Words: The Twentieth-Century Communist Discourse in an International Perspective*, ed. G. Bassi (Trieste: Edizioni Università di Trieste, 2019), 381–399.

[20] Ji, "The Power of Words," esp. 382–395.

To engage the masses in this project, the party taught them to overcome their aversion to violence by constantly using the savage language of class struggle. During the Cultural Revolution, for example, the Maoist propaganda apparatus taught people to revile and fear their victims as "hidden enemies" who looked like humans but had the natures of savage beasts and demons; it called them "wolves clad in the skins of sheep" and "man-eating smiling tigers"; and it described them as jackals, dogs, poisonous snakes, injurious vermin, devils, and vampires.[21] It also encouraged the revolutionary masses to drag them before "struggle meetings," accuse them of heinous crimes, assail them with revolutionary slogans, shout abuse, and demand that they be punished.[22] This constant linguistic dehumanization worked all too well, and on a conservative estimate the number of people killed during the Cultural Revolution was between 1.1 and 1.6 million.[23] It also worked well during the great campaign to suppress counterrevolutionaries during the early 1950s, when at least 712,000 real and alleged counterrevolutionaries were executed in response to well-orchestrated popular demand;[24] and it was effective during the land-reform campaign of the late 1940s and early 1950s, when up to a million or more members of landlord families were dragged before struggle meetings, dehumanized with the ferocious language prescribed by the party, and executed to "appease the revolutionary masses."[25]

The party's control of language and discourse, then, was an extraordinarily effective instrument of social coercion, and it was brutal when used as a weapon to create targets, dehumanize them, and legitimize their punishment and execution. However, its record as a *technology of*

---

[21] Ji, *Linguistic Engineering*, 188–204.

[22] Ji, *Linguistic Engineering*, 161–173; Fengyuan Ji, Koenraad Kuiper, and Shu Xiaogu, "The Formulae of Revolution," *Language in Society* 19 (1990), 61–79.

[23] Andrew G. Walder, "Rebellion and Repression in China, 1966–1971," *Social Science History* 38(34) (2014): 513–539; Yang Su, "Mass Killings in the Cultural Revolution: A Study of Three Provinces," in *The Chinese Cultural Revolution as History*, ed. Joseph W. Esherick, Paul G. Pickowicz, and Andrew G. Walder (Stanford, CA: Stanford University Press, 2006), 96–123; Su, *Collective Killings*; Xiaoxia Gong, "Perpetual Victims: Persecution of the Bad Classes during the Cultural Revolution," *China Information* 11(2/3) 1996): 35–53; Jonathan Unger, "Cultural Revolution Conflict in the Villages," *The China Quarterly* 153 (1998): 82–106. For specific focus on the links between language and violence, see Fengyuan Ji, "Language and Violence during the Chinese Cultural Revolution," *American Journal of Chinese Studies* 11(2) (2004): 93–117, and the more general treatment by Benjamin A. Valentino, "Why We Kill: The Political Science of Political Violence against Civilians," *Annual Review of Political Science* 17 (2014): 89–103.

[24] Kuisong Yang, "Reconsidering the Campaign to Suppress Counterrevolutionaries," 102–121.

[25] Ji, *Linguistic Engineering*, 69–71, and references at 320n4.

persuasion was mixed.[26] It worked splendidly with young people, who had unformed ideas and limited experience; and it worked well with adults when it acted in their favor, when it gave plausible interpretations of their experience, and when official discourse was their only source of information. However, people were generally skeptical when official mantras contradicted what they knew from their own lives. Members of the "bad classes," for example, did not believe the calumnies heaped upon them by official discourse, and the party's claims about the economic "successes" of the Great Leap Forward between 1958 and 1972 did not stop peasants from remembering that its policies had caused people in their village to starve to death, or from recalling those years as "the hunger crisis era" (*ji huang niandai*).

People also lost faith in revolutionary discourse during Mao's final decade because he so frequently reversed the official line to advance his own changing agendas. Before the Cultural Revolution, for example, official discourse had praised the party's leaders as paragons of revolutionary virtue, but once the revolution started the Mao-controlled media denounced most of them as capitalist roaders, revisionists, and traitors; in 1966, official discourse celebrated the Red Guards as revolutionary heroes, but once they had served Mao's purpose it told them to disband and denounced some of them as "counterrevolutionaries"; and in 1971, after spending years praising Mao's deputy, Lin Biao, as his "best student," the party unmasked him as a "traitor" and mobilized the revolutionary masses to attack him. For many, these repeated changes of line were too much. As one young man told the authors of *Chen Village*, "we came to see that the leaders up there could say today that something is round; tomorrow, that it's flat. We lost faith in the system."[27]

Linked to this loss of faith was a disheartening reality. After years of privation, loss of life, and endless class struggle, the country was still no closer to the harmony and prosperity of the promised Communist future. Indeed, Mao had abandoned the goal of social betterment, saying that it impeded the transition to socialism. He now believed that "nothing is certain except struggle" and that "it is quite possible the struggle will last for two or three hundred years."[28] This was a future that hardly anyone wanted to believe in. Many people wept when Mao died, but China was ready for a change.

---

[26] Ji, *Linguistic Engineering*, 285–317.
[27] Anita Chan, Richard Madsen and Jonathan Unger, *Chen Village: The Recent History of a Peasant Community in Mao's China* (Berkeley: University of California Press, 1984), 231.
[28] Lowell Dittmer, *China's Continuous Revolution: The Post-Liberation Epoch* (Berkeley: University of California Press, 1987), 41, 134.

Language and Hegemony in the Reform Era

After Mao's death, the new leader, Hua Guofeng, secured his position by arresting Mao's wife Jiang Qing and the others who made up the "Gang of Four," who had championed Mao's emphasis on class struggle and totalitarian controls. Hua had to rely increasingly on the support of moderates led by Deng Xiaoping, who had doubted aspects of Mao's revolutionary politics and suffered as a result. From 1978, these moderates gained the upper hand and began a far-reaching program of reform. They dismantled the system of dividing people into good and bad classes; they put an end to Mao's policies of constant revolutionary upheaval and class struggle; they stopped routinely censoring people's private correspondence; and they ceased trying to politicize people's private lives. Moreover, crucially for our purposes, they stopped forcing people to integrate Mao-quotes, political scripts, and revolutionary formulae into their conversations and daily lives. They also allowed unofficial discourses to proliferate provided they did not threaten the party's rule. In short, they put an end to the totalitarian form of linguistic engineering through which Mao had attempted to control people's lives and create new, revolutionary human beings.[29]

However, the relaxation of totalitarian controls did not put an end to linguistic engineering, which the party still uses in less coercive and ubiquitous ways to maintain party unity, express its theory, promote its policies, and ground discourses that enhance its standing. Linguistic engineering now operates at two levels of intensity. In official intraparty contexts, cadres have to use prescribed linguistic formulae that express the party's current line, promote its policies, foster its work culture, and ensure that the party speaks with one voice. Outside those contexts, use of official formulae is not required, either for party members or for ordinary people, but the party still promotes them vigorously through its propaganda apparatus, the media, and the education system.[30] Most people learn the formulae simply because they read and hear them so frequently, and this in turn enables the party to use them as familiar "anchors" for discourses that explain its policies, polish its image, promote its ideologies, and stabilize its rule.

One of the most important functions of official formulae in the Reform Era has been to instigate and sustain discourses that create the appearance of continuity in the party's history, theoretical development, and

---

[29] Fengyuan Ji, "Language, State, and Society in Post-Mao China: Continuity and Change," in *Legacies of Totalitarian Language in the Discourse Culture of the Post-Totalitarian Era*, ed. Ernest Andrews (Lanham, MD: Lexington Books, 2011), 183–207.
[30] Ji, "Language, State, and Society in Post-Mao China."

policies. They enable the party to claim a Maoist heritage for what is, in its substance, a determinedly anti-Maoist program that has involved decollectivizing agriculture, relaxing restrictions on private economic activity, giving market forces a role in the economy, cooperating with foreign capitalists, and adopting an "open door" policy toward foreign technology and investment.[31] This program has taken China at breakneck speed down the path that Mao would have condemned as the "capitalist road."

The problem facing Deng and his theoreticians was that they could not repudiate Mao's Thought without splitting the party and discrediting its Maoist past. The solution that they came up with was to pay fulsome tribute to the guiding spirit of Mao's Thought, while pointing out that he himself had said that he would be happy if 70 percent of his life's work consisted of achievements and only 30 percent of mistakes. This meant, said Deng, that instead of regarding Mao's words on any single issue as sacrosanct, the party had to interpret his Thought "as an integral whole" and focus on its "fundamentals." Deng then resurrected long-neglected statements from Mao about the importance of seeking truth from facts and set about establishing a new orthodoxy: that "seeking truth from facts, proceeding from reality and integrating theory with practice form the fundamental principle of Mao Zedong Thought."[32] When this line of argument won the support of the People's Liberation Army, Deng and the moderates carried the day.

The victory of the moderates produced a chain reaction that quickly transformed the party's dominant discourse. The conventions of party unity, as in Mao's time, required all cadres to *biaotai* (take a stand openly) in support of the new line, whether they agreed with it or not. Party members who had made Mao's word the criterion of truth now had to say that the most important thing was to "emancipate the mind," "seek truth from facts," remember that "practice is the sole criterion of truth," and recall the necessity of "proceeding from reality and integrating theory with practice." These slogans replaced Mao's "Never forget class struggle" and other revolutionary dicta, and once the cadres had mastered them in study sessions in late 1978 they became the cornerstones of a new discourse that was repeated up and down the country.[33]

When "seeking truth from facts" suggested that increasing the role of private enterprise and the market would boost economic growth, Deng and his allies devised an official language that depicted this change as

---

[31] Alan R. Kluver, *Legitimating the Chinese Economic Reforms: A Rhetoric of Myth and Orthodoxy* (Albany: State University of New York Press, 1996).

[32] Deng Xiaping, *Selected Works of Deng Xiaoping (1975–1982)* (Beijing: Foreign Languages Press, 1984), 128, 132.

[33] Ji, "Language, State, and Society in Post-Mao China."

a stage in the building of socialism. In this new language China, with its underdeveloped economy, was at "the primary stage of socialism" and, as orthodox Marxist theory had always stated, could advance to higher stages only by developing its productive forces. In doing that, it had to use the most effective means available – including private ownership, joint ventures, foreign investment, and market forces. This would not involve a reversion to capitalism because it would be superintended by a socialist state dedicated to reaching the level of development required for the transition to advanced socialism. Rather, it would involve the creation of a "socialist market economy" operating within the wider framework of "socialism with Chinese characteristics."[34]

In justifying these changes, Deng pointed out that Mao had adapted the thought of Marx, Lenin, and Stalin to Chinese circumstances and then claimed that by adapting Mao's own Thought he was just following Mao's example. Subsequent party leaders have all adopted a similar position, acknowledging the achievements of their predecessors and then following their example by devising linguistic formulae that express their own "advances" in the theory of "socialism with Chinese characteristics." They then put these formulae to work as *post facto* justifications for policies that they already decided to adopt and require all cadres to acknowledge their authority and submit to the party line by using them.

Deng's theoretical "advances" supplied the framework for the advances of his successors, who have all claimed to be building "socialism with Chinese characteristics." His immediate successor Jiang Zemin's doctrine of the "Three Represents" identified the party with China's new direction by stating that it represented China's "advanced productive forces," its "advanced culture," and "the fundamental interests of the overwhelming majority of the Chinese people." This placed the party at the head of the great technological, economic, and cultural forces that were transforming Chinese society, allowing it to claim credit for their benefits. It also allowed Jiang to say that the "overwhelming majority" whose interests the party represented included not just the workers and peasants but also the capitalists, who had risen again thanks to the economic reforms and were building "socialism with Chinese characteristics" by developing productive forces. Having finally reconciled with the capitalists, Jiang could now recruit them into the party and consolidate their loyalty. Party members who had opposed this now had to endorse it, and the "Three Represents" were enshrined in the party's constitution in 2002.

---

[34] Kluver, *Legitimating the Chinese Economic Reforms*, chapter 5.

Hu Jintao, in turn, adapted the party's theoretical and linguistic heritage to address the problems of rapid but uneven economic growth. He pointed out that a party representing the interests of "the overwhelming majority of the people" should not be promoting economic policies that caused vast regional and social inequalities. His solution was a "Scientific Development Concept" in which economic development remained "fundamental" but had to be "for the people, by the people, and with the people sharing its fruits." He then elaborated this concept of "putting people first" through a campaign to build a "New Socialist Countryside," aimed at reducing rural–urban disparities; and a campaign to build a "Socialist Harmonious Society" based on social justice, fairness, legality, and concern for the environment.[35] Such a society would require open debate on many topics, but it would also, of course, require censorship of "disharmonious" statements that had the potential to undermine the party's rule or subvert its fundamental objectives. As a result, "to harmonize" became an unofficial slang term for "to censor."[36]

The finely crafted evolution of the party's theory and language under Jiang and Hu owes much to theoreticians like Wang Huning, a member of the Politburo since 2012. These theoreticians have also ensured the continuity and coherence of official discourse under Xi Jinping, linking his theoretical advances to the foundations laid by his predecessors. Take, for example, Xi's principle of the "Two Combinations," which calls for the Sinification of socialist theory by combining it with "China's specific reality" and "China's excellent traditional culture."[37] The call to adapt socialist theory to Chinese reality is simply an application of Deng's doctrine of "socialism with Chinese characteristics." Similarly, the party has been attempting to co-opt "China's excellent traditional culture" since the mid 1980s, and by 2004 Hu Jintao had fused socialism with the Confucian concept of harmony in his call for a "Socialist Harmonious Society." Xi's "Two Combinations" is just the party's most recent attempt to use traditional values for its own purposes and position itself as the culmination of China's great civilization and long history.

Xi has also promoted linguistic formulae that stress his personal role in "the great rejuvenation of the Chinese nation." Only two years after becoming leader, for example, he began promoting a formula that placed

---

[35] Fengyuan Ji, "Linguistic Engineering in Hu Jintao's China: The Case of the 'Maintain Advancedness' Campaign," in *China's Thought Management*, ed. Anne-Marie Brady (London: Routledge, 2012), 90–106.

[36] Xuan Wang, Kasper Juffermans, and Caixia Du, "Harmony as Language Policy in China," *Language Policy* 15 (2016): 299–321.

[37] Tang Zhouyan and Wang Xueyuan, "*Jianchi 'Liangge jiehe'*" [Adhere to the two combinations], in *Hongqi wengao* [Red flag manuscript], May 2022, www.qstheory.cn/dukan/hqwg/2022-03/10/c_1128456414.htm.

him alongside Mao and Deng in the pantheon of great, era-defining leaders: "Mao made the Chinese people stand up, Deng Xiaoping made the Chinese people prosperous, Xi Jinping will make the Chinese people strong." Xi's special status was further confirmed in 2018 when the party abolished the two-term limit on holding office as president and wrote the formula "Xi Jinping Thought on Socialism with Chinese Characteristics for a New Era" into the Chinese constitution.

Xi's grand vision of China's future is conveyed by the "China Dream" (*Zhongguomeng*), a master-concept that harmonizes, extends, and adds luster to objectives that emerged under his Reform Era predecessors. At the heart of the Dream is the attainment of the objectives expressed by the "Two Centenaries":

(i) "To build a moderately prosperous society in all respects" by 2021, the hundredth anniversary of the CPC's founding.
(ii) "To build a modern socialist country that is prosperous, strong, democratic, culturally advanced, harmonious, and beautiful" by 2049, the hundredth anniversary of the founding of the People's Republic of China.

China's leaders and the media repeat these two slogans constantly, and the party's extraordinary success in modernizing and enriching the country since 1978 makes them credible. Indeed, China achieved the first objective on schedule when it became an upper-middle income country and eliminated absolute poverty by World Bank criteria in 2020.

Throughout the Reform Era, the party has derived enormous benefits from the way in which its carefully crafted linguistic formulae link all its policies to its theoretical heritage, create the illusion of a consistent line of development, and mimic the standardized terminology of science. This enables the party to argue that its theory is a *science of society* that guides policy decisions and is constantly tested and refined by observing policy outcomes. This contention in turn grounds the claim that China has performed spectacularly since 1978, not because it has abandoned Marxism in favor of theories borrowed from the capitalist West, but because it has remained true to its own Marxist tradition – a tradition whose stages of development are enshrined in Article 3(1) of the Chinese Constitution: "Marxism–Leninism, Mao Zedong Thought, Deng Xiaoping Theory, the Theory of Three Represents, the Scientific Outlook on Development, and Xi Jinping Thought on Socialism with Chinese Characteristics for a New Era." It is this evolving theory, with its "scientific" terminology, that underpins the party's claim that it alone is responsible for China's success and that it alone can be trusted with the country's future.

The official linguistic formulae have also been crucial to the party's success in using its propaganda apparatus and media to disseminate its message. Since the 1980s, most of the media has been at least partly commercialized, forcing it to produce material that attracts readers, listeners, viewers, and advertisers, and it reports freely on many matters. However, this has not meant that "the commercial 'bottom line' has undermined the 'Party line'" as once seemed likely.[38] The party still owns nearly all traditional media, its Central Propaganda Department superintends the media with a "guiding hand," and that guiding hand has become firmer under Xi Jinping. Journalists and editors know that there are boundaries that they cannot cross, and because these boundaries are vague at the margins they generally play safe by policing themselves. Social media, meanwhile, is subject to a variety of overt and algorithmic controls as well as pressure to self-censor. Crucially, all media people are briefed regularly on the latest official formulae and required to use them.[39] Under Xi Jinping, these formulae have also proliferated on billboards and electronic screens in public places, becoming a pervasive feature of the "linguistic landscape." They pass into common use because people are constantly exposed to them, and they structure public debate. When people discuss policies linked to the "Two Centenaries," for example, most will start out with the presumption that the policies are, in the words of a constantly repeated linguistic formula, intended to make China "prosperous, strong, democratic, culturally advanced, harmonious, and beautiful." To escape that presumption requires mental effort and a skeptical disposition because the initial "framing effect" of the linguistic formula is very strong.

The effects of constantly repeated linguistic formulae carry through to online political reporting and debate. As Shuyu Zhang notes in this volume (Chapter 6), since 2021 the party has restricted original news reporting to "whitelisted" news providers, with other media restricted to reprinting content from whitelisted ones. All news sources use the official formulae, as do the official social media accounts that have proliferated in response to Xi's call for the party to "march the mass line through the internet." The framing effect creates favorable terrain for supporting comments from individual cadres and a "volunteer army" of patriotic, proparty netizens – the most able of whom the party promotes as Key Opinion Leaders on multiple accounts and platforms. The result is

---

[38] David Shambaugh, *China's Communist Party: Atrophy and Adaptation* (Washington, DC: Woodrow Wilson Center Press, 2008), 108.

[39] Anne-Marie Brady, "Guiding Hand: The Role of the CCP Central Propaganda Department in the Current Era," *Westminster Papers in Communication and Culture* 3(1) (2006): 58–77, 63–66.

a massive online cheer squad that does not stop all debate but eventually overwhelms the voices of unorganized dissenters and creates at least the semblance of a consensus in favor of the official position. And, through it all, while the language of debate is often informal, it retains echoes of the official linguistic formulae that keep the cheer squad "on message."

Xi's determination to "march the mass line through the internet" is just one part of a wider attempt to ensure that the party's official discourse remains dominant. Under his leadership, the party has also erected the "Great Firewall of China," which bans Google and requires other internet search engines to use algorithms that filter out politically sensitive material; it has forced Christian, Buddhist, and Islamic leaders to "Sinicize" their discourse and teachings so that they align with the party's goals; and it has accelerated its drive to integrate Confucian concepts into official discourse.[40]

Under Xi, the party has also intensified its attempt to promote a new moral culture that will foster the emergence of a harmonious society under its rule. It sums up that new culture using keywords that identify the twelve Core Socialist Values: prosperity, democracy, civility, harmony, freedom, equality, justice, the rule of law, patriotism, dedication, integrity, and friendliness. Students learn these keywords by heart, and teachers elaborate their meaning. Along with the vision and the ethical system that they express, they are becoming part of tertiary curricula as well. They are celebrated in song, and the media extols them. Electronic screens on public transport carry video clips linking them to modern life and Chinese tradition, and prominently displayed posters list, explain, and illustrate them. And, of course, they anchor a wider moral discourse promoting virtuous and harmonious living under party rule. This moral discourse draws on traditional values as well as modern socialist ones, and it depicts the party as the culmination of the most creative forces in China's past. It is intended to fill the void created by the loss of faith in revolutionary Maoism, creating a fresh ethic that will bring the Chinese people together under a new hegemonic culture with the party at its core.

If the party is to command respect and rule effectively, its cadres have to be imbued with a good work culture. For this too, the party has always relied heavily on linguistic engineering. Mao made extensive use of slogans for educating and "rectifying" party cadres. The title of his 1944 speech "Serve the People" soon became the party's unofficial motto and it has been used to imbue an ethic of dedication and service in party

---

[40] Diana Fu and Emile Dirks, "Xi Jinping-Style Control and Civil Society Responses," *China Leadership* Monitor 69 (2021): 1–12; Richard Madsen, ed., *The Sinicization of Chinese Religions from Above and Below* (Leiden: Brill, 2021).

members ever since. In 2005–2006, for example, Hu Jintao's great "Maintain the Advanced Nature of the Communist Party" campaign required all seventy million party members to read "Serve the People." Cadres had to spend a minimum of forty hours studying it alongside other carefully selected political texts whose messages were encapsulated in linguistic formulae like the "Two Musts," the "Six Upholds," and "The Eight Upholds and the Eight Opposes."[41] They then had to use these formulae to critically analyze their own values, lifestyle, and work performance in handwritten "self-criticisms" while drawing up personal plans for reform. Finally, they had to implement Hu Jintao's Scientific Development Concept by "taking people as the basis" or "putting people first" in their orientation and work style.[42] Slogans like "People come first," "Practice the people-centered principle of development," and "To meet people's desire for a happy life is our mission" set the official values of their professional culture.

Pledges to "Serve the people" cannot rehabilitate the party's image if cadres take bribes and help themselves to public funds. So when Xi Jinping took office in late 2012 he launched his signature drive against corruption with a campaign to rid the party of the "Four Bad Work Styles" of "formalism, bureaucratism, hedonism, and extravagance," with the latter two targeting corruption. The fight against corruption has targeted some of Xi's opponents but is much wider, has had many successes, and is ongoing. It is also, of course, supported by slogans, study, and the Central Commission for Discipline Inspection of the Communist Party of China. Other efforts to improve the party's culture, reinforced by political formulae intended to guide the cadres as they go about their duties, have accompanied the anticorruption campaign. Among other things, the cadres must "Uphold Xi Jinping Thought on Socialism with Chinese Characteristics for a New Era," be guided by the "Four Comprehensives" and the "Four Awarenesses," obey the "Eight Musts," commit themselves to the party and its doctrines through the "Four Self-Confidences," and submit to the "Four Obediences." In other words, study materials and rote-learned linguistic formulae mold the working culture of party and state cadres in much the same way as the Confucian classics and rote-learned Confucian formulae molded the

[41] The "Two Musts," a Maoist numerical slogan first used in 1949, tells cadres: "We must be sure to make cadres continue to preserve a work style of humility, circumspection, free from arrogance and rashness; and we must be sure to make cadres continue to preserve a work style of hard work and struggle." Similarly, the "Six Upholds" (a slogan originating under Hu Jintao) and the "Eight Upholds and the Eight Opposes" (originating under Jiang Zemin) are numerical slogans designed to improve cadres' work style. The frequent use of numerical slogans to codify moral norms goes back to imperial times.
[42] Ji, "Linguistic Engineering in Hu Jintao's China."

working culture of imperial officials. There is no reason to believe that this very traditional method of promoting a good working culture has lost its effectiveness.

During the Mao era, the totalitarian form of linguistic engineering gravely handicapped the party's ability to formulate effective policies and promote economic growth because it encouraged both cadres and the Chinese people to take Mao's Thought as the criterion of truth, to recite political formulae when asked for their views, and to avoid empirical investigations that might result in "incorrect" conclusions. This stifled information flows, feedback, and creativity, sometimes with disastrous results. By contrast, the nontotalitarian linguistic engineering of the Reform Era is specifically designed to minimize these problems. The party now linguistically engineers both its cadres and the general population to "seek truth from facts," to remember that "practice is the sole criterion of truth," and to recall the necessity of "proceeding from reality and integrating theory with practice." This has created an empirically oriented working culture with many beneficial outcomes. These include the party's systematic attempts to get feedback on its policies and its extensive use of pilot projects to trial new initiatives before introducing them nationwide. This new culture has facilitated China's astonishing economic growth and social progress during the Reform Era, enhancing the party's reputation and consolidating its rule. Indeed, a credible nationwide survey conducted between 2003 and 2016 showed a large rise in public confidence in the government at all levels, with Chinese citizens rating it as "more capable and effective than ever before."[43] However, the survey also reveals that the government's ratings rose and fell in response to "real, measurable changes in individuals' material well-being." This raises the question of what will happen if China's protracted economic miracle is interrupted by the sort of severe downturn that is always possible in a market economy – even, perhaps, a "socialist market economy." Will that shatter confidence in the party's fitness to rule? And if it does, will it imperil the party's hold on power?

---

[43] Edward Cunningham, Tony Saich, and Jessie Turiel, *Understanding CCP Resilience: Surveying Chinese Public Opinion through Time* (Cambridge, MA: Harvard Kennedy School Ash Center for Democratic Governance and Innovation, 2020); Jessie Turiel, Edward Cunningham, and Tony Saich, "To Serve the People: Income, Region and Citizen Attitudes towards Governance in China," *The China Quarterly* 240 (December 2019): 906–935. Western readers often ask whether people in China feel free to tell interviewers what they think. On issues like this, most of them do; and in the early years of this survey their views about local party officials were often damning.

Language, Power, and the Stability of Communist Party Rule

In assessing the future of Communist Party rule in China, it is helpful to consider whether the discourse supporting the party's hold on power in the Reform Era is as deeply entrenched as the discourses that underpinned the imperial system of government and Communist Party rule during the Mao era. In imperial China, the Confucian discourse that linked rulers and people in a stable hierarchy benefited powerholders at every level of society, right down to senior males in remote villages. This discourse therefore had such deep roots in the social structure that everyone saw the advantages of using it to win the support of local powerholders, legitimate itself, and perpetuate the imperial ideal. This helped to stabilize the system of imperial rule for over 2,000 years. By contrast, the discourse that justifies the rule of the contemporary Communist Party is disseminated by the party from the top down and is not embedded in the interests of independent powerholders distributed throughout society. It has very shallow roots in a population that is also more diverse, mobile, fragmented, subject to foreign influences, and aware of alternative ideologies and models of government. It is therefore far less likely to endure.

The absence of deep popular commitment to the party's ideology, however, will not stop it from staying in power. During the Mao era, for example, the party won over the peasant majority with land reform, only to lose a lot of that support by taking the peasants' land and collectivizing it in the name of the "revolutionary masses." It lost still more support, especially in rural areas, when thirty million people and perhaps many more died as a direct result of its policies during the Great Leap Forward;[44] and its credibility took another battering during the chaos, bloodshed, and endless political mobilization of the ten-year Cultural Revolution (1966–1976). It is not at all surprising that, as we have seen, many people had lost faith in official discourse by the end of the Mao era.

The Chinese people's loss of revolutionary faith, however, did not threaten the party's grip on power because of three fundamental factors identified by Levitsky and Way's compelling study of "durable authoritarianism":[45]

---

[44] Jasper Becker, *Hungry Ghosts: China's Secret Famine* (London: John Murray, 1996); Frank Dikotter, *Mao's Great Famine: The History of China's Most Devastating Catastrophe, 1958–1962* (London: Bloomsbury, 2010); Jisheng Yang, *Tombstone: The Great Chinese Famine, 1958–1962* (New York: Farrar, Straus and Giroux, 2012).

[45] Steven Levitsky and Lucan Way, *Revolution and Dictatorship: The Violent Origins of Durable Authoritarianism* (Princeton, NJ: Princeton University Press, 2022), 4–5, 85–116.

(i) By the early 1950s, the party had destroyed every form of political, social, and economic organization that had the potential to challenge it.
(ii) Years of revolutionary war had given the party discipline, a strong collective spirit, and intense loyalty to Mao as the man who led it to victory. As a result, even when Mao purged most of his fellow leaders during the Cultural Revolution, they continued to profess their loyalty to him as the embodiment of the "Party Center."
(iii) The People's Liberation Army's leadership was integrated with the party's leadership, with a bond forged by years of common struggle. It steadfastly supported Mao, and its overwhelming power was enough to crush all challenges.

Within the framework of this structural imbalance of power – so heavily weighted in favor of Mao, the party, and the military – the control of language and discourse played a crucial role. The bond between the party and the military under Mao's leadership was based not only on their shared raw experience of war and revolution, but on how their political language refracted that raw experience into a shared and very distinctive worldview. Their unity and loyalty were based, too, on their members' constant collective study of the language and meaning of key Maoist texts, on their repeated use of Maoist dicta to appraise their own and other people's conduct, and on their practice of publicly endorsing the party line by repeatedly using the linguistic formulae that expressed it. In other words, both the party and the military were held together by an official language whose compulsory use united them behind the current line, structured their collective interpretation of experience, constructed the party as their primary community, and overrode all other affiliations.[46] The party and the military were therefore bound together as a single discourse community.

Linguistic engineering further entrenched the balance of power in the party's favor by limiting popular protest. Dissenters had difficulty identifying potential supporters because everyone had to use standardized words and slogans to model revolutionary attitudes; even when they knew that others shared their dissatisfaction, they were afraid to protest because they feared that the party would label them as "counterrevolutionaries," get the "revolutionary masses" to dehumanize them with savage slogans, and then demand that they be punished. When, against

---

[46] Apter and Saich, *Revolutionary Discourse in Mao's Republic*, chapters 3–4, 7–9, and appendix; Hua Gao, *Hongtaiyangshi zenyang shengqi de: Yanan zhengfeng yundong de lailongqumai* [How did the sun rise over Yan'an? A history of the rectification movement] (Hong Kong: Chinese University Press, 2000), chapters 10–11.

the odds, localized protests nevertheless occurred, the party's controls over discourse limited the "contagion effect" by making it difficult for the news to spread. In this way, Mao's linguistic totalitarianism reduced the amount of open protest, and with it the party's need to defend its power by using naked force.

Today, despite the more restrictive approach adopted by Xi Jinping, China has nothing approaching the rigid controls over language, discourse, and society that stifled protest during the Mao era. However, it has not needed them. Indeed, as we have seen, the party's popularity has soared, and its official discourse seems credible because it resonates with the progress that people see everywhere. But this simply brings us back to the question of what happens if China's economic miracle hits obstacles or even comes to an end. Will the lack of totalitarian controls make it ill equipped to deal with rising dissatisfaction and possible protests? This seems extremely unlikely. The party can impose stringent controls on social media and the internet, if it needs to; and, crucially, the structural balance of power is still tilted decisively in its favor – provided it retains the support of the military and the People's Armed Police, with their monopoly of armed force.

If a serious challenge to the party emerges, it may well resemble the Tiananmen protests in 1989, when official condemnation of the reform-minded late premier Hu Yaobang crystallized wider dissatisfaction, inspiring massive student-led protests that demanded reform. Both the party and the military were initially divided on whether to negotiate with the protesters or to repress them. When they decided on the latter, the military crushed the protests with ease. In retrospect, having seen how Communist governments in the Soviet Union and Eastern Europe were swept away through their failure to crush similar protests, the party has concluded that it made the right decision. As a result, it is now more likely to end protests quickly and decisively; and if it does that, it will remain in power. The outcome will be uncertain only if reformers within the party block repression so that they can strengthen their position by rallying popular support.

If the party stays in power by using force, linguistic engineering and the management of discourse will remain as important as ever. Its theoreticians will craft new discourses using carefully chosen keywords to define and deprecate the nature of the protest, characterize and condemn the protesters, praise the decisive action of the party's leaders, and erase the voices of the vanquished from the country's collective memory.

The party will also learn from its mistakes. In the spirit of the Reform Era, it will "seek truth from facts," it will ascertain the causes of popular discontent, and it will devise policies to remove people's grievances and improve their lives. It will then promote the new policies with discourses organized around carefully crafted linguistic formulae, it will attribute the success of the new policies to the party's "scientific theory," and it will patiently win back popular support. This is what the party did as it recovered from the disasters of the Mao era, and as it restored its reputation in the aftermath of the "Tiananmen incident." The strategy worked on both these occasions, and it will work again. It is without doubt already inscribed in the party's contingency plans for rebuilding its legitimacy after any future challenge to its rule.

5 Patriotic Nationalism as Commodity

Delia Lin

When Huawei's chief financial officer Meng Wanzhou was released from nearly three years of house arrest in Canada and flew as a free person into Shenzhen airport on the night of September 25, 2021, she was hailed as a national hero in China. Wearing a red dress, she delivered a passionate speech thanking the leadership of the Communist Party of China (CPC) and her "strong motherland," claiming, "where there is a Chinese flag, there is a beacon of faith. If faith has a color, it must be China Red."[1] This statement has since been converted into an iconic catchphrase, perfectly tethering personal faith to national pride. Businesses have quickly adopted "China Red" into a brand to boost their sales and popularity along with their political creed. For example, in December 2021, on its twentieth anniversary, the Chinese cosmetic brand Carslan (*ka zi lan*) released a new line of lipsticks that included the color "Flourishing China Red" (*shengshi zhongguo hong*). The expression for "flourishing" in Chinese – *shengshi* – refers both to specific, glorious historical periods and language used around the China Dream of "national rejuvenation." The cosmetic brand, therefore, successfully incorporated patriotic passion and national pride together with China's cultural fondness for the color red (traditional signifier of good fortune, wealth, and happiness) into the name. Here we see the convergence between commodity fetishism and the patriotic nationalist push that is reshaping the CPC's approach to ideological-affective governance in Xi Jinping-era China.

This chapter claims that ideological-affective governance is fundamental to CPC rule. I use this term to emphasize the cultivation of emotions that work hand in glove with ideological work. In other words, China's one-party authoritarian governance relies on the coalescing of ideological propaganda and the channeling of public emotions and individual affects to drive moral-political action. Like political scientist Christian Sorace, I prefer the language of *affect* instead of *emotion* to capture the governance

---

[1] Chen Qingqing and Shen Weiduo, "'If Faith Has a Color, It Must Be China Red': Patriotism Prevails as Meng Wanzhou Arrives on Home Soil," *Global Times* (September 25, 2021). www.globaltimes.cn/page/202109/1235069.shtml.

style, to suggest "fluid, socially mediated atmospheres, rather than discrete, psychological states."[2] As I show, the Confucian theory of heart-mind provides the cultural and philosophical foundation for ideological-affective unification. The resilience of the CPC's authoritarian one-party rule lies to a great extent in the CPC's ability to instill beliefs and mobilize the emotional energies of the masses to support the party's moral and political claim to be the ongoing, sole ruling party of China. Communism as a political belief system has gradually faded into the background since the introduction of a market-based economy. The party therefore needs to establish alternative belief systems to sustain its monopoly rule.

One such belief system is patriotic nationalism (*aiguo*). This chapter shows that patriotic nationalism, as illustrated by the lipstick example, has also transformed into a commodity, a fashion, an object of trade for profit. This encourages the elite and the general public alike to participate as consumers of nationalism, demonstrating their patriotic loves and hates through the commerce of both objects and ideas. Today's party propaganda embraces the consumer cultures that have evolved during forty years of economic reform, to make ideology not only popular but also profitable – unthinkable through the Mao era (1949–1976).

In the following sections, I introduce the philosophical roots of ideological-affective governance and examine the mechanisms for commodifying ideology in entertainment, media, and social media. Mass consumerism and the wired world enable the party to turn entrepreneurs into propaganda-fueled machines reaching far beyond the Great Wall of China.

Ideological-Affective Governance

Ideological-affective governance has its roots in the Confucian architecture of two millennia of imperial rule. In his study of the psychological and ethical foundations of how people's beliefs have been manipulated and controlled in socialist China, Donald Munro examines the psychological assumptions implicit in ideas of governance in Confucianism and socialism.[3] The typical liberal democratic attitude distinguishes between an individual's mind and their actions, between their intentions and deeds. Confucianism, Munro observes, folds them into one and assumes

---

[2] Christian Sorace, "The Chinese Communist Party's Nervous System: Affective Governance from Mao to Xi," *The China Quarterly* 248 (November 2021): 29–51, 30.
[3] Donald J. Munro, "Belief Control: The Psychological and Ethical Foundations," in *Deviance and Social Control in Chinese Society*, ed. Amy Auerbacher Wilson, Sidney Leonard Greenblatt, and Richard Whittingham Wilson (New York: Praeger, 1977), 14–36.

that actions are the consequence of what is known and believed. Therefore it is not only transgressions of behavior that are problematic, but the knowledge, belief, attitudes, and thoughts behind them, however trivial.[4]

Ideological-affective governance also has philosophical roots in the theory of human nature described by the philosopher Mencius (372–289 BCE), who was the first important philosopher to elaborate on Confucius's ideas. Munro notes that in contrast to Judeo-Christian traditions, Confucian philosophy anchors morality not in an anthropomorphic deity, but in social virtues that correspond with the four innate emotional qualities: sympathy corresponds with benevolence (*ren*), for example, scorn and shame with righteousness (*yi*), deference with propriety (*li*), and good judgment with wisdom (*zhi*).[5] Munro suggests that the Western dichotomies between facts and values, between reason and emotions, which originated with Plato, are not present in Confucian or other traditions of Chinese thought.[6] Rather, Chinese thinkers (early, mid imperial, and modern alike) tend to favor a "tight linkage of cognitive and emotional functions."[7] Munro differentiates early philosophical Confucianism (*rujia zhexue*) from "State Confucianism" (*guojia rushu*), the legacy of Dong Zhongshu (c. 179–c.104 BCE), who proposed "banning all other schools of thought and venerating only Confucianism" (*bachu baijia, duzun rushu*), taking it as the basis for imperial statecraft. Munro argues that whereas philosophical Confucianism distinguishes between morality and conformity to conventional rules, State Confucianism draws no distinction between the two.[8] The largely unchallenged primacy of "State Confucianism" as an albeit constantly evolving philosophy of governance over two millennia has shaped a political outlook in which morality, ideology, and affective power converge. The CPC has proven adept at taking advantage of this.

The CPC has an extraordinary and well-documented ability to mobilize people's emotional energy for revolutionary and political purposes and has done so throughout its history. As one of the first scholars to directly study what she calls the CPC's "emotion work," Elizabeth Perry highlights the attention to mass mobilization of emotions as a key ingredient in

---

[4] Delia Lin, *Civilising Citizens in Post-Mao China: Understanding the Rhetoric of Suzhi* (London: Routledge, 2017).
[5] Donald J. Munro, *The Concept of Man in Contemporary China* (Ann Arbor: University of Michigan Press, 1977); Donald J. Munro, "When Science Is in Defense of Value-Linked Facts," *Philosophy East & West* 69(3) (July 2019): 900–917.
[6] Munro, "When Science Is in Defense of Value-Linked Facts."
[7] Munro, "When Science Is in Defense of Value-Linked Facts."
[8] Munro, "When Science Is in Defense of Value-Linked Facts."

the CPC's revolutionary victory in 1949.[9] Michael Dutton describes the Chinese Cultural Revolution (1966–1976) as an "affective revolution"[10] through which the political friend/enemy dichotomy became intensively "felt." This worked, for example, through mass participation in acts of hate-filled political "struggle" (including ransacking people's homes and beating and torturing political and class enemies) as well as in acts of ecstatic devotion to Mao (million-strong rallies in Tiananmen Square, for instance). Political ideas thus left the abstract realm to touch people's inner selves.

Zheng Wang's seminal work on the patriotic education that began after the violent suppression of student-led protests for democracy in 1989 shows how the Norwegian scholar Johan Galtung's theory of the Chosenness–Myths–Trauma (CMT) complex sheds light on CPC strategies of ideological-affective governance.[11] According to this theory, chosenness refers to "the idea of being a people chosen by transcendental forces," which results in China from pride in the country's long civilizational history and contemporary achievements. Chosenness in combination with the forces of myth and trauma results in a collective megalo-paranoia syndrome, as embedded in the CPC's historical narrative of "One Hundred Years of Humiliation" and a particular brand of Chinese nationalism. Christian Sorace traces the CPC's conceptualization of gratitude (*gan'en*) from Mao to Xi as a way of connecting the party's narratives of legitimacy to people's emotional lives, entwining ordinary life in the official nervous system.[12] An example would be the ubiquity of the song "Without the Communist Party of China there would be no New China." Each time this uplifting tune is heard or sung, it reinforces the association of rising living standards with the CPC.

What I add to the literature on CPC's affective governance is consideration of the dimension of moral ideology, in the Confucian sense by which the standard of morality is measured by affective and emotional performance – for example, schoolchildren who write moving essays about their "China Dream" or citizens who express gratitude for the party and government for their good life. Because the Chinese philosophical tradition doesn't differentiate between reason and emotion, it gives the party

---

[9] Elizabeth Perry, "Moving the Masses: Emotion Work in the Chinese Revolution," *Mobilization* 7(2) (2002): 111–128.

[10] Michael Dutton, "Cultural Revolution as Method," *The China Quarterly* 227 (2016): 718–733, 718.

[11] Zheng Wang, *Never Forget National Humiliation: Historical Memory in Chinese Politics and Foreign Relations* (New York: Columbia University Press, 2012).

[12] Sorace, "The Chinese Communist Party's Nervous System."

ethical power to assign moral values to emotional sentiments. This allows them, for instance, to encourage love for the nation and gratitude for the party and discourage any mockery of national heroes, as ways of educating Chinese citizens to be "good" or "moral." Among the twelve "socialist core values" (*shehui zhuyi hexin jiazhi*) introduced at the Eighteenth Party Congress in 2012 is *aiguo*, patriotism, literally "love for the nation" or "loving the nation."[13] The twelve officially sanctioned moral virtues divide into the national values of prosperity, democracy, civility, and harmony; the social values of freedom, equality, justice, and rule of law; and the individual values of patriotism, dedication, integrity, and friendship. Patriotism heads the list of the four individual values. In his 2015 speech celebrating Model Workers for International Labor Day, Xi Jinping emphasizes that of the twelve socialist core values, patriotism is "the deepest, the most fundamental and the most enduring value."[14] Placing love for the nation at the heart of ideology and identifying it as a prerequisite of moral integrity means that the CPC endorses it as the basis for moral and political doctrine.

Aiguo, patriotic nationalism, thus has ideological, psychological, and emotional dimensions. Building on the work of Rogier Creemers and Susan Trevaskes,[15] I refer here to ideology in the sense of a set of beliefs and arrangement of ideas and ideals purposefully designed to drive political action. Ideology has been central to the People's Republic of China's social governance, politics, and institutions. The historian John Fitzgerald reminds us of the centrality of *aiguo* when he notes that the PRC's 1982 constitution implicitly justifies the CPC's continuing rule by its historical nationalist achievements.[16] As it states in the Preamble:

After waging hard, protracted and tortuous struggles, armed and otherwise, the Chinese people of all nationalities led by the Communist Party of China with Chairman Mao Zedong as its leader ultimately, in 1949, overthrew the rule of imperialism, feudalism, and bureaucrat-capitalism, won the great victory of the new democratic revolution and founded the People's Republic of China.

---

[13] Delia Lin and Susan Trevaskes, "Creating a Virtuous Leviathan: The Party, Law, and Socialist Core Values," *Asian Journal of Law and Society* 6 (2019): 41–66.

[14] Xinhua Net, "'*Ping yu' jin ren – Xi Jinping tan shehuizhuyi hexin jiazhiguan*" [Ping's "pinning" messages – Xi Jinping on socialist core values], Xinhua Net (December 8, 2016), www.xinhuanet.com/politics/2016-12/08/c_129395314.htm.

[15] Rogier Creemers and Susan Trevaskes, "Ideology and Organisation in Chinese Law: Towards a New Paradigm for Legality," in *Law and the Party in China: Ideology and Organisation*, ed. Rogier Creemers and Susan Trevaskes (Cambridge: Cambridge University Press, 2020), 1–28.

[16] John Fitzgerald, *Cadre Country: How China Became the Chinese Communist Party* (Sydney: UNSW Press, 2022), 129–130.

Thereupon the Chinese people took state power into their own hands and became masters of the country.[17]

Fitzgerald highlights two motifs of Chinese nationalism common to modern nationalism in general that the CPC cultivates effectively.[18] They are unity and uniformity. I suggest that *aiguo* goes beyond the emotional and psychological state of patriotic love. It is as much about constructing an ideological system for the "national imaginary"[19] as it is about cultivating and channeling political emotion. As discussed earlier (p. 98), this conflation of reason and emotion has roots in Chinese traditional philosophy. "Patriotic nationalism" therefore here denotes the Chinese sense of *aiguo* as it is used today.

In 2017, the CPC Central Committee and State Council issued "Opinions on Creating a Healthy Environment for Entrepreneurship Development, Promoting Excellent Entrepreneurial Spirit and Maximizing a Better Role of Entrepreneurs," stressing the party's leadership in building the entrepreneurial community, with patriotic nationalism as the first entrepreneurial spirit to be nurtured and promoted.[20] China's hybrid economy, in which market forces may be tempered or directed by the state, what we might call "party-state capitalism," enables the party to manipulate the market to reward the production of objects signaling patriotic nationalism, thereby transforming ideological and emotional patriotism into commodities to be traded for wealth and status. As ideology becomes a commodity, active mass participation in constructing and channeling beliefs and emotions supplements conventional top-down authoritarian forms of propaganda. Yet there is a paradox: As effective as commodification of ideology is in its popularization, it also undermines what ideologies set out to achieve – the making of true believers. The following sections present three examples.

Commercializing Patriotic Nationalism in the Entertainment Industry

Cinema and TV productions have always played a leading role in turning party-sanctioned values into mainstream values. Elevating *aiguo* to an

---

[17] For the English version of the 1982 State Constitution of the PRC, see https://aceproject .org/ero-en/regions/asia/CN/china-constitution-1982/view.
[18] Fitzgerald, *Cadre Country*, 133.
[19] Fitzgerald, *Cadre Country*, 132.
[20] "*Zhonggong Zhongyang Guowuyuan guanyu yingzao qiyejia jiankang chengzhang huanjing hongyang youxiu qiyejia jingshen geng hao fahui qiyeejia zuoyongde yijian*" [CPC Central Committee and State Council opinions on creating a healthy environment for entrepreneurship development, promoting excellent entrepreneurial spirit and maximizing a better role for entrepreneurs], PRC Central Government website, www.gov.cn (September 25, 2017).

ideological level makes it the arbiter of values for both entertainment-industry productions and personnel. The National Radio and Television Administration's Notice on "Enhancing the Management of Entertainment Programs and Personnel" ("the Notice"), issued on September 2, 2021, enshrines its central role in the production of entertainment programs. The National Radio and Television Administration (NRTA) is a ministry-level executive agency directly under the jurisdiction of the State Council; it is in charge of the administration and supervision of the state-owned radio and television industries. The Notice states "unequivocally" (*qizhi xianming*) that the entertainment industry's culture must be based on "loving the Party, loving the nation" (*aidang aiguo*) and "upholding moral and artistic standards" (*chongde shangyi*).[21] The Notice forbids radio and television broadcasting stations and online audio/video platforms from employing or hosting three types of people: those who hold "incorrect political views" and whose "hearts and minds deviate from the Party and the nation"; those who break laws and regulations and offend against social fairness and justice; and those who "act against public order and good morals."[22] The Notice requires radio and television programs to uphold "cultural confidence" (*wenhua zixin*) and "vigorously carry forward China's outstanding traditional culture, revolutionary culture and advanced socialist culture."[23]

The progressive commercialization of the ideology of patriotic nationalism has achieved at least three forms of success. First, making "patriotic" film and television productions has become profitable. Second, censorship processes that are unpredictable, opaque, and exacting have made cultural production with blatant, even sensational patriotic nationalist themes a safe investment. Third, the threat that any perceived violation of patriotic values may lead to public shaming and even unemployability makes industry personnel careful to police their own actions and speech so as to appear properly patriotic.

The first two forms concern the genre, theme, and content of entertainment products. At the time of writing, the top two highest-grossing films in China's box office history have had strong overtones of patriotic nationalism. Released on September 30, 2021, the war epic *The Battle at Lake Changjin* (*Changjin Hu*) had already taken a record US$890 million

---

[21] NRTA (National Radio and Television Administration Office), "*Guojia guangbo dianshi zongju bangongting guanyu jinyibu jiaqiang wenyi jiemu ji qi renyuan guanlide tongzhi*" [National Radio and Television Administration Office notice on enhancing the management of entertainment programs and personnel], National Radio and Television Administration Office website (September 2, 2021), www.nrta.gov.cn/art/2021/9/2/art_113_57756.html.
[22] NRTA, "Notice to Further Enhance Management."
[23] NRTA, "Notice to Further Enhance Management."

by the end of November 2021, surpassing the previous box office record-holder, the 2017 action blockbuster *Wolf Warrior 2* (*Zhan Lang 2*).[24] Outside China, both films have been widely dismissed as party propaganda intended to galvanize patriotic feelings and glorify the greatness of China and the heroism of its soldiers while condemning the cowardly West, especially the United States.[25] Films and television productions drawn from the history of the brutal conflict with Japan between 1937 and 1945, known in China as the War of Resistance against Japanese Aggression (the Anti-Japanese War), have long been used to construct patriotic nationalism. Yin Hong, the vice-president of the China Film Association, has astutely observed that such productions, which tie the fates of individuals or families to the fate of the nation, constitute China's quintessential patriotic culture, representing the "integration of family and the state as one" (*jiaguo yiti*).[26] This reinforces the traditional Confucian notion of the state as family writ large, with filial devotion to one's parents paralleled in the public realm by loyalty to one's ruler, hence tying individuals cognitively, morally, and emotionally to the state. The number of Anti-Japanese War films and television dramas has increased exponentially in the twenty-first century.[27] According to a widely cited report on how China's entertainment industry has profited from the war by then *Southern Weekly* journalist Fan Chenggang and his team,[28] in the fifty-five years between 1949 and 2004, China produced 150 or so Anti-Japanese War television dramas – but in 2004 alone, Chinese television broadcast over 20 such dramas and in 2012, 70. Fan and his team report that producers shifted to investing in Anti-Japanese War dramas as the safest path to official approval, after the NRTA's predecessor, the State

---

[24] Sara Merican, "'Battle at Lake Changjin' is China's All-Time Highest-Grossing Film," *Forbes* (November 29, 2021), www.forbes.com/sites/saramerican/2021/11/29/battle-at-lake-changjin-is-chinas-all-time-highest-grossing-film/?sh=756ece3cbf7; Xinhua, "'The Battle at Lake Changjin' Becomes New Highest-Grossing Film in China," *XinhuaNet* (November 25, 2021), www.news.cn/english/2021–11/25/c_1310332171.htm.

[25] Clifford Coonan, "Smash Hit War Movie 'Wolf Warriors 2' Flies Flag for a Resurgent China," *The Irish Times* (August 19, 2017), www.irishtimes.com/news/world/asia-pacific/smash-hit-war-movie-wolf-warriors-2-flies-flag-for-a-resurgent-china-1.3190847; Merican, "Battle at Lake Changjin."

[26] Hong Yin and Qingsheng Zhan, "*Dangdai Zhongguo wenhuade yingxiang duolengjing – guanyu Zhongguo kangzhan ticai yingshi chuangzuod duihua*" [The prism of contemporary Chinese culture: A conversation on Chinese film and television productions with the theme of China's war of resistance against Japanese aggression], *Journal of PLA Academy of Art* 3 (2015): 50–60, 60.

[27] Jemimah Steinfeld, "Screened Shots: The Chinese Film Industry's Obsession with Portraying Japan's Invasion during World War II," *Index on Censorship* 44(1) (2015): 103–106.

[28] Chenggang Fan and Shiwei Shao, "'*KangRi*' *zhe men shengyi*" [This "anti-Japanese" business], *Southern Weekly* (March 7, 2013), https://m.fx361.cc/news/2013/0307/202058.html.

Administration of Radio, Film, and Television, placed restrictions, in 2006 and 2009 respectively, on popular genres such as historical dramas (*guzhuang ju*) and wartime spy dramas (*diezhan ju*).[29]

Yet not all Anti-Japanese War productions are the same. Yin Hong describes a five-stage evolution in China's Anti-Japanese War productions, each stage featuring a theme driven by the key political messages of the times.[30] The first stage, prior to 1949, and especially during the war itself, saw a focus on mobilizing the masses for national defense. An example would be the charming and popular *Xiao wanyi'er* (*Little Toys*, 1933), starring Ruan Lingyu as a village woman who makes and promotes traditional toys as an alternative to foreign – including Japanese – imports. Another, *Fengyuan ernü* (*Children of Troubled Times*, 1935), features the song "March of the Volunteers," which later became the Chinese national anthem.

The second stage, from 1949 to 1966, shifted the focus from the conflict itself to the creation of revolutionary heroes and villains within the context of the war. Mass mobilization under the inspiration of Mao Zedong Thought is the theme of *Tunnel Warfare*, made in 1965, in which villagers under attack by the Japanese read Mao's *On Protracted War* and dig an extensive tunnel network under the village, eventually forcing the Japanese to retreat (*Tunnel Warfare* is reportedly the world's most watched film: 1.8 billion viewers by 2006 according to the military's August First Film Studio).[31] The war also features as part of the CPC's journey to victory depicted in the epic *The East Is Red* (1965).

During the Cultural Revolution (1966–76) there were hardly any films made apart from adaptations of model operas (*yangban xi*), a series of revolutionary theatrical works engineered by Jiang Qing, the wife of Mao Zedong. Yin Hong omitted the period and considered the early Reform Era from the late 1970s to the late 1980s to be the third stage of Anti-Japanese War films. Yin Hong calls these films "double variations" of patriotism and humanitarianism. By "humanitarianism," Yin Hong meant viewing the war not from a purely nationalistic perspective – hence glorifying the victory of the CPC and promoting patriotism – but acknowledging the devastating consequences of the war on people's lives. These films also acknowledged the Kuomintang's (KMT's) contribution to the war effort for the first time (as part of a new United Front appeal to Taiwan for "peaceful reunification"). For example, *The Xi'an Incident*

---

[29] Fan and Shao, "This 'anti-Japanese' business."
[30] Yin and Zhan, "The Prism of Contemporary Chinese Culture."
[31] David Lague and Jane Lanhee Lee, "Special Report: Why China's Film Makers Love to Hate Japan," *Reuters* (May 26, 2013), www.reuters.com/article/us-china-japan-specialreport-idUSBRE94O0CJ20130525.

(1981) was one of the pioneers that faced up to historical truth and depicted historical figures as flawed human beings, neither perfect heroes nor complete villains. The seminal films of the Fifth Generation of filmmakers, Chen Kaige's *Yellow Earth* (1984) and Zhang Yimou's *Red Sorghum* (1987), which were set against the backdrop of the Anti-Japanese War, broke the mold of propagandistic filmmaking.

In the fourth stage, beginning in the 1990s, just as the party launched its nationwide (and culture-wide) Patriotic Education Campaign to reorient the party's and the nation's ideological position in the post-Tiananmen period, nationalism became the main theme, emphasizing the sentiment of *jiaguo yiti*, or "family and the state as one." *Don't Cry, Nanking* (1995) tells the story of a Chinese doctor, his pregnant Japanese wife, and their children, who flee the Japanese occupation of Shanghai only to be caught in the Rape of Nanjing.

The fifth stage, beginning in the twenty-first century, saw the beginning of the commercialization of patriotism.[32] Productions were caught between fulfilling the party's requirement for energizing patriotism through ideological propaganda and the dictates of the market.[33] One of the most talked about Anti-Japanese War films of the era was Jiang Wen's *Devils on the Doorstep* (2000), which was popular but then banned because it failed to make the Japanese clear villains and the Chinese clear heroes. In order to meet the National Telecommunications Regulatory Authority's political demands while pleasing an increasingly choosy and entertainment-hungry audience, exaggerated and unrealistic "anti-Japanese war films and TV dramas" (*"KangRi" leiju*) emerged. For example, in the popular 2011 TV drama series *The Legendary Anti-Japanese War Hero* (*KangRi qixia*), a Chinese man takes on armed Japanese soldiers with kung fu, and there are scenes of him tearing apart Japanese soldiers with his bare hands.

Based on interviews with producers of war-themed film and television programs, as well as directors and actors, the work of reporter Mango, journalist Fan Chenggang, and others describes the uncertain and drawn-out censorship process ensuring that every detail of the entertainment products satisfies ideological requirements. This has impeded the artists' efforts to reflect more independently on the war or create complex, nuanced characters. In their widely quoted report, "This 'anti-Japanese' business," Fan and his coauthors included an anecdote: The director Ran Hao proposed to add an antiwar note to the end of his 2012 television drama series *The Legend of Gun Makers* (*Qiangshen chuanqi*) – a story

---

[32] Yin and Zhan, "The Prism of Contemporary Chinese Culture."
[33] Yin and Zhan, "The Prism of Contemporary Chinese Culture."

about a group of patriotic genius gunsmiths set during the Anti-Japanese War period – by having the protagonist suggest that his wife, who is making a toy handgun from bullet casings for their child, make a lock charm instead, a traditional Chinese numismatic charm blessing the wearers (especially young children) with peace, health, and longevity. This proposal, however, was rejected for "not aligning with the main [patriotic] theme."[34]

Vague and volatile guidelines, including patriotic standards employed in the censorship process, leave directors and screenwriters themselves to work out where the red lines are and how to interpret the guidelines in practice. This encourages politically safe decision-making. The director Xu Jizhou, whose work includes several television series set during the Anti-Japanese War, has commented that sometimes a single inappropriate line in the script can send the screenplay back for rewriting. After numerous censorial interventions Xu realized that taboos in work about the Anti-Japanese War films included negative depictions of the Chinese national character (such as Lu Xun's depiction of Ah Q in his *True Story of Ah Q*), the humanity of Japanese soldiers, and realistic portrayals of situations, people, and events that contradict official histories and propaganda.[35] For example, the expensive propaganda epic *The Eight Hundred* (2020), based on the historical defense of a Shanghai warehouse from the Japanese, had to cut and refilm the heroic "defense of the flag" scene because the flag being defended was that of the KMT.[36] Screenwriter Yu Fei told journalist Fan Chenggang that his interpretation of his red line was not to "make Japanese soldiers look good at all. They're mere ciphers, signifying blackest evil and it's not worth it to try to deviate from this color."[37] Mango goes further to argue that if filmmakers used to "dance with shackles on," today's film censorship apparatus has entirely reshaped China's film sector, whose personnel have "internalized" the "shackles" as part of their creative process.[38] For example, in the commercialization of patriotism, humanitarian concerns and historical facts often take a back seat to the nationalistic

---

[34] Fan and Shao, "This 'anti-Japanese' business."
[35] Fan and Shao, "This 'anti-Japanese' business."
[36] Steve Rose, "The Eight Hundred: How China's Blockbusters Became a New Political Battleground," *The Guardian* (September 18, 2020), www.theguardian.com/film/2020/sep/18/the-eight-hundred-how-chinas-blockbusters-became-a-new-political-battleground.
[37] Fan and Shao, "This 'anti-Japanese' business."
[38] Mango, "*Xingsu dangxia, xingsu yishu: buduan jinhuade Zhongguo dianying shencha zhidu*" [Shaping the present, shaping art: Continually evolving film censorship apparatus in China], *Wainao* (February 2, 2022), www.wainao.me/wainao-reads/evolving-censorship-of-chinese-film-02212022.

expression of hatred for the enemy, as Yin Hong notes.[39] Although based on a real battle, *The Battle at Lake Changjin*, for instance, focuses more on depicting a great Chinese victory against American imperialists than historical accuracy.[40]

Patriotism is increasingly becoming a foundational moral requirement for celebrities employed within the entertainment industry, and one they are expected to "perform." In 2014, the China Federation of Literary and Art Circles (CFLAC), an official "mass organization" for writers and artists, published an open letter (*changyi shu*) calling on writers and artists to demonstrate their practice of Socialist Core Values.[41] Netizens constantly police celebrities on the firmness and consistency of their expressions of patriotic sentiment.[42] A celebrity's perceived transgression of the patriotic moral ideal can put their career at risk.

The famous actor Zhang Zhehan's Yasukuni Shrine scandal is an excellent example. On the evening of August 12, 2021, photos surfaced online of Zhang posing in 2018 in front of cherry blossoms allegedly in the grounds of Japan's controversial Yasukuni Shrine (which pays homage to, among others, Japanese military officers implicated in war crimes during the Japanese invasion of China), and attending a wedding ceremony at Nogi Shrine (dedicated to a Japanese general who led forces against China in the Sino–Japanese War of 1894–1895) the following year. Despite posting a long apology on his Weibo account the very next day, Zhang lost sponsorship deals, and his social media accounts and his presence were removed from China's online platforms within a couple of days.[43] On August 15, 2021, the China Association of Performing Arts (CAPA), a semiofficial national association for entertainers and management companies, called for a boycott of Zhang.[44] Three months later, CAPA released their ninth (black)list of "immoral artists," including

---

[39] Yin and Zhan, "The Prism of Contemporary Chinese Culture."
[40] James Carter, "The Real Battle at Lake Changjin," *SUP China* (December 1, 2021), https://supchina.com/2021/12/01/the-real-battle-at-lake-changjin/.
[41] CFLAC, "*Wenyi gongzuozhe jianxing shehuizhuyi hexin jiazhiguan changyishu*" [Open letter to call for writers' and artists' implementation of socialist core values], CFLAC.org (August 29, 2014), www.cflac.org.cn/wywzt/2014/wenyijianxing/changyishu/201408/t20140829_267943.html.
[42] See, for example, Baijiahao, "*Aiguo taidu jiandingde nianqing yiren: Huang Zitao baqi nu dui, Wang Jiaer cheng: Wo shi Zhongguoren*" [Young performing artists with unequivocal patriotic stand: Zitao Huang's powerful rage and Jackson Wang's claim "I'm Chinese"], *Baidu*.com (2021), https://baijiahao.baidu.com/s?id=1711963805718433322&wfr=spider&for=pc.
[43] Bingqing Yang, "China's Nationalist Cancel Culture," *The Diplomat* (September 5, 2021), https://thediplomat.com/2021/09/chinas-nationalist-cancel-culture/; Jessica Jones, "China's Extreme Cancel Culture and Increasingly Hostile Online Environment," *The China Story* (June 14, 2022), www.thechinastory.org/chinas-extreme-cancel-culture-and-increasingly-hostile-online-environment/.
[44] Jones, "China's Extreme Cancel Culture."

actor Zhang Zhehan.[45] The prior ban lists only included "immoral" livestreamers. The inclusion of Zhang in CAPA's list of "immoral artists" made filmmaker Li Xuezheng, the vice-chairperson of the China TV Artists Association, question the authority of CAPA to do so.[46] On January 1, 2022, Li Xuezheng posted his interview with Zhang on his Weibo account.[47] In the interview, Zhang repeatedly insisted that he had never entered the Yasukuni Shrine itself and that his love for the party and motherland was unwavering; he pointed out that both his mother and late father were members of the party.[48] Unless Zhang Zhehan can clear his name, he will remain a "traitor to the Chinese" (*hanjian*) as charged by enraged netizens and will be unable to return to the industry. On January 10, 2022, Li Xuezheng's own Weibo account with over 1.6 million fans was banned.[49]

The Enterprise of "Telling China's Story"

Another example comes from business. Entrepreneurs see manufacturing anti-Western patriotic nationalism as a business opportunity. Two representative players in the enterprise of "telling China's story" are Rao Jin and US-educated venture capitalist Eric X. Li. The US–China Perception Monitor (*ZhongMei yinxiang*), an online publication of the Carter Center's China Focus, published an anonymous article detailing how Rao and Li grew their media enterprises through capitalizing on popular patriotic and nationalistic fervor and the CPC's ambition to "seize the discursive power" (*zhengduo huayu quan*), a major theme of the Xi era.[50]

Eric X. Li, whose citizenship remains a mystery (some reports suggest that he is a US citizen while others claim that he is a Chinese citizen), holds a BA in economics from the University of California, Berkeley, an MBA from the Graduate School of Business at Stanford University, and

---

[45] VCT News, "*Zhuming zhipian ren Li Xuezheng zhiyi Zhongyanxie yue quan zao Weibo jin yan*" [Famous producer Li Xuezheng's Weibo banned for questioning CAPA], *VCT News* (January 11, 2022), https://vct.news/news/afd638bd-c882-4a5a-a984-5e1e972dd4a3.

[46] Lim Yian Lu, "Zhang Zhehan Denies Entering Yasukuni Shrine, Says He's Willing to be Investigated," *Yahoo! News* (January 11, 2022), https://au.news.yahoo.com/zhang-zhehan-denies-entering-yasukuni-shrine-willing-investigated-063158363.html.

[47] VCT News, "Famous producer Li Xuezheng's Weibo banned."

[48] Lim, "Zhang Zhehan Denies Entering Yasukuni Shrine."

[49] VCT News, "Famous producer Li Xuezheng's Weibo banned."

[50] USCNPM, "*Jinqian youxi: Jin Canrong, Hu Xijin deng 'wujue' beihoude caopanshou*" [Money Game: The traders behind the "five greats" such as Canrong Jin and Xijin Hu], *US–China Perception Monitor* (2021), www.uscnpm.com/model_item.html?action=view&table=article&id=25588.

a PhD in political science from Fudan University. Li founded one of China's first venture capital firms, Chengwei Capital (formerly known as Chengwei Fund), in 1999. Chengwei Capital has kept a low profile despite funding large corporations such as YouKu and raising a single investment of US$1.5 billion in 2021 to support businesses and entrepreneurs.[51] The official website of the firm is empty apart from a few lines of brief overview on the home page. According to PEDaily. cn (*touzi zhe*), an investment news and content platform, Chengwei Capital's senior consultant is entrepreneur Mao Daolin, son-in-law of Hu Jintao, general secretary of the CPC in 2002–2012.[52] Eric X. Li's venture capital firm may be out of the public eye, but he has been among the most outspoken and eloquent voices pitching the CPC's authoritarian governance model to the global audience, claiming its superiority to Western liberal democracy. Li also reportedly provided key support to Rao Jin's patriotic venture – April Media – when Rao Jin approached Li with his business proposal in 2010.[53]

A graduate in engineering physics from Tsinghua University, Rao Jin was perhaps the first entrepreneur within China to build a private business on the commercial promise of patriotism. In early 2008, just months after US president George W. Bush presented the Dalai Lama with the US Congressional Gold Medal, mass protests broke out in Tibet against party-state repression of Tibetans. The state met the protests with force, and dozens of Tibetans were killed. Pro-Tibetan, anti-CPC demonstrators converged on different stages of the Olympic torch relay in April, creating a public relations nightmare for Beijing. Seeing other young Chinese citizens at home and abroad outraged by international criticism of China and the disruption of the Beijing Olympics' torch relay, Rao, only twenty-three at the time, saw an opportunity for a new business model: a private media outlet that rallies what he calls patriotic "April youths" (*siyue qingnian*) supporting the state media to "seize the discursive power" for China on the global stage.[54] Rao launched a "patriotic" website called Anti-CNN to counter the information broadcast by CNN

---

[51] China Venture, "*Chengwei ziben: xian wei renzhide Changqing jijin, du jiao shou mingzhong lü chao 1/3, gang didiao mu zi 15 yi Mei yuan*" [Chengwei Capital: The little known Chengwei Ventures Evergreen Fund, Unicorns' success rate reaches 1/3, recently raises US$1.5 billion keeping a low profile], ChinaVenture (June 28, 2021), www.chinaventure.com.cn/news/80–20210628–362895.html; PEDaily, "*Chengwei ziben*" [Changwei Capital], PE Daily website (2022), https://zdb.PEDaily.cn/company/show7267/#inv-box.
[52] PEDaily, "Chengwei Capital."
[53] USCNPM, "Money Game."
[54] People.cn, "*Fan CNN wangzhan chuangshi ren rao jin tan caogende aiguo zhengcheng*" [Jin Rao, founder of website Anti-CNN on the journey of grassroots patriotism], People.com.cn (December 17, 2008), https://web.archive.org/web/20130510144519/http://media.people.com.cn/GB/8535196.html.

and other major Western media outlets, claiming that their reports about the brutality of the Chinese police were lies and distortions, fundamentally biased against China and the Chinese people.[55]

Rao firmly believed that a nation's "soft power" (*ruan shili*) relies on its discourse power – how strong its voice is globally – and that as China's "hard power" (*ying shili*) grew so should its "soft power."[56] To achieve this, Rao proposed that all domestic media, state and private, "unanimously work against the outsider" (*yizhi duiwai*), raising the voice of the nation and the state on the global stage. In his view, a private media portal had an advantage over state media: Not only could it be viewed as an independent source of information but also, being less restrained than media representing official party and state positions, it could present more radical viewpoints.[57] This is essentially a more radical (and commercialized) version of the operations of the daily tabloid *Global Times*. Founded in 1993 and operated by the *People's Daily*, the CPC's paramount mouthpiece, the *Global Times* is widely considered as an unofficial voice of Beijing's more belligerent views; as Hu Xijin, its former editor-in-chief and party secretary, once told Quartz, "They [officials from the party center] can't speak willfully, but I can."[58]

In 2009, Rao revamped Anti-CNN into a comprehensive site called April Media (*siyue wang*), the name resonating with "April youths." Rao reportedly received 10 million RMB (approximately US$1.4 million) from Chengwei Capital for establishing April Media.[59] In Rao's words, April Media would be an upgraded "new patriotic cultural product" (*xin aiguo zhuyi wenhua chanye*).[60] According to China's leading corporate credit information provider Qixinbao, Rao established April Huawen (Beijing) Culture and Media Co., Ltd. (hereafter referred to as April Huawen) in 2007.[61] April Media became the key site operated by April Huawen.

April Huawen is the main company under the April Huawen Syndicate, for which Rao is the legal representative. Qixinbaoao shows that apart from April Huawen, there are six other companies for which Rao is the

---

[55] People.cn, "Jin Rao."
[56] People.cn, "Jin Rao."
[57] People.cn, "Jin Rao."
[58] Zheping Huang, "Inside the Global Times, China's Hawkish, Belligerent State Tabloid," *Quartz* (August 9, 2016), https://qz.com/745577/inside-the-global-times-chinas-hawkish-belligerent-state-tabloid/.
[59] USCNPM, "Money Game."
[60] Ming Zeng, "*Siyue wang fenlie quan guocheng: chuanglizhe gongkuan mai fang, biaomei chi kongxiang*" [How April Media splits: The founder purchases private home with company money, cousin becomes the phantom employee], *Southern Weekly* (December 19, 2013), https://news.qq.com/a/20131219/010689_all.htm?pc.
[61] Qixin, "*Siyue huawen (Beijing) wenhua chuanmei youxian gongsi*" [April Huawen (Beijing) Culture and Media Co., Ltd.], Qixin website (2022), www.qixin.com/company/3789922c-1e85-41de-839e-8c09d7041ef8.

legal representative, all under the umbrella of the April Huawen Syndicate.[62] One of the six is Beijing Zhongyi Nettian Information Technology Co., Ltd., established by Rao as early as 2005, which manages official Weixin (WeChat) pages (*gongzhonghao*) for key patriotic and nationalistic opinion leaders such as Jin Canrong, Sima Nan, Li Su, and Li Yi.[63]

April Media never achieved the wide popularity Rao envisioned for it. In fact, the business nearly fell apart during its early years after key team members resigned. They cited irreconcilable differences with Rao in their views on patriotism. April Media's first editor-in-chief Tang Jie wanted the site to learn from the *Global Times*, focusing on producing knowledge-base content about patriotism and China identity (*Zhongguo rentong*) such as promoting official CPC thought and history, but Rao was more interested in self-promotion and sensational anti-West nationalist opinion pieces.[64] The staff's frustration was exacerbated by Rao's poor management. It was alleged that he had defrauded the company, purchasing private properties with company funds and placing his cousin on the payroll as a phantom employee.[65] Reporter Du Qiang published an article on the labor disputes between Rao and his employees in the influential weekly newspaper *Southern Weekly*, titled "April Youths Defending Their Rights."[66] In this article, Du Qiang points out that Rao shows no interest in patriotism as a doctrine but treats it as a milch cow, but since this type of business is encouraged by the government, sensible "business logic" does not apply; so much so that despite Rao's mismanagement of funds no legal charges were laid against him and investors still continued to invest in Media April.[67] Indeed, in 2020, Rao was among the thirty recipients of the 2020 Beijing Model Youth (*Beijing qingnian bangyang*) award from the Beijing Committee of the Communist Youth League in recognition of his outstanding contribution to promoting Chinese culture through April Huawen.[68]

Despite the problematic operations of Anti-CNN and April Media, their business concept inspired the launch of a far more successful

---

[62] Qixin, "April Huawen (Beijing) Culture and Media Co., Ltd."
[63] Harpre Ke, "Tracing Control and Influence at Guancha News," *Medium* (May 1, 2021), https://medium.com/doublethinklab/tracing-control-and-influence-at-guancha-news-5 4219a0f8203; USCNPM, "Money Game."
[64] Zeng, "How April Media splits."
[65] Zeng, "How April Media splits."
[66] Qiang Du, "*Nanfang renwu zhoukan: qi di Siyue wang*" [*Southern Weekly* figures: inside stories of April Media]. *China Digital Times* (October 14, 2013), https://chinadigital times.net/chinese/318047.html.
[67] Du, "*Southern Weekly* figures."
[68] Jing Liu, "*30 ming qingnian huo ping 'Beijing qingnian bangyang'*" [Thirty youngsters awarded "Beijing exemplary youth"], *Beijing Youth Daily* (December 7, 2020), www.ch inanews.com.cn/sh/2020/12-07/9355770.shtml.

nationalist news site called Observer, or Guancha.cn, cofounded by Eric X. Li himself in 2011.[69] As of June 16, 2022, Guancha's Weibo account had 18.75 million followers compared to April Media's 158,000. Eric X. Li presents himself as a political scientist. He publishes provocative opinion pieces in influential newspapers and magazines including *The New York Times*, *The Economist*, and *Foreign Affairs*. His TED Talk in 2013 and conversation with Francis Fukuyama on Guancha in 2015 have earned him international fame. China analyst Damien Ma and reporter Benjamin Carlson observe that, despite his flimsy logic, Li's mastery of Western-style debate and argument makes him an appealing and persuasive public intellectual and perhaps one of the CPC's most powerful weapons in the discourse wars.[70] Apart from being a trustee or board member of a number of institutes and art organizations, both domestic and foreign, such as Fudan University's China Institute, the Shanghai-based China Europe International Business School, and the University of California's Berkeley Art Museum and Pacific Film Archive, Li is a member of the Advisory Council of the International Institute for Strategic Studies (IISS), the think tank that runs the annual Shangri-La Dialogue, also known as the Asia Security Summit.[71] By comparing his influence across Google, Wikipedia, YouTube, Twitter, Instagram, and Facebook with everyone else in the world, People.ai, an artificial intelligence platform for enterprise revenue, estimates Eric X. Li's net worth to be US$630 million as of June 2022.[72] This hypothetical net worth does not indicate Li's actual income but is tied to his prominence on social media platforms (numbers of followers, fans, likes, and retweets for instance).

Blogger Ma Ning and Harpre Ke, a researcher with Doublethink Lab (an online platform focusing on digital authoritarianism), have examined the intertwined relationships between Guancha, Eric X. Li, Chengwei Capital, and party-endorsed nationalist public intellectuals as well as the CPC's influence in Guancha since the organization's inception.[73] For example, Guancha has its genesis in Social Observer magazine, published

---

[69] USCNPM, "Money Game."
[70] Damien Ma, "What It Means to Be a Rising Public Intellectual in China," *The Atlantic* (February 28, 2012), www.theatlantic.com/international/archive/2012/02/what-it-means-to-be-a-rising-public-intellectual-in-china/253610/; Benjamin Carlson, "When a TED Talk Is a Propaganda Tool," *Salon* (August 11, 2013), www.salon.com/2013/08/11/ted_talk_is_propaganda_tool_for_chinese_communism_partner/.
[71] IISS (International Institute for Strategic Studies), The Advisory Council, IISS website, 2022, www.iiss.org/governance/the-advisory-council.
[72] PeopleAi, "Eric X. Li Net Worth," *People Ai* (no date), http://peopleai.com/fame/identities/eric-x-li.
[73] Ning Ma, "*Guanchazhe wang, Chunqiu zonghe yanjiuyuan yu Hua'er jie ziben*" [Guancha.cn, Chunqiu Institute and Wall Street Capital], *China Digital Times*,

by the Shanghai Academy of Social Sciences (SASS), a state entity partially financed by the State Council and the Shanghai city government.[74] Ma reveals that the cofounder of Chengwei Capital is Feng Bo, husband of Deng Xiaoping's granddaughter.[75] Ke details how Eric X. Li and Chengwei Capital are deeply connected with party-endorsed nationalist public intellectuals such as Chen Ping (an economist and research fellow of Fudan University's China Institute), Zhang Weiwei (a former interpreter with the Chinese Foreign Ministry and director of Fudan University's China Institute), and Hu Xijin (former editor-in-chief and party secretary of the *Global Times*).[76] Two companies under Guancha Syndicate are the entities behind the official WeChat accounts for Chen, Zhang, and Hu.[77] All of them are devoted to promoting China's political system and demonstrating its superiority to the history, cultures, and institutions of Western liberal democracy.[78] The official website of Fudan University's China Institute describes Zhang Weiwei as the director of the China Institute; Li is its Advisory Committee Chair.

These connections are far from being obvious or widely known. One has to look to realize that the networked enterprises involved in answering Xi Jinping's call to "tell China's story well" have created a profit-making factory for creating and recreating the ideology of statism and nationalism as popular patriotic rhetoric, making propaganda no longer the sole realm of the state. As Rao Jin envisaged with Anti-CNN, private or "independent" media can be a less restrained, more radical, and more outspoken force pushing aback against the West.

Patriotism as Wealth Code on Self-Media

The statement "Patriotism is a good business" (*aiguo shi men hao shengyi*) has become a phenomenon in the age of self-media (*zimeiti*).[79] The term "self-media" as used on Chinese social media mostly refers to independently operated accounts that produce original content but are not

---

May 26, 2016. Viewed January 25, 2022, https://chinadigitaltimes.net/chinese/439003.html; Ke, "Tracing Control and Influence."

[74] Ma, "Guancha.cn, Chunqiu Institute and Wall Street Capital"; Ke, "Tracing Control and Influence."

[75] Ma, "Guancha.cn, Chunqiu Institute and Wall Street Capital."

[76] Ke, "Tracing Control and Influence."

[77] Ke, "Tracing Control and Influence."

[78] Delia Lin, "The Construction of Political Superiority," in *China Story Yearbook 2020*, ed. Jane Golley, Linda Jaivin, and Sharon Strange (Canberra: ANU Press, 2021), 12–21.

[79] Ping Ding Shan Net Friends, "*Aiguo, jingran bianchengle yimen shengyi?*" [How has patriotism turned into a business?], Ping Ding Shan Net Friends (2021), www.163.com/dy/article/GL4R43DG0534GPGU.html.

registered with an official agency such as Xinhua.[80] One popular form is online short videos made through one of the short-video apps such as Douyin (the Chinese version of TikTok), Kuaishou, Xigua Video, and Bilibili. The account holder, or vlogger (*bozhu*), earns money according to their traffic, that is, the volume of likes, shares, and followers. In addition, vloggers with a large fan base can create their own business empire through media advertising and other sources. Unlike the entrepreneurs and influential public intellectuals in the previous examples who are supported by wealthy venture capitalists, many vloggers rely on MCNs (Multi-Channel Networks) and KOLs (Key Opinion Leaders) to get a leg up. He Jia, an online public-speaking trainer, shared top five tips for success from a Douyin vlogger with over 10 million fans: a popular video should be: (1) hilarious: the video must make people laugh; (2) teary: the video must be moving; (3) exotic: for example, foreigners eating Xinjiang lamb skewers; (4) beautiful: for example, a traveler sharing aerial photographs; and (5) self-deprecating: allow the audience to make jokes at your expense.[81] Patriotism is regarded as the "secret code for flow" (*liuliang mima*) – the thing that guarantees a smashing success – as it can be used to create "teary" stories. Numerous account holders post identical patriotic content – typically sensational, untruthful, but certain to be widely shared on social media. One famous example features vloggers telling stories in tears describing how, during a recent tourist trip to the Chinese border, brave Chinese soldiers shielded them in case the enemies on the other side took potshots at them while they were taking landscape photos near the border.[82] The same storyline has been used by different vloggers with slight changes to the details: Some say they were on the China–Japan border (failing to realize that the said border is actually in the middle of the sea), and others claim to be by the Yalu River, bordering China and North Korea. These vloggers all end with sobbing and teary eyes expressing how grateful they are for being born in a great nation.[83] There are also numerous videos made by non-Chinese live streamers rhapsodizing on how much they love China as they share their day-to-day lives in China.[84] Russian *wanghong* (internet celebrity) Vladislav Yuryevich Kokolevskiy (known by his Chinese name Fulafu) is one such example: His "I want to be a Chinese" video attracted 3 million

---

[80] Reuters, "Chinese Social Media Platforms to 'Rectify' Financial Self-Media Accounts," *Reuters* (August 28, 2021), www.reuters.com/world/china/chinese-social-media-platforms-rectify-financial-self-media-accounts-2021-08-28/.

[81] Jia He, "*Duan shipin shi ruhe zhuanqiande*?" [How to earn money from short videos?], *Zihu* (2022), www.zhihu.com/question/26912865.

[82] Ping Ding Shan Net Friends, "How has patriotism turned into a business?"

[83] Ping Ding Shan Net Friends, "How has patriotism turned into a business?"

[84] Ping Ding Shan Net Friends, "How has patriotism turned into a business?"

viewers.[85] Some vloggers are more sophisticated in their approach to "loving China" videos. American vlogger Jerry Kowal (known by his Chinese name Guo Jierui) is an excellent example. He is hailed by mainstream Chinese media outlets, such as China Central Television (CCTV), *Guangming Daily*, and *China Newsweek*, as a "war correspondent" (*zhandi jizhe*) for his Bilibili videos on the severe impact of the COVID-19 pandemic in the US and how the US should learn from China's own response to COVID-19.[86] Jerry Kowal joined Bilibili in 2017, but within five years he had gained over 7 million fans on his Bilibili channel, and each of his short videos attracts millions of viewers.

Conclusion

Ideological-affective governance has been at the heart of CPC rule. As the ideology of patriotic nationalism is linked to entrepreneurialism and mass consumerism, we see blurring of the boundaries between state and populist nationalism, and between the official and unofficial purveyors of propaganda.

The party steers the direction of ideology and approved political emotion, through speeches from the party general secretary, through the CPC Central Committee, the State Council, or government agencies issuing Opinions and Notices on professional/entrepreneurial development. But the party behaves more like a giant venture capitalist and chief consultant of an emotional, ideational, and ideological manufacturing syndicate with numerous ambitious CEOs and players, both inside the party-state system (*tizhinei*) and outside (*tizhiwai*). The ideological direction the party steers affects every phase of business growth – funding, censorship, strategy, planning, and publicity.

With the view of making profit from patriotic propaganda at the grassroots, ideology is no longer disseminated via a linear top-down process. Yet the CPC also needs to ensure that all of these many voluntary agents of influence stay within bounds and does damage control if and when they go off the rails.

---

[85] Xin Gu, "*Youzhe shang bai wan fenside waiguo wang hong yong shipin jilu Meiguo xinguan yiqing*" [A foreign internet celebrity with millions of fans records the effects of COVID-19 in the US with videos], *China News* (April 27, 2020), https://web.archive.org/web/20200710183209/http://dw.chinanews.com/chinanews/content.jsp?id=9168959.

[86] Gu, "A foreign internet celebrity."

6   Manufacturing Consent and "Correct Collective Memory"

Shuyu Zhang

The media are indispensable in manufacturing consent in public discourse. The official media in China use relatively subtle and skillful opinion manipulation rather than overt and crude censorship, as well as digital propaganda. Under Xi Jinping's leadership, the digital propaganda approach of the Communist Party of China (CPC) has matured. The updated "regime of truth and memory" now features a complex structure of official government accounts, official media outlets, and Key Opinion Leaders (KOLs, *yijian lingxiu*), who act collaboratively to manufacture consent and to correct "collective memory" – the narrative which society and individual members of that society consent to agree on.[1] These agents navigate the fine line between propaganda and persuasion, tailoring their interpretation of the past to appeal to their young, patriotic audience. By manipulating the historical consciousness of their audience, they contribute critically to the party's longevity and legitimacy.

This study focuses on discourse across one of China's largest social media platforms, Weibo. The state has dominated this social media platform since its inception, and increasingly so in the past decade through the "digital propaganda matrix," a close-knit network of accounts belonging to official government organizations, state-run media outlets, and "patriotic individuals." This network acts collectively to alter the discourse and collective memory to suit the authority's grand narrative and interests. Wielding the cudgels of nationalism and populism, they rage against "foreign powers," their "accomplices," and the competing versions of the past that they represent – in the case of COVID-19, for example, a less competent and sympathetic vision of PRC authority.

In view of the emancipating influence of digital media on how information is diffused and memory fabricated, this chapter also considers the postmodernist notion of a "productive" form of censorship, one less concerned with overt censorship that silences unpopular opinions than

---

[1] Motti Neiger, "Theorizing Media Memory: Six Elements Defining the Role of the Media in Shaping Collective Memory in the Digital Age," *Sociology Compass* 14(5) (2020): 1–11.

it is with the "incitement of discourse" to promote its own favored narratives.[2] When the state's memory-making is challenged with alternative and more personal accounts of the past, the propaganda apparatus tackles this liberalizing amount of free-flowing information by inviting bottom-up participation from the general public in both censorship and state-led memory construction.

The party-state's digital propaganda apparatus and censorship mechanism was put to the test by China's Zero-COVID policy. Thanks to social media, the illusion propagated by the official media matrix has been increasingly contested with personal, vernacular accounts of China's pandemic experience. These include *The Diary of Fang Fang*, a Wuhan-based writer's testimony of her experience during the city's seventy-six-day lockdown, as well as reports made by "citizen journalists" and the public with their smartphones. They challenged, contravened, and tarnished the glowing image of competent authority constructed in the official, authoritative memory, epitomized in a self-aggrandizing White Paper published on China's COVID-19 response.

This paper shows how the propaganda matrix – which has become more connected, multidirectional, and all-encompassing under Xi – tackles the dissonance in experiences amplified by the internet. While the digital propaganda matrix may not entirely succeed in wiping out conflicting accounts, it achieves a silence that reveals an underlying acquiescence, willing or manufactured, among the public. The resulting revised and corrected collective memory bolsters the party's legitimacy and longevity.

Propagandist Matrix: New Media, New Order

China now constitutes the world's largest digital society, with the total number of internet users sitting at just over 1.051 billion as of August 2022.[3] The colossal volume and velocity of information generation and distribution is a nightmare for any censor and autocrat. It is a commonly held view in liberal democracies that the free flow of information created through broader participation in public discourse may further the cause of political liberalization, even democracy – bringing about the end of dictatorship.[4] The decade under the Hu–Wen

---

[2] Matthew Bunn, "Reimagining Repression: New Censorship Theory and After," *History and Theory* 54(1) (2015): 25–44; Michel Foucault, *The History of Sexuality: An Introduction* (New York: Vintage Books, 1980).

[3] China Internet Network Information Center, *The 50th Statistical Report on Internet Development in China* (2022), www.gov.cn/xinwen/2022–09/01/content_5707695.

[4] Jonathan Benney and Jian Xu, "The Decline of Sina Weibo: A Technological, Political and Market Analysis," in *Chinese Social Media: Social, Cultural and Political Implications*, ed. Mike Kent, Katie Ellis, and Jian Xu (New York: Routledge, 2017), 221–235; Juha

administration certainly saw confirmation of this optimistic prospect, when the increasingly vibrant new ecology of digital media presented potential ideological challenges to the party-state.[5]

Commercialized internet news sites were eager and incentivized to report on societal incidents fast and first-hand. Professional press filled the information void left by state and official media, who were hushed by propaganda directives not to send reporters or to investigate the incidents, for example during the 2008 Sichuan earthquake and 2011 Wenzhou high-speed train collision.[6]

The year 2010 saw China welcome "the Genesis of Microblogging,"[7] as major internet players in China, such as Sohu, Netease, Tencent, and Sina, each rolled out their version of microblogging portals. Microblogging promoted users who were on site at large-scale emergencies, citizen journalists in their own right, allowing real-time images and footage to become available to the burgeoning crowd online before making its way into newspapers. The agenda-driving potential of social media has made it unprecedentedly hard for the party-state to control the narratives and public sentiment, as exemplified in the 2015 Tianjin explosion.[8]

Before Xi's time, CPC leadership responded to the emergence of the internet with a combination of control and appropriation.[9] The Internet News Management Office, established in 2000, prevented commercial news websites from gathering news. They could only edit and relay news reported in mainstream and state-owned media, who were entrusted to correct and guide public opinion through swift reporting under the vision of then-president Hu Jintao. Pre- and postpublication/posting censorship remained a common practice, and online silencing was usually accompanied by real-life coercion, if the information caused

---

A. Vuori and Lauri Paltemaa, "The Lexicon of Fear: Chinese Internet Control Practice in Sina Weibo Microblog Censorship," *Surveillance and Society* 13(3–4) (2015): 400–421.

[5] Gloria Davies, "Chinese Social Media, 'Publicness' and One-Party Rule," in *Routledge Handbook of New Media in Asia*, edited by Larissa Hjorth and Olivia Khoo (New York: Routledge, 2015), 179–190; Ronggui Huang and Xiaoyi Sun, "Weibo Network, Information Diffusion and Implications for Collective Action in China," *Information, Communication & Society* 17(1) (2014): 86–104.

[6] Yanfang Wu, David Atkin, Yi Mou, Carolyn A. Lin, and T. Y. Lau, "Agenda setting and micro-blog use: An analysis of the relationship between Sina Weibo and newspaper agendas in China," *The Journal of Social Media in Society* 2(2) (2013): 8–25.

[7] Sina Weibo, *Zhongguo Weibo Yuannian Shichang Baipishu* [White Paper on the Chinese Market in the Genesis of Weibo], 2010. Accessed October 3, 2023. https://baike.baidu.com/item/中国微博元年市场白皮书/6025166.

[8] Xiaoping Wu, "Discursive Strategies of Resistance on Weibo: A Case Study of the 2015 Tianjin Explosions in China," *Discourse, Context and Media* 26 (2018): 64–73.

[9] David Bandurski, "Can the Internet and Social Media Change the Party?" in *Routledge Handbook of the Chinese Communist Party*, ed. Willy Wo-Lap Lam (New York: Routledge, 2017), 372–390.

unwanted disruption beyond the digital sphere.[10] Still, traditional top-down censorship, such as blacklisting and manual deletion, was put to the test, given the netizens' increasingly innovative ways of circumventing the censors.[11]

At the same time, the party-state has been adept in using the internet as a polyglossia to its advantage, amplifying proregime voices through paid commentators, the "fifty-cents army" (*wumao dang*).[12] Nonetheless, many of their laughable attempts at astroturfing – masking pro-state posts as grassroots voices – ended in ridicule and fiasco.[13] Much of the Hu–Wen administration's effort to encourage police to engage with the online masses through official microblogs was also to no avail: the Market White Paper published by Sina Weibo[14] recorded only forty-one government accounts and sixty accounts run by local-level Public Security Bureaus.

Acutely aware of what this social media Goliath was capable of, on assuming power in 2012 Xi Jinping began amassing a formidable force to defend his rule: an "internet army," adept in combat in the latest battleground for public discourse. In his 2013 speech to the National Propaganda and Thought Work Conference, Xi urged his top propagandists to "fully appreciate the characteristics and art of this war" and "form a strong internet army."[15]

The new media calls for "new order" and more "productive and constructive forms of 'structural' censorship."[16] New censorship, as Matthew Bunn observes in his essay "Reimagining Repression," was recast "from a negative, repressive force, concerned only with prohibiting, silencing, and erasing."[17] Instead, it incites, elicits, and creates new forms of discourse, new forms of communication, and new genres of speech. In a bid to "stave off the one-foot-tall devils with ten-foot-tall virtues" (*mogao yichi daogao*

---

[10] Beina Xu and Eleanor Albert, "Media Censorship in China," *Council on Foreign Relations* 25 (2014): 243. www.cfr.org/backgrounder/media-censorship-china.
[11] Rongbin Han, *Contesting Cyberspace in China: Online Expression and Authoritarian Resilience* (New York: Columbia University Press, 2015).
[12] Rongbin Han, "Manufacturing Consent in Cyberspace: China's 'Fifty-Cent Army'," *Journal of Current Chinese Affairs* 44(2) (2015): 105–134.
[13] Benney and Xu, "The Decline of Sina Weibo"; Han, "Manufacturing Consent in Cyberspace."
[14] Sina Weibo, *White Paper on the Genesis of Weibo* (2010).
[15] China Digital Space, *Xi Jinping Bayijiu jianghua jingshen chuanda tigang quanwen* [Full text of Xi Jinping's speech on August 19, 2013] (November 2013), https://chinadigitaltimes.net/space/习近平"8·19"讲话精神传达提纲全文.
[16] Sei Jeong Chin, "Institutional Origins of the Media Censorship in China: The Making of the Socialist Media Censorship System in 1950s Shanghai," *Journal of Contemporary China* 27(114) (2018): 956–972; Joy Zhang and Michael Barr, "Harmoniously Denied: Covid-19 and the Latent Effects of Censorship," *Surveillance and Society* 19(3) (2021): 389–402.
[17] Bunn, "Reimagining Repression," 26.

yizhang), Xi commands his internet army to speak loudly to drown out "the devils" while imparting "virtues" to a susceptible public.

To update the party-state's approach to censorship and propaganda, Xi launched the online "mass line" (*qunzhong luxian*) campaign in 2016, using an old Maoist method of developing policies by consulting the "masses" and then applying an ideological framework to their proposals. The campaign called on party and government bodies at all levels to "march the mass line through the internet."[18] It encouraged government agencies and officials to strengthen their online presence and interact more closely with the public by "regularly go[ing] online to look around and understand what the masses think and want."[19]

While this may be interpreted as party surveillance of its digital territory, it nonetheless shows that the party is acutely aware of the role of social media in its participatory "persuasion" campaign in the internet age, what Maria Repnikova and Kecheng Fang call "authoritarian participatory persuasion 2.0."[20] They write that online propaganda under Xi allows, even invites, controlled public participation in spreading officially endorsed information and channeling opinions on issues of governance through official digital platforms, such as the Weibo accounts of local governments.

A policy document issued by the State Council in 2016, Document No. 61, *Notice on an Enhanced Response to Public Discourse on Governance Affairs in Transparent Governance Work*, gave substance to Xi's requirement that the party should adapt to governance in the digital age. The *Notice* includes innovative use of the phrase "public discourse on governance affairs" (*zhengwu yuqing*), as an upgrade from "public discourse on the internet" (*wangluo yuqing*).[21] The phrase change sounded the bugle for the party-state's troops to advance on the battlefield of online discourse – calling on official government accounts to more closely integrate their roles in both public service and public discourse management.

Following the official launch of the "mass line campaign," a burgeoning number of government agencies and individual officials made their online debut using Weibo. Between 2012 and 2016, the number of agency and official Weibo accounts increased from 60,064 to 152,390. By 2020, the

---

[18] Benney and Xu, "The Decline of Sina Weibo."
[19] E. Hou, *2016 nian zhongguo zhengwu weibo juzhen fazhan baogao* [Development report on official Weibo matrix]. Research Institute of Communication and Public Affairs, Communication University of China (2017), https://data.weibo.com/report/file/view?download_name=2614e19e-ba0a-5944-a9a4-20d85cf8097b&file-type=.pdf.
[20] Maria Repnikova and Kecheng Fang, "Authoritarian Participatory Persuasion 2.0: Netizens as Thought Work Collaborators in China," *Journal of Contemporary China* 27(113) (2018): 763–779, 772.
[21] Hou, "*Development report on official Weibo matrix*."

number had risen to 164,522, comprising 125,098 accounts run by government agencies and 39,424 run by government officials.[22]

The functions of these official accounts are twofold. On the one hand, they aim to bolster the party's legitimacy through what Ashley Esarey and Qiang Xiao call "communication designed to guide citizens' thoughts and actions and elevate support for the regime."[23] On the other hand, they also provide an element of public service that seeks to win hearts and minds through routine life hacks and plain-language news and policy updates.[24]

For example, the official Weibo account of the Shanghai Municipal People's Government, *Shanghai Announcement*, frequently communicates government policies to its nine million followers and, during the pandemic outbreak, streamed government press conferences on a daily basis. Despite the overall official tone, the account strives to humanize itself whenever it can, most notably in its daily weather forecast, in which its followers are addressed as "little buddies" (*xiaohuoban*) and kindly reminded to carry an umbrella when showers are likely. These accounts, and how they present themselves through content and discursive tactics, represent the party-state's adaptive efforts to demonstrate its "people-centered" and community-service principles while subtly disguising their functions in information control.[25]

Since 2014, the Leading Small Group for Comprehensively Deepening Reform, headed by Xi, has launched two additional campaigns to promote the digitalization of mainstream news media, "Internet Plus" and "Network Convergence" (*wangluo ronghe*). While the former encourages traditional news outlets to expand their reach among its increasingly internet-savvy population,[26] the latter outlines how to transform traditional news formats into new multimedia that are more visual, more animated, and more interactive.

The two campaigns help the party-state give traditional journalism a fresh face and thereby avoid being outflanked by more interactive and competitive new media. The success is evident: The official Weibo

---

[22] Sina Weibo Data Center, *Weibo 2020 Yonghu fazhan baogao* [2020 official report on Weibo users] (2021), https://data.weibo.com/report/reportDetail?id=456.

[23] Ashley Esarey, "Winning Hearts and Minds? Cadres as Microbloggers in China," *Journal of Current Chinese Affairs* 44(2) (2015): 69–103, 71.

[24] China Internet Network Information Center, *50th Statistical Report*; Repnikova and Fang, "Authoritarian Participatory Persuasion 2.0."

[25] Repnikova and Fang, "Authoritarian Participatory Persuasion 2.0."

[26] Lei Guo, and Yiyan Zhang, "Information Flow within and across Online Media Platforms: An Agenda-Setting Analysis of Rumor Diffusion on News Websites, Weibo, and WeChat in China," *Journalism Studies* 21(15) (2020): 2176–2195; Maria Repnikova and Kecheng Fang, "Digital Media Experiments in China: Revolutionizing Persuasion under Xi Jinping," *China Quarterly (London)* 239 (2019): 679–701.

accounts of party organs and state-run news outlets have enjoyed wide popularity. Those of the *People's Daily*, Xinhua News Agency, and CCTV News have 150 million, 108 million, and 130 million Weibo followers, respectively, and the numbers are still growing.

Nonetheless, the party-state's ambition for government new media does not stop at innovative formatting and a considerable following. It has a vision for greater control and influence on online discourse through "an official new media matrix" (*zhengwu xinmeiti juzhen*). The matrix usually features one main flagship account with the largest number of followers, and a network of niche affiliate accounts, each with a comparatively smaller yet varied audience. As shown in Figure 6.1, the "Xinhua News Agency matrix" on Weibo consists of Xinhua News Agency as the flagship and its nine affiliates, such as Xinhua International, Xinhuanet, and Reference News.

Figure 6.1 Xinhua News Agency: Weibo matrix.

As envisioned in the State Council's 2018 document, *On Promoting the Sound and Orderly Development of Government New Media*, the matrix entails the presence of official media as the "more authoritative sources for announcements and responses." While each has its distinct audience and specialty, these accounts serve the common goal of amplifying the main account's message, in support of its agenda. The digital collaboration within the matrix is done not only through frequent liking, commenting, and reposting between accounts to maximize their digital presence, but also by diversifying a coherent message across a range of channels and in a variety of forms, be it caricature, editorial, or short clips.[27]

Policy further paves the way for official government accounts and media outlets to become the most credible, if not the only, news sources. Under the watch of the Cyberspace Administration of China – the enforcement agency overseeing information control and censorship on the internet – the party's whitelisting (*baimingdan*) scheme safeguards official media as the favored voices in the pluralistic world of online expression. First enacted in 2016 and reiterated in 2021, the whitelisting scheme divides online news service providers into three categories. Only those in the first category are allowed to report on current affairs, hence the "whitelist." The other two categories, non-news entities and republication entities, are only permitted to reprint content produced by those in the first category.

In the latest revision of the list in 2021,[28] hundreds of official public accounts on China's biggest social media platforms, WeChat and Weibo, joined the whitelist. Politically credible media outlets or propaganda departments at the national, provincial, or prefectural level own or directly run most of these accounts. Meanwhile, the whitelist allows the party-state to mute voices in online public discourse that are either critical of or otherwise deemed unhelpful to its information agendas.[29] Several prestigious news agencies, including Caixin – known for its credible and in-depth investigative journalism – were removed from the latest whitelist out of official concern for their "seriousness and credibility."

---

[27] Jian Meng, Zengyu Pei, and Xiang Xing, "Woguo xinwen fabu zhidu jianshe zhong de chuanboxue sikao" [Thoughts on the communication of China's press release system], *Chuanmei guancha [Media Observer]* 10 (2021): 22–28; Yanhong Zhou, "Xinmeiti shidai zhengwu xinmeiti chuanbo celue yanjiu" [Communication strategies of official media in the new media era], *Xinwen yanjiu daokan [Journal of News Research]* 11(7) (2020): 128–129.

[28] The Cyberspace Administration of China, *Zuixinban hulianwang xinwen xinxi gaoyuan danwei mingdan* [The latest internet news information source list] (2021), www.cac.gov.cn/2021-10/18/c_1636153133379560.htm.

[29] David Bandurski, "China Updates Rules on News Reposting," *China Media Project* (October 21, 2021), https://chinamediaproject.org/2021/10/21/china-updates-rules-on-reposting-news/.

The changing media landscape in the digital era propelled the party-state to raise its game in order to maintain its assertive, monopolizing control over online discourse. Propaganda under Xi innovates and transforms official media to appeal to its audience through a refreshed appearance and ubiquitous presence across platforms, while at the same time centralizing and limiting the production and dispersal of news through a tightly woven social media matrix and whitelisting. In a supposedly decentralized world of new media, this new order reestablishes the dominance of state-approved sources over contravening, critical accounts. It clears the stage for a scene change in the digital media landscape – new forms of propaganda that build on an increasingly fervent digital nationalism and especially cater to a younger, more patriotic generation of Chinese netizens.

Digital Propaganda: By the Youth, for the Youth

Xi is acutely aware that the key to renewed, effective propaganda and thought work lies with the grassroots (*jiceng*). To talk to the wider online population, propaganda needs to speak the language of the internet and the people.

Accordingly, the party singles out "patriotic bloggers" who have risen to prominence, glorifying them as Key Opinion Leaders who can be harnessed to amplify pro-regime content. They are usually self-made propagandists, quite distinct from the previous wave of paid commentators known as the "fifty-cent army," who attempt to influence online discourse through "astroturfing" – posing as grassroots voices while extensively posting proparty content, when they are in fact organized and sponsored by the party.[30]

The new band of patriotic bloggers differentiate themselves by calling themselves the "voluntary fifty-cent army" (*ziganwu*) – literally, the fifty-cent army that supplies its own rations. They display a genuine faith in the party and its commitment to rejuvenate the nation, together with distrust of Western liberal–democratic ideals. They portray themselves as not only more patriotic, but also more rational than most citizens "in defending the nation against online sabotage and emphasizing facts and logic."[31]

These "facts and logic" embed new forms of pro-state discourse, usually nationalist and sometimes populist in nature and cloaked in varied media forms and increasingly adept opinion-manipulation tactics. The bloggers' grassroots beginnings, and their command of internet language

---

[30] Benney and Xu, "The Decline of Sina Weibo"; Han, "Manufacturing Consent in Cyberspace."
[31] Han, *Contesting Cyberspace*, 15.

and online pop culture, allow them to market state propaganda in a more appealing and effective way than state media outlets such as the CCTV. They tend to steer clear of top-down, hegemonic discourse that would put off fellow netizens. Instead, they preach their patriotic gospel through multimedia forms such as video streaming, animation, and satirical content, which cater to a younger audience.

Patriotic KOLs have a strong presence not only on social media platforms, but also on platforms that specifically target a younger viewership. With an estimated 80+ percent of its users between the ages of eighteen and thirty-five, Bilibili[32] is hailed as the go-to website for China's Gen Z. Its young, patriotic users, along with its transformation from a subcultural, ACG (animation, comics, and games) video-streaming website to a mainstream knowledge-sharing platform, set the stage for patriotic KOLs in producing "professional user-generated videos" that feature ACG patriotism – patriotism through anime.

The ACG-style animation, *Year Hare Affair* (*Nanian natu naxieshi*), created by animator Lin Chao and solely distributed on Bilibili, represents one of the most successful attempts to appeal to younger viewers. First launched in 2015 and in its seventh season in 2025, the animation articulates the official patriotic narratives and national identity through clever metaphors and ideologically vested euphemisms.[33] With the conceptual metaphor of China as the hare, Lin features China's military and diplomatic activities after 1900 with an emphasis on its docile and innocuous nature, which is, in the artist's words, "harmless to humans and animals alike" (*renchu wuhai*).

However, Chinese idiom has it that "even a rabbit will bite when cornered" (*tuzi jile ye hui yao ren*). This conceptual metaphor serves as a victimization narrative that fits in the strategy of narrating the officially sanctioned history of China after 1949. This self-victimization is applied generously throughout the show to explain acts of aggression as retaliation and refusal to fall victim again to other allegorical animals. Some usual perpetrators include the bald eagle (the US), the bull (the UK), and the chicken-turned-crane (Japan). In revisiting China's humiliations and suffering, *Year Hare Affair* also provides historical reference and reasoning for Xi's "China Dream." The show calls on every single hare to put in their share of

---

[32] Bilibili is a Chinese video-streaming site that first gained its popularity for its ACG (animation, comics, and games) content and real-time scrolling chat function, also known as "bullet chat" (*danmu*). The combination of popular culture and interactive internet experience contributes to the preponderance of Bilibili users predominantly born after the 1990s.

[33] Xuanxuan Tan, "China Is a Hare: The Articulation of National Identity in Year Hare Affair," *Empedocles: European Journal for the Philosophy of Communication* 9(2) (2018): 159–175.

effort in "building China as a powerful nation," which amplifies Xi's message that "China's dream is every Chinese person's dream."[34]

The allegory was so well received among the netizens that it began to transcend the ACG community and reach a larger and more mainstream cohort on social media, propagating the creation and use of hare-related internet slang on Weibo, where "we hares" (*wotu*) is now commonly used as an amiable nickname for China among self-identified patriots. The hare metaphor resonates with them, portraying a national identity that is docile yet not submissive, especially not to foreign powers, while at the same time implying that this is only possible because of the leadership and statecraft of the "hare" (*tùzi*), not the "baldhead" (*tūzi*), a near-homophonic metaphor used to depict Chiang Kai-shek and pre-1949 China ruled by the Kuomintang.

There are also less allegorical and more antagonistic efforts to persuade youth to be patriotic. One of the latest examples is Wuheqilin,[35] who has amassed a whopping 3.46 million followers on Weibo for his deliberately provocative, anti-Western political content in the form of computer-generated images. The self-claimed "court painter" (*gongting huashi*) frequently has his content reposted by state media within and beyond the Great Firewall. Nonetheless, his drawings are well received by the masses and the "royals" alike. He was hailed a national hero, and a grassroots rebuttal to the West's attacks on China's internal affairs, after an official account tweeted an image that he created purporting to show an Australian soldier slitting the throat of an Afghan child, resulting in an angry response from the then Australian prime minister Scott Morrison.

Under his pinned Weibo post that features his ever-growing collection of artworks denigrating the "West" – the US to the fore – the most-liked comment reads, "How Qilin feels resonates so much in me. And I hold the same view. The double standard of the Americans (*laoMei*) in the past few years converted me from an 'angry youth' (*fenqing*) discontented with Chinese society, to one who is not." This comment shines light on the effectiveness of digital propaganda in its newer forms, while reflecting the changing mentality among this new generation of the Chinese audience who are subject to intensified xenophobic and nationalist sentiments in Chinese society, especially in the post-COVID-19 era.

---

[34] Tianru Guan and Tingting Hu, "The Conformation and Negotiation of Nationalism in China's Political Animations: A Case Study of Year Hare Affair," *Continuum* 34(3) (2020): 417–430.

[35] His pseudonym combines the first part of a phrase, *wuhe zhizhong* meaning "the black-haired masses" (i.e. the common people) with *qilin*, the name of a mythical creature that appears during the reign of exceptionally wise leaders.

"Little pinks" (*xiao fenhong*) are a burgeoning population of young Chinese netizens who voluntarily consume and promulgate fervent nationalist rhetoric, traditionally spouted by Chinese political elites to promote CPC legitimacy and gain diplomatic leverage domestically and abroad.[36] Contrary to the depiction of them as an "army of trolls," "little pinks" represent the complex, dynamic nature of China's new youth.

In tracing its genealogy, Liang Yu identifies three waves of "new patriotism," starting as early as 2008 – the year of the Beijing Olympics when China re-entered the global stage as a modern country and great power.[37] The country's economic success and ascension in the global order engendered national pride and recovery from the "century of humiliation" (*bainian zhi chi*), as well as confidence in the "China model" (*Zhongguo moshi*), a political system and governance model promoted from 2010 as a viable alternative to democracy for developing countries. The Arab Winter, followed by the Arab Spring in the early 2010s, further confirmed this confidence, while casting doubt on online criticism of the party-state for its incompatibility with Western ideologies and liberal–democratic values. China's growing middle class further contributed to the population's strong confidence in the nation, as well as in themselves, their sense of self-esteem closely attached to the national identity.

Today, "new patriotism" captures a varied and inherently messy constellation of cybernationalists, each approaching patriotism with a slightly different perspective: overseas-educated students who deromanticize and subsequently distance themselves from Western ideals; "patriots" who have faith in the China Model and pride in a rising China; populists who see China as a victim of Western hegemony; and, lately, fangirls who adopt "fan club culture" in their patriotism. Despite their internal differences, what they do share among themselves and with the archetypal "little pinks" – the more politically active members of the Fengyi site,[38] from where the implicitly derogatory label

---

[36] Yiben Ma, "Online Chinese Nationalism and Its Nationalist Discourses," in *Routledge Handbook of Chinese Media*, ed. Gary D. Rawnsley and Ming-yeh T. Rawnsley (London: Routledge, 2015), 221–234; Florian Schneider, *China's Digital Nationalism* (Oxford: Oxford University Press, 2018).

[37] Liang Yu, "Xiaofenhong de xipu, shengtan yu zhongguo qingnian de weilai" [The genealogy and ecology of "the little pinks" and the future of China's youth], *Wenhua zongheng [Beijing Cultural Review]* 5 (2021): 98–108.

[38] Fengyi used to be a subsection of the female-dominant, pink-themed website Jinjiang. According to Yanrui Xu and Ling Yang, with 93 percent female users, Jinjiang is the largest women's literature website in China. See Yanrui Xu and Ling Yang, "Forbidden Love: Incest, Generational Conflict, and the Erotics of Power in Chinese BL Fiction," *Journal of Graphic Novels and Comics* 4(1) (2013): 30–43.

"little pinks" derives[39] – is that they are young people who idolize their country and their identity as Chinese, equipped with well-versed internet dialect to express this sentiment.

The new forms of digital propaganda cater to, and at the same time play to, the population's pride and confidence in the nation and in themselves, as well as this newfound digital competence. It does not rely on overt censorship or stale preaching from above, but on a dynamic conversation between the select "Masses" and the party. There is a symbiotic relationship between online patriots – little pinks, KOLs, and "voluntary fifty-centers" – and the party-state. The party-state values bloggers' efficacy at marketing propaganda in a digital- and youth-friendly way. At the same time, open affirmation from the party-state, through reposting, featured interviews, and invitations to appear on talk shows as "example youth" (*bangyang qingnian*),[40] adds to KOLs' credibility as "true patriots," thereby helping them attract even more followers. The large and still-growing population of online party supporters powers the digital propaganda "mass line," promoting nationalist sentiments from the bottom up.

The online representations of the country's pandemic experience provide an illuminating example of how productive censorship functions to invite the public to co-create a "correct collective memory" that fits the grand narrative of the party-state. The following section is neither an exhaustive account nor a value judgment about the truth or accuracy of different versions of the past. Rather, it demonstrates how the digital propaganda matrix works to prioritize the official narrative while suppressing alternative accounts. Furthermore, as a microcosm of the hostility against the West offline, digital nationalism can manifest in a rather aggressive fashion toward Western powers and their supposed delegates who dare to be critical of the regime,[41] hence contributing to the collusion of the public in participatory censorship of voices that obstruct the making of "correct collective memory."

---

[39] Kecheng Fang and Maria Repnikova, "Demystifying 'Little Pink': The Creation and Evolution of a Gendered Label for Nationalistic Activists in China," *New Media & Society* 20(6) (2018): 2162–2185.

[40] China Digital Times, *Gongqingtuan Zhongyang chupin: bangyangqingnian yanjiang jiemu Yu Shijie Shuo* [Produced by Communist Youth League: Model youth talk show Hey, The World] (May 18, 2021), https://chinadigitaltimes.net/chinese/666138.html.

[41] Rongbin Han, "Withering Gongzhi: Cyber Criticism of Chinese Public Intellectuals," *The International Journal of Communication* 12 (2018): 1966–1987.

Manufacturing "Correct Collective Memory"

A City of Two or More Tales

Memory-making in the digital era is characterized by a plurality of voices – events from the past are represented and remembered in various forms by netizens, "a new mass [that] constantly snap, post, record, edit, like, link, forward and chat" online.[42] Despite the party-state's long-standing, highly controlled policy on national memory construction as "a reconstruction of the past in the light of the present" – specifically, the present need to justify the CPC's continued monopoly on power[43] – the new memory ecology of social media allows fragmented, marginalized, and alternative narratives to be heard, raising questions as to whose memory gets to define "collective memory." The discrepancy in collective memories was witnessed in the city of Wuhan at the outbreak of COVID-19, when the party-state's prioritized top-down narratives were contravened by multiple, contesting tales of pandemic experiences on Chinese social media.

During her regular press briefing on June 8, 2020, then Foreign Ministry spokesperson Hua Chunying defended the State Council's White Paper, *Fighting COVID-19: China in Action*,[44] which provided a commendatory account of Beijing's coronavirus response. Hua stated that it was published "to keep a record" and ensure that "the history of the combat against the pandemic" is not "tainted by lies and misleading information" but "recorded with the correct collective memory of all mankind." The White Paper consists of four main narratives: a swift response at the initial stage of the outbreak; well-coordinated prevention and control measures steered by the party; a joining of forces across the nation to send aid and resources; and international solidarity and cooperation in fighting the pandemic.

As much as the party-state wants to install its official narrative as the definitive version of the past, it needs to work out how best to engage and persuade the broad online public. Critics called out the official narrative on its selective amnesia regarding the grimmer details of the pandemic, its opacity especially stark when contrasted with earlier and more personal "first drafts of history." Among these "first drafts" was a chronicle by the

---

[42] Andrew Hoskins, "Memory of the Multitude: The End of Collective Memory," in *Digital Memory Studies: Media Pasts in Transition*, ed. Andrew Hoskins (New York: Routledge 2017), 85–109, 86.
[43] Florian Schneider, "Mediated Massacre: Digital Nationalism and History Discourse on China's Web," *The Journal of Asian Studies* 77(2) (2018): 429–452.
[44] The State Council Information Office (PRC), *Fighting COVID-19: China in Action* (June 2020), www.scio.gov.cn/zfbps/32832/Document/1681809/1681809.htm.

established Chinese writer Wang Fang, better known by her pseudonym Fang Fang. On January 25, 2020, two days after the central Chinese city of Wuhan was locked down, Fang Fang began to keep a daily record of her life in the city. The sixty diary entries of Fang Fang's *Diary* fill in the gaps of the White Paper with their descriptions of ordinary citizens' helplessness and suffering, especially during the early days of the lockdown. It also details the incompetence and malfeasance of local officials, whose initial reaction was to suppress information on the outbreak.[45]

Unsurprisingly, the authorities perceived Fang Fang's alternative history as a threat. Integrated into and amplified by the ecology of digital media, her personal account had ceased to be personal. Nationalist, sometimes populist, sentiments were weaponized by different participants in the digital propaganda matrix who work in collaboration to chop down "representatives of foreign powers" such as Fang Fang, while at the same time guiding the creation of collective memory with the broad (but curated) participation of netizens raising their diversified and deafening voices to drown out any potential dissonance.

Participatory Censorship

The Diary of Fang Fang was swiftly targeted by censors, and Fang Fang's Weibo account was suspended on January 29, 2020. Yet by the time she completed the final diary entry, she had over four million followers, and the diary entries were read and reposted by millions of people across different social media platforms. The diary was initially well received as an on-the-ground account of the city in lockdown by an outspoken and respected novelist. Her supporters, many of them middle-aged like herself or older, saw her as a hero who held government officials and agencies accountable for their mishandling of the outbreak by honestly relaying her experience among the apocalyptic sights of Wuhan during the sudden lockdown.[46]

However, readers' opinions began to polarize. Some questioned the veracity of Fang Fang's reports, accusing her of "hearsay."[47] Some accused her diary of having an anti-government undertone and of

---

[45] Lintao Qi, "Source Text Readers as Censors in the Digital Age: A Paratextual Examination of the English Translation of Wuhan Diary," Perspectives: Studies in Translation Theory and Practice 31(2) (2021): 1–15; Zhang and Barr, "Harmoniously Denied."

[46] Liang Yu, "*Ba Fangfang Riji maizai chuntianli*" [Bury the Diary of Fang Fang in spring], Bilibili (2020), www.bilibili.com/read/cv5336787.

[47] Liangni Sally Liu, Guanyu Jason Ran, and Yu Wang, "Bold Words, a Hero or a Traitor? Fang Fang's Diaries of the Wuhan Lockdown on Chinese Social Media," in *Global Reflections on Covid-19 and Urban Inequalities. Volume 2: Housing and Home*, ed.

deliberately finding fault with authorities' actions. In an interview with China News Service, an official news outlet affiliated with the central government's United Front Work Department, Fang Fang denied the allegations, saying that she was merely "venting and grieving" and that her account was "absolutely consistent with the government's position."[48]

The interview did not assuage the skeptics, and after it emerged that the diary was being translated into English and German for fast-tracked global publication as *Wuhan Diary: Dispatches from a Quarantined City*, critics said it was being used by anti-China forces to support their conspiracy theories about the virus's origins and unjustified attacks on China. Presales of the book began on April 8, 2020, the day of Wuhan's reopening: highly inconvenient timing for Beijing as China faced what New York–based Consul-General Huang Ping called the "finger-pointing and politicization" of its pandemic handling from some Western leaders, particularly then US president Donald Trump.[49]

Patriotic bloggers took on the task of amplifying the public fury and perpetuating a second round of censorship – this time driven by netizens themselves. Many KOLs saw it as a chance to reinforce "political correctness" in the Chinese context: in other words, to uphold the party-state's long-held dictum to "accentuate the positive and minimize the negative" when it comes to reporting China's affairs to an international audience. They wanted to "keep the family feud on this side of the door" (*jia chou bu wai yang*; roughly equivalent to the warning against publicly airing one's "dirty laundry").

On his Weibo account, Wuheqilin posted a satirical image entitled "Crown a Jester" and dedicated it to "China's most influential writer," with an explicitly sarcastic tone condemning Fang Fang for garnering international fame and influence by appealing to "the West." It featured Fang Fang in a court jester costume, kneeling and presenting a blood-drenched book with a knife embedded in it to a uniformed white man on a throne fiddling with a dog chain as if pondering whether she should be "rewarded" with it, while a gallery of Western journalists capture the moment. It accused her of "handing over the knife" with which her "Western sponsors" could attack China.

Brian Doucet, Pierre Filion, and Rianne van Melik (Bristol: Bristol University Press, 2021), 97–108.

[48] Chinese News Service, "*Zuojia Fangfang he tade 'Wuhan riji'*" [Fang Fang the writer and her Wuhan Diary], *China News* (February 2020), www.chinanews.com.cn/cul/2020/02-22/9100825.shtml.

[49] Edith Lederer, "China Calls for Solidarity Not 'Finger-Pointing' on Virus," *ABC News* (April 22, 2020), https://abcnews.go.com/US/wireStory/china-calls-solidarity-finger-pointing-virus-70276357.

The post was quickly picked up and reposted by state media and official accounts, including the official Communist Youth League account. Thanks to the attention from above, the picture attracted 176,000 likes and 47,000 reposts on Weibo alone, with many asking in the comments if they could repost it to other social media platforms, including Instagram. Those who believed that Fang Fang was an opportunist who profited from Wuhan's suffering flooded her comments with criticism, questioning her intentions and even accusing her of being a "liar" or a "traitor." Even residents who had experienced the struggle firsthand were quick to distance themselves from such anger and wild accusations. The well-known gong-ringing daughter, trying to save her sick mother after she was refused admission to the local hospital, condemned Fang Fang for making her an unwilling accomplice in defaming China (*tuo xia shui*, "dragging someone into (troubled) water") and "weaponizing" her gong-ringing story. "Please do not include me in your diary. I don't wish to go abroad," she wrote in her Weibo account "Gong-ringing me" (*qiaoluo de wo*).

The nationalist Guancha Syndicate joined in the patriotic zeal and featured Wuheqilin in a profile, "He Fought Tooth and Nail against Anti-China Forces so that More Patriotic Youth Can Speak Up." This was not only an official nod to, but also an explicit call for, greater participatory patriotism from the younger generation, which was justified and aggrandized as grassroots revolt against Western hegemony. Hu Xijin, then *Global Times* editor-in-chief, posted:

> the public has every right to express their strong dissatisfaction for The Diary of Fang Fang. This represents an important aspect of the plurality [of our society]. Many people would feel differently about the Diary now that they have witnessed a much more severe humanitarian crisis going on in the pandemic-ridden US and can reconsider the combat against the outbreak in Wuhan in a larger context.

In a similar anti-Western/anti-liberal tone, on his official WeChat account, Liang Yu, a prominent journalist at Guancha and academic at Shanghai's Fudan University, described the pro- and anti-Fang Fang debate as "not a war between left and right, but between old and new."[50] He criticized Fang Fang and her generation of "public intellectuals," who "held onto their outdated historical narrative shaped by the Cultural Revolution and attacked any questions for being conservative outcries – just like Don Quixote against the windmills," implying that their fear of totalitarianism was unfounded. He commended the "younger generation" who opposed Fang Fang on social media for being aware of

---

[50] Yu, "Bury the Diary of Fang Fang."

"the rise of a great nation (*daguo jueqi*)" and for realizing the fundamental, hegemonic conflicts between the West and China, "as exemplified in the Sino–US conflicts."

What these patriotic individuals propagated sat well with the more ambitious political agenda of the digital propaganda matrix. Over the course of the pandemic, China's official media launched an intensive "information" campaign which, as Zhao Xin puts it, contrasted a positive "us" with a negative "US,"[51] and this has continued since. The discursive strategy presents a selection of facts that put the US in a negative light and accords with the party-state's attempts to shift the blame for the COVID-19 outbreak from China to the US. CCTV News Online led a discussion series on different countries' management of the COVID-19 pandemic, with trending hashtags including "#Ten patients fighting over one hospital bed in Alaska," "#Almost all Americans are exposed to high infection risk," and "#Young Americans dying from Coronavirus."

In retaliation for the US call for further investigation into the pandemic's origins, the propaganda matrix engaged in a full-on campaign to shift the spotlight from Wuhan to Fort Detrick. The state-run news outlet *Global Times* started a petition on its official Weibo account calling for the World Health Organization (WHO) to investigate the US military base at Fort Detrick and the possibility that COVID-19 was deliberately leaked from a lab there. The petition attracted more than twenty-five million signatures. Other state media, CCTV and *People's Daily* to the fore, echoed and fortified this narrative by manipulating the anti-Western and anti-Japanese complexes of the people. Aside from an hour-long special report on "the dark history behind Fort Detrick," CCTV dropped a trending topic on "Dirty Deals between the Japanese Unit 731 and Fort Detrick" on a politically sensitive date, September 18, 2021. On the same day ninety years earlier, Imperialist Japan invaded Manchuria and, subsequently, started the Sino-Japanese War, during which Unit 731 conducted lethal human experiments and biological weapons manufacturing. CCTV thus implied that the pandemic was another attempt by the West and Japan to wage biological and chemical war on Chinese civilians.

Digital propaganda fosters a sense of common duty to maintain "the greater good and the positive," seeks to create an inspiring patriotic discourse that is hegemonic, if superficially diverse, and functions as "an impersonal form of control."[52] It mediates public discourse by

---

[51] Zhao Xin, "How China's State Actors Create a 'Us vs US' World during Covid-19 Pandemic on Social Media," Media and Communication 8(2) (2020): 452–457.
[52] Bunn, "Reimagining Repression," 41.

prescribing an intolerance of "unpopular opinion" and "negative energy" and gives an authoritative warrant for the public to censor such views, views that Fang Fang supposedly displayed in her diary. By conflating "the unfavorable" with "the incorrect," and "the incorrect" with "the unpatriotic," patriotic KOLs successfully drummed up nationalist sentiment into acts of participatory censorship against Fang Fang, while official government accounts and media outlets largely remained backstage, focusing on reinforcing the grand narrative justifying the party-state rule – the construction of "correct collective memory."

Co-constructing Memory

The state media dropped the phrase "correct collective memory" after a public backlash. It is now nowhere to be found on the official social media accounts of major state media outlets. Nonetheless, they did not drop the idea. The construction of memory in the digital era still occurs in a state-guided and state-guarded online space. It does not matter whether the topic is the Russian invasion of Ukraine, China's trade war with the US, or the specific subject of this study, the pandemic.

With their enhanced discourse power as the most authoritative, if not the only, source of COVID-related news and information, state actors and official media can privilege certain narratives over others. The whitelisting placed official media outlets even higher in the apex of the information pyramid, while nonstate actors had to adopt the wording and, inevitably, content of official news stories. However, as a public sphere for information sharing, social media allows different individuals to tell alternative versions of the past. Official accounts need to compete with other, more personal and vernacular stories. One way to ensure that the official narratives continue to prevail is through maximizing state media's digital presence with an overflow of information, which in turn manipulates the Weibo algorithm to further their goals.

According to the *Weibo Official 2020 Users Report*,[53] official accounts and state-backed media in 2020 collectively contributed over 6.07 million microblog posts related to the COVID-19 pandemic, generating a readership of over 364.7 billion clicks. The massive number of posts granted Chinese official media the communication privilege to set the agenda for everyone. The top ten most-discussed pandemic-related Weibo topics in 2020 (examples shown in Table 6.1) all emphasized in some way the party-state's proactive actions in combating the pandemic: *zhanyi* (战疫),

---

[53] Sina Weibo Data Center, *2020 Official Report on Web Users*.

a homonym for going into war (战役), or defending the people against the pandemic, *kangyi* (抗疫).[54]

State media and official accounts' ability to curate content in these trending topics was safeguarded by not only the sheer number of posts, but also their authoritative status as topic "hosts," or moderators, with the power to recommend, pin, and delete posts, as well as to block users from posting. Without exception, these trending topics were all "hosted" by high-profile state or party bodies, such as the Ministry of Public Security and the Communist Youth League; local-level agencies, such as the Wuhan People's Government; or state-affiliated organizations, such as the *China Women's News*, the organ of the All-China Women's Federation under the watch of the National Congress and Executive Committee.

In fact, according to the *Statistical Report on Weibo Trending Topics*, over 80 percent of all trending topics were led by official accounts at national or local levels.[55] In 2022, Weibo further adjusted its algorithm on trending topics in accordance with the *Guideline on Developing a More Civilized and Well-Regulated Cyberspace*, published by the CPC Central Committee and the State Council. Official control over agenda-setting is further heightened through Weibo's algorithm that "prioritizes central (national) media, local media, other official media and industrial media" and "assigns precedence to mainstream media and official institutions' reports on major social negative news," according to the *Weibo Trending Topics* account.

The contents in these top trending topics share a key theme imbued with "positive energy" (*zheng nengliang*, a new term arising from official sources): the organized and united fight against the COVID-19 pandemic, and how various ministries joined forces under party leadership. For example, pictures and videos of police on the front line, made by local public security departments, called on the public to "pay [the police] tribute" by liking or commenting on them. These posts would then be actively reposted by other government departments in the same province on their own Weibo accounts, not simply as a gesture of cordiality, but more for the maximized dissemination of approved topics and content through the communication matrix.

Official accounts also acted in collective efforts to sanitize and take ownership of the term "diary" by attributing positive energy to its meaning, hence moving it away from the contested memory of *The Diary of*

---

[54] Sina Weibo Data Center, *2020 Official Report on Web Users*.
[55] Sina Weibo, *Weibo resoubang shuju baogao* [Statistical Report on Weibo trending topics] (2021), https://weibo.com/u/1658035485?layerid=4730266733773684.

Table 6.1 *State-led memory-making through Weibo hot topics hosted by official accounts*

Topic	Media	No. of views	No. of comments
#*Wuhan Riji* (武汉日记, "Wuhan Diary")	CCTV News	10,270 million	5.23 million
#*zhanyi daka xingdong* (战疫打卡行动, "'Clocking In' Campaign to Fight the Pandemic")	Weibo Public Welfare	6,100 million	12.76 million
#*Wuhan kangyi riji* (武汉抗疫日记, "Fighting the Wuhan Outbreak Diary")	Weibo Reading	930 million	324,000
#*jilupian Wuhan riji* (纪录片武汉日记, "Documentary: Wuhan Diary")	CCTV	300 million	319,000

Fang Fang. Many threads and hashtags posted by official media outlets such as CCTV News included the word "diary" in their purportedly bottom-up, participatory memory keeping, for example, "#Wuhan Diary" and "#Diary of Fighting the Wuhan Outbreak" (more examples in Table 6.1). The topic "#Documentary: Wuhan Diary," hosted by CCTV News to promote one "inhouse" video of the same name, attracted over 300 million views and was widely praised for its storytelling technique that "easily wet eyes."

By taking over and flooding the "diary" hashtag with both official and grassroots posts, official media sought to offset the impact of Fang Fang's account, acting as both agenda setter and effective censor. The public were encouraged to "clock in" (*daka*) and post about their experiences fighting the pandemic in these threads, no matter how big or small and in whichever form – writing, photos, or even short videos.

Chenxiaotao (Momo), an artist based in Tianjin, posted using her manga skills. Her artwork personified Wuhan as its city dish, hot-dry noodles in sesame paste (*reganmian*), lying in a hospital bed in isolation, while other cities – also represented by their signature dishes: Tianjin as Chinese crepes (*jianbingguozi*), Sichuan as hotpot, and Guangzhou as yum cha – cheer Wuhan on from behind the glass wall. The close-to-the-heart personification in the form of anime resonated with netizens who found it "cute and heart-warming at the same time." The *People's Daily* picked up on the trend and hosted a series of follow-up topics that carried on the foodie theme.

The state-led online commemoration and memory construction we have seen in the case of the pandemic is a model of public participation in guided memory-making. The propaganda matrix amalgamates varied and unconnected personal memories into a collective recollection promoted via state-created hashtags for maximum influence. The acceptable version of the past serves the interests not only of China's elites but also of social cohesion and the manufacture of consent. Joy Zhang and Michael Barr, in examining the sociopolitical impact of China's censorship, see this as an important part of the party-state's success in "bending the population into acquiescing to a harmonious denial of its collective prospects and how it curtails the global response."[56] This is needed to stabilize social order and society so that the party-state can realize its vision of the "great rejuvenation of the Chinese nation" and the Chinese dream.

Can You Still Hear the People Sing?

The propaganda matrix that once silenced Fang Fang is still in effect; if anything, these mechanisms have become stronger or more efficient in the time since they were used against Fang Fang. More cities were rushed into draconian and ill-managed lockdowns, creating a growing number of "cities with two or more tales," such as Beijing, Shanghai, and lately, Shenzhen.

Nonetheless, the party-state's updated censorship apparatuses have become more adept and efficient in quieting down the "negative energy," or, as Xi says, "resolutely fight[ing] against any words and acts that distort, doubt or deny Zero-COVID policy." The matrix can guide attacks on those who post inconvenient alternative views or perspectives, or bury them through careful manipulation of hashtags. However, as illustrated by its handling of the pandemic, it cannot fully silence or annihilate diverging narratives. Remembrance and commemoration of officially disfavored narratives continue.

An example on Weibo is the account of Doctor Li Wenliang, which has been compared to a Chinese digital wailing wall. On December 30, 2019, Doctor Li alerted other medical professionals about the appearance of "patients with SARS-like symptoms" in a WeChat group. He was subsequently punished for this whistleblowing and later died from the disease in hospital on the front line of the pandemic on February 7, 2020. His final Weibo post reads: "Today I received my positive PCR result. The other shoe dropped. Finally [Doge emoji[57]]." His updates stopped there,

---

[56] Zhang and Barr, "Harmoniously Denied," 390.
[57] This is a meme that has evolved to convey irony in the Chinese internet.

but the comments and likes on Weibo continued long after his death. As of September 2022, there were over 1 million comments and 4.28 million likes. People continued to commemorate Doctor Li – addressing him affectionately as "Old Li" (*lao Li*) and telling him mundane details of their life, reflections, and daily greetings, along with occasional outbursts of emotion: "Before they did not acknowledge it was here, now they do not acknowledge it is gone." When more than seventy cities were put into partial or full lockdown since August 2022, the comment section under Doctor Li's last Weibo was filled with complaints about "lockdown norms": daily testing, restricted movement, "remaining silent and in place" (*jing mo*), and an unstable supply of necessary food, medication, and services – including medical treatment for conditions other than COVID.

These are only a few of the abundance of internet outcries in the online sphere during the pandemic. However, there is rarely any desire to elevate contested voices into contested politics. Netizens practice assiduous self-censorship; rarely do the commemoration and discontent turn into questions on the party-state's reliability and legitimacy. This may be partly attributed to the success of the propaganda matrix in promoting and internalizing in the population the party's vision of how their lives in lockdowns should be seen and remembered, best visualized by none other than Wuheqilin: Zero-COVID shuts China's gate to a swarm of snakes, who viciously attack the efforts of people in hazmat suits, seeking every chance to slither through from overseas (Figure 6.2). The image continues the xenophobic narrative which supported participatory censorship on Fang Fang and the like – "lying flat" with COVID is just another conspiracy of "foreign powers and their representatives," to which neither Shanghai nor China must fall victim. The population becomes bound to this narrative shaped by the propaganda matrix and complicit in the CPC's shaping of collective memory through silencing contravening voices. Commemoration and complaints are limited to the online sphere, while society as a whole practices "forgetting," willingly or unwittingly.

At the same time, "forgetting," as an act of self-censorship, is also an indication of people's real fear of the censorial authority as the anaconda coiled in an overhead chandelier,[58] the strike of which can inflict actual offline harm. During the Shanghai lockdown, WeChat account Strawberry Fields Forever posted a six-minute clip, *Voice of April*, documenting "voices wiped off the Chinese Internet since the Shanghai lockdown" and "things

---

[58] Perry Link, "The Anaconda in the Chandelier: Chinese Censorship Today," *The New York Review of Books* 49(6) (2002): 1230–1254.

 乌合麒麟
22-4-30 15:38
#上海新增1249例本土确诊8932例本土无症状#
上海的战士们加油 希望尽快清零

 1.2万   1.1万 15.4万

Figure 6.2 Wuheqilin Cheers on "Fighters in Shanghai." In the picture, he writes, "Shanghai Must Not Fall."

shouldn't have happened and should not be forgotten" – residents chanting for food and a mother knocking door to door begging for medicine. Netizens raced with censors in "relay posting" the video, taking active measures to evade censorship, such as dubbing party propaganda videos with the original sound, so that it could reach the next viewer. The evasion of online censorship appeared to be effective as the video was reposted over 100,000 times before it was taken down. Nonetheless, offline censorship is alive and active, as the account owner begged people "not to give the video further publicity," writing: "Nothing has happened [to me] for now, but my family is really concerned."

Conclusion

This chapter investigates how the party today demonstrates its omnipresence in the realm of ideology less in traditional types of propaganda, such as *People's Daily* editorials, than through its strategic use of digital media. Most notable in its updated propaganda and media control apparatuses is the party's online propaganda matrix, an internet army of official and state-endorsed accounts. Envisioned by Xi to counter the "devils" in the digital realm with party-aligning "virtues," this matrix exercises censorship in both its traditional repressive form and a more productive form, preaching "political correctness" in a more digital- and youth-friendly way.

As spelled out in this chapter, through the party's sanitation of the digital record on its pandemic response, the matrix engaged various control mechanisms and digital-era propaganda in an attempt to augment the nation's collective memory. This involves state media under the party's direction using their official accounts to promote trusted "patriots" within the digital sphere, from KOLs to "little pinks," to amplify their message and drown out the voices of their critics. By mobilizing populist nationalist sentiments, especially among younger netizens, the digital propaganda matrix co-opts the online population into engaging in participatory censorship. They censor and silence alternative accounts of the past that contest the party-state narrative, in the belief that they are being "patriotic" against anti-China forces and their Western sponsors. The propaganda matrix both censors and simultaneously produces content in a way that encourages participation and seeks to manufacture consent. Those who wish to remember nonsanctioned versions of the past can avoid participating in the collective forgetting that is facilitated by digital propaganda so long as their contested memories never make the transition from online commemoration to offline activism. The online matrix, coupled with extensive surveillance, exercises an incredible degree of control of its citizens offline, ensuring for the Chinese party-state a "purified" internet ecology.

The party's success in censoring unpopular individual accounts of COVID underscores its evolution from an authoritarian to a techno-totalitarian organization, and technology plays an important role in enabling this. The party has been remarkably adaptable in the face of the internet, originally perceived as an inevitable force of liberalization and, consequently, a threat to its stability and prolonged existence. Particularly under Xi's leadership, the party has fortified itself with contemporary insights into new media and technological prowess, leveraging these to shape public sentiment through populist authoritarianism. Instead of attempting to "nail Jell-O to the wall," the CPC has approached the problem of the internet more efficiently, inventing and marketing an appealing alternative for the online masses. Nonetheless, the filtered facts and distorted history risk causing China to view itself and the world through a single, increasingly polarizing and binary lens, making it more susceptible to the influence of demagogues and absolutists. This has a clear chilling effect, not only encouraging the practice of self-censorship for fear of public ostracism and official persecution, but also making people less willing to take action in civil movements that might challenge the party's reign.

7 Neo-Maoist Sticks and Nationalist Carrots
Maintaining Party Cohesion in the New Era

Fengming Lu

Cohesion in an authoritarian ruling party is critical to regime survival. Many would regard the pre-2012 Communist Party of China (CPC), which maintained control of all levels of government and the military for decades and established institutional channels of recruitment and promotion, as a successful authoritarian ruling party and nothing like the Communist Party of the Soviet Union (CPSU) in the late 1980s. Xi Jinping, however, who took over as China's paramount leader in 2012, still fears a Soviet-style collapse as his worst nightmare and is obsessed with what he sees as the CPC's lack of cohesion. Xi believes that Gorbachev's policy of *Glasnost* (transparency), which allowed party members to express dissident views and party organizations to operate autonomously, turned members and even leaders of the CPSU into champions of Western ideologies, leading to the collapse of the Soviet Union. To maintain party cohesion and unity, Xi refers to Mao's idea of the party's line as *"wangdao"* (the benevolent way), and of party discipline as *"badao"* (the coercive way). Both are indispensable.[1]

In his first term as party general secretary (2012–2017), Xi primarily employed disciplinary instruments (the "coercive" way), and his main focus was "vertical cohesion," an effective and responsive chain of top-down command. After his rule became more established in 2015, he began to strengthen the party's "horizontal cohesion" as well, especially its political control over the government, state-owned enterprises, and other state-controlled institutions. Following brief background summaries, the first half of this chapter analyzes Xi's use of coercion, institutional oversight, and personnel reforms to strengthen the party's organizational

---

[1] Xi Jinping, *"Yanming zhengzhi jilü, zijue weihu dang de tuanjie tongyi"* [Make political discipline stricter and consciously maintain the party's solidarity and unity], in *Shibada yilai zhongyao wenxian xuanbian, shang* [Selection of Important Documents since the 18th Party Congress, Vol. I] (Beijing: Central Party Literature Press, 2013), 131–134, 133–134.

cohesion, which paved the way for a more centralized (and personalized) control over the whole party.

During his second term (2017–2022), with the rise of Wang Huning as the CPC's ideological chief, Xi began to implement his "benevolent way" by constructing a more comprehensive ideological rationale to maintain and even improve the party's capacity to mobilize. Although Xi has not matched Mao and Deng's successes in revising party history to stigmatize rival factions, there have been modest successes in an alternative ideological strategy to place the party at the center of nationalist myth. This rebrands the party as the only organization capable of seeking and realizing the national rejuvenation of China, with Xi as navigator. Patriotism is also called on to encourage party elites and members to voluntarily support and conform to the party. In the second half of this chapter, I delineate how Xi has tweaked the party's official historical narrative and mission, and other ideological strategies to mobilize party cadres and members.

Disciplinary and Organizational Measures: Iron Fists, Institutional Oversight, and Personnel Reforms

Disciplinary Crackdowns and Institutional Oversight

The CPC established discipline inspection commissions (*jilü jiancha weiyuanhui*) in 1949, along the lines of Soviet "party control" institutions, and subsequently renamed them as control commissions (*jiancha weiyuanhui*) in 1955. However, the party control system was unimportant in enforcing party discipline throughout the Mao era. Instead, Mao relied on political campaigns to forge party discipline and unity.[2] Following Deng's economic reform, the CPC Central Commission for Disciplinary Inspection (CCDI) and CDIs at lower levels were restored. One of their initial tasks, especially under the leadership of Chen Yun (1978–1987), was upholding the authority of central planners in Beijing and tackling reformist experiments and policy relaxations in coastal provinces.[3] Since the 1990s, the mission of the CDIs has been gradually depoliticized and has shifted toward anticorruption: intraparty investigations into disciplinary violations unrelated to corruption, policy deviations, and dissent have been rare.[4]

---

[2] Graham Young, "Control and Style: Discipline Inspection Commissions since the 11th Congress," *The China Quarterly* 97 (1984): 24–52.

[3] Yang Jisheng, *Zhongguo gaige niandai de zhengzhi douzheng (xiudingban)* [Political Struggles in China in the era of reform, revised edition] (Hong Kong: Cosmos Books, 2010), 193–195.

[4] Ling Li, "The Rise of the Discipline and Inspection Commission, 1927–2012: Anticorruption Investigation and Decision-Making in the Chinese Communist Party," *Modern China* 42(5) (2016): 447–482.

While many scholars argue that regime survival is not at stake for the post-1989 CPC,[5] Xi is demonstrably concerned about regime stability and durability. He has been particularly concerned about broadly defined disciplinary violations beyond corruption, which might ultimately erode the authority of the party and its leader. He has described the party discipline under his predecessors Jiang Zemin and Hu Jintao as "lax and weak."[6] Xi's signature anticorruption campaign now encompasses disciplinary crackdowns aiming to improve party cohesion. As Xi elaborated to the CCDI, party cohesion is crucial to the survival of the CPC regime:

> The leadership role of the Party ... is also reflected in the Party's tight-knit organizational system and strong organizational capabilities. A flabby and loose organization cannot work properly and get things done. If a party organization is like a roadside inn (*dachedian*) or a big marketplace where anyone can come and go freely, will the Party's "core strength" remain intact? Can we still unite the people around the Party? We must seriously work on organizational discipline ... across the whole Party.[7]

Some of Xi's concerns[8] have involved corruption: He was furious that some senior cadres were "not taking the organization seriously," some clandestinely holding permanent residence in other countries or sending their families abroad to live. But his most grave concern has been the failing top-down chain of command and control, as well as centrifugal forces and factionalism within the party. In his unpublished address to the CPC Central Committee in 2014, Xi stressed:[9]

---

[5] Andrew J. Nathan, "Authoritarian Resilience," *Journal of Democracy* 14(1) (2003): 6–17; Dali L. Yang, *Remaking the Chinese Leviathan: Market Transition and the Politics of Governance in China* (Stanford, CA: Stanford University Press, 2004); Ann M. Florini, Hairong Lai, and Yeling Tan, *China Experiments: From Local Innovations to National Reform* (Washington, DC: Brookings Institution, 2012); Joseph Fewsmith, *The Logic and Limits of Political Reform in China* (New York: Cambridge University Press, 2013).

[6] Xi Jinping, "*Juesheng quanmian jiancheng xiaokang shehui, duoqu xinshidai Zhongguo tese shehuizhuyi weida shengli*" [Secure a decisive victory in building a moderately prosperous society in all respects, Strive for the great success of socialism with Chinese characteristics for a new era], in *Shijiuda yilai zhongyao wenxian xuanbian, shang* [Selection of important documents since the 19th Party Congress, Vol. I] (Beijing: Central Party Literature Press, 2017), 1–50, 5.

[7] Xi Jinping, "*Yanming dang de zuzhi jilü, zengqiang zuzhi jilü xing*" [Make the Party's organizational discipline stricter and strengthen the sense of organizational discipline], in *Shibada yilai zhongyao wenxian xuanbian, shang* [Selection of important documents since the 18th Party Congress, Vol. I] (Beijing: Central Party Literature Press, 2014), 764–772, 766.

[8] Ibid., 768.

[9] Xi Jinping, "*Zai Zhonggong shibajie sizhongquanhui dierci quanti huiyi shang de jianghua*" [Speech at the Second Plenary Session of the Fourth Plenum of the 18th CPC Central Committee], http://theory.people.com.cn/n1/2016/0819/c406714-28650314-2.html.

Since the 18th Party Congress, the Party Central has repeatedly underscored that party members and cadres, leading cadres in particular, must strictly obey political disciplines and political rules. In recent years, many party organizations ... think that so long as cadres are not corrupt, other issues are negligible, and there is no need to pursue them, and they even don't want to pursue them. Some cadres also think that so long as they are not corrupt, they are fine. Other issues are not serious. Nothing to worry about.

Dominated by such an idea, some cadres ignore political discipline and the political rules of the Party. To pursue their so-called official careers and influence, some engage in cronyism and exclude colleagues with different views, some form cliques and factions, some make false allegations anonymously and manufacture rumors, some collect followers and lobby for votes,[10] some hand out official posts and make promises, some go their own way, overtly obeying but covertly disobeying, some are irresponsive to command and issue groundless criticism of the Party Central, etc. Some of them are extremely bold and reckless! Those problems often do not get the attention of regional and departmental Party organizations. Even if they pay attention to those problems, they do not sanction those acts according to party regulations and state laws. That is wrong, and we must correct it.[11]

Xi's disciplinary crackdowns have led to severe punishment of party officials who have disobeyed or even expressed dissenting views of Xi's decisions. For the first time, the 2015 revision of the "Regulations on Disciplinary Actions by the CPC" specified punishment for "violations of political disciplines and political rules."[12] The 2018 revision further targeted violations of the "Two Upholds" (*liangge weihu*): "upholding General Secretary Xi Jinping's core position on the CPC Central Committee and in the Party as a whole, and upholding the Party Central's authority and its centralized, unified leadership."[13] While senior party members investigated and punished after 2014 were charged primarily with corruption, many of them, especially those in key and powerful posts, were also investigated for "severe violations of political disciplines and political rules." Sun Zhengcai, one of those previously mooted as Xi's successors, and Lu Wei, China's former cyberspace czar, were accused of implicitly disobeying or deceiving the Party Central and

---

[10] Here, Xi refers to party cadres casting approval votes for their colleagues or superiors in democratic recommendations (*minzhu tuijian*), which is discussed later (p. 149). See Junqi Feng, "*Zhongxian ganbu*" [Zhong County's cadres], PhD thesis, Peking University (2010); and Qingjie Zeng, "Democratic Procedures in the CCP's Cadre Selection Process: Implementation and Consequences," *The China Quarterly* 225 (2016): 73–99.

[11] I refer to official translations whenever possible. But I also notify readers if official translations intentionally deviate from the literal meanings.

[12] "*Tuchu zhengzhi jilü he zhengzhi guiju*" [Highlighting political disciplines and political rules], *Zhongguo jijian jiancha bao* [*China Discipline Inspection Daily*] (November 11, 2015), https://news.12371.cn/2015/11/19/ARTI1447900500007108.shtml.

[13] See the CPC CCDI's official comparison table of the two revisions: www.ccdi.gov.cn/toutiao/201808/W020180827575451993853.pdf.

selectively implementing its policies. The disciplinary crackdowns also target rank-and-file functionaries and party members for expressing dissent from the party's policies, particularly Xi's signature policies such as bans on extravagance, and Sinicization (cultural assimilation). A former administrator of the Economic Development Zone in Jiaxing, Zhejiang province, was accused of "issuing groundless criticism of the Party Central" (*wangyi zhongyang*) for saying that Xi's antiprivilege Eight-Point Regulations (*ba xiang guiding*) were too rigid.[14] In another case, the party expelled a herder in Xinjiang and publicly criticized him for concealing his party membership from the organizers and participants to attend prayers.[15]

The party's disciplinary enforcement arms have been extended to broader disciplinary violations, including common bureaucratic problems such as shirking responsibilities and poor policy implementation, or not sufficiently showcasing one's "ideals and convictions" and not being communist enough. In 2017, several ethnic Uyghur party functionaries were punished and demoted by the local CDI because of not properly performing weekly mandatory national flag raising ceremonies in Uyghur villages, or for not daring to smoke in front of local religious leaders (presumably this was being too deferential to Muslim elders).[16] CDIs have even targeted local officials whose policy implementation deviates from Xi's instructions, partially reviving Chen Yun's practice of using CDIs to curb policy experiments. Xiao Yi, former party secretary of Fuzhou, Jiangxi, was investigated by the central inspection team in 2020 because he endorsed an energy-consuming cryptocurrency mining project and an internal-combustion-engine car plant, both contrary to Xi's "new development philosophy" of a greener economy. Xiao eventually received a life sentence and featured as a prominent negative example in a 2023 official documentary produced by the CCDI.[17]

[14] "*Duoci gongkai wangyi Zhongyang baxiang guiding, jieguo zai zheli kandao le ta*" [Openly issuing multiple groundless criticisms of the Party Central, and this is how he ends up], Disciplinary Commission of the CPC Zhejiang Provincial Committee and Zhejiang Provincial Supervisory Commission (May 15, 2019), www.zjsjw.gov.cn/yixiankuaixun/201905/t20190515_2611475.shtml.

[15] "*Xinjiang Huo'erguosi shi yi dangyuan yinman shenfen duoci canjia zongjiao huodong, bei kaichu dangji*" [A party member in Korgas, Xinjiang, expelled for attending religious activities multiple times without revealing identity], *Pengpai Xinwen* [The Paper] (May 29, 2017), www.sohu.com/a/144504035_260616.

[16] "*Xinjiang Hetian yi cun zhishu bei liudangchakan yinian: xubao manbao sheng guoqi canyu renshu*" [A village party secretary in Hotan, Xinjiang receives a one-year probation from the party for inflating numbers of participants in national flag raising ceremonies], *Pengpai Xinwen* [The Paper] (April 11, 2017), https://m.thepaper.cn/kuaibao_detail.jsp?contid=1659637.

[17] "*Weigui gei 'wakuang' qiye rongzi 24 yi yuan! Xiao Yi an xijie baoguang*" [2.4 billion yuan of unlawful finance for "cryptomining" firm! Details exposed in the case of Xiao Yi],

Xi has beefed up the party's control (and ultimately, his own control) over government agencies, state-owned enterprises (SOEs), universities, and other public institutions (*shiye danwei*).[18] Under Jiang and Hu, local governments had considerable room to take initiatives and adapt central policies, and the State Council (the cabinet) largely operated autonomously from the party, especially in economic affairs. Despite the SOEs' importance in the Chinese economy, especially since the late 1990s, the party's role was limited to appointing top executives and creating an "integrated fragmentation" of the party's political control.[19] Although public institutions have been under tighter party control since 1989, many of them, especially universities engaging in global competition, have enjoyed enough autonomy to incentivize innovation and productivity.[20]

Xi revived and strengthened existing institutional practices such as central inspections and the work of leading groups (*lingdao xiaozu*), "leading Party member groups" (*dangzu*), and party committees and instituted novel ones such as annual work reporting, to tighten the control over these "blind spots." Central inspections, headed by disciplinary or retired officials, whose interests often conflict with the inspected localities or institutes by design, have been regularly sent down to conduct anticorruption probes, along with investigations on implementation of central policies and adherence to formal rules, at lower-level governments since 2012.[21] Since 2019, inspections have been further expanded, to scrutinize the party's control over ministries and departments and to check for violations of political discipline and rules or failures to implement Xi's signature policies.[22] Often chaired by the general secretary, leading

Pengpai Xinwen [The Paper] (January 9, 2023), https://m.thepaper.cn/newsDetail_forward_21492525.

[18] Chien-wen Kou. "The Reshaping of the Chinese Party-State under Xi Jinping's Rule: A Strong State Led by a Political Strongman," in *Political and Social Control in China: The Consolidation of Single-Party Rule*, ed. Ben Hillman and Chien-wen Kou (Canberra: ANU Press, 2024), 21–52.

[19] Kjeld Erik Brødsgaard, "Politics and Business Group Formation in China: The Party in Control?" *The China Quarterly* 211 (2012): 624–648.

[20] Li Wang, "Higher Education Governance and University Autonomy in China," *Globalisation, Societies and Education* 8(4) (2010): 477–495.

[21] Yukyung Yeo, "Complementing the Local Discipline Inspection Commissions of the CCP: Empowerment of the Central Inspection Groups," *Journal of Contemporary China* 25 (97) (2016): 59–74.

[22] "*Zhongyang xunshi gongzuo lingdao xiaozu bangongshi zhuyao fuzeren jiu 'guanyu zhongyang buwei, zhongyang guojia jiguan bumen dangzu (dangwei) kaizhan xunshi gongzuo de zhidao yijian (shixing)' da jizhe wen*" [Answers of a primary responsible official of the Office of the Central Inspection Work Leading Group on the "Guideline of Inspection Works on Central Ministries, Administrations, and Leading Party Member Groups (Party Committees) of Central State Agencies (Provisional)" to the press], *Zhongguo*

groups have facilitated policy coordination and the party boss's oversight of specific policy issues for decades. Since 2012, Xi has chaired meetings of existing leading groups much more frequently and established a dozen new ones, so that he can directly intervene in other policy domains that traditionally belong to the State Council. Some were elevated into CPC Central Commissions in his second term. The most prominent one is the "Leading Small Group on Comprehensively Deepening Reform," established in 2013 and elevated into a central commission in 2018. Xi has chaired its meeting bimonthly and issued specific instructions on a wide range of policy issues, particularly economic policies, making it a "shadow State Council."[23]

Leading party member groups were designed in the 1950s to ensure the CPC's full control over ministries headed by noncommunists. Xi boosted their roles to facilitate the party's control over the government. Xi also expanded the institution (previously used in the Ministry of Foreign Affairs) of "dual-command," that is, assigning a separate party secretary to monitor the minister (even when the minister is a CPC member), in ministries such as the People's Bank in 2018 and the Ministry of Public Security in 2021. Leading party member groups in a few other government agencies, such as the State Taxation Administration and the General Administration of Customs, were elevated into party committees in 2018.[24] Since 2018, in the name of "strengthening and maintaining the centralized and unified leadership of the Party Central," Xi has ordered all other Politburo members to submit an annual work report, covering how they have implemented his instructions and reported to him, for review and comment. In the annual work reports, other Politburo members are required to summarize how they have studied Xi Jinping Thought and implemented Xi's instructions in the past year. Elevating Xi from the host of Politburo and Politburo Standing Committee meetings to boss of other members, this new rule further transformed the

---

jijian jiancha bao [China Discipline Inspection Daily] (June 17, 2019), http://fanfu.people.com.cn/n1/2019/0617/c64371-31156112.html.

[23] Susan L. Shirk, "China in Xi's 'New Era': The Return to Personalistic Rule," *Journal of Democracy* 29(2) (2018): 22–36, 23.

[24] See Gao Xin, "*Yehua Zhongnanhai: Gong'an Bu de shuangshouzhang zhi yu Wang Xiaohong de zhengzhi weilai*" [Night talks about Zhongnanhai: The dual-command system of the Ministry of Public Security and the political prospects of Wang Xiaohong], Radio Free Asia (November 22, 2021), www.rfa.org/mandarin/zhuanlan/yehuazhongnanhai/gx-11222021145314.html; and Jiang Jie, "*Yingji Guanli Bu dangzu weihe gai she dangwei*" [Why was the Leading Party Member Group of the Ministry of Emergency Management transformed into a Party Committee], Renmin Ribao Zhongyang Chufang: yiben zhengjing gongzuoshi [The Central Kitchen of People's Daily: Yibenzhengjing Workshop] (April 9, 2020), www.hubpd.com/c/2020-04-09/955900.shtml.

Politburo from a coordinating body of factions and powerful leaders into a top-down, cohesive institution, at the expense of power sharing and collective leadership.[25]

Since 2015, the CPC has launched a series of reforms that elevate its role in SOE corporate governance, alienating or even antagonizing external shareholders and foreign investors. The party secretary of an SOE must serve as its chairman, to "execute the Party's will," and can override decisions by the board of directors.[26] In 2014, the CPC similarly reinforced party secretaries' oversight of universities.[27] The most prominent example is Peking University, before 2018 a hub of dissenting views and student activism, particularly regarding labor rights and the MeToo movement, before 2018. Qiu Shuiping, a Peking University alumnus and former political tutor who had "little experience of running a school" but "spent years in China's legal system," was appointed the party secretary of Peking University expressly to suppress pro-Marxist student activists.[28]

Xi is particularly angry at critics of the party-state within the party, as he explained in his 2013 address to the CCDI:

But there are a small number of party members and cadres whose sense of political discipline is weak, who take an ambiguous stand on issues of principle and major matters. Some publicly express dissident views on major political problems that involve the Party's theory, line, and general and specific policies ... Some party members and cadres even say and do whatever they want. Some even intentionally challenge political principles that are clearly regulated by the Party, speaking with a big mouth and without concern for any rule, just so that they can show off their so-called "abilities" and be cheered by rival forces. They are not ashamed but proud of it. These problems ... do great harm to the cause of the Party. The Party

---

[25] "*Zhongyang Zhengzhiju tongzhi xiang Dang zhongyang he Xi Jinping zongshuji shuzhi*" [Comrades of the Politburo report annual works to the Party Central and General Secretary Xi Jinping], *Xinhua She* [Xinhua News Agency] (March 21, 2018), www.xinhuanet.com/politics/2018-03/21/c_1122569929.htm.

[26] Orange Wang and Zhou Xin, "China Cements Communist Party's Role at Top of Its SOEs, Should 'Execute the Will of the Party,'" *South China Morning Post* (January 8, 2020), www.scmp.com/economy/china-economy/article/3045053/china-cements-communist-partys-role-top-its-soes-should.

[27] "*Zhonggong Zhongyang bangongting yinfa 'guanyu jianchi he wanshan gaodengxuexiao dangwei lingdao xia de xiaozhang fuze zhi de shishi yijian'*" [The General Office of the Central Committee of the CPC issues "Implementation opinion on upholding and improving the President Responsibility System under the Supervision of the Party Committee"], Xinhua She [Xinhua News Agency] (October 15, 2014), www.gov.cn/zhengce/2014-10/15/content_2766861.htm.

[28] Christian Shepherd, "China's Peking University Tightens Party Control, Curbs Activism," *Reuters* (November 14, 2018), www.reuters.com/article/us-china-education-peking/chinas-peking-university-tightens-party-control-curbs-activism-idUSKCN1NJ1IP.

leaves no room for "special" party members who are not bound by party regulations and state laws or even override the Party Charter and the Party organization.[29]

Xi further noted that even members of "western political parties" are subject to party discipline.[30] Stemming from his notion that the Soviet Union collapsed simply because the CPSU allowed members to speak freely, Xi believes that even a handful of internal party critics and sympathizers with liberal Western democracy might endanger party cohesion and threaten regime survival: They must be expelled and punished. The 2015 and 2018 revisions of the "Regulations on Disciplinary Actions" codified punishment of party members who "act or speak in a manner inconsistent with the Party's critical principles, resulting in negative consequences."[31] Punishment is much harsher than what intraparty dissidents like Fang Lizhi and Liu Binyan were given in the 1980s. A prominent case involved Ren Zhiqiang, a CPC member, a former executive of a state-owned real estate firm, and an outspoken critic of the party on Weibo before 2014. After writing and disseminating an open letter attacking Xi shortly after the 2020 COVID-19 outbreak, the sixty-nine-year-old former real estate tycoon was quickly investigated, arrested, and sentenced to an unusually severe sentence of eighteen years in prison.[32]

Squeezing Intraparty Democracy and Centralizing Personnel Management

So-called intraparty democracy, such as limited competition in Central Committee elections and participation of a broader group of elites in political selection, was nominally present in the CPC before the Cultural Revolution. Yet the "democracy" in democratic centralism was constantly vulnerable to manipulation from the top: first the Comintern and later Mao himself. Despite the failed political liberalization in the 1980s, the post-Mao CPC has maintained several key institutions that promote intraparty democracy and inclusiveness. A small (around 10 percent) margin of competitiveness has been allowed in

---

[29] Xi, "Make the Political Discipline Stricter," 133.   [30] Ibid., 133–134.
[31] "*Wangyi Zhongyang dazheng fangzhen cuozai 'wang'*" [Issuing groundless criticisms of the Party Central's grand policies and guidelines is mistaken in "Groundless"], *Xuexi shibao* [Study Times] (November 19, 2021), https://www.shobserver.com/wx/detail.do?id=425353.
[32] Chris Buckley, "China's 'Big Cannon' Blasted Xi. Now He's Been Jailed for 18 Years," *New York Times* (September 22, 2020), www.nytimes.com/2020/09/22/world/asia/china-ren-zhiqiang-tycoon.html.

elections of full and alternate members to the CPC Central Committee since 1982.[33] Unpopular candidates were either eliminated (including the antiliberal propagandist Deng Liqun in 1987 and Xiao Yang, the high-profile reformist party secretary of Chongqing, in 1992)[34] or humiliated by ranking last among alternate members (such as Xi himself in 1997). Straw polls, known as "democratic recommendation" (*minzhu tuijian*) and "public election and ballots" (*gongxuan piaojue*) have been used at all levels from township and county appointments to members of the Politburo and its Standing Committee.[35] "Open examinations" (*gongkai zhaokao*) for senior offices, which are open to active public servants (mostly party members), have also been popular in Chinese subnational administrations since the 1990s and received a boost during Hu Jintao's second term.

While these institutions facilitate power sharing and expand both inclusiveness and competitiveness in elite recruitment, they dilute the party's hierarchical control over personnel management. Xi has opposed those measures for decades, even before being humiliated by his poor ranking in the election of alternate Central Committee members at the Fifteenth Party Congress (1997). When serving as the party secretary of Fuzhou (1990–1996), he complained that many who scored well in open examinations performed poorly in actual posts, even claiming that exam preparations distracted officials from normal duties, akin to similar complaints from Zhang Tiesheng, the anti-

---

[33] Fengming Lu and Xiao Ma, "Is Any Publicity Good Publicity? Media Coverage, Party Institutions, and Authoritarian Power-Sharing," *Political Communication* 36(1) (2019): 64–82.

[34] Deng was eliminated in the election of full members and quit the election of alternate members. Xiao was eliminated in the election of full members and ranked at the bottom of alternate members.

[35] "Democratic recommendation" does not involve genuine public elections, but it introduced some competitiveness in the pool of party and government officials. The Organization Departments of the regional CPC committee (one administrative level above the locality) first prepare a cadre roster as a pool of candidates and subsequently invite several hundred participants into a recommendation meeting. The participants come from five groups: the incumbent leaders of the locality's Party and government apparatus; those who have retired from the locality's leadership posts; the leaders of the locality's functional departments and mass organizations; the leaders of the various subdivisional offices/townships; and a small number of the representatives of democratic satellite parties and noncommunists. They are asked to fill in a candidate's name to match each of the available offices on secret ballots, known as recommendation forms. The task force then counts votes among each group, summarizes the result, and interviews about a hundred participants for detailed information. The vote counts, the gathered information, and a list of recommended appointments are reported to the regional Party committee for the final decision. For detailed discussions about the "democratic recommendation," see Feng, *Zhong County's Cadres*, and Zeng, "Democratic Procedures in the CCP's Cadre Selection Process."

intellectual hero who turned in a near-blank answer sheet in the restored university entrance exam in 1973 and was later celebrated by Jiang Qing.[36] After becoming the paramount leader, Xi unleashed an all-out offensive on the institutions of intraparty democracy and inclusiveness. At his first party organizational work conference as top leader, Xi argued that these institutions undermined the party's control over political appointments and jeopardized horizontal cohesion. According to Xi, it was irresponsible, even stupid, for the party to give up its centralized control of cadres:

> We must promote the Party's roles of leadership and gatekeeping in cadre selection and appointments ... The Party controls the cadres! If the votes determine everything, how can we implement the principle of "Party in Charge of Cadre Management" (*dang guan ganbu*)? Who best knows the virtue, merits, and performance of cadres? It should be the leadership team, leaders in charge, and the organization department ... If [they] cannot make verdicts about which cadres are strong or weak (in performance), they are failing in their duties![37]

Xi said that if the voting results didn't accord with the party's assessment of candidates' "virtues, merits and performance," the party leaders and organization departments needed to investigate and decide on their own. He continued: "On the transparency of cadre management: what should be transparent? Transparent to whom? In what ways? How transparent should it be? You (the party organization departments) must deliberate carefully. You cannot just turn the solemn job of cadre management into 'talent shows' (*xuanxiu*) or 'gesture politics' (*zuoxiu*)." Xi stressed that the party's evaluation of performance should be the main criterion for promotion, not "competitive selection." He cautioned that the party should neither set quotas for elected cadres nor make every process of evaluation a competitive one. By promoting these practices, Xi Jinping has centralized, personalized, and deinstitutionalized personnel appointments among both the centrally controlled *Nomenklatura* (Party-appointed leadership positions) and lower-level offices controlled by lower-level party authorities. As a result, the discretion of Xi Jinping and lower-level party secretaries has become more dominant in political selection and personnel appointments.

Xi's words sent a clear signal to the whole party, particularly the Central Organization Department and party organization departments

---

[36] Editorial Office of the Interview Records at the Central Party School, *Xi Jinping zai Fuzhou* [Xi Jinping in Fuzhou] (Beijing: Central Party School Press, 2020), 103.

[37] Xi Jinping, "*Zai quanguo zuzhi gongzuo huiyi shang de jianghua*" [Speech at the National Organizational Work Conference], in *Shibada yilai zhongyao wenxian xuanbian, shang* [Selection of important documents since the 18th Party Congress, Vol. I] (Beijing: Central Party Literature Press, 2013), 336–355, 345–347.

at lower levels. The personnel management practices that allow broader participation and more transparency significantly declined after 2012.[38] The 2014 and 2019 revisions of the "Regulations on the Selection of Party and Government Leading Cadres" further codified Xi's ideas on centralized personnel control. In the 2019 revision, new institutional restrictions and conditions were applied to straw polls and open examinations.[39] Provisions in earlier versions concerning the open and competitive recruitment of senior officials were deleted in the 2019 update, which contained new rules for institutionalizing cadre evaluations by the party organization departments. Granting more discretion to party leaders and organization departments strengthened the party's hierarchical control over personnel management. The use of straw polls was also abolished at higher levels. A Xinhua News Agency-featured story revealed that straw polls, used in the selection of Politburo members before 2012, were abolished in 2017 because they left room for "nonorganizational activities" (*feizuzhi huodong*).[40] Instead, Xi adopted a more centralized means of one-on-one interviews with stakeholders and retired leaders.[41]

Another significant sign of tightened and centralized party control is the diminishing expression of dissent in intraparty elections. The election of alternate CPC Central Committee members at the Nineteenth Party Congress (2017) contrasted dramatically with the elections in the Jiang and Hu eras. Although one still finds unpopular figures such as Yao Zengke (a protégé of Wang Qishan, Xi's anticorruption czar in the first term) at the bottom, more were listed according to the first-order and neutral "stroke order" method, suggesting delegates' reluctance to cast disapproval votes. Separately, an analysis finds that National People's Congress (NPC) approval rates for some official reports had risen by more than 10 percent, to over 95 percent since 2012.[42] While this is attributed to elite consensus over Xi's agenda, it is more likely that Xi's

---

[38] Zeng, "Democratic Procedures in the CCP's Cadre Selection Process."
[39] See a comparison table prepared by the Organizational Department of the CPC Guangdong Provincial Committee: https://mp.weixin.qq.com/s/lIGaSNavBs_qjNH4K0xtPA.
[40] In the CPC, the term "nonorganizational activities" usually refers to unauthorized lobbying and campaigning activities for lucrative positions.
[41] "*Linghang xinshidai de jianqiang lingdao jiti: Dang de xinyijie zhongyang lingdao jigou chansheng jishi*" [A strong leadership body that pilots the new era: A record of the generation of the party's new central governing body], Xinhua She [Xinhua News Agency] (October 26, 2017), www.xinhuanet.com/politics/19cpcnc/2017-10/26/c_112 1860147.htm.
[42] Neil Thomas, "Xi Jinping Is Gaining Support from Party Elites, the Numbers Say," *SupChina* (March 4, 2021), https://supchina.com/2021/03/04/xi-jinping-is-gaining-support-from-party-elites-the-numbers-say/.

measures of suppressing intraparty democracy and centralizing controls over party elites have worked.

In addition to suspending his predecessors' reforms, Xi has adopted some personnel management initiatives to enhance party cohesion. Since promoting engineers and other intellectuals en masse to official positions in the 1980s as part of the "Four Cadre Transformations" (*ganbu sihua*) reforms to make cadres more "revolutionary, youthful, educated, and professional," the CPC has rarely appointed professionals and business leaders to the public sector as senior provincial or ministerial officials. Although senior executives were frequently rotated across giant SOEs during the Jiang and Hu eras,[43] only a handful of princelings managed to switch from SOE heads to provincial leaders.[44] The de facto separation of political and business career tracks in the CPC exacerbated "fragmented authoritarianism" and undermined horizontal cohesion. After 2012, Xi embarked on systematically transferring SOE executives, particularly those from the defense industry, into regional party and government positions. Among thirty-one provincial party secretaries in 2023, three, all of whom had spent decades in arms and space industries,[45] were transferred from SOEs after 2012. Zhang Guoqing, who was promoted from party secretary of Liaoning to vice premier in early 2023, also spent decades in the state-owned defense conglomerate Norinco before 2012. Senior state bankers Guo Shuqing and Jiang Chaoliang were also appointed as provincial leaders.[46] According to a Brookings Report, such appointments allow Xi to curb localism and factionalism in provincial governments and enable the party to exert more direct control.[47]

Dubious Attempts to Create a Historical Myth

Although the CPC has stopped using "line struggles" (*luxian douzheng*) since adopting the second "Resolution on Party History" in 1981, creating heroes and villains in the party's history remains a classical and convenient strategy to strengthen party cohesion. This strategy dates

---

[43] Richard McGregor, *The Party: The Secret World of China's Communist Rulers* (New York: Harper Perennial, 2010).
[44] Lu and Ma, "Is Any Publicity Good Publicity?"
[45] They are Ma Xingrui (Xinjiang), Tang Dengjie (Shanxi), and Yuan Jiajun (Chongqing).
[46] Guo now serves as the Chairman of the Banking and Insurance Regulatory Commission, and Jiang was removed from the post of party secretary of Hubei shortly after the COVID-19 outbreak.
[47] Cheng Li and Lucy Xu, "The Rise of State-Owned Enterprise Executives in China's Provincial Leadership," Brookings Institution (February 22, 2017), www.brookings.edu/opinions/the-rise-of-state-owned-enterprise-executives-in-chinas-provincial-leadership/.

back to Stalin's 1938 *History of the Communist Party of the Soviet Union (Bolsheviks): A Short Course* (hereafter, *Short Course*), which portrayed Lenin and Stalin as the sole ideologically righteous Bolshevik leaders. By depicting the Bolsheviks' history as a series of battles between a Leninist–Stalinist "correct" party line and various "mistaken" lines, the *Short Course*'s historical revisionism established Stalin's ideological superiority, shaped collective memory, and forged a historical myth that strengthened party unity.[48] Creating a historical myth from the party's history relies on compiling an authoritative and (over)simplified account in which the incumbent leader has navigated the party on its successful course. Personalizing the historical narrative as his own through ideological indoctrination campaigns, a leader such as Stalin convinces the whole party of his brightness and competence, so that they follow him with conviction.

During the Yan'an Rectification Campaign (1942–1945), Mao copied Stalin's strategy and combined a party-wide ideological remolding campaign that involved exhaustive study of Mao's writings with intensive indoctrination in a new historical narrative. Akin to Stalin's *Short Course*, the "Resolution on Certain Issues in the History of Our Party" (hereafter "the first Resolution") in 1945 depicts the party's history between 1927 and 1937 as a continuous struggle between the correct Maoist line and the incorrect Wang Ming line, attributing the party's failures before 1935 (including the fall of the Jiangxi Soviet) to Wang Ming's "dogmatic" line (and implicitly, Moscow's instructions). According to Mao's revisionist historical myth, Mao correctly sinicized Marxism and rescued the party from Moscow's remote control in the early stage of the Long March. The Maoist account, codified into the first Resolution, was so successful that almost the whole party was convinced that Mao was the sole leader who could lead the CPC to further victories.[49] The following generations of party members absorbed this binary picture of the party's historical path. Although some Chinese historians have questioned the accuracy of the Maoist historical myth since the 1980s,[50] the first Resolution has remained almost unchallenged within the CPC.

---

[48] Paul H. Avrich, "The *Short Course* and Soviet Historiography," *Political Science Quarterly* 75(4) (1960): 539–553; Graeme Gill, *Symbols and Legitimacy in Soviet Politics* (New York: Cambridge University Press, 2011).

[49] Gao Hua, *Hong Taiyang shi zenyang shengqi de: Yan'an Zhengfeng Yundong de lailong qumai* [How the red sun rose: The origin and development of the Yan'an Rectification Movement, 1930–1945] (Hong Kong: Chinese University Press, 2000).

[50] See Huang Daoxuan, *Zhangli yu xianjie: Zhongyang Suqu de geming, 1933–1934* [Tensions and limits: The revolution in the Central Soviet Area, 1933–1934] (Beijing: Social Sciences Literature Press, 2011).

The second Resolution, "Resolution on Certain Questions in the History of Our Party since the Founding of the People's Republic of China," released in 1981 under Deng, deals with the thorny evaluation of Mao's role after 1949. It creatively redefined the central tenet of Mao Zedong Thought as "Seeking Truth from Facts" (*shishi qiushi*), successfully excluding Mao's policy failures from any evaluation of the party's legitimacy and achievements. The second Resolution was able simultaneously to acknowledge both Mao's errors and his contributions, thus maintaining the legitimacy of the party-state and justifying Deng's deviations from Mao's line and policies. More importantly for the party's unity under Deng, the second Resolution openly criticized Mao's chosen successor Hua Guofeng and compared achievements since 1978 to the "stagnation" under Hua, paving the way for Deng's administration into the next decade. As the party subsequently purged the "Three Kinds of Persons" who arose in the Cultural Revolution[51] along with Hua and his supporters from key offices at all levels, the second Resolution successfully unified the party, reorienting it toward economic development and legitimizing Deng's reforms.

The second Resolution was considerably more ambiguous than the first. Following Deng's principle of "recording in broad strokes, not in detail," it generally sheds favorable light on Mao, ironically leaving room for eroding its own authority. Since the 1990s, orthodox and neo-Maoists have questioned the second Resolution's interpretation of the party's history and reclaim "positive" elements from the post-1957 Maoist era, or even the Cultural Revolution.[52] Historians such as Han Gang have also questioned the historical accuracy of depicting Hua as one of the villains.[53]

Although Xi has never openly opposed the second Resolution, in speeches and policies he has substantially challenged Deng's narrative. In one of his first speeches as general secretary,[54] Xi claimed that the second thirty years of the PRC's history (1979–2009) cannot be

[51] Officially, "Three Kinds of Persons" (*san zhong ren*) refer to "those who rose to prominence by following the counterrevolutionary cliques of Lin Biao and Jiang Qing in 'rebellion,' those who are seriously factionalist in their ideas, and those who indulged in beating, smashing and looting."
[52] Feng Chen, "An Unfinished Battle in China: The Leftist Criticism of the Reform and the Third Thought Emancipation," *The China Quarterly* 158 (1999): 447–467.
[53] See Han Gang, "*Guanyu Hua Guofeng de ruogan shishi*" [Some historical facts about Hua Guofeng], *Yanhuang chunqiu* 2 (2011): 9–18, and "*Guanyu Hua Guofeng de ruogan shishi (xu)*" [Some historical facts about Hua Guofeng, part 2], *Yanhuang chunqiu* 3 (2011): 9–17.
[54] Xi Jinping, "*Guanyu jianchi he fazhan Zhongguo tese shehuizhuyi de jige wenti*" [Several problems regarding upholding and developing socialism with Chinese characteristics], in *Shibada yilai zhongyao wenxian xuanbian, shang* [Selection of important documents since

used to negate the first thirty years (1949–1979). To endorse Xi's reform of establishing dozens of Central Leading Groups in the party to override the State Council, a WeChat article by *People's Daily* favorably compared it to Mao setting up leading groups in the CPC Central Committee in 1958.[55] As Mao's leading groups aimed at the takeover of the state apparatus by the party in preparation for the Great Leap Forward, the 1958 leading group reform was criticized in Deng's historical narrative as overcentralization, erosion of the collective leadership, and violation of the separation of party and state. Such Maoist "errors" have increasingly been reendorsed in Xi's New Era. The third Resolution, produced under Xi, reduced the criticism of Mao's errors into a single paragraph of 330 Chinese characters.

Xi regards the "Resolution on the Major Achievements and Historical Experience of the Party over the Past Century" (hereafter "the third Resolution"), which accompanied the party's centenary anniversary in 2021, as equally important and as authoritative as the first two in its attempt to forge a new collective memory of post-2000 party history. However, it has not identified specific villains, such as Wang Ming in the first Resolution and Lin Biao, Jiang Qing, or even Hua Guofeng in the second, that might strengthen Xi's role as the central protagonist. Over 85 percent of the first Resolution detailed how the party had suffered from the "dogmatic" lines, contrasting them with the brightness of Mao's line and criticizing the "dogmatists." Although Deng was more prudent in exposing and criticizing Mao's errors, the second Resolution devoted one-quarter of the text to criticizing Mao's post-1957 errors. Moreover, it was forceful about Hua, concluding bluntly that "obviously, it is impossible that he could correct the leftist errors within the Party, and more importantly, restore good traditions of the Party." These humiliating, party-wide denunciations killed Hua's political career and paved the way for party unity under Deng's leadership.

The third Resolution spent two-thirds of the text praising the CPC's achievements under Xi's leadership since 2012. The villain against which the whole party can be mobilized is vague and ambiguous: No specific group of people, but the party's weak control of corruption and its lack of discipline before 2012. Criticisms of the "Old Era," the antithesis of Xi's "New Era," were soft, brief, and vague at best. While reviewing problems

---

the 18th Party Congress, Vol. I] (Beijing: Central Party Literature Press, 2013), 109–118, 112.

[55] "*Xinxiliang juda! Duo ming Zhengzhiju weiyuan lianxu fawen tan jigou gaige*" [Hugely informative! Multiple Politburo members write on the administrative reform], *Xiakedao* (March 17, 2018), https://xw.qq.com/cmsid/20180317A1GB5V00.

during the first thirty years of the Reform and Opening, the third Resolution claimed that:

> the Party has remained soberly aware that changes in the international environment have brought about many new risks and challenges and China faces no small number of long unresolved, deep-seated problems as well as newly emerging problems regarding reform, development, and stability. Moreover, previously lax and weak governance has enabled inaction and corruption to spread within the Party and led to serious problems in its political environment, which has harmed relations between the Party and the people and between officials and the public, weakened the Party's creativity, cohesiveness, and ability, and posed a serious test to its exercise of national governance.

Unlike the first two Resolutions, the third Resolution failed to draw a clear line between heroes and villains, or champions of the incumbent's "correct line" versus the predecessor's "mistaken" lines or those who committed political errors. In the first two Resolutions, forceful criticisms of previous leaders signaled that the incumbent leader had solved the problems they caused, reshuffled the key offices, and formed a unified Politburo. The leader is thus ready to unify the party under a new agenda.[56] The third Resolution indicates that although Xi has thoroughly purged the ranks of the party and reorganized some of its key power structures, he still needs continuity, and his divorce from the previous party line is still incomplete. Since the third Resolution did not successfully establish a convincing historical and ideological myth to justify the historical inevitability of Xi's rise and his superiority over his predecessors, a good-versus-bad storytelling hardly improved party cohesion.

Instead of relying on the legitimization of a new party orthodoxy, the third Resolution attempts to justify Xi's rule and forge party unity based on two less provocative and intrusive approaches. The first was to highlight Xi's anticorruption campaign as a key contribution. The Resolution introduced the new phrase "self-revolution" (*ziwo geming*), meaning that the party can eliminate corruption on its own, without an independent anticorruption authority, rule of law, and free press, as the final one of ten key tenets of the party's centenary experience.[57] The second represents

---

[56] Forceful and blunt words in propaganda are also an effective way to shape the recipients' perceptions of the regime's tight control over social order. See Haifeng Huang, "Propaganda as Signaling," *Comparative Politics* 47(4) (2015): 419–444.

[57] Interestingly, the official English version translated *ziwo geming* into the less provocative "self-reform" (*ziwo gaige*). See https://language.chinadaily.com.cn/a/202111/18/WS6195aa45a310cdd39bc75fe0_9.html. The rest of the "ten key tenets" include "upholding the Party's leadership," "putting the people first," "advancing theoretical innovation," "staying independent," "following the Chinese path," "maintaining a global vision," "breaking new ground," "standing up for ourselves" (lit. "daring to struggle," which is discussed later, p. 167), and "promoting the united front."

a subtle, gradual, and cumulative strategy for forging party – and national – cohesion: the construction of a nationalist myth crediting the party with the central role in a 100-year struggle to restore China's pride and standing as great power. While the third Resolution underscored Xi's achievements and depersonalized and underplayed those of previous leaders, particularly Jiang and Hu, all were integrated into a continuous historical narrative in which the CPC leads China toward rejuvenation.

The Party's New Mission: In the Vanguard of National Rejuvenation

After the 1989 Tiananmen protests, the CPC switched the focus of official propaganda to patriotism and nationalism, portraying the party as the custodian of China's national interests.[58] Xi is not the first CPC leader to advocate nationalism, but his rewriting of the CPC's mission represents the first effort to create a systematic nationalist strategy for unifying the party. Only a few days after becoming general secretary in 2012, Xi warned his Politburo colleagues that "ideals and convictions" (*lixiang xinnian*) are the "calcium" of party spirit.[59] Yet the "ideals and convictions" are by no means orthodox communist doctrines. Two weeks after his inauguration, when visiting the "Road to Rejuvenation" Exhibition at the National Museum, which covers post-1840 Chinese history, Xi first put forward the concept of a "China Dream" of "the great rejuvenation of the Chinese nation."[60]

However, Xi did not fully embark on an ideological campaign to rewrite the party's mission until 2017, when he had largely finished a campaign of eliminating political rivals, curbing corruption, and building a broader support base within the party as well as among the general public. Xi launched three intraparty ideological or "educational" campaigns

---

[58] Suisheng Zhao, "Chinese Nationalism and Its International Orientations," *Political Science Quarterly* 115(11) (2000): 1–33; Peter Hayes Gries, *China's New Nationalism: Pride, Politics, and Diplomacy* (Berkeley: University of California Press, 2004); Susan L. Shirk, *China: Fragile Superpower* (New York: Oxford University Press, 2008).

[59] Xi Jinping, "*Jinjin weirao jianchi he fazhan Zhongguo tese shehuizhuyi xuexi xuanchuan guanche dang de shibada jingshen*" [Grasp firmly the principle of upholding and developing socialism with Chinese characteristics, study, promote, and implement the spirit of the 18th Party Congress], in *Shibada yilai zhongyao wenxian xuanbian, shang* [Selection of important documents since the 18th Party Congress, Vol. I] (Beijing: Central Party Literature Press, 2012), 72–82, 72–73.

[60] Xi Jinping, "*Zhongguo meng, fuxing lu*" [The Chinese dream, the path of rejuvenation], in *Shibada yilai zhongyao wenxian xuanbian, shang* [Selection of important documents since the 18th Party Congress, Vol. I] (Beijing: Central Party Literature Press, 2012), 83–84, 84. See also Jane Golley, Linda Jaivin, Ben Hillman, and Sharon Strange (eds.), *China Dreams* (Canberra: ANU Press, 2024).

between 2012 and 2017,[61] all focusing on reinforcing the message of the anticorruption campaign and building up Xi's personal authority within the party. The loosely defined "China Dream," aiming to inspire citizens rather than party elites and cadres, served as the primary ideological slogan.[62] In 2017, Xi began his second term, and largely finished consolidating his power, installing Wang Huning as the chief party theoretician. Xi first introduced the CPC's new "aspiration and mission" (*chuxin shiming*) at the Nineteenth Party Congress: "to seek happiness for the Chinese people and rejuvenation for the Chinese nation."[63]

The CPC is an authoritarian ruling party with a defining ideology, in charge of a party-state.[64] Its "soft" mechanism for maintaining party cohesion is dramatically different from that of political parties in liberal democracies, which offer evolving policy programs with a guiding ideological agenda. During the post-Mao era, the pragmatic Deng took lessons from the defeat of Mao's radical ideology and Japan's economic miracle, setting concrete, tangible, and materialistic mid-term and long-term goals, such as quadrupling the Gross National Product in twenty years, to motivate the whole party toward economic development.[65]

Since 2001, however, Chinese party elites, particularly theoreticians, have increasingly regarded Deng's performance-based legitimacy as an unsustainable or even precarious method for mobilizing the masses and unifying the party, because the CPC, after all, cannot guarantee high economic growth forever: if China's economy stumbles, the party's performance-based legitimacy will suffer. Another concern coincides with the widespread belief in the West that economic growth, openness, and a growing middle class will eventually lead to popular support for liberal democracy.[66] Party theoreticians worry that if the people's

---

[61] They were namely "the Campaign to Educate Party Members about the Mass Line," "the Special Education Program of the Three Stricts and Three Earnests," and "Two Studies and One Action Education Campaign."

[62] Willy Lam, "Xi Jinping's Ideology and Statecraft," *Chinese Law & Government* 48(6) (2016): 409–417.

[63] Xi, "Secure a Decisive Victory in Building a Moderately Prosperous Society," 1.

[64] The CPC's official ideologies range from Marxism–Leninism to their Sinicized versions dating back to Mao Zedong Thought, with the most recent and dominant one being "Xi Jinping Thought on Socialism with Chinese Characteristics for a New Era."

[65] Ezra F. Vogel, *Deng Xiaoping and the Transformation of China* (Cambridge, MA: Belknap, 2011), 361, 387.

[66] For prominent proponents of the modernization theory, which argues that economic development breeds a middle class that aspires to democracy, see Seymour Martin Lipset, "Some Social Requisites of Democracy: Economic Development and Political Legitimacy," *American Political Science Review* 53(1) (1959): 69–105; Robert A. Dahl, *Polyarchy: Participation and Opposition* (New Haven, CT: Yale University Press, 1971); and Samuel P. Huntington, *The Third Wave: Democratization in the Late Twentieth Century* (Norman: University of Oklahoma Press, 1991).

material needs are satisfied, they will demand a higher degree of political participation, a more pluralist and inclusive society, and freedoms of speech, press, and association, which would undermine or even endanger the CPC's single-party rule.[67] To preserve party cohesion in the face of such challenges, Hu Jintao tried to walk a fine line between ideological continuity and flexibility, while maintaining the party's performance-based legitimacy and appeal. The party did foster "patriotic education," but the myth of national rejuvenation was not elevated to be the party's dominant mission. Averaging two-digit annual economic growth, Hu implemented reforms that distributed more resources to the underdeveloped countryside, such as a social security system covering all Chinese, and launched an intraparty campaign to "Preserve the Party's Advanced Nature" that attempted to indoctrinate the then seventy million CPC members in new concepts of Sinicized Marxism. However, these represented little more than modifying Jiang Zemin's elitist "Three Represents" in a more populist direction.[68]

The third Resolution makes clear Xi's belief that the party's ideology under Jiang and Hu was insufficient to hold the party together: "misguided ideas often cropped up, including money worship, hedonism, ultra-individualism, and historical nihilism; online discourse has been rife with disorder; and certain leading officials demonstrated ambiguity in their political stance and a lack of fighting spirit. These phenomena have all had a serious impact on people's thinking and the environment for public discourse." The Resolution asserted that the party must "bolster Chinese spirit, Chinese values, and Chinese strength to consolidate a common ideological foundation for the concerted efforts of all Party members and all Chinese people." Unlike Deng, Xi has not set tangible material objectives for the party. He wants to unify the party based on a stronger adherence to ideology rather than access to material resources and benefits. In his January 2018 address to newly promoted officials who entered the CPC Central Committee and provincial-level offices some months earlier, Xi reiterated that ideological conviction, rather than

---

[67] Heike Holbig, "Remaking the CPC's Ideology: Determinants, Progress, and Limits under Hu Jintao," *Journal of Current Chinese Affairs* 38(3) (2009): 35–61, 43.

[68] According to "Three Represents," the CPC represents the development trends of advanced productive forces, represents the orientation of an advanced culture, and represents the fundamental interests of the overwhelming majority of the people of China. This concept marks the CPC's turn from a nominal vanguard party of the working class to a "whole people's party" and, more importantly, legitimizes the admission of capitalists into the Party (Holbig, "Remaking the CPC's Ideology"; Heike Holbig and Bruce Gilley, "Reclaiming Legitimacy in China," *Politics & Policy* 38(3) (2010): 395–422).

material spoils, would hold the party together over the long term and would even prevent the regime from collapsing:[69]

> as the largest political party in the world, our Party must behave in a way commensurate with this status, but being a big establishment like ours carries its own difficulties. It's hard to manage such a large political party well, and it's even harder to build such a large party into a strong Marxist ruling party. A Marxist political party is not organized based on interests but on shared ideals and convictions. ... Belief in Marxism, along with socialist and communist convictions, are communists' political souls and spiritual pillars for withstanding all kinds of trials. We often say that "if the foundation is not sturdy, the earth will move and the mountains will shake." If convictions are not sturdy, the earth will move and the mountains will shake as well. Didn't the dissolution of the Soviet Union, the collapse of the CPSU, and the upheavals in Eastern Europe all follow the same logic? The CPSU seized political power with twenty thousand members, defeated Adolf Hitler with two million members, but lost power when it had twenty million members. ... during the upheaval, nobody stood up like a man, and nobody came out to resist. Why? It is because ideals and convictions simply evaporated.

Although Xi deplores the fall of communism in Eastern Europe, he does not want to revive Marxism and communism as the CPC's "ideals and convictions." In his 2019 address to the Politburo colleagues about the party's aspirations and mission, Xi misrepresented the meaning of this line in *The Communist Manifesto*: "the proletarian movement is the self-conscious, independent movement of the immense majority, in the interest of the immense majority."[70] Following the flawed logic that Marxism simply means representing the interests of the "immense majority," Xi claims that since its foundation, the CPC has chosen "seeking happiness for the Chinese people and rejuvenation for the Chinese nation as its aspiration and mission" precisely because the CPC is "equipped with Marxism." To convince the whole party that the party has popular support and needs to be unified under his leadership, Xi has systematically promoted a nationalist party ideology.

Revising History with Xi as the Navigator

The dominant feature of Xi's ideological strategy is a thorough revision of the party's history to portray Xi as the indispensable navigator on the road

---

[69] Xi Jinping, "*Tuijin dang de jianshe xin de weida gongcheng yao yiyiguanzhi*" [We must be persistent in advancing the new grand project of party building], *Qiushi* [Seek truth] (October 2, 2019), www.xinhuanet.com/politics/leaders/2019-10/02/c_1125068791.htm.

[70] Xi Jinping, "*Laoji chuxin shiming, tuijin ziwo geming*" [Remember the aspiration and mission, advance self-revolution], in *Shijiuda yilai zhongyao wenxian xuanbian, zhong* [Selection of Important Documents since the 19th Party Congress, Vol. II] (Beijing: Central Party Literature Press, 2019), 118–124, 118–119.

to national rejuvenation. Following the CPC's post-1989 nationalist turn, the 2002 revision of the party's Charter renamed the party as the vanguard not just of the Chinese working class, but also of the Chinese people and nation. Xi has even more radically revised the party's history into one of seeking "national rejuvenation," totally abandoning the narrative of class struggle. In the third Resolution, the word "class" (*jieji*) only appeared 7 times, compared with over 100 times in the second Resolution. The third Resolution squeezed the party's post-1957 "errors" into one paragraph, focusing instead on how the party saved the Chinese nation from the bullying and humiliation that began with the Opium Wars, and reelevated China into the status of a great power. Similarly, textbooks for the Party History Campaign minimized the CPC's failures, highlighting its self-proclaimed consistency and competence in realizing national rejuvenation. In the 531-page *A Brief History of the CPC*, failures from the Great Leap Forward to the Cultural Revolution were compressed into 3 pages in a 33-page chapter, "Explorations and Tortuous Development of the Socialist Construction." The rest of the chapter celebrated achievements between 1957 and 1978, including China's first atomic bomb, its first satellite launch, and winning United Nations membership.[71]

After enumerating the CPC's achievements in national rejuvenation, the third Resolution revealed the new catchphrase "Two Establishes" (*liangge queli*), which centers Xi in the narrative:

The Party has established Comrade Xi Jinping's core position on the Party Central Committee and in the Party as a whole and established the guiding role of Xi Jinping Thought on Socialism with Chinese Characteristics for a New Era. This reflects the common will of the Party, the armed forces, and Chinese people of all ethnic groups, and is of decisive significance for advancing the cause of the Party and the country in the new era and for driving forward the historic process of national rejuvenation.

Ceremonies and Symbols

The "Two Establishes" soon became a key mantra of the "Party History Learning and Education Campaign," particularly for senior officials to signal their loyalty. But Xi and his ideological mastermind Wang Huning obviously regard conventional intraparty ideological campaigns as insufficient to unify the party around Xi. Their distinct ideological strategy is the heavy use of ceremonies and symbols. Studies of nationalism, particularly banal

---

[71] Writing Group of the Book, *Zhongguo Gongchandang Jianshi* [A Brief History of the Communist Party of China] (Beijing: People's Press and History of the Communist Party of China Publishing House, 2021), 184–216.

nationalism, show how ceremonies and symbols forge national unity by building a sense of community and belief in historical myths.[72] Xi and Wang have long held similar ideas. When visiting Shaoxing as the party secretary of Zhejiang in 2005, Xi learned that the Shaoxing municipal government could only organize large-scale ceremonial tributes to the legendary first king of the Xia dynasty, Yu the Great, credited with taming the Great Flood around the twenty-second century BCE, every five or ten years because of budget constraints and the central government's restrictions on holding grand ceremonies. Lecturing local leaders that Yu the Great wasn't just the pride of Shaoxing or Zhejiang but was a national symbol of China, Xi instructed Shaoxing officials to hold grand tributes to Yu annually, because "Yu represented the national spirit; people should commemorate Yu's 'sense of responsibility for the nation and the state.'"[73] Wang expressed similar thoughts after watching the 1994 National Day Ceremony on TV: "a nation must have its own ceremony: it's the best way for a nation to sense its own wholeness and greatness."[74]

The CPC have held numerous ceremonies and rituals since 1949. But most ceremonies, such as the grand National Day Parades and Xi's 2015 Victory Day Parade, in which 12,000 soldiers marched with 500 pieces of military equipment on display, were organized as national events rather than being exclusively prepared for the party.[75] Xi's and Wang's thoughts on forging the sense of party unity through ceremony first came to fruition in 2021, the party's centenary, when the CPC organized party-centered ceremonies on an unprecedented scale. Since 1959, the CPC's anniversary ceremonies have been held inside the Great Hall of the People. For the first time, the 2021 centenary anniversary was held in Tiananmen Square. Hosting an outdoor rally of 70,000 people during Beijing's hot and humid summer, with its unpredictable thunderstorms, presented immense logistical challenges. The ceremony was held at the unusually early hour of 8 am. The program featured unprecedented rituals including a military flyover, a gun salute, and representatives of the Communist Youth League and the Young Pioneers taking a pledge of loyalty.

---

[72] Thomas Hylland Eriksen, "Formal and Informal Nationalism," *Ethnic and Racial Studies* 16(1) (1993): 1–25; Tim Edensor, *National Identity, Popular Culture and Everyday Life* (New York: Routledge, 2020).
[73] Editorial Office of the Interview Records at the Central Party School, *Xi Jinping zai Zhejiang, shang* [Xi Jinping in Zhejiang, Vol. I] (Beijing: Central Party School Press, 2021), 244.
[74] Wang Huning, *Zhengzhi de rensheng* [The Life of Politics] (Shanghai: Shanghai People's Press, 1995), 172–173.
[75] The only exception may arguably be the National Party Congresses, which highlight the CPC's authority in a ceremonial way Guoguang Wu, *China's Party Congress: Power, Legitimacy, and Institutional Manipulation* (New York: Cambridge University Press, 2015).

Other carefully orchestrated events helped construct a strong sense of the party's unity throughout the centenary celebration. Xi decided to build a dedicated CPC history museum shortly after the 2017 Nineteenth Party Congress. The Museum of the CPC, rivaling the National Museum in size, opened in June 2021, aiming to "enhance Party cadres' and members' belief in Marxism and communism, their belief in socialism with Chinese characteristics, and their confidence in the great rejuvenation of the Chinese nation." It was also designed as "a spiritual home and shrine for Communists' education and purification."[76] Besides regular exhibitions of party history, the CPC Museum has a large, dedicated hall for party members renewing their oath to the CPC: Xi and other CPC leaders did so during their inaugural visit.[77] Song and dance performances featured in previous anniversaries were staged inside the Great Hall of the People. The cultural "epic show" for the party's centenary, named "the Great Expedition" (*weida zhengcheng*),[78] however, took place at the National Stadium – "the Bird's Nest" – on June 28, 2021.[79] The choice of venue showcased the grandness of the performance. The term "epic show" clearly aims to evoke the 1965 spectacular "The East Is Red: A Song and Dance Epic," the climax of Maoist art-cum-historical narrative. Following his complete overhaul of the National Honor System in 2015, Xi conferred new "July 1 Medals" on June 29, 2021, to honor outstanding CPC members. A Xinhua News Agency editorial reviewing the centenary celebrations said that the grand ceremonies "unified thought, concentrated strength, inspired people, and boosted morale."[80]

Noneconomic Achievements, Party Spirit, and Continuous Mobilization

Since 2012, the CPC has increasingly relied on noneconomic achievements, spiritual motivation, and continuous mobilization to maintain party cohesion, as economic development has, as anticipated, slowed

---

[76] The original Chinese word for "purification" here is *xili*, which also means baptism.
[77] Wu Xiangdong, "*Zhongguo Gongchandang lishi zhanlanguan: zhanshi Zhongguo Gongchandang fendou lishi de jingshen diantang*" [The Museum of the CPC: A spiritual shrine that exhibits the history of struggle of the CPC], *Qiushi* [Seek truth] (August 16, 2021), www.qstheory.cn/dukan/qs/2021-08/16/c_1127760410.htm.
[78] The official translation was softened into "the Great Journey."
[79] The National Stadium is not equipped with a retractable roof. Therefore, the date was not confirmed until the very last minute again because of the frequent and unpredictable summer thunderstorms in Beijing.
[80] "*Erjin maibu congtou yue: Zhongguo Gongchandang chengli 100 zhounian qingdian qishi*" [With firm strides we are crossing its summit: Lessons from the centenary of the CPC], Xinhua She [Xinhua News Agency] (July 14, 2021), www.xinhuanet.com/politics/2021-07/14/c_1127656102.htm.

down and faces thorny challenges ahead. Since 2014, once-dramatic economic growth gradually dropped to 6–7 percent right before the COVID-19 pandemic, which means fewer distributable resources are available to buy off elites and citizens. China has also faced an increasingly adverse international environment since 2017. Worsening relationships with the United States and other Western powers hurt China's trading and international-facing sectors as well as transnational elites who benefit from trade and connection with the West. Therefore, Xi needs to convince other party elites, and ordinary Chinese as well, that they need to make sacrifices for the desirable but distant vision of national rejuvenation. Vladimir Lenin argued that, rather than focus on day-to-day economic needs and incremental gains, genuine revolutionaries should mobilize workers to fight for a socialist revolution that would profoundly improve workers' lives in future but entail significant sacrifices in the present.[81] Xi's exhortations to the party to be prepared to bite the bullet for the cause of national rejuvenation are in a similar vein. Since his political report at the Nineteenth Party Congress, and similar to Mao's warning that a revolution is "not a dinner party, or writing an essay, or painting a picture, or doing embroidery," Xi has repeatedly warned the party that the path to national rejuvenation "will be no walk in the park, and it will take more than drum beating and gong clanging to get there. Everyone in the Party must be prepared to work even harder toward this goal."

Later in 2017, Xi coined a related, cryptic assertion that has been frequently repeated by him and other Chinese officials since then: "The world today is undergoing profound changes unseen in a century." Clearly, Xi (probably Wang Huning as well) anticipated a bumpy ride ahead in 2017: This assertion suggests growing tensions and conflicts between a declining United States and a rising China. However, difficulties and challenges in Xi's second term were greater than anticipated. The intensifying US–China trade war and rising tensions between not just the US and China but China and other countries, the COVID-19 pandemic, China's unsustainable zero-COVID strategy, and even the 2022 Russia–Ukraine War, have all turned out to be seriously divisive within the CPC.[82] Xi needs to provide more than just warnings, he needs motivations for party elites and rank-and-file cadres to stick together.

[81] Vladimir Ilyich Lenin, "What Is to Be Done? Burning Questions of Our Movement," in *Lenin's Selected Works, Vol. 1* (Moscow: Foreign Languages Publishing House, 1902), 119–271.
[82] Xi Jinping partially admitted the more adverse environment by coming up with a new evaluation in August 2020: "the COVID-19 pandemic has further accelerated the profound changes … the world has entered a period of new turbulence and

As economic performance is no longer sufficient to guarantee party cohesion, Xi has focused on the CPC's noneconomic achievements. The third Resolution's summary of Xi's accomplishments did not mention concrete economic achievements. Instead, it celebrated Xi's anticorruption campaign, alongside his grand strategies and signature policies including creating a "Chinese" identity that transcends ethnicity (such as Uyghur or Han),[83] the ceremonies and rituals, the Poverty Alleviation Campaign, environmental protection ("clear waters and green mountains are as valuable as mountains of silver and gold"), comprehensive military reform, the Belt and Road Initiative, hardline policies toward Hong Kong and Taiwan, and, unsurprisingly, his COVID-19 response. Between 2020 and 2022, the state media have praised COVID-19 containment as a key CPC achievement under Xi and one that has outperformed the West, whose handling of the pandemic has been "disastrous." Xi further linked this to the national rejuvenation: "we must promote the spirit of fighting COVID-19 across society, and transform the spirit into a great strength for comprehensively building a modern socialist country and realizing the great rejuvenation of the Chinese nation."[84]

Xi seems to genuinely believe that the spiritual motivation of a revolutionary party can shape the mindsets of party elites and rank-and-file members today. In his 2018 address to the new full and alternate members of the Central Committee, Xi stressed that the CPC is "both a Marxist ruling party and a Marxist revolutionary party." Therefore, to get work done, the CPC needs to harness the revolutionary passion and spirit that emerged during the revolution.[85] For the first time, and right ahead of the centenary anniversary, the CPC summarized and promoted as many as ninety-one types of the party's revolutionary spirit, labeling them "the spiritual genealogy of Chinese Communists" (*Zhongguo gongchandangren*

transformation (*dongdang bianqe qi*). In the next period, we will face a more adverse external environment, and we must be prepared for a series of new risks and challenges." See "*Xi Jinping: zai jingji shehui lingyu zhuanjia zuotanhui shang de jianghua*" [Xi Jinping: Speech at the Symposium with experts in economic and social affairs], Xinhua she [Xinhua News Agency] (August 24, 2020), www.xinhuanet.com/politics/leaders/2020-08/24/c_1126407772.htm.

[83] Officially coined as "Forging a Sense of Community for the Chinese Nation."
[84] Xi Jinping, "*Zai quanguo kangji xinguan feiyan yiqing biaozhang dahui shang de jianghua*" [Speech at the Commendation Conference for the National Response to COVID-19], in *Shijiuda yilai zhongyao wenxian xuanbian, zhong* [Selection of important documents since the 19th Party Congress, Vol. II] (Beijing: Central Party Literature Press, 2020), 682–696, 691.
[85] "*Yiyiguanzhi jianchi he fazhan Zhongguo tese shehuizhuyi*" [Be persistent in upholding and developing socialism with Chinese characteristics], *Renmin Ribao* [People's Daily] (January 6, 2018), www.xinhuanet.com/politics/2018-01/05/c_1122218424.htm. Xi's discussion about the CPC as a revolutionary party is deleted in the published, abridged version.

jingshen puxi). The spiritual genealogy is a hodgepodge of concepts ranging from the "Spirit of Jinggangshan" and the "Spirit of the Jiangxi Soviet" to the "Spirit of the women's volleyball team,"[86] the "Spirit of entrepreneurs," and the "Spirit of fighting COVID-19."[87] The CPC claimed that these spirits can "motivate party members, cadres, and the masses to promote glorious revolutionary traditions" and "form great spiritual strength for realizing the great rejuvenation of the Chinese nation." As Andrew Nathan argues, the promotion of the "Ninety-One Spirits" reflects the third Resolution's revisionist historical narrative.[88] But it also carries a useful message that the CPC is capable of overcoming all sorts of difficulties at will, and thus its leader's orders should be followed.

As neither noneconomic achievements nor spiritual motivations can fully substitute for concrete economic spoils, the CPC has increasingly invoked, even fueled, antagonism against and tensions with the United States and other Western countries, so that the party can rally the party elites and members around the flag of "national rejuvenation," shifting blame for suboptimal economic performance onto the West's bullying. Poststructuralist studies of populism have found that one effective strategy of nationalist populists such as Narendra Modi and Donald Trump is to construct negative images of foreign Others, including states, transnational elites, refugees, or international institutions. The foreign Other is portrayed as a threat to one's own people, their identity, and their well-being, so that populist politicians can use the fear and sense of insecurity to mobilize the people and unite them in a common front.[89] Xi goes one step further: It is necessary to maintain constant tensions between China and the foreign Others (the United States and other Western countries) to safeguard the national rejuvenation from their sabotage.

---

[86] Jinggangshan was the CPC's first "revolutionary base area" (1927–1929), which was established under Mao's idea of "encircling the cities from the rural areas." Jiangxi Soviet was the CPC's largest revolutionary base area in the early 1930s. The CPC founded the Chinese Soviet Republic and set out on the Long March there. The Chinese women's volleyball team is one of the most successful national sports teams in China, winning ten world champion titles, including five consecutive ones in the 1980s.

[87] "*Zhongguo Gongchandangren jingshen puxi diyipi weida jingshen zhengshi fabu*" [The first batch of great spirits of the spiritual genealogy of the Chinese Communists is formally released], Xinhua She [Xinhua News Agency] (September 29, 2021), www.gov.cn/xinwen/2021-09/29/content_5640143.htm.

[88] Fang Bing, "*Bainian dangqing zaiji, Zhonggong chuangzao de 91 zhong jingshen he wei zhen*" [In the lead-up to the party's centenary: Which of the 91 spirits created by the CPC are genuine?], *Voice of America* (June 20, 2021), www.voachinese.com/a/ccp-centennial-91-spirits-which-one-is-real-ccp-spirit-20210619/5935568.html.

[89] Thorsten Wojcewski, "'Enemies of the People': Populism and the Politics of (In)security," *European Journal of International Security* 5(1) (2020): 5–24; Thorsten Wojcewski, "Populism, Hindu Nationalism, and Foreign Policy in India: The Politics of Representing 'the People,'" *International Studies Review* 22(3) (2020): 396–422.

Accordingly, the CPC has exploited the trade war, the arrest of Meng Wanzhou, allegations against human rights abuses in Xinjiang, criticism of crackdowns in Hong Kong, and the origins of COVID-19 to fuel preexisting anti-American and anti-West sentiments. But the anti-West propaganda does not simply target the masses; it also promotes party cohesion. It is in Xi's interests to proclaim the inevitability of American decline and Sino-American conflict. National rejuvenation in the age of "profound changes unseen in a century" (*bainian weiyou zhi dabianju*) is bound to provoke more clashes with the West. Clearly, the party's new mission implies a more aggressive and hardline stand against the West. By stirring up tensions, Xi manages to ensure that so long as there is turbulence on the international front (or perception of turbulence), it will be hard to argue for a change of leadership. The third Resolution supports this logic. To foil the West's efforts at containment and achieve national rejuvenation, the whole party must stand firm:

> The Central Committee is acutely aware that, confronted with various types of external encirclement, suppression, disruption, and subversion, we must not be misguided or intimidated, and we must fight to the end with any forces that would attempt to subvert the leadership of the CPC and China's socialist system, or to hinder or obstruct China's advance toward national rejuvenation. Constant concessions will only invite more bullying and humiliation.

The *People's Daily*'s official catechism of Xi Jinping Thought reveals that Xi insisted on asserting that the party needed to carry out "a great historical struggle with many contemporary features" when he drafted Hu Jintao's political report to the 2012 Eighteenth Party Congress.[90] After the outbreak of the trade war, Xi became increasingly obsessed with the idea of "struggle" (*douzheng*), especially within the party. In an unpublished 2019 address to younger cadres undergoing training at the Central Party School, Xi mentioned the word "struggle" fifty-six times. The third Resolution even names the spirit of "daring (or having the courage) to struggle" (*ganyu douzheng*) as a key lesson from the party's history:[91]

---

[90] Hu Jintao, "*Jianding buyi yanzhe Zhongguo tese shehuizhuyi daolu qianjin, wei quanmian jiancheng xiaokangshehui er fendou*" [Firmly march on the path of socialism with Chinese characteristics and strive to complete the building of a moderately prosperous society in all respects], in *Shibada yilai zhongyao wenxian xuanbian, shang* [Selection of important documents since the 18th Party Congress, Vol. I] (Beijing: Central Party Literature Press, 2012), 1–44.

[91] The official translation intentionally softened *ganyu douzheng* into "standing up for ourselves." In the Cultural Revolution, the official translation of the same term was more straightforward: "Dare to struggle, dare to fight." To convey the actual meaning of this term accurately, I have modified the official translation and adopted a more literal translation.

Having the courage to struggle and the mettle to win provides the Party and the people with inviolable strength. The Party's and the people's achievements have not come from nothing, nor were they given to us by others; they were earned through persistent struggle. The Party was born amid domestic turmoil and foreign aggression, tempered by numerous tribulations, and has grown strong by surmounting difficulties. No matter how powerful the enemy, how difficult the journey, or how grave the challenges, the Party has never lost heart or backed down, and has never hesitated to make necessary sacrifices. It has remained unyielding despite all setbacks, fighting for our people, our country, and our nation, as well as our shared ideals and convictions. We should grasp the contemporary features of the great new struggle, seize historical opportunities, and get a head start. If we carry forward the fighting spirit, build up our ability, and rally the will and strength of the whole Party and the entire nation, we are sure to overcome any risks or challenges, whether foreseeable or otherwise.

Although the aforementioned catechism does not name any specific enemy, it enumerated several kinds of struggle, including not only anticorruption but also "wars of thoughts and public opinion" initiated by "rival forces," struggles against "unilateralism, trade protectionism, and international bullying," and "maintaining national dignity and interests." Ultimately, the catechism argues that such "great struggles" are indispensable for "realizing people's desire for a better life and the great rejuvenation of the Chinese nation."[92] A *People's Daily* analysis of the "ten tenets of historical experience," however, revealed the identity of the foreign Other. Prominent examples of great struggles include "resolutely countering the United States' bullying acts in the economy, trade, and technology," "refuting slanders and lies" (allegations of human rights abuses in Xinjiang and elsewhere), and "withstanding and striking back at suppression and containment by other powers."[93]

Conclusion: Xi's Neo-Maoist Strategy for Party Cohesion

Before 2012, party elites and members had some autonomy to pursue their own material or factional interests and limited autonomy to express dissident views under the umbrella of the party. Xi's blunt disciplinary crackdowns and far tighter political control have significantly reduced

---

[92] "*Wanshan pangbo you zhufeng (Xi Jinping xinshidai zhongguo tese shehuizhuyi sixiang xuexi wenda (50)): guanyu jianchi he jiaqiang dang de quanmian lingdao*" [Ten thousand mountains have a main peak (Catechism of Xi Jinping Thought on socialism with Chinese characteristics for a new era (50)): On upholding and strengthening the all-round leadership of the party], *Renmin ribao* [People's Daily] (September 28, 2021), http://theory.people.com.cn/n1/2021/0928/c40531-32239280.html.

[93] Li Gang, "*Jianchi ganyu douzheng: shenke renshi dang de bainian fendou lishi jingyan*" [Upholding the spirit of daring to fight: A deep understanding of the party's experience of struggle in the past century], *Renmin ribao* [People's Daily] (December 17, 2021), http://opinion.people.com.cn/n1/2021/1217/c1003-32310208.html.

room for such behavior, demanding that party members should adhere to the party line everywhere, even in private conversation and WeChat groups of former classmates or friends, and should not watch or read unauthorized materials. Such harsh discipline over party members was common in the Maoist era, particularly the late stage of the Cultural Revolution. One of Xi's favorite sayings is his paraphrase of Mao's 1973 quote: "Party, government, military, civilian, and academic, east, west, south, north, and center, the Party leads everything."[94] The omnipresence of the party reminds people of "the monopoly on leadership of the Party" (*dang de yiyuanhua lingdao*) in the 1970s. Even Xi's rotation of senior officials echoes Mao's frequent rotation of officials across different sectors. Meanwhile, Xi has also revived some of Chen Yun's conservative policies for more centralization, such as using the CCDI to curb local policy deviations and sanctioning intraparty dissidents. In 2023, Zhu Jiamu, Chen Yun's former personal secretary, even admired the fact that "many correct claims about party and state governance promoted by Comrade Chen Yun have been increasingly implemented by the Party Central since the 18th Party Congress," which "would be the best consolation to Comrade Chen Yun."[95]

Nevertheless, Xi's disciplinary and organizational strategy comes with economic costs. The great expansion of the party's monitoring role has consumed enormous fiscal resources. The party's deeper involvement in ("supervision" of) the business world has estranged foreign shareholders and investors. Frequent party-led inspections often undermine lower-level party cadres' productivity.[96] More party oversight means more unproductive bureaucrats on the payroll. No direct evidence shows that Xi is very concerned about any of those things. Instead, he is even more ambitious about cementing the party's political control and unity. In his speech at the 2018 National Organizational Work Conference, Xi asserted that while the party's control over SOEs is "relatively good" at the headquarters or parent company level, it is much weaker in subsidiaries.[97] Similarly, while the party's leadership role is quite

---

[94] Mao's original words in 1973 were, "the Politburo supervises everything: Party, government, military, civilian, and academic, east, west, south, north, and center."

[95] "*Hongse toutiao: jinian Chen Yun tongzhi shishi 28 zhounian jidian huodong zai Babaoshan geming gongmu juxing*" [Red headline: Memorial ceremony for the 28th anniversary of the death of Comrade Chen Yun held at Babaoshan Revolutionary Cemetery], *Zhong hong wang* (April 13, 2023), www.crt.com.cn/news2007/news/HStop/2023/4/23413104915704350KGH0AII5H5JE52.html.

[96] Erik H. Wang, "Frightened Mandarins: The Adverse Effects of Fighting Corruption on Local Bureaucracy," *Comparative Political Studies* 55(11) (2022): 1807–1843.

[97] Xi Jinping, "*Zai quanguo zuzhi gongzuo huiyi shang de jianghua*" [Speech at the National Organizational Work Conference], in *Shijiuda yilai zhongyao wenxian xuanbian, shang*

"clear" in universities, "there is still a large gap in extending the Party's leadership throughout university administration, academic courses, and educating students." The party's leadership in K-12 [primary and secondary] schools, hospitals, and research institutes, he claimed, "has not been well established." The party-building work across "social organizations, particularly academic and professional associations, has not yet made a breakthrough." He also criticized "noises" within the party arguing that there was enough centralization in the party during Xi's first term and there should be more intraparty democracy, dubbing the proponents as "confused" or "having ulterior motives."[98] Clearly, Xi's project of exerting the party's political control over every corner of national and party life is not yet finished.

Xi's ideological strategy, which is different from past CPC leaders', is even more intriguing. He did not follow Mao's and Deng's divisive approach of completely revising party history and labeling villains. As Xi cannot openly denounce his predecessors and still needs to preserve consistency and continuity in the party's history, he has chosen a less provocative and intrusive approach to highlighting his indispensableness to the party: conventional ideological indoctrination, a more nationalist party ideology, heavy use of ceremonies and symbols, and constant mobilization of party cadres and members. Since the Twentieth Party Congress, "national rejuvenation" has further evolved into two contesting ideological taglines, "Chinese-style modernization," presumably developed by former political scientist Wang Huning, and "modern Chinese civilization," promoted by the new propaganda chief Li Shulei, previously trained as a literary critic. On the surface, the ideological strategy seems to hold the party together. The recent wave of voices attempting to divide Xi and the CPC received no open support within the party.[99] But ideological strategies may fail or backfire as well. The intensive use of rituals and symbols may reinforce obedience but cannot generate genuine support.[100] Fueling

---

[Selection of important documents since the 19th Party Congress, Vol. I] (Beijing: Central Party Literature Press, 2018), 554–574, 561.

[98] CPC Central Institute of Party History and Literature (ed.), *Xi Jinping guanyu quanmian congyan zhidang lunshu zhaibian, 2021 ban* [Xi Jinping on exercising full and strict governance over the party, 2021 edition] (Beijing: Central Party Literature Press, 2021), 38.

[99] Prominent examples include George Soros's prediction that Xi would soon be toppled within the party: www.georgesoros.com/2022/01/31/george-soros-on-china-remarks-delivered-at-the-hoover-institution, and Lingling Wei's unfounded speculation that Li Keqiang would counterbalance Xi Jinping in 2022 and onward (Lingling Wei, "China's Forgotten Premier Steps Out of Xi's Shadow as Economic Fixer," *The Wall Street Journal* [May 11, 2022], www.wsj.com/articles/china-premier-li-keqiang-xi-jinping-11652277107).

[100] Lisa Wedeen, *Ambiguities of Domination: Politics, Rhetoric, and Symbols in Contemporary Syria* (Chicago: The University of Chicago Press, 1999).

xenophobic sentiments among the people limits the leader's options and room for backing down in international bargaining.[101] Until the next political stress test, we may not know whether Xi's ideological strategy is really working.

The CPC's long-standing concerns about performance-based legitimacy – its vulnerability in economic downturns – may explain Xi's comprehensive ideological strategy. Yet it is difficult to understand why Xi is so obsessed with abstract motivations such as "serving the people" or "achieving national rejuvenation" while he rarely mentions, and sometimes appears to despise, extrinsic motivations such as material rewards and career advancements. As Xi said to senior disciplinary officials: "Leading cadres should be particularly grateful to and in awe of the organization and the people. They should be content with their rank, fame, fortune, and salary. They must know the limits of material comforts and personal benefits."[102] The CPC does nominally set higher moral bars for senior cadres, but very few post-Mao CPC leaders put as heavy a weight on moral motivations and intangible, symbolic targets as Xi. This is particularly intriguing given that extrinsic, material, and tangible motivations, especially given that the party provides institutional access to spoils of power, have been the dominant explanation for single-party regimes' cohesion and durability for decades.[103] Economists have also maintained that career advancement motivates Chinese officials to deliver economic growth.[104]

---

[101] Jessica Chen Weiss, "Authoritarian Signaling, Mass Audiences, and Nationalist Protest in China," *International Organization* 67(1) (2013): 1–35; Jessica Chen Weiss and Allan Dafoe, "Authoritarian Audiences, Rhetoric, and Propaganda in International Crises: Evidence from China," *International Studies Quarterly* 63(4) (2019): 963–973.

[102] Xi Jinping, "*Chongzheng xingzhuang zai chufa, yi yongyuan zai lushang de zhizhuo ba quanmian congyan zhidang yinxiang shenru*" [Repack for a new start: Persistently on the road to comprehensively intensifying the party's self-governance], in *Shijiuda yilai zhongyao wenxian xuanbian, shang* [Selection of important documents since the 19th Party Congress, Vol. I] (Beijing: Central Party Literature Press, 2018), 192–200, 194–195.

[103] Barbara Geddes, "What Do We Know about Democratization after Twenty Years?" *Annual Review of Political Science* 2(1) (1999): 115–144; Jason Brownlee, *Authoritarianism in an Age of Democratization* (New York: Cambridge University Press, 2007); Beatriz Magaloni, "Credible Power-Sharing and the Longevity of Authoritarian Rule," *Comparative Political Studies* 41(4–5) (2008): 715–741; Milan W. Svolik, *The Politics of Authoritarian Rule* (New York: Cambridge University Press, 2012).

[104] Eric Maskin, Yingyi Qian, and Chenggang Xu, "Incentives, Information, and Organizational Form," *Review of Economic Studies* 67(2) (2000): 359–378; Hongbin Li and Li-An Zhou, "Political Turnover and Economic Performance: The Incentive Role of Personnel Control in China," *Journal of Public Economics* 89(9) (2005): 1743–1762; Chenggang Xu, "The Fundamental Institutions of China's Reforms and Development," *Journal of Economic Literature* 49(4) (2011): 1076–1151; Li-An Zhou, *Zhuanxing zhong de difang zhengfu: guanyuan jili yu zhili, di'er ban* [Local governments in transition: Officials' incentives and governance] (Shanghai: Truth & Wisdom Press, Shanghai Joint Publishing, and Shanghai People's Press, 2017).

The role of the party's ideology in today's CPC, especially in maintaining the party's unity, cannot be fully understood independent of Xi's personal background and character. Xi is pragmatic: He regards national rejuvenation as a more realistic motivation than orthodox communist doctrines and utopian visions. But he is simultaneously a voluntarist. Possibly influenced by Mao during his sent-down years in Liangjiahe, Xi has long celebrated the spiritual and ideological molding of human will via moral transformation, because he believes it is a primary mover of social and economic changes. In 1991, a Japanese homemaker asked Xi for impressions on his first visit to Japan. In response, Xi spoke highly of how human effort and will, rather than institutional and material incentives, had transformed Japan into the world's second-largest advanced industrial economy:

> Japan's technology is advanced. Many high-rise buildings, and plants are well equipped too. But the industrial modernization is not my primary concern, because all those things can be achieved through human agency. In the near future, you will see all of them in China as well. But one thing really impressed me deeply. I visited many industrial plants, and workers had a really good work ethic: no one slacking off or doing nothing in particular. I saw that the countryside was tidy and clean, and farmers were very hard working. What makes Japan so developed and its economy growing so fast is that every class is hard working. That is the key thing we really should learn from.[105]

In this regard, Xi resembles Mao, not Deng, who believed that economic development and rising living standards shielded the CPC from the collapse of communism that had occurred in Eastern Europe. Xi, with his emphasis on human will, seemed to have a poor understanding of why Chinese workers and peasants were "less hard working" than their Japanese counterparts: It was not because Chinese workers in SOEs and peasants on public communes lacked ideological motivation, but because they were not institutionally and materially incentivized to work hard. It is questionable whether "the spirit of hard work" and high morale are sustainable under a worsening economy. In post-bubble Japan, the common strong work ethic of overtime-working "salarymen" did not prevent the bubble from bursting and the economic recession. Working overtime, partially a consequence of unhealthy corporate culture, became increasingly less common there.[106]

---

[105] Editorial Office of the Interview Records at the Central Party School, *Xi Jinping zai Fujian, shang* [Xi Jinping in Fujian, Vol. I] (Beijing: Central Party School Press, 2021), 47.

[106] Ironically, overtime working has been increasingly common across Chinese government agencies and private firms, where it is not a result of a hard-working spirit and high morale, but in fact quite the opposite.

While Xi's nationalism-based mythology surrounding the party's mission has apparently held the party together throughout the storms of the trade war and the COVID-19 pandemic, whether an ideology-based approach will be sustainable still ultimately depends on factors outside the CPC's control. External shocks, economic policy stumbles, the crackdowns on Big Tech companies, the real estate industry, and private tutoring in 2021, popular discontent with the draconian and expensive lockdowns needed to preserve the "zero-COVID" strategy amid the Omicron variant (which ultimately led to the White Paper Movement in late 2022), and an even more hostile international environment (including toward Xi's "no-limits" friendship with Putin) all consume immense state resources and pose challenges that nationalist myth-making, ideological mobilization, and the vision of national rejuvenation cannot solve in themselves.

8 Co-opting the Private Sector

Minglu Chen

Since Aristotle, classic theories of democracy have convincingly established the correlations between wealth and democracy, as well as the role of private business owners as the driving force of democratic changes. Joseph Schumpeter points out the causal relationship between the rise of capitalism and the emergence of modern democracy.[1] He saw capitalist revolution as a process by which a social structure where the wealth-creating bourgeoisie were the humble subjects of the ruling class was replaced by another social structure which safeguarded the bourgeoisie's own interests and provided them with a social status to match their economic resources. Modernization theory argues that the more well-to-do a society is, the more likely it is to democratize. This is because economic development leads to urbanization, industrialization, rising living standards, and increased educational opportunities, all of which create a middle class that acts both as a driver and a necessary condition of democratization.[2] Barrington Moore also notes how capitalism and democracy have arisen hand in hand and points to the indispensable role that the urban middle class has played in the latter. Hence the famous statement: "no bourgeoisie, no democracy."[3]

Yet China's development under the rule of the Communist Party of China (CPC) challenges these conventional understandings of the correlation between wealth and democracy. Despite the unprecedented growth and prosperity over the past decades, the authoritarian system has neither collapsed nor embraced democracy, and the rising middle class has not demanded it, either. This invites the question of why China's economic liberalization has not created a business class that advocates political change. This chapter argues that the answer lies in both the

---

[1] Joseph Schumpeter, *Capitalism, Socialism and Democracy* (New York: Harper & Brothers, 1942).
[2] Seymour Martin Lipset, "Some Social Requisites of Democracy: Economic Development and Political Legitimacy," *The American Political Science Review* 53(1) (1959): 69–105.
[3] Barrington Moore, *Social Origins of Dictatorship and Democracy: Lord and Peasant in the Making of the Modern World* (New York: Beacon, 1969), 418.

communist party-state's capacity to control and adapt, and private entrepreneurs' ability to safeguard their interests.

Since the introduction of the policy of reform and opening in the late 1970s, China has experienced unprecedented economic growth. For most of the past four decades, the Chinese economy enjoyed a double-digit growth rate. In 2011, China overtook Japan as the world's second-largest economy. Over the decades, the private economic sector has become increasingly significant. In 2017, there were more than 27 million private enterprises in the country with overall registered capital of more than 16.5 trillion RMB, contributing more than 60 percent of the national GDP.[4] As of August 2022, 47 million enterprises in China were privately owned, accounting for 93.3 percent of all Chinese enterprises.[5] China's economic development has resulted in the accumulation of wealth in private hands and concerns about the security of property rights.[6] The Property Law protecting property rights was not adopted until 2007, and land ownership and use rights are separated in the country.

According to the conventional understanding of the correlation between economic development and democracy, these developments could have profound implications for the CPC rule. Minxin Pei describes them as "the self-destructive political dynamics inherent in an autocracy caught up in rapid socioeconomic change."[7] Defying predictions, however, one-party rule has not withered, nor collapsed, nor embraced democratization,[8] instead becoming stronger and more entrenched. China's private entrepreneurs generally support the CPC.[9] Instead of democratization, China's economic development is characterized by what Kellee S. Tsai calls "capitalism without democracy."[10]

---

[4] People.com.cn, "*Jiezhi 2017 nian minying qiye chao 2700 wan jia, minying jingji zhan GDP bizhong chao 60%*" [As the end of 2017 there are more than 27 million private enterprises, counting for more than 60% of GDP], People.com.cn (September 6, 2018), http://finance.people.com.cn/n1/2018/0906/c1004-30276612.html.

[5] The Central People's Government of the People's Republic of China, "*Minying qiye shuliang 10 nian fan liang fan, zai qiye zongliang Zhong zhan bi jiu cheng*" [The number of private enterprise has doubled in 10 years, counting for 90 percent of all Chinese enterprises] (October 12, 2022), www.gov.cn/xinwen/2022-10/12/content_5717756.htm.

[6] Yasheng Huang, *Capitalism with Chinese Characteristics: Entrepreneurship and the State* (Cambridge: Cambridge University Press, 2010).

[7] Minxin Pei, *China's Trapped Transition: The Limits of Developmental Autocracy* (Cambridge, MA: Harvard University Press, 2006), 20.

[8] Gordon Chang, *The Coming Collapse of China* (New York: Random House, 2001).

[9] Jie Chen and Bruce Dickson, *Allies of the State: China's Private Entrepreneurs and Democratic Change* (Cambridge, MA: Harvard University Press, 2010).

[10] Kellee S. Tsai, *Capitalism without Democracy: The Private Sector in Contemporary China* (Ithaca, NY: Cornell University Press, 2007).

Why has economic development and the rise of private entrepreneurs under the CPC rule not only not resulted in democratic transition but also actively reinforced party rule? This is the question to be answered in this chapter. It is true that this issue has been explored repeatedly by various scholars from different perspectives. Drawing upon the existing scholarship, this chapter aims to unveil the complex state–business relationship in contemporary China. Focusing on the institutional means of co-option and policy input in the Chinese political system, it argues that the rise of the business class does not challenge the CPC's rule, not just because of the alliance between business owners and the party-state where the former depends on the latter for business success and the latter depends on the former for economic growth. Despite the socioeconomic changes, the party is able to maintain its control over the private sector, through adapting its ideology, policies, and institutions. By doing so, it has created a space for private entrepreneurs to represent their interests in the policy-making process. At the same time, private entrepreneurs are not just passively complying with the party's orders but also actively negotiating with the party in both informal and formal ways to safeguard their interests. These mechanisms mean that even if there is friction or a gap between the interests of the business community and the party, the business community and the rising middle classes are generally more inclined to support the party than they are to push back against its rule.

Evolving Policies, Ideology, and Institutions

China's rapid economic growth over the last decades and the party-state's need to maintain such intensive growth has affected the relationship between the party-state and the private business sector. Since the start of China's reform and opening, the CPC has actively and proactively adapted its policies, ideology, and organizations to better suit the evolving socioeconomic reality and accommodate the newly (re)emergent business class, the first since 1949 that the party has encouraged to flourish. Its ability to adapt and reform itself helps explain the party's longevity.[11]

The party-state is a hierarchical system that incorporates different interests and agendas at different levels. Policy setting at the national level, policy implementation at the subnational levels, and competition between local governments, as well as individual officials' preferences and aspirations, all have an impact on private sector development.

---

[11] David Shambaugh, *China's Communist Party: Atrophy and Adaptation* (Berkeley: University of California Press, 2008).

The party reintroduced private ownership into the economy in 1979, when it made the pragmatic decision to allow urban youth who had been sent "up to the mountain and down to the countryside" during the Cultural Revolution to return to the cities and engage in individual enterprise, such as bicycle repair shops or tea stalls.[12] In 1981, the party-state issued the landmark document "Several Decisions on Finding New Ways, Developing the Economy and Solving the Problem of Unemployment in the Cities," which referred to individual business owners as "socialist laborers" and described individually owned businesses as "a necessary supplement to socialist state-owned businesses."[13] This description was written into the Fourth Amendment of the Constitution of the People's Republic of China a year later. In 1997, the party's Fifteenth Congress further confirmed that "the non-public economy is a significant component of China's socialist market economy," and this was written into *The Fifth Amendment of the Constitution of the People's Republic of China* in 1999.[14] The change of wording signified that the private economy had lost its marginal status and had been placed on an almost-equal footing with the state-owned and collective sectors.

An increasing number of CPC members were becoming private entrepreneurs. Many former government officials and state-owned enterprise managers took the risk of "jumping into the business sea" (*xia hai*) to set up their own businesses. Meanwhile, the party considered recruiting private entrepreneurs as members to promote economic development, in the words of Bruce Dickson in his book *Red Capitalists in China*, so as not to "shut itself off from the best supply of human resources."[15] But Marxism–Leninism and Mao Zedong Thought do not provide ideological justification for the party to recruit private entrepreneurs, the sort of people formerly labeled "class enemies" who had been "beaten down." In 2000, the CPC finally overcame the ideological barrier, with the "Three Represents" Theory proposed by then party secretary-general Jiang Zemin. The "Three Represents" assert that "the Party should represent the developmental needs of the advanced social productive

---

[12] See "*Geti siying jingji fazhan 30 nian*" [30 years development of individual and private economy], *Dongbei xinwen wang* [Northeast News Online] (August 27, 2008), www.scio.gov.cn/wszt/wz/Document/535785/535785.htm.

[13] The CPC Central Committee and the State Council, "*Guanyu guangkai menlu, gaohuo jingji, jiejue chengshi jiuye wenti de ruogan jueding*" [Several decisions on finding new ways, developing economy and solving the problem of unemployment in the cities], issued on October 17, 1981, www.100test.com/html/330/s_330066_33.pdf.

[14] The National People's Congress of China, *Zhonghua Renmin Gongheguo Xianfa Xiuzheng An* [Amendment to the Constitution of the PRC], www.people.com.cn/item/faguiku/xf/F01-A1050.html.

[15] Bruce J. Dickson, *Red Capitalists in China: The Party, Private Entrepreneurs, and Prospects for Political Change* (Cambridge: Cambridge University Press, 2003), 8.

forces, the promotion of advanced culture, and the fundamental interests of the greatest majority of people."[16] Since then, party documents and leaders' speeches have explicitly affirmed the role of the private economy in promoting "the fundamental interests of the greatest majority of people" and acknowledged private entrepreneurs as an advanced social productive force.

The CPC has further opened its doors to the private sector by providing educational programs for private entrepreneurs through the Party School system. In the 1990s, the Central and local party schools began to offer special classes and higher education programs in management, finance, law, and philosophy, designed to cater to people in the private economic sector.[17] Although the Central Party School stopped providing such courses in 2008 in order to focus on training party-state officials, the local party schools continue to function as direct channels for the CPC to provide education and training programs for private business owners.[18] Private entrepreneurs are reported to choose to study these subjects at the party schools in order to gain better understanding of party policies and build connections with party-state officials.[19]

Adaptive Methods of Party Control

The party-state needed to rely more and more on the private sector for its contribution to gross value added, tax revenue, and employment, so much so that Minxin Pei could point in 2006 to "the significant decline of the state's role in the economy."[20] Certainly, the size of the state-owned sector decreased while the private sector grew. But this does not necessarily mean that "the state's control ... has greatly eroded as a direct result of its declining presence in the economy," as Pei has suggested.[21] Private business owners still have to rely on the state for loans, policy interpretation, public resources such as land, and its exclusive authority to issue licenses and implement regulations. Research reveals a significant

---

[16] Zemin Jiang, "*Zai xinde lishi tiaojian xia women dang ruhe zuodao 'sange daibiao'*" [How can the CCP achieve the "Three Represents" under new historical circumstances], *Dang de wenxian* [Literature of the Chinese Communist Party] 3 (2001): 3–5.

[17] Minglu Chen, *Tiger Girls: Women and Enterprise in the People's Republic of China* (New York: Routledge, 2011).

[18] "*Zhonggong Zhongyang bangong ting yifa 'Guanyu jiaqiang xin shidai minying jingji tongzhan gongzuo de yijian'*" [CCP Central Office issued "Opinions on enhancing United Front work on private economy in the new era"], www.mee.gov.cn (2009), www.mee.gov.cn/zcwj/zyygwj/202009/t20200917_798796.shtml.

[19] "*Qiyejia dangxiao gangke cheng xin shishang*" [It has become a new trend for private entrepreneurs to take courses in party schools], sina.com.cn (2009), http://style.sina.com.cn/news/2009-11-17/100751424.shtml.

[20] Pei, *China's Trapped Transition*, 2.   [21] Pei, *China's Trapped Transition*, 3.

increase in private businesses' need to connect with the national government over the past twenty years to navigate "a politically uncertain environment" and to build "robust connections to minimize political hazards."[22] The party exercises power over the private sector through its ongoing supervision, training, and regulation of business. After nearly four decades of economic reform, the party-state's control over the private sector has not weakened, although the forms the control takes have adapted under the changing circumstances.

Business Associations

Since the 1990s, the CPC has shifted from a central command system by which the party-state directly ordered and dominated the economy to a system of state corporatism. Under state corporatism, various associations emerged to ensure the party's oversight of the business sector – despite being officially described as "nongovernmental."[23] These associations include the All-China Federation of Industry and Commerce (ACFIC), the Private Enterprises Association (PEA), and the Self-Employed Laborers Association (SELA), as well as different business chambers affiliated with the ACFIC. All have hierarchical structures corresponding to China's territorial administrative jurisdictions, ranging from the national to subnational. Despite their "nongovernmental" status, these associations are established often on the initiative of the party-state at various levels. The party-state effectively controls these associations through appointing their officers, allocating budgets, and paying staff salaries.

The development of the ACFIC exemplifies how the party-state's control over business has evolved to adapt to changing socioeconomic conditions. The CPC established the ACFIC in 1953 as a successor to the pre-1949 chambers of commerce. Run under the aegis of the party's United Front Department, it sought to obtain support from the business sector for the party, which then moved to put private businesses under state control.[24] At the height of socialization, during which private enterprises, capital, and equipment were absorbed by the state, it stopped functioning, only resuming its work in 1979. In the early years of economic reform and

---

[22] Yuhua Wang, "Beyond Local Protectionism: China's State-Business Relations in the Last Two Decades," *The China Quarterly* 226 (2016): 319–341, 320.

[23] Jonathan Unger and Anita Chan, "China, Corporatism, and the East Asian Model," *The Australian Journal of Chinese Affairs* 33 (1995): 29–53; Jonathan Unger, "'Bridges': Private Business, the Chinese Government and the Rise of New Associations," *The China Quarterly* 147 (1996): 795–819.

[24] Gerry Groot, *Managing Transitions: The Chinese Communist Party, United Front Work, Corporatism, and Hegemony* (New York: Routledge, 2003).

opening, the ACFIC recruited members from businesses of all sorts, including the state sector. But over the course of the 1990s, it increasingly prioritized the private sector, until 1997, when it formally excluded the state-owned sector from membership. The changing composition of the ACFIC leadership also reflects the increasing significance of the private sector. Private sector entrepreneurs only started to serve as leaders of the ACFIC in 1993. Since the CPC officially opened its door to the private sector in the early 2000s, private sector entrepreneurs have dominated ACFIC leadership positions.[25] The increased number of private sector entrepreneurs in the ACFIC's membership and leadership, however, has not led it to develop into an autonomous business organization. Instead, Chen and Huang's research reveals that despite changes the ACFIC still functions as a United Front organ to garner business support and remains a key tool of the party-state's economic governance.[26] It reports directly to the CPC's United Front Department, and its administrative staff are civil servants on the party-state's payroll. At subnational levels, the ACFIC often shares offices with local party-state departments. A major part of its daily operation is to offer workshops and training sessions to propagate party ideology promote party policies on the private sector among private entrepreneurs.

Nevitt's examination of the Self-Employed Laborers' Association of Tianjin Municipality reveals that local government appointed its leadership and its staff were civil servants.[27] A significant part of the association's budget comes directly from the local state. Consequently, its institutional loyalty lies with the party-state. Likewise, Kenneth W. Foster's 2002 research on business associations in Yantai City, Shandong Province, reinforces this argument.[28] Instead of being the site of business autonomy, the associations he studied were directly established by the party-state. They were located within the office buildings of local party-state agencies, which provided these associations with financial and administrative assistance, so that they essentially functioned as "appendages" of local party-state agencies. All the evidence argues against the conclusion that the private sector's rise has weakened the communist party-state's control over society or the economy. By removing the possibility of independent business associations that might

---

[25] Minglu Chen and Donya Huang, "The Institutional Origin of Private Entrepreneurs' Policy Influence in China: An Analysis of the All-China Federation of Industry and Commerce," *Journal of Chinese Governance* 4(3) (2019): 267–291.
[26] Chen and Huang, "The Institutional Origin of Private Entrepreneurs' Policy Influence."
[27] Christopher Earl Nevitt, "Private Business Associations in China: Evidence of Civil Society or Local State Power?" *The China Journal* 36 (1996): 25–43.
[28] Kenneth W. Foster, "Embedded within State Agencies: Business Associations in Yantai," *The China Journal* 47 (2002): 41–65.

challenge party policies or rule, and both creating an oversight mechanism and fostering dependency of the private sector on the party-state, the party actively strengthens its hold over what otherwise might be more independent actors.

People's Congresses, People's Political Consultative Conferences, Minor Political Parties

In the post-reform era the party-state has used two formal institutions as important channels for inclusion and co-option: the People's Congresses and the People's Political Consultative Conferences. The People's Congresses function as China's legislatures and the People's Political Consultative Conferences as advisory bodies. Together with the CPC and the government, they are referred to as "the four sets of leadership" (*si tao banzi*) in Chinese politics. Like the party and the government, the People's Congresses and the People's Political Consultative Conferences operate within a hierarchical system that recognizes jurisdictions ranging from the national to the township levels. Thus the National People's Congress is the highest, national-level version of the legislatures at provincial and lower levels, and the Chinese People's Political Consultative Congress is the highest, national-level advisory body. On paper, the People's Congress deputies are elected to represent different constituents and groups within the population (such as territorial administrative jurisdictions, workers, and rural residents). Members of the People's Political Consultative Conferences are nominated by their affiliated sectors (the minor political parties, the Federation of Industry and Commerce, religious groups, and the Women's Federation, for example) to include key elite groups such as business owners. In practice, the CPC controls both institutions by overseeing nominations.[29] By inviting the participation of private entrepreneurs to be members of these bodies and allowing them official channels for their otherwise potentially disruptive requests and dissenting opinions, the CPC is able to co-opt them as putative partners in governance. For example, in both the People's Congress and People's Political Consultative Conference of Taiyuan City in Shanxi Province, private entrepreneurs occupied about a quarter of the seats (24 percent in the congress and 28 in the consultative conference) in 2014, which makes the private sector the second most represented category apart from party-state officials and leaders of mass

---

[29] Chuanmin Chen, "Getting Their Voices Heard: Strategies of China's Provincial People's Congress Deputies to Influence Policies," *The China Journal* 82 (2019): 46–70; Xiaojun Yan, "Regime Inclusion and the Resilience of Authoritarianism: The Local People's Political Consultative Conference in Post-Mao Chinese Politics," *The China Journal* 66 (2011): 53–75.

organizations such as the Women's Federation, trade unions, and the Communist Youth League.[30] These organizations are constitutionally independent but in practice are state-led and form an essential part of the party's mass line.

While the "Three Represents" provided the Communist Party with the ideological rationale for admitting private entrepreneurs, research suggests that, in practice, it has not inspired many business owners to seek CPC membership proactively.[31] Instead, the "Three Represents" acknowledge the existing reality – that many private entrepreneurs were already CPC members,[32] many being previous government officials or managers of state-owned enterprises who quit their jobs to "jump into the sea" and found their own businesses in the 1990s.[33] Despite the common assumption that CPC membership is a crucial political asset of China's business owners, recent research has revealed that the party has increasingly become an "old boys' club."[34] Men who were already CPC members before the establishment of their enterprises benefit more from their party membership than men who are late-joiners (those who joined the CPC after the start of their business activities) and party outsiders. On the other hand, women's business successes have not been contingent upon CPC membership.

While CPC membership itself might have lost its appeal among some business owners in the post-reform era as it is no longer the key to prestige and opportunities,[35] the private sector's membership in minor political parties[36] has been picking up in contemporary China. Research reveals

---

[30] Minglu Chen, "Local Governance: The Roles of the People's Congresses and the People's Political Consultative Conferences," in *Handbook of the Politics of China*, ed. D. S. G. Goodman (Cheltenham: Edward Elgar, 2015), 104–117.

[31] Chen, *Tiger Girls*.

[32] Dickson, *Red Capitalists in China*; Björn Alpermann, "'Wrapped Up in Cotton Wool': Political Integration of Private Entrepreneurs in Rural China," *The China Journal* 56 (2006): 33–61.

[33] "Catchphrases Etched in History," *China Daily* (2008), www.chinadaily.com.cn/30years/2008-12/18/content_7316538.htm.

[34] Minglu Chen, Benjamin Goldsmith, and Shaun Ratcliff, "Chinese Entrepreneurs, the Party-State, and Gender: Women Succeed in Business without the CCP," *Journal of East Asian Studies* 3 (2022): 391–409.

[35] Bruce J. Dickson and Maria Rost Rublee, "Membership Has Its Privileges: The Socioeconomic Characteristics of Communist Party Members in Urban China," *Comparative Political Studies* 33(1) (2000): 87–112.

[36] Apart from the CPC, there are eight minor political parties in China's political system: the China Democratic League (CDL), the China Association of Promoting Democracy (CAPD), the China Democratic Construction Association (CDCA), the Revolutionary Committee of the Chinese Kuomintang (RCCK), the Chinese Peasants' and Workers' Democratic Party (CPWDP), the Jiusan Society (JS), the China Zhi Gong Party (CZGP), and the Taiwan Democratic Self-Government League (TDWGL). These minor political parties had their origins in pre-1949 China, and the CPC courted their

that private entrepreneurs are seeking membership in the minor political parties as a pathway to the People's Political Consultative Conferences.[37] In a People's Political Consultative Conference in a northern provincial capital, for example, about 30 percent of all members are affiliated with one of the minor political parties. Among its private sector entrepreneur members, nearly 40 percent are members of minor parties.[38]

Theoretically, the relationship of the minor political parties with the CPC is one of "long-term coexistence and mutual supervision (*changqi gongcun, huxiang jiandu*)." But in reality, the minor parties work under the leadership of the CPC and form an important part of the CPC's United Front.[39] Thus membership serves as another means of CPC control. The party-state oversees the minor parties' nomination to the People's Political Consultative Conferences, as well as appointing staff and allocating their budgets. For instance, the annual budget report released by the China Association for Promoting Democracy's Sichuan Committee in 2021 reveals that it received an annual grant of 8 million RMB from the Sichuan provincial government.[40] The China Democratic League in Hubei reported an annual budget of 9.7 million RMB from the Hubei provincial government.[41] Evidently the minor political parties rely almost entirely on government transfers for their daily expenditures. In 2005, the China Democratic Construction Association (CDCA) in Hainan proposed through the provincial People's Political Consultative Conference that the provincial government provide more funding to the committee of the minor political parties.[42] The proposal pointed out that the provincial CPC Committee's Organization Department received an annual funding

support for the Communist revolution. Post-1949, they remained as important parts of the CPC's United Front.

[37] Chen, *Tiger Girls*.

[38] Minglu Chen, "From Economic Elites to Political Elites: Private Entrepreneurs in the People's Political Consultative Conference," *Journal of Contemporary China* 24(94) (2015): 613–627.

[39] "*Zhongguo Gongchan Dang tong minzhu dangpai hezuo de jiben fangzhen*" [Basic guidelines on the Chinese Communist Party's cooperation with democratic parties], Chinese Peasants and Workers Democratic Party (2004), www.ngd.org.cn/jzlmbf/dclm/blcqjycj/zsjs/zcxx/1481.htm.

[40] "*Zhongguo Minzhu Cujin Hui Sichuan sheng weiyuan hui 2021 nian bumen yusuan bianzhi shuoming*" [Explanations on the China Association of Promoting Democracy's Sichuan committee's budget planning], Sichuan Provincial Finance Department (2021), http://czt.sc.gov.cn/sczt/c106345/2021/3/14/f291dc09ddb0472c829211964f1ffbe4.shtml.

[41] "*Zhongguo Minzhu Tongmeng Hubei Sheng Weiyuan Hui 2019 nian yusuan gongkai*" [Publication on the Hubei Province Committee of China Democratic League 2019 Budget], Hubei Government (2019), www.hubei.gov.cn/xxgk/czyjs/qt/mmhb/201902/t20190215_1381555.shtml.

[42] "*Guanyu zengjia minzhu dangpai caizheng bokuan de jianyi*" [Suggestions on increasing financial allocation for democratic parties], Hainan Government (2006), www.hainan.gov.cn/zxtadata-1593.html.

of 1.3 million RMB to provide training to Communist Party officials, while all the minor political party committees combined received 30,000 RMB through the CPC Committee's United Front Work Department for the same item. The proposal explained in detail how the lack of government funding made it hard for the minor political party committees to provide training to their officials, pay for business and field research trips, and cover expenses such as senior officials' housing costs and telephone bills.

The party expects, and gets, value for money. Once private sector entrepreneurs are recruited into the People's Congresses, the People's Political Consultative Conferences, and the minor political parties, they are expected to participate in activities organized by the assemblies and parties, among which the most significant is propagation and promotion of CPC ideology and policies. For example, the website of the Hubei CDCA has a section on "Important News," which provides a list of key topics, including CPC policies, news from the CPC congress annual meetings, and President Xi Jinping's speeches.[43] Members are expected to study Communist Party history and policies through frequent participation in workshops, training sessions, reading groups, speech contests, and field trips. The Hubei CDCA website reports an entrepreneur member hosting the local CDCA committee's group studying the communiqué of the Nineteenth CPC Central Committee's Sixth Plenum at his company.

Communist Party Branches

In 2012, the CPC moved to strengthen its presence in the private sector by establishing Party cells within nonstate enterprises, regardless of their size.[44] Party authorities at county level and above were required to establish Nonstate Economic Organizations and Social Organizations Working Committees (*fei gongyouzhi jingji zuzhi yu shehui zuzhi gongzuo weiyuanhui*) in charge of party building in the private sector and to assign professional staff to facilitate the process. Research shows that by the end of 2012, nearly all private enterprises in Anhui Province had established party organizations.[45]

An excellent example of how the party-building campaign was carried out is the establishment of a CPC committee in Xiaomi Corporation, China's

---

[43] See the official website of the China Democratic Construction Association Hubei Committee: www.hbmj.gov.cn/c/mjyw.html.
[44] Xiaojun Yan and Jie Huang, "Navigating Unknown Waters: The Chinese Communist Party's New Presence in the Private Sector," *The China Review* 17(2) (2017): 37–63.
[45] Yan and Huang, "Navigating Unknown Waters."

largest manufacturer of smartphones. In a media interview, an administrator of the company commented that the establishment of the CPC committee was the result of "care and attention" (*guanxin*) from the party. "[Since 2014], Xiaomi has been repeatedly visited by officials from the Organizational Department and the Social Work Commission of the CPC Beijing Committee, as well as the CPC Haidian District Committee Haidian Industrial Park Working Committee. They investigated the situation of party building in Xiaomi and suggested that a Communist Party committee be established."[46] Many senior officials, including the deputy secretary-general of the Beijing CPC Committee and the deputy director of the Beijing CPC Committee Organization Department attended the inauguration of the committee at Xiaomi. Clearly, the party adopted a top-down mobilization approach here to realize its goal of infiltrating and controlling the private sector. Presumably, repeated visits from senior party officials had put pressure on the company's management to establish such a committee.

Yan and Huang report that private entrepreneurs were concerned that a Communist Party presence within their enterprises would weaken their control over their own businesses. The Communist Party responded by recruiting these business owners into formal institutions offering some form of empowerment, such as the Communist Party itself, and the People's Congresses and People's Political Consultative Conferences, as well as the business associations previously mentioned. The author's own research shows that the party-state also gives out awards and honorary titles to private entrepreneurs, which convey status, prestige, and privileges, as well as perhaps a degree of political protection from regulation or punishment.[47] Some business owners, however, have come up with their own strategies for coping with the party's demands for representation within their enterprises. One private entrepreneur revealed in an interview that he had appointed his driver as the secretary of the Communist Party branch in his company. "This ensures my authority within the company," he explained.[48]

Accepting Authoritarianism

It is safe to say that the party's efforts to co-opt private business owners and insinuate itself into the private business sector have been worthwhile investments of time and resources, as they reap, with some exceptions, the political loyalty of the business class. Research over various periods has revealed that China's private businesses are not promoters of political

---

[46] "*Xiaomi you le 'dangwei shuji'*" [Xiaomi has got a "Party secretary"], sina.com.cn (2015), https://business.sohu.com/20150703/n416128939.shtml.
[47] Chen, "From Economic Elites to Political Elites."
[48] Private interview, July 27, 2009.

change.⁴⁹ Instead, they generally support the CPC's rule and the status quo. The business class overwhelmingly believes that the CPC's reforms have improved the policy environment for the private sector and that existing political institutions are able to represent their interests. Hong Kong-based political scientist Kellee S. Tsai's 2007 research shows that being politically embedded within the party-state enhances private entrepreneurs' social and political status and can translate into economic benefits: entrepreneurs with institutional connections find it easier to obtain loans and investment from both public and private sources.⁵⁰ In addition, as China's economy is not entirely free-market, connections with the party-state help private entrepreneurs gain access to market information, as well as receive favorable treatment from governmental departments and/or officials in policy implementation.⁵¹ All these benefits incentivize private business owners to seek institutional connections with the party-state.⁵²

While the benefits from such institutional connections might largely explain the support given to the regime by business owners, there are other plausible reasons too. Research done by Jie Chen and Bruce Dickson reveals that being embedded in the CPC or other institutions including business associations is positively correlated to private entrepreneurs' political loyalty.⁵³ But they argue that these business owners' own understanding of liberal democratic values plays a bigger role in determining their regime support or the lack thereof. It is unsurprising that democratic values reduce support for an undemocratic regime: The more private entrepreneurs are in favor of democratic principles, the less likely they are to support the current system.⁵⁴

Tsai's 2007 study of Chinese business owners in twelve provinces reveals a shared prodemocracy attitude among private entrepreneurs. In general, they had a highly positive impression of the term "democracy," believing that democracy had a positive effect on national economic development and should not be associated with policy inconsistency. Notably, a majority of the private entrepreneurs surveyed in the research agreed that, despite having its problems, democracy is better than other forms of government.⁵⁵

---

[49] Tsai, *Capitalism without Democracy*; Chen and Dickson, *Allies of the State*; Jie Chen and Bruce Dickson, "Allies of the State: Democratic Support and Regime Support among China's Private Entrepreneurs," *The China Quarterly* 196 (2008): 780–804; Teresa Wright, *Accepting Authoritarianism: State–Society Relations in China's Reform Era* (Redwood City, CA: Stanford University Press, 2010).
[50] Tsai, *Capitalism without Democracy*.
[51] Chen, "From Economic Elites to Political Elites."
[52] Wright, *Accepting Authoritarianism*.
[53] Chen and Dickson, "Allies of the State"; Chen and Dickson, *Allies of the State*.
[54] Chen and Dickson, *Allies of the State*.
[55] Tsai, *Capitalism without Democracy*.

Chen and Dickson found that the overwhelming majority of the private entrepreneurs surveyed in 2006–2007 in five coastal provinces considered it was desirable to hold competitive elections to choose key leaders of the government at various levels.[56] But both studies argued that despite holding such beliefs, the business class was unlikely to challenge the CPC's rule or promote democratic change. This is in part because Chinese private entrepreneurs' understanding of the concept of democracy is considerably different from the commonly accepted notions in the West of multiparty competition, rule of law, and individual rights.

This helps make sense of the seeming paradox that on the one hand private entrepreneurs favor democracy and democratic values, and on the other hand they so easily accept authoritarian rule. Tsai points out that the party-state leadership often describes "democracy" in politically desirable terms, even if their conception of the term is neither based on liberal democratic principles nor reflected in their own practices. And such conceptualization has been internalized by the business owners.[57] When asked how they understood the exercise of democratic rights, those business owners gave the example of participants in meetings voting by raising their hands, which is the model used in the party and People's Congresses. Chen and Dickson's survey produced similar results.[58] The respondents associated competitive elections with the party-state's practice of holding single-candidate elections for important leadership positions. In other words, the "democracy" envisaged by China's private sector entrepreneurs is not necessarily at odds with the one-party system.

Similarly, members of the Chinese middle class in general demonstrate a high degree of "rights consciousness," strongly supporting the protection of individual rights to work, education, free information, privacy, and travel.[59] But their support for political freedoms such as the rights to demonstrate and organize is much less strong. In situations where political freedom could impede social order and stability, private entrepreneurs surveyed tended to prioritize the latter.[60] Again, this is likely due to how individual rights have been conceptualized by the communist party-state. The policies of the PRC have long emphasized social order and stability while subordinating individual rights and freedoms to state, social, and collective interests.[61] The internalized belief in the relative

---

[56] Chen and Dickson, *Allies of the State*.   [57] Tsai, *Capitalism without Democracy*, 95.
[58] Chen and Dickson, *Allies of the State*.
[59] Jie Chen and Chunlong Lu, "Democratization and the Middle Class in China: The Middle Class's Attitudes toward Democracy," *Political Research Quarterly* 64(3) (2011): 705–719.
[60] Chen and Dickson, *Allies of the State*.
[61] Liantai Liu, "*Woguo Xianfa wenben zhong zuowei renquan xianzhi liyou de sige liyi fanchou zhi guanxi*" [The relationship between the four types of interests used to restrict human rights in China's constitution], *Falü kexue* [Science of Law] 4 (2006): 37–44.

importance of social order over that of individual rights could well prompt private entrepreneurs to support authoritarian rule.[62]

Despite their political participation and rights consciousness, China's private entrepreneurs are more concerned with day-to-day issues of running their business. When institutional affiliations do not help and democratic values are not the concern, private entrepreneurs have informal strategies to navigate the system and make it work for them. They rely on patron–client connections with party-state officials, or *guanxi*.

Patron–client relationships and favoritism are by no means specific to China. But as Mayfair Yang points out, as post-reform Chinese society changes so quickly, the practice of *guanxi* is becoming more complex too.[63] In the 1990s, as Wank reports, private entrepreneurs sometimes forged personal ties with officials through kinship, leaning on shared experiences in childhood or youth, or simply providing gifts to officials.[64] Such practices continue, but over the past two and a half decades, private entrepreneurs have found new ways to approach and connect with party-state officials, such as employing incumbent or retired officials as paid employees or advisers.[65] These officials bring their connections and contacts to the enterprises. More recently, business owners have been able to build connections with officials by attending China's elite business schools such as the independent Cheung Kong Graduate School of Business in Beijing and the China Europe International Business School in Shanghai, where senior political leaders were also invited to study until 2014.[66] Recent research found that informal connections between business owners and political leaders can also be formed through institutional channels.[67] When official meetings and inspection trips bring the two groups together, private entrepreneurs can utilize these ties to lobby directly to government officials.

Although the forms of clientelist connections and the ways to forge them have evolved alongside larger socioeconomic changes, their nature

---

[62] David L. Wank, "Private Business, Bureaucracy, and Political Alliance in a Chinese City," *The Australian Journal of Chinese Affairs* 33 (1995): 55–71.
[63] Mayfair Mei-hui Yang, "The Resilience of *Guanxi* and Its New Deployment: A Critique of Some New *Guanxi* Scholarship," *The China Quarterly* 170 (2002): 459–476.
[64] David L. Wank, "The Institutional Process of Market Clientelism: Guanxi and Private Business in a South China City," *The China Quarterly* 147 (1996): 820–838.
[65] Chen, *Tiger Girls*.
[66] "*Guanyuan xiandu ling yi EMBA tuixue chao, ming xiao zhaosheng ruijian 4 cheng*" [The ban on officials taking training programs triggers a wave of withdrawals from EMBA courses: Privileged universities lose 40 percent of their recruits], people.com.cn (2015), http://finance.people.com.cn/n/2015/0319/c1004-26715293.html.
[67] Jun Li and Jing Vivian Zhan, "Environmental Clientelism: How Chinese Private Enterprises Lobby under Environmental Crackdowns," *The China Quarterly* 255 (2023): 679–696.

remains the same. Through establishing and maintaining personal connections with the powerful, private entrepreneurs are able to expand their business and create wealth for themselves. In other words, they need to depend on party-state officials in exchange for business opportunities. So long as private entrepreneurs can benefit from the clientelist connections, they can make the system work for them. Like other ways in which the party connects with the business community, clientelism tends to enforce the party's power over it.

Private Entrepreneurs' Interest Expression and Policy Influence

The CPC-led regime is stable because, among other things, it has successfully turned the potentially hostile force of private business owners into its ally. Yet the party-state does not solely rely on top-down control. It also needs to accommodate the policy requests and other interests of key groups such as private entrepreneurs. As a group, private entrepreneurs are especially enthusiastic to participate in assemblies and organizations that allow them to offer opinions and advice on policymaking. A survey with cotton sector entrepreneurs in 2002–2004 reveals that 80 percent of them agreed with the statement that "rich people should have more political influence" than the poor.[68] Without any formal or informal mechanisms to have their demands met, private entrepreneurs could turn against the party-state.

Authoritarianism does not automatically meet certain functional requirements of stable governance, one of which is the ability to allow key groups in the society the opportunity to have their interests represented, registered, and dealt with. In recent years, business owners appear to have been able to collectively represent their policy interest and lobby for them.[69] One recent study conceptualizes China's private entrepreneurs as a "strategic group," in other words one that has developed long-term strategies to influence policymaking to safeguard its

[68] Alpermann, "Wrapped Up in Cotton Wool."
[69] Chen, "Local Governance"; Chen, "From Economic Elites to Political Elites"; Gunter Schubert and Thomas Heberer, "Private Entrepreneurs as a 'Strategic Group' in the Chinese Polity," *China Review* 17(2) (2017): 95–122; Thomas Heberer and Gunter Schubert, "Weapons of the Rich: Strategic Behavior and Collective Action of Private Entrepreneurs in China," *Modern China* 45(5) (2019): 471–503; Yingying Ji, "Emerging State–Business Contention in China: Collective Action of a Business Association and China's Fragmented Governance Structure," *China Information* 32(3) (2018): 463–484; Chen and Huang, "The Institutional Origin of Private Entrepreneurs' Policy Influence"; Dongya Huang and Minglu Chen, "Business Lobbying within the Party-State: Embedding Lobbying and Political Co-optation in China," *The China Journal* 83 (2020): 105–128.

interests.[70] Gunter Schubert and Thomas Heberer argue that it is the party-state's control over economic resources that brings these people together.[71] Exposed to the institutional constraints of the Chinese system, their shared discontent has helped to forge a common identity and willingness to act together to voice their demands.

In China's political system, while People's Congresses, People's Political Consultative Conferences, and business associations provide forums for voicing sectional interests, the nature of authoritarian rule limits their role as representative institutions. The previous sections have described how the party-state has used these institutions and organizations as a new means of extending its control over business. At the same time, through their involvement in these formal institutions, private entrepreneurs may contribute both to the creation of climates of opinion on various issues and to incremental change in policies.

In her 2015 article, the author examines the roles of the People's Congresses and People's Political Consultative Conferences in the Chinese political system and argues that at subnational levels, the local congresses are increasingly playing a genuine supervisory role and the consultative conferences an effective advisory role.[72] This is seen in local People's Congresses rejecting government work reports and appointment nominations and the People's Political Consultative Conferences actively soliciting suggestions from the public and setting up mechanisms to ensure that their policy proposals are taken seriously by the party-state. In general, as delegates to the two bodies, private entrepreneurs are able to submit proposals, express opinions, and provide advice on the party-state's work that seek to advance their interests as a group.[73]

Schubert and Heberer describe business associations as "an important platform ... that provides a useful complement to the individualistic network strategies employed by private entrepreneurs."[74] Among other things, they organize meetings between government departments and banks with entrepreneurs to negotiate credit arrangements and communicate their members' policy concerns and suggestions to the government at different levels. But the authors question whether such actions have an actual impact on decision-making. Yingying Ji confirms that business associations can affect local governments' decision-making, through

---

[70] Schubert and Heberer, "Private Entrepreneurs as a 'Strategic Group'"; Heberer and Schubert, "Weapons of the Rich."
[71] Schubert and Heberer, "Private Entrepreneurs as a 'Strategic Group.'"
[72] Chen, "Local Governance." [73] Chen, "From Economic Elites to Political Elites."
[74] Schubert and Heberer, "Private Entrepreneurs as a 'Strategic Group,'" 109.

organized collective activism such as appealing to higher-level governments and attracting media attention from outside the local jurisdiction.[75]

Business associations may also act as institutionalized channels for expressing the interests of private entrepreneurs and their opinions on policy by submitting proposals to the People's Political Consultative Conferences. Once the consultative conferences forward these proposals to relevant government departments, the departments are required to investigate and respond to the issues raised. At both national and local levels, the consultative conferences establish channels for government departments and vested interests to communicate with each other.[76] This in turn enables direct interaction and negotiation between business owners and policymakers who may be seeking more economic resources to be allocated to the sector as well as changes in existing laws and policies.

The All-China Federation of Industry and Commerce plays an essential role in this process, by acting as a bridge between its affiliated business associations and the People's Political Consultative Conferences.[77] The ACFIC and the subnational Federations of Industry and Commerce are an important constituency of the People's Political Consultative Conferences, and they sit above various business associations at national and subnational levels. Each year, the ACFIC submits collective proposals in the names of its affiliated business associations to the People's Political Consultative Conference. These proposals may concern the interests of the overall private economic sector, particular industries, or specific business association or enterprises. Research shows that between 2009 and 2016, at the national level, nearly 20 percent of the ACFIC's collective proposals resulted in new policies or policy changes.[78]

Despite its increasing influence, the business class does not pose a challenge to the CPC's rule. Firstly, their policy inputs work within the party-state's opinion synthesis system, with the People's Congresses, the People's Political Consultative Conferences, and business associations functioning as institutions of inclusion. Secondly, when making policy proposals, business owners understand that they need to carefully toe the "party line" to make suggestions that are not controversial and do not challenge the party-state rule. This means they need to avoid trouble while ensuring positive feedback from policymakers that in many cases has eventually led to policy change. Instead of carving out an autonomous space, Chinese private entrepreneurs still rely upon the party-state to voice and advance their interests.

---

[75] Ji, "Emerging State–Business Contention in China."
[76] Chen, "Local Governance"; Huang and Chen, "Business Lobbying within the Party-State."
[77] Huang and Chen, "Business Lobbying within the Party-State."
[78] Huang and Chen, "Business Lobbying within the Party-State."

Conclusion

Returning to the question posed at the beginning of this chapter, how do we understand the lack of correlation between economic development and a push for democratic change in China? In other words, why does the rising entrepreneurial class defy the predictions of conventional theories that rising wealth leads to greater demands for democratization? This chapter argues that this is due to the adaptive nature of the party-state and its complex, co-optive relationship with the private economic sector.

The communist party-state is not a rigid system solely reliant on coercion to stay in power. It has a long tradition of and institutionalized means for accommodating different interests. In adjusting to the changing socioeconomic conditions brought about by the introduction of economic reform and the rise of the private economy, the communist party-state has actively reformed and updated its policy orientation, formal institutions, and official ideology so as to best tap into the human and material resources of the private sector. By recruiting business owners into the membership of the Communist Party, welcoming them into the People's Congresses, the People's Political Consultative Conferences, the eight minor political parties, and various business associations, it binds their interests to its own. Its control over the sector has been further strengthened by the move in 2012 to require private enterprises to host their own party branches.

Enfolded within the system, private entrepreneurs do not feel the need to challenge one-party rule. While sympathetic to democratic values and individual rights, this group generally prefers social order over individual liberty. And they can voice their individual or collective interests and demand policy changes through informal and formal channels. The party's strength and resilience here lie in its ability to convince such groups as private entrepreneurs to accept and even support authoritarianism, because they are able to make the system work for themselves.

This is not to argue that the party refrains from using coercive forces in its rule over the private sector, when it perceives private interests to be undermining state interests and challenging the authority of the party itself. In 2020, Jack Ma, founder of Alibaba, openly criticized China's banks for behaving like "pawn shops," and China's financial regulators for being obsessed with minimizing risks, so as to limit innovation.[79] This led him to disappear from public view for more than a year and his Ant

---

[79] Karen Maley, "Lessons for Australia in Jack Ma's Fall from Grace," *Financial Review* (2021), www.afr.com/companies/financial-services/lessons-for-australia-in-jack-ma-s-fall-from-grace-20210107-p56sc5.

Group being fined US$2.78 billion. In 2022, Didi Chuxing, China's biggest ride-hailing company, was fined US$1.2 billion and forced to delist from the New York Stock Exchange for violating several national cybersecurity laws.[80] Such high-profile crackdowns have led some scholars to conceptualize China's current economic model as "party-state capitalism," where "the Party-state's political survival trumps developmental goals."[81]

However, this does not terminate the state–business alliance. Facing economic slowdown and declining confidence of private business owners, in July 2023, the CPC Central Committee reiterated the significance of the private sector and offered a thirty-one-point plan to create a favorable environment for private enterprises and build a "close and clean state–business relationship."[82] Although the impact of this national initiative is yet unclear, at subnational levels, as long as the private sector remains local governments' major source of revenues, the alliance between the local governments and private enterprises will stay strong.

---

[80] Julie Zhu, Yingzhi Yang, and Kane Wu, "China Fines Didi $1.2bln but Outlook Clouded by App Relaunch Uncertainty," *Reuters* (2022), www.reuters.com/technology/china-fines-didi-global-12-bln-violating-data-security-laws-2022-07-21/.

[81] Margaret Pearson, Meg Rithmire, and Kellee S. Tsai, "Party-State Capitalism in China," *Current History* 120 (2021): 207–213.

[82] "*Zhonggong Zhongyang Guowu Yuan guanyu cujin minying jingji fazhan zhuangda de yijian*" [Opinions of CPC Central Committee and the State Council on developing and strengthening the private economy], www.gov.cn (2023), www.gov.cn/zhengce/202307/content_6893055.htm.

9 China's Adaptive State Capitalism and Its International Sources

Wendy Leutert and Sarah Eaton

Once viewed as a declining vestige of the planned economy era, Chinese state-owned enterprises (SOEs) today are bigger, stronger, and more active abroad than ever before. SOEs contribute an estimated one-quarter of national GDP in the world's second largest economy.[1] They channel investment to critical industries in China, providing over three-quarters of domestic investment in infrastructure and half the investment in coal and oil.[2] They dominate Chinese equity markets, accounting for approximately 40 percent of total market capitalization and 50 percent of company revenues for the Shanghai and Shenzhen stock exchanges.[3] And Chinese SOEs themselves are now among the largest firms by revenue globally, with ninety-seven SOEs from mainland China and Hong Kong ranking on the 2023 Fortune Global 500 list.[4]

However, Chinese SOE performance continues to lag far behind that of private firms. State firms frequently act as "asset maximizers" rather than "profit maximizers."[5] Although SOEs account for nearly a third of China's industrial assets, they contribute less than a fifth of total industrial profits. Return on assets, a standard measure of how efficiently a company generates profits from its assets, was only 3.0 percent for SOEs compared with 6.7 percent for private firms in China as of

---

[1] For estimates of SOEs' contribution to China's GDP, see Andrew Batson, "The State Never Retreats," *Gavekal Dragonomics* (October 2020) and Chunlin Zhang, "How Much Do State-Owned Enterprises Contribute to China's GDP and Employment?" (Washington, DC: World Bank, 2019).

[2] "Fiscal Monitor – April 2020," Online Annex 3.1. "China: State-Owned Enterprises Remain Key Players," International Monetary Fund (IMF) (April 2020). www.imf.org/en/Publications/FM/Issues/2020/04/06/fiscalmonitor-april-2020#Chapter%203.

[3] See also Daniel H. Rosen, Wendy Leutert, and Shan Guo, *Missing Link: Corporate Governance in China's State Sector* (San Francisco: Asia Society, 2018), 9.

[4] SASAC: "*2023 nian 'Caifu' shijie 500 qiang jiexiao, guozi jianguan xitong 85 jia qiye bang shang youming*" [2023 Fortune Global 500 announces, 85 companies in the state-owned assets supervision system make the list] (August 2, 2023).

[5] Nicholas R. Lardy, *The State Strikes Back: The End of Economic Reform in China?* (Washington, DC: Peterson Institute for International Economics, 2019).

the second quarter of 2020.[6] Approximately one-quarter (by assets) or more than one-third (by number) of Chinese SOEs are loss-making.[7] The debt of SOEs as a percentage of GDP soared to a record high of more than 142 percent in 2020.[8] The large role of SOEs in China's state capitalist model thus entails high economic costs in terms of efficiency and profitability.

Yet the ruling Communist Party of China (CPC), under the leadership of Xi Jinping, remains firmly committed to SOEs because they serve critical functions for the state. State-owned enterprises support stability by providing urban employment and welfare and by maintaining low prices for key inputs. They serve a redistributive function subnationally by channeling investment to develop infrastructure in poorer interior provinces.[9] China's government routinely leverages SOEs to respond to economic, political, and social crises like stock market volatility, protests, and pandemics.[10] In addition, SOEs advance Chinese industrial policy by directing capital to develop targeted technologies and sectors like artificial intelligence and electric vehicles. State-owned enterprises also play a leading role in domestic and international initiatives, such as the Belt and Road Initiative (BRI). In this chapter, we show that a large state-owned economy is both a key and enduring pillar of China's state capitalist model and a critical source of the CPC's enduring power.

In particular, we highlight that international policy inputs and pressures to change have played a surprisingly significant role in how China has governed and restructured SOEs to pursue dual political and economic aims. Chinese policymakers have consistently navigated pressures from abroad while engaging foreign actors and ideas. Beginning in the late 1970s, as China began to overhaul its state sector, policymakers engaged intensively with Japan and the World Bank for ideas, examples, and

---

[6] Rhodium Group and Asia Society Policy Institute, China Dashboard: State-Owned Enterprise Policy Reform (Winter 2021), https://chinadashboard.gist.asiasociety.org/winter-2021/page/state-owned-enterprise.

[7] "Fiscal Monitor – April 2020," Online Annex 3.1. "China: State-Owned Enterprises Remain Key Players," International Monetary Fund (IMF) (April 2020), www.imf.org/en/Publications/FM/Issues/2020/04/06/fiscalmonitor-april-2020#Chapter%203.

[8] Karen Yeung, "China Debt: Highly-Leveraged State Firms Could Threaten 'Efficient Growth,' Private Investment Post-Pandemic," *South China Morning Post* (February 8, 2021).

[9] Andrew Batson, "The State of the State Sector," *Gavekal Dragonomics* (March 2017).

[10] SASAC: "*Guozi wei caiqu youli cuoshi weihu gupiao shichang wending*" [SASAC takes effective measures to safeguard stock market stability] (July 8, 2015); Keith Zhai, "Exclusive: China Prods State Firms to Boost Investment in Crisis-Hit Hong Kong – Sources," *Reuters* (September 12, 2019); SASAC: "*Yangqi zhan yi tujian*" [Illustrated compendium of central SOEs' war against the epidemic] (April 24, 2020).

material assistance. In the 1990s, as China negotiated to join the World Trade Organization, Chinese leaders' concerns about intensified competition with foreign firms motivated renewed efforts to build internationally competitive "national champions" – large, central government-owned enterprises in strategic sectors. American and international legal and financial communities also played a key part in repackaging large industrial Chinese SOEs for public listing in Hong Kong and overseas. Since the 2000s, Chinese policymakers have interacted with Singapore to study its government ownership agency Temasek as they designed a national system to manage state-owned assets and developed corporate governance institutions for SOEs.

This research advances a growing body of scholarship about the significance of international actors and ideas in China's economic transformation during the post-Mao reform era. Such studies include Isabella Weber's 2021 *How China Escaped Shock Therapy: The Market Reform Debate*, which traces how Chinese economists and officials in the 1980s engaged with, embraced, and ultimately rejected ideas from abroad about radical price reform. Julian Gewirtz's 2017 *Unlikely Partners: Chinese Reformers, Western Economists, and the Making of Global China* argued previously that Chinese officials and scholars' interactions with foreign economists, and their travels abroad between 1976 and 1993, catalyzed the country's economic reinvention. Other studies have demonstrated the powerful effects of Sino-Japanese exchanges on Chinese industrial policies and SOE restructuring on the resurgence of large SOEs in China despite market reforms.[11] Most recently, *New Political Economy* published a special section in 2021 on "China and the Transnational Circulation of Developmentalism."[12]

This chapter defines the concept of state capitalism and situates it in the literature on adaptive governance. It examines what we term China's "adaptive state capitalism" through the lens of SOE restructuring. By analyzing the pathways through which Chinese policymakers have engaged with ideas and actors from abroad during the reform era, we identify how international engagement can affect domestic policymaking – and, ultimately, help the CPC retain power.

---

[11] Sebastian Heilmann and Lea Shih, "The Rise of Industrial Policy in China, 1978–2012," Harvard-Yenching Institute Working Paper Series 17(7) (2013); Wendy Leutert, "Sino-Japanese Engagement in the Making of China's National Champions," *New Political Economy* 27(6) (2021): 1–15; Sarah Eaton, *The Advance of the State in Contemporary China: State–Market Relations in the Reform Era* (New York: Cambridge University Press, 2016).

[12] Sarah Eaton and Saori N. Katada, "A Critical Node: The Role of China in the Transnational Circulation of Developmentalist Ideas, Policies and Practices," *New Political Economy* 27(6) (2021): 1–9.

Adaptive State Capitalism

We define state capitalism as an economic system that combines market institutions with a strong form of state guidance exercised, in part, through large SOEs in strategic sectors. As debate continues about whether a new model of CPC-centered state capitalism may be emerging under Xi Jinping,[13] we build on Andrew Batson's definition of state capitalism as "the coexistence of state and private companies and the combination of a market economy with an authoritarian and interventionist government."[14] Although state authorities exercise growing leverage over the management and commercial decision-making of private enterprises in China,[15] we focus here on SOEs. This is because these firms are still the state's most important tool for mobilizing resources and directing economic activity.[16]

The CPC's strategies for guiding the state sector since the late 1970s have been inventive and adaptive. The Chinese authoritarian state has demonstrated a surprising capacity to navigate through formidable challenges. In his seminal 2008 article on policy experimentation and its relation to China's economic rise, Sebastian Heilmann attributes China's successful market transformation to the party-state's "unusual adaptive capacity," made possible by an "institutional structure that, despite ubiquitous uncertainties, enables it to try out alternative approaches to overcome long-standing impediments to economic development, tackle newly emerging challenges, and grasp opportunities when they open up."[17] Investigating the roots of this adaptive capacity, Heilmann and Elizabeth J. Perry identify a distinctive "guerilla policy style" honed in revolutionary CPC base areas during the 1930s.[18] In recent years, debate has emerged

---

[13] Jude Blanchette, "From 'China Inc.' to 'CPC Inc.': A New Paradigm for Chinese State Capitalism," *China Leadership Monitor* (December 1, 2020), www.prcleader.org/blanchette; Wendy Leutert and Sarah Eaton, "Deepening Not Departure: Xi Jinping's Governance of China's State-Owned Economy," *The China Quarterly* 248 (2021): 200–221; Margaret M. Pearson, Meg Rithmire, and Kellee S. Tsai. "China's Party-State Capitalism and International Backlash: From Interdependence to Insecurity," *International Security* 47(2) (2022), 135–176.

[14] Andrew Batson, "Some Facts about China's State Capitalism," in *Chinese State Capitalism: Diagnosis and Prognosis*, ed. Scott Kennedy and Jude Blanchette (Washington, DC: Center for Strategic and International Studies, 2021), 9–14, 9.

[15] Daniel Koss, "Party Building as Institutional Bricolage: Asserting Authority at the Business Frontier," *The China Quarterly* 248 (2021): 222–243; Curtis J. Milhaupt and Wentong Zheng, "Beyond Ownership: State Capitalism and the Chinese Firm," *Georgetown Law Journal* 103 (2014): 665–722.

[16] Yongnian Zheng and Yanjie Huang, *Market in State: The Political Economy of Domination in China* (New York: Cambridge University Press, 2018), 380.

[17] Sebastian Heilmann, "Policy Experimentation in China's Economic Rise," *Studies in Comparative International Development* 43(1) (2008): 1–26, 1.

[18] Sebastian Heilmann and Elizabeth J. Perry, "Embracing Uncertainty: Guerrilla Policy Style and Adaptive Governance in China," in *Mao's Invisible Hand*, ed.

about whether the shift to a "top-level design" approach under Xi Jinping – a more centralized and top-down approach to reform – is constraining China's adaptive capacity.[19]

One perspective on China's SOE reform process portrays it as highly adaptive. Policymakers showed both prudence and creativity by delaying a potentially catastrophic downsizing of the state sector until the economy had grown sufficiently to absorb large-scale unemployment. Only in the late 1990s did Premier Zhu Rongji finally make an ambitious push to privatize smaller and underperforming SOEs, despite social resistance to the state's rollback of its traditional employment and welfare guarantees.[20] As Chen Li writes in *China's Centralized Industrial Order*, institutional adaptation in China's state sector extends back to the late 1950s.[21] He further notes that since the 1990s, "continuous learning, experimentation and adaptation of CPC central bureaucracy ... has not only brought about the rise of China's 'national champions' in finance, but also sustained critical support for the entire 'national team.'" The gradual and experimental approach to SOE reforms from 1978 to 2018 was "typical" of China's approach to reform more generally.[22] "Policy feedback loops" characterized by overlapping – instead of strictly sequencing – policy experimentation and implementation efforts have facilitated adaptive policymaking.[23] This adaptability, in turn, has bolstered the Communist Party's hold on power despite it being a revolutionary party overseeing an increasingly marketized economy.

Another school of thought argues that the state's management of SOEs is instead a prime example of the "limits of developmental autocracy."[24]

Sebastian Heilmann and Elizabeth J. Perry (Cambridge, MA: Harvard University Press, 2011), 1–29.

[19] Anna L. Ahlers and Gunter Schubert, "Nothing New under 'Top-Level Design'? A Review of the Conceptual Literature on Local Policy-Making in China," *Issues & Studies* 58(1) (2022): 1–34; Wen-Hsuan Tsai, Hsin-Hsien Wang, and Ruihua Lin, "Hobbling Big Brother: Top-Level Design and Local Discretion in China's Social Credit System," *The China Journal* 86(1) (2021): 1–20; Xuedong Yang and Jian Yan, "Top-Level Design, Reform Pressures, and Local Adaptations: An Interpretation of the Trajectory of Reform Since the 18th CPC Party Congress," *Journal of Chinese Governance* 3(1) (2018): 25–48.

[20] Barry Naughton, *The Chinese Economy: Adaptation and Growth* (Cambridge, MA: MIT Press, 2018).

[21] Chen Li, *China's Centralized Industrial Order: Industrial Reform and the Rise of Centrally Controlled Big Business* (New York: Routledge, 2014), 146.

[22] Ligang Song, "China's 40 Years of Reform and Development: 1978–2018," in *China's 40 Years of Reform and Development: 1978–2018*, ed. Ross Garnaut, Ligang Song and Cai Fang (Canberra: ANU Press, 2018), 345–374, 345.

[23] Wendy Leutert, "Innovation through Iteration: Policy Feedback Loops in China's Economic Reform," *World Development* 138 (2020): 1–11.

[24] Minxin Pei, *China's Trapped Transition: The Limits of Developmental Autocracy* (Cambridge, MA: Harvard University Press, 2006).

In this view, the greatest beneficiaries of "partial reform" of the state sector are corrupt officials in SOEs and government posts who have amassed illicit fortunes through their connections to protected state-run industries. One such figure is Lai Xiaomin, the disgraced former head of state-owned finance firm China Huarong Asset Management, who was rumored to have a trove of gold bars and a collection of luxury cars among items seized by anticorruption investigators in 2018.[25] Minxin Pei argues that rent-seeking officials like Lai have worked effectively behind the scenes of Chinese economic policy to protect their opportunities for corruption by preventing the opening of lucrative sectors such as finance, telecommunications services, and energy to competition from the private sector.[26] By effectively defending their monopolistic privileges, the argument goes, these powerful insiders impede adaptation.[27] By the closing years of Hu Jintao's tenure as leader, Wu Jinglian, a liberal economist and leading advocate of SOE reform, had grown deeply concerned about stalled SOE reforms and argued in a bold op-ed in *Caijing* that it was the result of "vested interests," namely "state-owned monopolies and government departments [who] have been enjoying the fruits of reform for a long time and further reform will harm their interests."[28] Writing a decade later, Barry Naughton found that the SOE bottleneck remained in place: "crucial questions about the role of SOEs and the most appropriate institutions to run them efficiently remain unanswered, and no clear consensus has emerged on the future evolution of the state sector."[29]

Common to both perspectives on SOE reform is a focus on the domestic story: policymakers pursuing market transformation "without a map,"[30] embracing a gradualist approach tailored to China's national conditions.[31] For those viewing this process through the lens of adaptive governance, Chinese policymakers inventively and iteratively balanced the interests of key stakeholders (such as urban workers or the line ministries in control of SOEs) with broad reform imperatives (including stabilizing the financial system and promoting private sector development). To skeptics, China's SOE reforms ran aground on the strong

---

[25] Helen Davidson, "China Sentences Top Banker to Death for Corruption and Bigamy," *The Guardian* (January 5, 2021).
[26] Pei, *China's Trapped Transition*; Minxin Pei, *China's Crony Capitalism* (Cambridge, MA: Harvard University Press, 2017).
[27] Pei, *China's Trapped Transition*; Pei, *China's Crony Capitalism*.
[28] Wu Jinglian, "*Zhongguo jingji 60 nian*" [The Chinese Economy at 60], *Caijing* [Finance] (September 28, 2009).
[29] Naughton, *The Chinese Economy*, 358.
[30] Andrei Shleifer and Daniel Treisman, *Without a Map: Political Tactics and Economic Reform in Russia* (Cambridge, MA: MIT Press, 2001).
[31] Isabella M. Weber, *How China Escaped Shock Therapy: The Market Reform Debate* (New York: Routledge, 2021).

and deep networks of patron–client relations in the Chinese bureaucracy. In both accounts, it is actors and institutions within China that shaped the narrative of SOE reform.

Both perspectives neglect the international sources and pressures shaping China's adaptive state capitalism. By contrast, we regard the international system as an important source of both policy inputs and pressures to change. Following Peter Gourevitch's insight, expressed in his article "The Second Image Reversed: The International Sources of Domestic Politics," that "the international system is not only a *consequence* of domestic politics and structures but a *cause* of them" [emphasis added],[32] we believe that the economic and political pressures associated with China's opening to world markets catalyzed the restructuring of Chinese SOEs throughout most of the reform era.

Yet for a variety of reasons, this is often overlooked. One reason is that SOEs have been an enduring feature of the Chinese economic landscape since 1956, when CPC leaders declared the nationalization of Chinese industry complete – despite the introduction of market reforms in the late 1970s. The contribution of SOEs to China's economy has remained remarkably stable for nearly a quarter of a century at about 25 percent of GDP.[33] Second, SOEs are embedded in the bureaucracy of the Chinese state; their leaders are CPC- and government-appointed officials with formal administrative rank equivalent.[34] Third, China's preservation of state ownership has been a persistent source of tension with its major trade partners, who contend that state support to SOEs prevents fair competition.

China's Adaptive State Capitalism

International Engagement in the Reform Era

The start of the reform and opening movement in the late 1970s catalyzed greater engagement between China and the world. With the support of Mao's successor Hua Guofeng and subsequent top leader Deng Xiaoping, high-ranking Chinese officials led diplomatic delegations around the globe, from Hong Kong to Japan to the United Kingdom. In 1978 alone, twenty-one Chinese delegations led by thirteen vice-premiers and National People's Congress vice-chairmen

---

[32] Peter Gourevitch, "The Second Image Reversed: The International Sources of Domestic Politics," *International Organization* 32(4) (1978): 881–912, 911.
[33] Andrew Batson, "The State Never Retreats," *Gavekal Dragonomics* (October 1, 2020).
[34] Wendy Leutert and Samantha A. Vortherms, "Personnel Power: Governing State-Owned Enterprises," *Business and Politics* 23(3) (2021): 419–437.

visited fifty-one countries.³⁵ Foreign governments meeting Chinese delegations were eager to forge closer diplomatic ties with Beijing – and to position themselves for access to Chinese markets. Beyond pledges of loans and technology imports to Beijing, foreign governments also established new channels for transnational exchanges of people and ideas at all levels. For example, in 1978, the United Kingdom pledged to place hundreds of Chinese students in British universities, dispatch British lecturers in science and technology to China, provide materials on management science, and establish an English Language Institute, among other things.³⁶ In the late 1970s, China's leadership, eager to emulate Japan and West Germany's rapid postwar economic growth, invited the economists Ōkita Saburo and Sakisaka Masao of Japan and Armin Gutowski of West Germany to serve as the first international economic advisers to the State Council.

Deng Xiaoping's reformist policies accelerated cross-border movements of people and ideas between China and other countries throughout the 1980s. The Chinese leadership deepened its engagement with the United States through high-level state visits and the expansion of official, cultural, and educational exchanges.³⁷ Beijing also embraced closer ties within Asia, looking to Hong Kong, Japan, and Singapore as it formulated policies ranging from the restructuring of SOEs to the development of special economic zones. Members of the Chinese diaspora played an important role in facilitating some of these exchanges. However, the Tiananmen Square protests and massacre of civilians in June 1989 ended China's diplomatic honeymoon, with sanctions and condemnation replacing engagement.

Following a post-Tiananmen period of retrenchment, the Chinese leadership then sought to correct its diplomatic course while continuing economic reforms. In the immediate aftermath of Tiananmen, "neoconservatives" held sway in Beijing and cautioned against further reforms which might encourage expansion of the private sector and contraction of the state sector. Seeking to avoid the Soviet Union's fate, neoconservatives argued in an influential 1991 internal report that shoring up state ownership was the key to the CPC's survival: "Party control of the asset economy is advantageous in stabilizing and advancing reform of the political system. If the Party owned the assets, political stability would

---

³⁵ Frederick C. Teiwes and Warren Sun, "China's New Economic Policy under Hua Guofeng: Party Consensus and Party Myths," *The China Journal* 66 (2011): 1–23, 14.
³⁶ United Kingdom Department of Education and Science internal document, September 13, 1978, British Archives. Document on file with authors.
³⁷ Robert L. Suettinger, *Beyond Tiananmen: The Politics of US–China Relations 1989–2000* (Washington, DC: Brookings Institution Press, 2004).

have a carrier."[38] Opposed to retrenchment, eighty-seven-year-old Deng Xiaoping seized the opportunity of an official tour of China's southern region to pull the rug out from under the neoconservatives in Beijing with a series of speeches calling on local leaders to have a "daring spirit" in pursuing economic development and for those leaders who stand in the way of reform to "go to sleep" (*shei fandui geming, jiu rang shei shuijiao qu hao le*).[39] Deng's Southern Tour served to reinvigorate the reform drive and paved the way for both restoring relations with Western countries and Jiang Zemin's declaration of China's "socialist market economy."[40]

China's international integration grew at the dawn of the twenty-first century. It joined the World Trade Organization (WTO) in 2001 after a lengthy and contested negotiation process. Entry to the WTO benefited CPC legitimacy in the short term by assuring China's representation in a leading international organization and by supporting continued economic reforms and growth. Starting from the 1990s, American and international financial and legal communities became some of Beijing's most important international sources of policy ideas and practices – and in the case of SOE restructuring, also a key partner in their implementation. By contrast, China–Japan relations deteriorated as the new century neared, with the exit of key diplomatic "bridge builders," the end of the shared Soviet threat, the waning importance of Japanese economic and technical assistance, and growing military tensions.[41]

Since the 2010s, international engagement between China and the world has continued to deepen. Within Asia, transnational exchanges expanded even as territorial disputes – between China and states including Japan, Vietnam, and the Philippines – stoked regional tensions. Moscow again became a key diplomatic partner for Beijing, but no longer a main source of ideas for economic policymaking. And China itself has increasingly become a seller as well as a shopper in the global marketplace of policy ideas. Beijing is reshaping the landscape of international relations and development by establishing new multilateral institutions like the Asian Infrastructure Investment Bank, which was launched in 2016,

---

[38] Quoted in Xin Gu and David Kelly, "New Conservatism: Intermediate Ideology of a New Elite," in *China's Quiet Revolution: New Interactions Between State and Society*, ed. David S. G. Goodman and Beverly Hooper (Melbourne: Longman Cheshire St. Martin's Press, 1994), 219–233, 226.

[39] Sina, "*Chongwen Xiaoping nanxun jianghua: shei fandui geming, jiu rang shei shuijiao qu hao le*" [Revisiting Xiaoping's speech on the southern tour: Whoever opposes the reform should go to sleep] (November 12, 2018).

[40] This concept affirmed that diverse economic elements could coexist while simultaneously upholding the continued dominance of state ownership. Jiang Zemin, Report to the National Party Congress (October 12, 1992).

[41] Ezra F. Vogel, *China and Japan: Facing History* (Cambridge, MA: Harvard University Press, 2019).

and by relying heavily on state-backed export credits to finance the development of commercial infrastructure projects abroad.[42]

However, China's enduring commitment to a state-led model of economic development has generated trade frictions at the WTO and with the United States. In a communication to the WTO in 2018, for example, the United States harshly criticized what it characterized as "China's trade-disruptive economic model."[43] Under the Biden administration, the Office of the United States Representative resolved to counter China's "state-centered and non-market trade practices including Beijing's non-market policies and practices that distort competition by propping up SOEs, limiting market access, and other coercive and predatory practices in trade and technology."[44] And there now appears to be far less openness to ideas and practices from overseas under China's current leader Xi Jinping, rolling back decades of growing international engagement that had preceded the COVID-19 pandemic.[45]

Linking the International and Domestic

Transnational flows of people and ideas can occur via many means, including but not limited to international advisers, exchanges, the study of foreign examples (e.g. other countries' companies and national economies), joint projects, and diaspora linkages. Since 1949, the Chinese government at central and local levels has routinely invited foreign experts to serve formally as economic advisers (*jingji guwen*) or to provide analysis to Chinese policymakers through more informal channels like personal exchanges. These international interlocutors ranged from Soviet experts during the 1950s, to officials and economists from Japan, West Germany, the United States, Hungary, and the United Kingdom serving as formal and informal policy advisers during the 1970s and 1980s, and to American and international businesspeople and lawyers in the 1990s and 2000s.

---

[42] Gregory Chin, "Asian Infrastructure Investment Bank: Governance Innovation and Prospects," *Global Governance* 22 (2016): 11–26; Kristen Hopewell, "Power Transitions and Global Trade Governance: The Impact of a Rising China on the Export Credit Regime," *Regulation and Governance* 15(3) (2021): 634–652.
[43] US Delegation to the WTO, "China's Trade-Disruptive Economic Model," Communication from the US to the WTO General Council (July 11, 2018).
[44] USTR (Office of the United States Trade Representative), "Fact Sheet: The Biden–Harris Administration's New Approach to the U.S.–China Trade Relationship" (October 4, 2021).
[45] This shift is evident most recently in the 2021 ban on foreign textbooks in primary and junior high schools in Beijing. Wan Lin, "Beijing Bans Foreign Textbooks in Primary, Junior High Schools as Regulation Continues," *Global Times* (August 11, 2021).

International exchanges also facilitate cross-border movements of people and ideas. They encompass in-person meetings as well as other forms of communication between individuals across national borders, such as written correspondence, social media exchanges, and video conferencing. Formal overseas study tours, involving small numbers of official and academic participants traveling overseas for the purpose of noncommercial exchange, extend a long-standing Chinese official domestic practice of inspection (*kaocha*).[46] Semiformal exchanges between individuals can also take place in settings like government-facilitated academic conferences or on the sidelines of official meetings, whereas unstructured informal exchanges between individuals can occur both in person and remotely through mediums like letters, telephone calls, and now video conferencing. Such exchanges enable firsthand access to information; however, they are typically limited in scope and duration.

The study of international examples is a key channel for the transnational movement of ideas. This practice ranges from analyses of the structure and development of national economies at the macro-level to detailed reports about individual foreign companies at the micro-level. The most common format involves case studies using secondary source materials and/or primary data collected through in-person visits or exchanges with foreign actors. In theory, the study of international examples enables policymakers to incorporate large amounts of data, draw upon diverse sources, and apply a broad chronological and comparative lens to the challenges at hand. In practice, problems with access to information limit the number and scope of international examples examined.

Such transnational movements of people and ideas serve key functions for domestic policymaking. First, they provide a source of new policy approaches. This is particularly important in more closed political and economic systems and when domestic channels for information flows among government bodies, companies, and citizens are limited. International examples and exchanges are especially valuable for late-developing countries because they enable them to learn from others' successes – and failures. In some cases, international examples and exchanges can provide strategic cover for ideas that might face domestic opposition,

---

[46] Such inspection typically involves officials reviewing developments at lower levels of government administration or in different localities at the same level. Domestic and international inspection share the common aim of information collection; however, domestic inspection also has a supervisory function absent in international inspection. On overseas study tours, see also Xiao Donglian, "*Zhongguo gaige chuqi duiwai jinyande xitong kaocha he jiejian*" [Systematic investigation and referencing of foreign experiences in the early stage of China's reform], *Zhonggong dangshi yanjiu* [CCP history research] 4 (2006), 25.

Table 9.1 *Mechanisms through which international engagement can affect domestic policy-making*

Firsthand experience through direct observation overseas or in-person exchanges sited in China or abroad
Formal oral/written reporting to higher-level leaders
Informal communications with higher-level leaders
Presentations at government-convened meetings of officials and enterprise representatives
Circulation of case studies in internal government journals
Talks delivered in venues outside state bureaucracy to targeted audiences (e.g. academics) which then provide inputs to domestic policy-making

---

either because they are untested at home or because they are perceived as unsuited to the prevailing political, economic, or social viewpoints.

The most immediate way international engagement can affect domestic policymaking is direct experience: when Chinese officials or researchers observe or engage with international actors in China or overseas. The Chinese bureaucracy can also disseminate information and ideas from abroad and incorporate them into the policy process through formal oral and written reports or private, informal communications. Another potential avenue is presentations at government-convened meetings involving hundreds of officials and enterprise representatives. Information and ideas from overseas can also circulate within the bureaucracy in the form of case studies or articles in internal government reference materials. See Table 9.1 for a summary of mechanisms through which international engagement can influence domestic policy.

Case Study: Chinese State-Owned Enterprise Restructuring, 1970s–2010s

During the reform area, Chinese policymakers routinely sought out and selectively adopted policy ideas and practices from abroad. The growing international integration of the PRC, both economic and political, amplified external actors' ability to engage with Chinese officials and experts – though such engagement did not always influence domestic policymaking. The history of Chinese state-owned enterprise restructuring from the late 1970s through the 2010s detailed in this section is a case in point.

1970s–1980s

Beginning in the late 1970s, Chinese policymakers studied the emerging economic powers of East Asia and engaged with the World Bank while determining how to restructure SOEs. Japan's rapid postwar economic growth prompted China to turn first to its neighbor. The Chinese leadership was especially interested in globally competitive, semiautonomous Japanese enterprise groups, such as Nippon Steel and Panasonic. Through a series of exchanges with Japan, Chinese officials and economists studied the corporate structure and operations of these enterprise groups. They published detailed analyses and recommendations for restructuring SOEs to upgrade their technologies and improve their economic performance so as to advance China's developmental objectives.

Study tours to Japan and Japanese economists' observations about China's economy and enterprises contributed to Chinese policymakers' growing support for horizontal linkages among various state-owned production facilities in China. These subsequently expanded to include joint operational decisions and finally asset consolidation.[47] The organizational structure of Japanese enterprise groups also offered solutions to dilemmas arising from state ownership, such as how to increase access to capital without privatization and how to balance monopoly with competition. As China set up its first stock exchanges, enterprise groups could flexibly encompass different types of ownership: Individual subsidiaries could be publicly listed, while the holding company and the overall group remained state-owned. Unlike earlier efforts in which SOEs simply issued stock to employees and other enterprises, this reform encouraged some SOEs to partially privatize their assets by publicly issuing shares on domestic and international equity markets.[48] Chinese policymakers cited the example of Japanese enterprises to justify creating shareholding enterprises (*gufen qiye*). A delegation to Japan from the National State-Owned Assets Administration Bureau, for example, concluded after a month of studying Japan's NEC Corporation that minority shareholding would not threaten state control and oversight,[49] and it could even promote improved performance and governance.[50]

Japan also provided an example of oligopolistic competition, in which companies within an enterprise group competed internally, while

---

[47] Economic Research Reference Materials, *Riben pengyou dui woguo jingji gongzuode kanfa he jianyi* [Japanese friends' views and suggestions on China's economic work] (Beijing: Zhongguo shehui kexue chubanshe, 1981).

[48] Wang Mengkui and Xing Junfang, *On the Issue of Shareholding* (Beijing: Zhongguo jingji chubanshe, 1987).

[49] The Nippon Electric Company, Limited, was renamed NEC Corporation in April 1983. NEC, "Corporate Profile: History," www.nec.com/en/global/about/history.html.

[50] National State-Owned Assets Administration Bureau, *Riben qiye jituan yu guoyou zichan guanli* [Japanese enterprise groups and state-owned asset management] (Beijing: Jingji kexue chubanshe, 1993), 36–37.

different enterprise groups competed within a single industry externally.[51] The global success of Japanese enterprise groups deepened Chinese policymakers' commitment to developing internationally competitive SOEs with cross-regional and cross-industry operations, economies of scale, and advanced technological capabilities.[52]

At the international level, the World Bank was an important early broker of capital and ideas about state-owned enterprise reform for Chinese policymakers. China rejoined the World Bank in 1980 following high-level dialogue between its president, Robert McNamara, and Deng Xiaoping in April of that year.[53] The World Bank quickly provided China with loans for a series of development projects, delivered training programs for officials, and provided analysis of its economy via field missions, joint dialogues, and desk research.[54] High-level Chinese officials judged the World Bank's first 1981 report on the Chinese economy to be of such great value that they requested a second report, which the Bank published in 1985.[55] Both reports identified state-owned enterprise reform as a top priority.[56] In addition, the World Bank also organized formal and informal exchanges between Chinese economic bureaucrats and its own and

---

[51] Shangquan Gao and Fulin Chi, *Reforming China's State-Owned Enterprises* (Beijing: Foreign Languages Press, 1997).

[52] CPC Central Committee, *Zhonggong zhongyang guanyu jianli shehuizhuyi shichang jingji tizhi ruogan wentide jueding* [Decisions of the CPC Central Committee on several issues concerning the establishment of a socialist market economic system] (November 14, 1993).

[53] Harold Karan Jacobson and Michel Oksenberg, *China's Participation in the IMF, the World Bank, and GATT: Toward a Global Economic Order* (Ann Arbor: University of Michigan Press, 1990).

[54] For a list of all World Bank-supported projects in China between fiscal year 1981 and 2018, see World Bank Office, Beijing, *The World Bank Group in China: Facts and Figures, 1980–2018* (Beijing: World Bank Office, Beijing, 2018), 1–12. On the World Bank's 1981 and 1985 reports about the Chinese economy, see Zhong Wei, "*Zhongguo gaige chuqide sixiang jiefang, Zhongwai jiaoliu he lilun changxin*" [Ideological emancipation, international exchange, and theoretical innovation in the early stage of China's economic reform], *Zhongguo jingjishi yanjiu* [Chinese economic history research] 6 (2019): 146–159. For a personal account of early Bank engagement with China, see Caio Koch-Weser, "Transcript of Oral History Interview with Caio Koch-Weser held on December 21, 1992," World Bank Archives, Oral History Program, 1992.

[55] Wei, "Ideological Emancipation," 157.

[56] For instance, the 1981 report echoed the endorsement of enterprise group formation to boost technological upgrading, productivity, and product quality "by establishing more enterprises and organizations that cut across the administrative boundaries between industrial ministries" (World Bank, *China: Socialist Economic Development, Volume 1: The Economy, Statistical System, and Basic Data* (Washington, DC: World Bank, 1983), 26). The 1985 report urged that "to be efficient, enterprises must be motivated to improve their economic performance; they must have some freedom of maneuver; they must be faced with economically rational prices; and they must be subjected to competition" (World Bank, *China: Long-Term Development Issues and Options* (Washington, DC: World Bank, 1985), 8).

other foreign economists, including on the increasingly urgent issue of loss-making SOEs.[57] In 1983 and 1984, the World Bank held what it assessed internally to be highly impactful workshops with the Chinese Academy of Social Sciences on state guidance of industry and structural change, noting: "Collaboration between the World Bank and CASS teams was close throughout and a consensus emerged on major points of analysis and policy recommendations."[58] Throughout the 1980s, the World Bank formally and informally provided Chinese policymakers with external assessments and recommendations about SOE restructuring.

1990s

In the 1990s, international pressures shaped Chinese policymakers' thinking and their efforts to build a "national team" of large state-owned enterprise groups in strategic sectors. Negotiation with the United States and other governments over China's membership in the World Trade Organization in the late 1990s renewed domestic policy debates about how the state could still steer the economy in the context of market liberalization demanded by the WTO.[59] Chinese policymakers came to view nurturing a pilot group of state-owned large enterprise groups in key sectors as a crucial defense against the growing presence of foreign firms in these sectors and a way to preserve national interests in a rapidly changing economy. As one State Council Research Group document framed it: "In the context of a high degree of economic openness, in which market competition is intense and the private sector is weak, large state-owned enterprise groups should be established to safeguard the interests of the nation."[60] In the aviation sector, for example, planners worried that Chinese firms would be unable to compete with

---

[57] Julian Gewirtz, *Unlikely Partners: Chinese Reformers, Western Economists, and the Making of Global China* (Cambridge, MA: Harvard University Press, 2017).

[58] World Bank, "World Bank, 'Collaborative Research with China – Phase II,' project report prepared by Gene Tidrick, submitted on September 2, 1986," World Bank Archives, Folder "673–14 Collaborative Research with China – Phase II – 1v," Folder ID: 1315007, p. 9. "Chinese scholars were interested in the research project largely for the opportunity it afforded to become familiar with Western analytical techniques and to view the Chinese economy in international perspective. Chinese policymakers were interested in obtaining an independent assessment of the effects of reforms begun in 1978 and in recommendations for further reforms" (World Bank, "World Bank, 'Collaborative Research with China,'" see pp. 4–9).

[59] Eaton, *The Advance of the State in Contemporary China*; Peter Nolan, *China and the Global Economy: National Champions, Industrial Policy, and the Big Business Revolution* (New York: Springer, 2001); Dylan Sutherland, *China's Large Enterprises and the Challenge of Late Industrialisation* (New York: Routledge, 2003).

[60] State Council Research Office Research Group, "*Woguo suoyouzhi jiegou biangede qushi he duice yanjiu zong baogao*" [Research report on trends in ownership change and

large multinationals like McDonnell Douglas, opening China up to a risky dependence on foreign suppliers. Facing such "powerful competitors," the answer was to "quickly adjust the organizational structure of enterprises; encourage competition; promote alliances and mergers; and allow some strong enterprises that are in line with the country's industrial policy to grow rapidly stronger."[61] This thinking underpinned the Jiang Zemin administration's decision in 1995 to "hold onto" large SOEs while "letting go" of small SOEs as part of the process of reducing the size of the state sector. It also informed later efforts to expand the scale and enhance the competitiveness of "national champion" SOEs under the slogan of "making them bigger and stronger" (*zuoda zuoqiang*).

American and international legal and financial communities were also deeply involved in the restructuring of large industrial Chinese SOEs prior to public listing in Hong Kong and overseas. Describing China Mobile's initial public offering (IPO) as "God's work by Goldman Sachs," Carl Walter and Fraser Howie observe: "International markets introduced Chinese companies to world-class investment bankers, lawyers, and accountants and brought their legal and financial technologies – the entire panoply of corporate finance, legal and accounting concepts, and treatments that underpin international financial markets – to bear on China's SOE reform effort."[62] As one American lawyer who participated in the IPOs of several of the largest Chinese SOEs recalled about the broader effect of such interactions on domestic policymaking in China: "At that time, China would almost never ask for specific advice on questions [related to policymaking]. But they would have a whole bunch of people in meetings that really weren't part of the companies that were being restructured or so forth. So they learned as they went along."[63] Successful IPOs of SOEs outside China contributed to national prestige and revenues – demonstrating the CPC's capacity to carry out the most capitalistic of moves: listing companies on stock markets.

2000s–2010s

In the twenty-first century, China continued to develop centrally controlled, partially privatized large SOEs by extracting and restructuring

countermeasures], *Jingji yanjiu cankao ziliao* [Reference materials for economic research] 43 (1994): 1–35, 27.

[61] Dawei Liu, "*Guanyu qiye jituanhua zhanlüede sikao*" [Thoughts on the enterprise group strategy], *Jingji yanjiu cankao ziliao* [Reference materials for economic research] 58 (April 12, 1996): 2–10, 2.

[62] Carl Walter and Fraser Howie, *Red Capitalism: The Fragile Financial Foundation of China's Extraordinary Rise* (New York: John Wiley & Sons, 2012), 177.

[63] Author interview with retired American lawyer, by phone, May 2019.

productive assets from the government bureaucracy. Domestic debate about the design of the national State-owned Assets Supervision and Administration Commission (SASAC), which was established in 2003, directly referenced international models like Singapore's state-owned holding company Temasek.[64] Officials and economists in China proposed a variety of competing designs: vesting management authority in the State Council; setting up a state-owned assets management committee under the Standing Committee of the National People's Congress (NPC); establishing a hybrid system of dual NPC and State Council authority; or creating a state-owned assets management bureau under the Ministry of Finance.[65] China's leaders ultimately chose the first approach. It created SASAC as a special commission of the State Council; its mission was to carry out investor functions in the management of state-owned assets.

Singapore and Temasek also provided crucial inspiration for the development of corporate governance institutions for SOEs, especially during SASAC's early years.[66] In 2004, SASAC's inaugural director Li Rongrong led an eight-person delegation on a study tour to Singapore. Upon his return, Li commended Temasek's approach of dispatching a state investor representative to government-linked companies' (GLCs') boards of directors, thus replacing top-down administrative management with delegated participation in corporate decision-making.[67] In 2004, SASAC and the Central Organization Department tapped seven central government-owned SOEs to pilot restructuring as wholly state-owned firms. They were all to establish boards of directors at the group company level, with a minimum of two external directors chosen by SASAC.[68] Li repeatedly invoked the lessons from Singapore, observing in 2006: "The experience of Temasek, a state-owned enterprise, is worth learning, and the most

---

[64] Temasek was established in 1974 under the authority of the Ministry of Finance to manage a portfolio of government-linked companies with the aim of improving their financial performance.

[65] For examples of these competing approaches, see Dexiang Zhang, Xiaowen Zhang, and Xiaoyan Zhang, "*Jianli xinxingde guoyou zichan guanli yunying tixi*" [Establishing a new type of state-owned assets management operations system], *Tigaiwei neibu cankao* [System Restructuring Commission internal references] 17 (1994).

[66] SASAC, *Li Rongrong jiu guozi jianguan gongzuo he yangqi gaige fazhan qingkuang da jizhe wen* [Li Rongrong answers reporters' questions on state-owned assets supervision and the reform and development of SOEs] (December 19, 2006).

[67] Li Wanquan, "*Li Rongrong lun dongshihui jianshe*" [Li Rongrong discusses board of directors establishment], *Qiye wenming* [Enterprise civilization] 7 (2007): 7–10, 7.

[68] SASAC, *Guanyu zhongyang qiye jianli he wanshan guoyou duzi gongsi dongshihui shidian gongzuode tongzhi* [Notice on central SOEs establishing and improving wholly state-owned enterprises board of directors pilot work] (June 9, 2004). See also Rosen, Leutert, and Guo, "Missing Link: Corporate Governance in China's State Sector."

important thing is its corporate governance structure."[69] In this case, Singapore's lesson for China concerned the importance of SOEs having boards of directors at the group company level with at least some external directors among their members. By the beginning of 2008, seventeen of these pilot enterprises had set up boards composed of more than 50 percent external directors. The following year, SASAC expanded the scope of the experimental scheme to twenty-four central SOEs.[70] Throughout this period, SASAC frequently conducted exchanges with Temasek, ranging from the SASAC–Temasek Directors Forum to reciprocal leadership visits.[71]

The Temasek model appealed to Chinese policymakers because it satisfied the legal requirements of SOEs to operate within a market economy under professional management, but without having to relinquish state ownership.[72] However, unlike SASAC, Temasek observes the principles of "nonintervention" and "nonpreference" in its dealings with state firms.[73] Beyond appointing the members of GLC boards, Temasek does not otherwise intervene in the management of firms. And neither Temasek nor the Singaporean government intervenes in markets to give GLCs competitive advantage.

Important differences in China's situation limit the replicability of the "Singapore model." First, China's state-owned economy is far larger than that of Singapore, as is the size of some of its largest SOEs. As SASAC's inaugural director Li Rongrong once noted: "The assets of one of our central SOEs, such as the State Grid Corporation of China, are basically equivalent to all of Temasek's assets [combined]."[74] Second, Singapore's Temasek model is significantly less market interventionist than China's SASAC model. Legal researcher Wei Jie Nicholas Ng describes SASAC's approach as the "antithesis" of Temasek's nonintervention and nonpreference principles "insofar as the National Champions Model is ingrained

---

[69] Li, "Li Rongrong discusses board of directors establishment," 8.
[70] Ning Shao, *Guoyou qiye gaige shilu* [The reform of SOEs in memoir] (Beijing: Jingji kexue chubanshe, 2014), 542.
[71] As of 2020, twenty-seven sessions of the SASAC–Temasek Directors Forum have been held. *Jianchi zheng qi fenkai, mingque gongneng dingwei, qianghua duoyuanhua juece – Xinjiapo Danmaxi kaochade qishi* [Adhere to the separation of government and enterprises, clarify functional positioning, and strengthen diversified decision-making – Inspiration from visiting Temasek in Singapore], *Guozi baogao* [State-owned assets report] (March 8, 2020).
[72] Deng Feng, "Indigenous Evolution of SOE Regulation," in *Regulating the Visible Hand? The Institutional Implications of Chinese State Capitalism*, ed. Benjamin L. Liebman and Curtis J. Milhaupt (New York: Oxford University Press, 2015), 3–28, 13.
[73] Wei Jie Nicholas Ng, "Comparative Corporate Governance: Why Singapore's Temasek Model Is Not Replicable in China," *New York University Journal of International Law and Politics* 51 (2018): 211–249.
[74] Li, "Li Rongrong discusses board of directors establishment," 8.

with pervasive governmental intervention and is rife with state preference."[75] State-owned enterprises also continue to serve myriad strategic functions for the state apart from revenue generation and profit maximization. These functions, which include financial crisis management, promotion and maintenance of social stability, and, in recent times, epidemic response, are all vital to the resilience of party rule.[76]

Corruption remains a serious challenge in China's state sector. Since 2012, Xi Jinping's ongoing anticorruption campaign has targeted SOEs and uncovered evidence of executive and employee embezzlement, bribes, and lavish perks like 25,000 RMB (~3,900 USD) lunches.[77] The Central Commission for Discipline Inspection (CCDI) carried out four rounds of antigraft inspections targeting central government-owned SOEs – at two firms in 2013, ten firms in 2014, forty-three firms in 2015, forty-two firms plus SASAC in 2019, and twenty-seven firms in 2023 – as well as far-reaching inspections of SOEs owned by local governments.[78] However, Chinese SOEs' byzantine structures, weak oversight, and rapidly growing international portfolios all complicate efforts to curb corruption in China's state sector.

Conclusion

This chapter provides a counterpoint to characterizations of SOE governance as the CPC's economic Achilles' heel and the domain of Chinese reform most resistant to change and outside ideas. Today, China continues to defy its major trade partners' expectations that full privatization is inevitable.[79] Our analysis suggests that Chinese policymakers successively and actively sought out suitable policy inputs from abroad and

---

[75] Ng, "Comparative Corporate Governance," 226.
[76] See for example SASAC, *Guoziwei caiqu youli cuoshi weihu gupiao shichang wending* [SASAC takes effective measures to safeguard stock market stability] (July 8, 2015); Keith Zhai, "Exclusive: China Prods State Firms to Boost Investment in Crisis-Hit Hong Kong – Sources," *Reuters* (September 12, 2019); SASAC, *Yangqi zhanyi tujian* [Illustrated compendium of central SOEs' war against the epidemic] (April 24, 2020).
[77] Laura Zhou, "Senior Executives of Power Utility State Grid Punished over Lavish Lunch," *South China Morning Post* (March 25, 2015).
[78] *Zhongyang jiwei jianchabu wangzhan yi fabu yangqi pi cha lingdao 64 ren* [CCDI Inspection Department website announces 64 central SOE leaders have been investigated], *Xinhua News* (January 4, 2016); CCDI, *Shijiujie zhongyang disan lun xunshi zhenggai jinzhan qingkuang quanbu gongbu* [Situation of the third round of inspection and rectification of the 19th Central Committee] (March 22, 2020); CCDI: *Ershijie zhongyang diyilun xunshi duixiang gongbu* [Announcement of the targets of the first round of inspections of the 20th Central Committee of the CCP] (March 27, 2023).
[79] Stephen Paul Green and Guy Shaojia Liu, "Introduction," in *Exit the Dragon? Privatization and State Control in China*, ed. Stephen Paul Green and Guy Shaojia Liu (London: Wiley-Blackwell, 2005), 10.

tailored them to China's distinctive situation. We find that key episodes in CPC governance and reform of the state sector during the reform era – the development of state-owned enterprises and enterprise groups, the decision to develop a "national team" of large SOEs, the listing of state firms on stock exchanges, the design of a national system to manage state-owned assets, and the development of corporate governance institutions in SOEs – have all been shaped through interaction with international players and forces.

Our analysis thus helps to explain the resilience of the Chinese Communist Party today, more than a century after its founding in 2021. China's state capitalist system is both subject to and supports CPC rule. Yet China's state capitalism is neither static nor a product of domestic experimentation alone. Deeper global integration during the reform era has amplified the international system's importance as a key source of policy inputs and pressures to change. This global context increasingly shapes nominally domestic Chinese policymaking about state-owned enterprise restructuring and a host of other policy issues. Even as domestic policy experimentation and openness continue to wane under Xi Jinping, China's adaptive state capitalism supports the ongoing endurance and evolution of CPC rule.

10 Digital Power
Technological Leadership, Smart Governance, and Ideological Control

John Lee and Katja Drinhausen

Introduction

For over a quarter century, the Communist Party of China's (CPC's) top leaders have recognized that "informatization" – the application of digital information and communication technology (ICT) – is key to achieving development goals and social stability and improving the People's Republic of China's (PRC's) position vis-à-vis the world's leading nations. Despite former US president Bill Clinton's prediction that trying to control the internet would be like "nailing jello to a wall," the CPC has managed to maintain a high degree of control over cyberspace, while leveraging the internet as a multiplier for economic growth and technological progress. The development of digital technologies has not only fueled the country's digital economy and international competitiveness, but it has also provided new tools for surveillance and censorship.

Yet the CPC's leaders perceive significant threats from the digital environment. This stems from the nature of the internet – a system that was originally designed for the quick and relatively uncontrolled flow of information – and from the dominance of digital ICT by nations they see as hostile to China, especially the United States. Xi Jinping's accession to supreme CPC leadership in late 2012 was followed by the elevation of cybersecurity as a coequal policy priority with informatization, and by the continuous extension of the party-state's control to every corner of cyberspace.

As the US has moved to cut China off from access to cutting-edge semiconductors and other critical technologies on which cyberspace is built, achieving greater self-reliance in these technologies has become a first-order priority for Beijing. China's response to the challenge

This chapter builds on previous work by the authors in "The CCP in 2021: Smart Governance, Cyber Sovereignty and Tech Supremacy," in *The CCP's Next Century: Expanding Economic Control, Digital Governance and National Security*, MERICS Paper on China, 2021, and covers developments until September 2024.

presented by American regulations will determine whether it can achieve the CPC's development goals, including the "great rejuvenation of the Chinese nation" envisioned by Xi Jinping, thus helping to cement the legitimacy of the party and the stability of its rule.

This chapter provides an overview of the CPC's management of cyberspace and how it is being harnessed to the party's vision for China, as well as how it helps keep the party in control. First, we review the institutional framework that has evolved under Xi Jinping's rule over the last decade, which amounts to creation of a new system of bureaucratic clusters (*xitong*) to manage cyberspace as a distinct field of policy.[1] Second, we examine how cyberspace is being utilized for more effective governance and delivery of public services within China. Third, we describe the party-state's employment of digital technologies and the internet for mass surveillance and control. Fourth, we explain China's position in the transnational ICT landscape and its quest for greater self-reliance in the technologies of cyberspace. In this context, we consider the implications of increased US export controls and their potential to hobble China's technological progress – or accelerate the division of the world into technological spheres of influence. Finally, we draw these threads together to consider what the CPC's approach to cyberspace means for China's future and for that of the world.

Central Leadership over Cybersecurity: Institutional Actors

Over the past decade, China has developed an institutional system to manage cyberspace and digitally networked technologies across society.[2] This system aims to coordinate and supervise the application and enforcement of the rapidly expanding network of legislation, regulation, and policy covering every area of cyberspace. For instance, Beijing is building "a legal regime creating a comprehensive protection matrix for all data, personal or otherwise, from the perspective of national security and the public interest," an ambition for comprehensive data governance that has yet to be matched by any other national government.[3] Chinese regulators are now pushing into fields where they are global pioneers, in

---

[1] Rogier Creemers, *Report: China's Cyber Governance Institutions* (Leiden Asia Centre, January 5, 2021), https://leidenasiacentre.nl/en/report-chinas-cyber-governance-institutions, p. 5.
[2] See generally John Lee, *Cyberspace Governance in China: Evolution, Features and Future Trends* (Asie.Visions 129, July 2022, IFRI – Institut français des relations internationales).
[3] Rogier Creemers, "China's Emerging Data Protection Framework," *Journal of Cybersecurity* 8(1) (2022): tyac011.

areas including articulating user rights and technical standards for the transparency of algorithms.[4]

In Xi Jinping's words, the purpose of all this institutional and regulatory innovation is to implement the "Party center's uniform leadership over cybersecurity and informatization work."[5] It has effectively created a new functional administrative system that cuts across formal bureaucratic lines and is designed to better transmit the party center's intentions through all agents of policy, including quasi-state and private actors. The main elements of this system coalesced over the 2010s as China articulated and implemented relevant laws, regulations, and policies.[6]

At the top is the Central Commission for Cybersecurity and Informatization (CCCI), which in 2018 was upgraded in status from a Central Leading Small Group (CLSG) to a Commission, cementing its role in the government apparatus.[7] The Leading Small Group had itself been upgraded in 2014 from an earlier body responsible for promoting national informatization. The 2014 reform added cybersecurity to this preceding group's titular responsibilities. The new priority on security was informed by Edward Snowden's disclosures about US cyberespionage and the vulnerabilities they revealed in China's digital networks. Xi Jinping became chair of this new CLSG, with two other Politburo Standing Committee members as deputy chairs, including then premier Li Keqiang.[8]

At the outset, the CCCI included the heads or deputy heads of powerful party and state agencies: these include, among others, the Central Propaganda Department, Central Political-Legal Commission, Central Military Commission, People's Liberation Army General Staff, Ministry of Public Security, Ministry of Industry and Information Technology, Ministry of Science and Technology, Ministry of Finance, and the

---

[4] John Lee, Eric Zhang, and Rogier Creemers, *China's Standardisation System: Trends, Implications and Case Studies in Emerging Technologies* (Leiden Asia Centre, April 2022), https://leidenasiacentre.nl/chinas-standardisation-system-trends-implications-and-case-studies-in-emerging-technologies/.

[5] *"Xi Jinping: Zizhu chuangxin tuijin wangluo qiangguo jianshe"* [Xi Jinping: Advance indigenous innovation and build a cyber superpower], Xinhua (2018), www.xinhuanet.com/politics/2018-04/21/c_1122719810.htm.

[6] Creemers, *China's Cyber Governance Institutions*.

[7] Rogier Creemers, Paul Triolo, Samm Sacks, Graham Webster, and Ziaomeng Lu, "China's Cyberspace Authorities Set to Gain Clout in Reorganization," *DigiChina* (blog), Stanford University (March 26, 2018), https://digichina.stanford.edu/work/chinas-cyberspace-authorities-set-to-gain-clout-in-reorganization/.

[8] *"Zhongyang wangluo anquan he xinxihua lingdao xiaozu chengli: cong wangluo daguo mai xiang wangluo qiangguo"* [Central Commission on Cybersecurity and Informatization Leading Small Group is established: Marching from a cyber great power towards a cyber superpower], People.cn (2014), http://politics.people.com.cn/n/2014/0301/c1001-24499049.html.

National Development and Reform Commission. This broad membership reflected recognition by China's most senior leaders that the development and management of cyberspace has fundamental impacts on all aspects of society and so requires centralized direction and coordination. As Xi declared at the CCCI's inaugural meeting: "cybersecurity and informatization are two driving wheels of a single vehicle ... there is no national security without cybersecurity, and no modernization without informatization."[9]

The CCCI's administrative and executive office is the Cyberspace Administration of China (CAC), which also evolved from an earlier body that was charged with regulating communications over the internet. The CAC has itself acquired significant policymaking and regulatory responsibilities. Some of these include overseeing the entities that manage the global internet addressing system (DNS) within China and national computer network emergency response; monitoring China's tiered national cybersecurity alert state; leading the regulatory articulation of China's Personal Information Protection Law; initiating cybersecurity reviews into critical information infrastructure (CII) operators and internet platform providers under China's Cybersecurity Law; and guiding implementation of the Five-Year Plan for National Informatization adopted in December 2021.

The CAC's expanding influence comes from its character as a "dual-badged" entity that exists as both a state and a CPC organ under the direct supervision of the CPC Central Committee.[10] Because of the CAC's expanding regulatory role, the ambiguity around its scope of authority and its compliance with Chinese administrative law – including, for example, the right of private entities to appeal the CAC's decisions – presents a dilemma to entities operating in Chinese cyberspace, including foreign ones. Its exercise of government functions cannot be clearly distinguished from its behavior as a CPC organ; the institution itself asserts both identities.[11] This is an example of how, since rising to power, Xi Jinping has reversed the previous trend toward separating state and party. The imperative to reassert the party's authority over the sphere of governance is especially acute for data security. The CCCI's existence is evidence of the CPC's judgment that the Chinese economy's headlong rush into the

---

[9] "*Xi Jinping: Ba woguo cong wangluo daguo jianshe chengwei wangluo qiangguo – gaoceng dongtai*" [Xi Jinping: Build China from a cyber great power into a cyber superpower – high-level dynamics], Xinhua (2014), http://news.xinhuanet.com/politics/2014-02/27/c_119538788.htm.
[10] State Council Notice Concerning Establishment of Institutions, State Council 2018, www.gov.cn/zhengce/content/2018-03/24/content_5277121.htm.
[11] See generally Jamie Horsley, "Behind the Facade of China's Super-Regulator," *DigiChina* (blog), Stanford University (August 8, 2022), https://digichina.stanford.edu/work/behind-the-facade-of-chinas-cyber-super-regulator/.

digital age was creating unacceptable exposure to dangerous ideas and "hostile foreign forces."

The CAC's growing range of competencies over cyberspace regulation in China has involved it in a power struggle with the Ministry of Public Security (MPS). The MPS supervises China's long-established multilevel protection system (MLPS), a graded system of security requirements for information systems. It has extensive powers that include the ability to physically or remotely access digital systems, copy proprietary data, and require operators to explain how their systems are configured.[12] The MPS was put in charge of "guiding and supervising" the protection of CII across China by regulations effective September 2021.[13]

Alongside the MPS, the Ministry of State Security (MSS), China's foreign intelligence and counterintelligence service, has authority to vet personnel who staff the cybersecurity teams which the September 2021 regulations require all CII operators in China to establish.[14] The US and several allied governments accused the MSS in 2021 of conducting international cyberespionage activities to advance China's commercial interests.[15] The MSS has access to the work on testing software vulnerabilities of various Chinese institutes such as the China Information Technology Security Evaluation Center (CNITSEC). Researchers have speculated that such close links work to benefit the MSS's cyber exploitation capabilities.[16] The MSS has close links to CNITSEC.

The Ministry for Industry and Information Technology (MIIT) plays a leading role in the development of digital ICT in China and has some regulatory powers that shape China's cybersecurity environment. It manages a telecoms equipment certification system that exists alongside the MLPS and the emerging regime of CII protection and has regulatory authority over the DNS within China.[17] The ministry supervises

---

[12] "*Gongan jiguan hulianwang anquan jiandu jiancha guiding*" [Public security organs internet security supervision and inspection regulations], Gov.cn (2018), www.gov.cn/gongbao/content/2018/content_5343745.htm.

[13] Paul Triolo, Samm Sacks, Graham Webster, and Rogier Creemers, "After 5 Years, China's Cybersecurity Rules for Critical Infrastructure Come Into Focus," *DigiChina* (blog), Stanford University, August 18, 2021, https://digichina.stanford.edu/work/after-5-years-chinas-cybersecurity-rules-for-critical-infrastructure-come-into-focus/.

[14] Triolo, Sacks, Webster, and Creemers, "After 5 Years."

[15] The White House (US), "The United States, Joined by Allies and Partners, Attributes Malicious Cyber Activity and Irresponsible State Behavior to the People's Republic of China," media release (July 19, 2021), www.whitehouse.gov/briefing-room/statements-releases/2021/07/19/the-united-states-joined-by-allies-and-partners-attributes-malicious-cyber-activity-and-irresponsible-state-behavior-to-the-peoples-republic-of-china/.

[16] Jon Lindsay, Tai-Ming Cheung, and Derek Reveron (eds.), *China and Cybersecurity: Espionage, Strategy, and Politics in the Digital Domain* (Oxford: Oxford University Press, 2015), 11.

[17] Creemers, "China's Cyber Governance Institutions," 13–14.

cyberspace vulnerability databases and a national vulnerabilities information-sharing platform. It also works with CAC and MPS on threat reporting and mitigation.[18] Its affiliated research institute, the China Academy for Information and Communication Technologies (CAICT), is leading development in various ICT fields, including in partnership with foreign organizations (for example, the Sino-German Industrie 4.0 collaboration on intelligent manufacturing).[19] The institute has started to perform regulatory functions in this context: In 2021, for example, it began issuing "trustworthy AI" certifications for facial recognition software.

The development of technical standards will in many instances shape how cyberspace governance works in practice. As in other countries, in China this involves extensive inputs by industry associations and dedicated multistakeholder committees. Notable among these is the National Information Security Standardization Technical Committee (TC260), which is headed by the CAC's deputy director and brings together senior bureaucrats from various agencies alongside Chinese and (for certain working groups) foreign ICT businesses. To give an example of how TC260 influences cyberspace governance, it has led development of national data classification and grading standards. These include guidelines for identifying "important data," a key term that appears in the framework laws (described in what follows). The term lacks a clear definition yet is critical to determining compliance obligations for cross-border data transfers out of China.[20]

At a technical level, the interface between Chinese cyberspace and the outside world is shaped by bodies like CAICT, TC260, and international standards development organizations in which representatives of Chinese firms and state agencies participate. At the diplomatic level, the Ministry of Foreign Affairs leads China's participation in the United Nations-based dialogue processes for discussing international cyberspace norms. Below the intergovernmental level, other Chinese organizations engage in structured discussions with foreign stakeholders about the principles that should regulate cyberspace internationally. Notably, the China Institute of Contemporary International Relations, which is affiliated to the MSS and provides analysis to China's senior leaders, conducts "track 1.5" (between government officials and experts) and facilitates "track 2" international dialogues (between experts).[21]

---

[18] Rogier Creemers, "China's Emerging Data Protection Framework," *SSRN* (November 16, 2021), https://papers.ssrn.com/sol3/papers.cfm?abstract_id=3964684.

[19] "Sino-German Industrie 4.0 Cooperation," *Platform Industrie 4.0*, www.plattform-i40.de/IP/Redaktion/EN/Dossiers/china.html.

[20] "*Shuju anquan jishu shuju fenlei fenji guize*" [Data security technology – Rules for data classification and grading], tc260.org.cn (March 2024), https://www.tc260.org.cn/upload/2024-03-21/1711023239820042113.pdf.

[21] Creemers, "China's Cyber Governance Institutions," 16–17.

The Regulatory "Direction of Travel": Framework Policy and Legal Documents

The foregoing is a selective description of the main actors in an extensive web of state and quasi-state entities that influence China's cyberspace governance. This bureaucratic cluster works within a policy and legal framework which is being progressively refined through the introduction of subordinate regulations and technical standards. None of these documents is a definitive body of regulation for a particular field or a specific administrative direction comparable to, respectively, the European Union's General Data Protection Regulation or US presidential executive orders.[22] Rather, the evolving regulations indicate the leadership's policy priorities and regulatory "direction of travel." Details about how they will apply in specific situations are possibly still years away in some cases.[23]

China's National Cybersecurity Strategy and Strategy for International Cooperation in Cyberspace enshrine key principles, notably cyberspace sovereignty, law-based governance, and the interlinked nature and equal priority given to security and development.[24] The Cyberspace Strategy lays out principles for transforming global cyberspace governance and contains proposals for building a "community of common destiny in cyberspace." These proposals, which Xi Jinping announced to the UN General Assembly in 2015, had been introduced at the Chinese state-hosted World Internet Conference in Wuzhen earlier that year.[25] The Fourteenth Five-Year Plan for National Informatization, issued by the CCCI in late 2021, outlines policy priorities and thematic work programs for development of Chinese cyberspace over the period 2021–2025, addressing both security and development.[26]

---

[22] Compare, for example, President Trump's executive order on securing the US national ICT supply chain: "Securing the Information and Communications Technology and Services Supply Chain," Federal Register (Executive Order 13873, May 15, 2019), www.federalregister.gov/documents/2019/05/17/2019-10538/securing-the-information-and-communications-technology-and-services-supply-chain.

[23] Creemers, "China's Emerging Data Protection Framework," *Journal of Cybersecurity*, 7.

[24] "*Guojia wangluo kongjian anquan zhanlüe*" [National cybersecurity strategy] (December 2016), www.cac.gov.cn/2016-12/27/c_1120195926.htm; "*Wangluo kongjian guoji hezuozhan*" [International strategy for cooperation on cyberspace] (March 2017), www.xinhuanet.com/politics/2017-03/01/c_1120552767.htm.

[25] "*Xi Jinping 'si xiang yuanze' he 'wu dian zhuzhang' cheng quanqiu gongshi*" [Xi Jinping's "four principles" and "five-point proposal" become global consensus] (December 2016), www.cac.gov.cn/2016-12/29/c_1120209665.htm.

[26] Rogier Creemers and Paul Triolo, "Analyzing China's 2021–2025 Informatization Plan: A DigiChina Forum," *DigiChina* (blog), Stanford University (January 24, 2022), https://digichina.stanford.edu/work/analyzing-chinas-2021-2025-informatization-plan-a-digichina-forum/.

The Cybersecurity Law (CSL), Data Security Law (DSL), and Personal Information Protection Law (PIPL) provide the legal framework for a comprehensive regulatory regime for cyberspace, the substantive content of which is progressively being filled out. The CSL, which came into effect in 2017, establishes a range of security-related requirements, notably for technical cooperation with state security organs, and for data localization and security review by state agencies in certain situations for certain types of data. The PIPL and the DSL, which both came into effect in late 2021, deal respectively with "personal information" and with the general management of the data economy for both national security and social development purposes. However, these laws only provide foundational obligations, which are being articulated by a growing mass of administrative activity and regulation. Provisions on Promoting and Regulating Cross-Border Data Flows promulgated by CAC, which took effect in March 2024, integrate and articulate obligations across the CSL, DSL, and PIPL.[27] These include mandatory security review of data exports across China's border in specific circumstances, led by the CAC.[28] Obligations are based on terms such as "important data" and "critical information infrastructure operator," which are not defined in Chinese law.

The scope of these terms will be determined by executive agencies on a sectoral basis, according to systematized rules that are still under development. For example, regulations specific to the automotive sector define some types of "important data" in the case of data collected by intelligent and connected vehicles.[29] One of the apparent objectives is to build in the flexibility needed to adapt to changing circumstances. For instance, interim measures published by MIIT in February 2022 devolve responsibility for cataloging "important data" in the context of "industrial data" and "IT data" to handlers of such data types. These catalogs must be filed with MIIT's local offices and include details about cross-border transfers.[30]

---

[27] "*Cujin he guifan shuju kuajing liudong guiding*" [Provisions on promoting and regulating cross-border data flows] (March 2024), https://www.cac.gov.cn/2024-03/22/c_1712776611775634.htm.

[28] Samm Sacks, Krystal Chen Zeng, and Graham Webster, "Moving Data, Moving Target: Uncertainties Remain in China's Overhauled Cross-Border Data Transfer Regime," *DigiChina* (blog), Stanford University (October 25, 2024), https://digichina.stanford.edu/work/moving-data-moving-target/.

[29] "*Qiche shuju anquan guanli ruogan guiding (shixing)*" [Several provisions on automobile data security management (for trial implementation)] (August 2021), https://www.gov.cn/zhengce/zhengceku/2021-09/12/content_5640023.htm.

[30] "*Gongxinbu jiu 'gongye he xinxihua lingyu shuju anquan guanli banfa (shixing)' zheengqiu yujian*" [Ministry of Industry and Information Technology on the "industrial and information technology sector data security management measures (for trial implementation)" for

"Data handling" is defined by the DSL as "collection, storage, use, processing, transmission, provision, disclosure, etc." of "any information in electronic or other form."[31] The DSL also asserts extraterritorial jurisdiction over data-handling activities outside China that "harm national security, the public interest, or the lawful rights and interests of citizens or organizations of the PRC." It can thus be assumed that any data transfers inside China or involving Chinese entities may be subject to the exercise of authority by Chinese state agencies, even if the target of such action is outside the borders of the PRC.

On the development side of the cyberspace policy agenda, the DSL directs state agencies to "standardize data transaction behavior, and cultivate a data transaction market," comparable to foreign data economy-oriented regulatory initiatives like the European Union's draft digital services act package.[32] On the security side, the DSL mandates a national system of data security measures graded by the data's category and importance and is based on the catalogs of "important data" structured by region and sector of activity. This data protection system will sit alongside other state-run structures such as the Corporate Social Credit System, a national database of compliance records for every legal entity in China.[33]

This brief discussion illustrates both the comprehensive scope of China's fast-evolving cyberspace regulatory regime and the degree of uncertainty about how it will apply in specific situations. It also illustrates how government is often simultaneously centralized and decentralized in the PRC. The combination of multiple sweeping objectives and iterative implementation has produced a governance system that is far from optimally rationalized, which inevitably makes it less efficient. In March 2022, a senior figure at a research institute affiliated to the Ministry of Finance blamed regulatory confusion and related compliance burdens for slowing growth in China's digital economy and for the low foreign-market share of China's internet platform giants.[34]

---

comments] (September 2021), https://wap.miit.gov.cn/gzcy/yjzj/art/2021/art_dcb6cc8d9f5c414eabd7070871996525.html.

[31] Digital Security Law (DSL), Article 2, Article 3.
[32] DSL, Article 19; "The Digital Services Act Package," European Commission (November 24, 2022), https://digital-strategy.ec.europa.eu/en/policies/digital-services-act-package.
[33] Kendra Schaefer, *China's Corporate Social Credit System: Context, Competition, Technology and Geopolitics* (Report, Trivium Research, November 16, 2020), www.uscc.gov/sites/default/files/2020-12/Chinas_Corporate_Social_Credit_System.pdf.
[34] "*Liu Shangxi weiyuan ti'an: guanyu jinyibu tisheng woguo shuzi jingji guoji jingzheng li*" [Proposal by Committee Member Liu Shangxi on further enhancing the international competitiveness of China's digital economy] (March 2022), www.chineseafs.org/cky

However, this system also gives China's top leaders a growing understanding of what is happening throughout Chinese cyberspace. This puts them in a better position to broker outcomes among different actors, while ideally leaving those actors flexibility to push ahead with regulation and policy according to their particular fields. The party-state's influence over cyberspace has outpaced that of other national governments in breadth and increasingly in depth, while tethering it to the CPC's wider developmental and political goals. Whether this stimulates or hinders the growth of China's digital economy remains to be seen. But it will improve Chinese authorities' control over all aspects of national cyberspace, and thereby China's overall cybersecurity situation, which remains parlous given the scale of the nation's expanding dependence on digital networks.[35]

Data as a Factor of Production: Leading the Fourth Industrial Revolution

China's government sees leadership in key digital technologies and applications, coupled with control over digital information, as central to economic and systemic competitiveness. In line with this ambition, it has rapidly driven forward the expansion of the country's internet and strives to stay at the forefront of new technological developments. China's telecoms operators had installed around 4 million 5G telecoms base stations by September 2024, thereby providing all urban and most rural areas access to speedy connections.[36]

The number of Chinese internet users reached 1.1 billion in August 2024, a penetration rate of roughly 78 percent.[37] Chinese citizens account for one-fifth of global internet users.[38] Life in China has gone digital, as services, sales, and payments have moved online, especially in the 2010s, which saw the rise of globally known platform companies such

---

newsmgr/newsContent_queryOneNewsRecord?retVal=cnzkdtxw&zyflag=1&searchFlag=2&newsid=0304163743_27673014.

[35] *Cyber Capabilities and National Power: A Net Assessment* (Report, International Institute for Strategic Studies, June 28, 2021), www.iiss.org/blogs/research-paper/2021/06/cyber-capabilities-national-power.

[36] "China Rolls Out 1.6 Million 5G Base Stations, All Rural Villages Having Access to Broadband," *Global Times* (May 17, 2022), www.globaltimes.cn/page/202205/1265842.shtml.

[37] *Global Times*, "Number of Internet Users in China Rises to 1.1 Billion; Internet Penetration Rate Reaches 78%," *Global Times* (August 29, 2024), https://www.globaltimes.cn/page/202408/1318873.shtml.

[38] Compare number of internet and social media users worldwide as of February 2025, compiled by Statista: www.statista.com/statistics/617136/digital-population-worldwide/.

as Alibaba and Tencent, but also a sprawling sector of online service providers, retailers, and communication platforms. Chinese tech companies have flourished in this environment: China's internet companies are among the biggest global players.

China's leaders, aware that China was a latecomer in previous rounds of transformative change, see the development of digital technologies and the country's digital economy as key to lead in the fourth wave of industrial evolution. It frames and treats data as a "key factor of production" – similar to land, labor, capital, and technology – and thus necessitating increased state control.[39] Since late 2023, Xi and policy organs across the party-state administration increasingly talk about unleashing "new productive forces" to propel China's economy forward.[40] This is part of a broader conceptual emphasis on establishing a new development model built strongly on new technologies – a strategic focus reflected in the CPC's Third Plenum resolution in July 2024.[41] Using "top-level design," an approach of guiding policy from the pinnacle of party-state authority, the CPC aims to control and harness economic digitalization and the internet for its overarching goal of "socialist modernization and national rejuvenation."[42]

This new conceptual outlook focuses on the value of data for both the economy and governance.[43] The top leadership and provincial leaders across the country have drawn up new policies to pool data and allow it to circulate beyond the companies or organs that originally collected it.[44]

---

[39] Qiheng Chen, "China Wants to Put Data to Work as an Economic Resource – But How?," *DigiChina* (blog), Stanford University (February 9, 2022), https://digichina.stanford.edu/work/china-wants-to-put-data-to-work-as-an-economic-resource-but-how/; Dave Yin, "China Is Laying the Groundwork to Nationalize Private Companies' Data," *protocol* (June 16, 2021), www.protocol.com/china/china-national-security-data-exchange.

[40] Arthur R. Kroeber, "Unleashing 'New Quality Productive Forces': China's strategy for technology-led growth," *Brookings* (June 4, 2024), www.brookings.edu/articles/unleashing-new-quality-productive-forces-chinas-strategy-for-technology-led-growth/.

[41] Katja Drinhausen, Max J. Zenglein, and Rebecca Arcesati, "Having It Both Ways: Third Plenum Promises Reforms and Doubles Down on Xi's Grand Vision," *MERICS: Mercator Institute for China Studies* (August 2, 2024), https://merics.org/en/comment/having-it-both-ways-third-plenum-promises-reforms-and-doubles-down-xis-grand-vision.

[42] Cao Shumin, "*Yi xinxihua shuzihua qudong yinling Zhongguoshi xiandaihua*" [Informatization and digitalization are the drivers of Chinese-style modernization], *Red Flag Manuscript* 2023/2 (January 20, 2023), www.qstheory.cn/dukan/hqwg/2023-01/20/c_1129303314.htm.

[43] Chen, "China Wants to Put Data to Work."

[44] Barry van Wyk, "The Chinese Government Wants a Data Trading Market, But It May Never Happen," *The China Project* (October 11, 2022), https://thechinaproject.com/2022/10/11/the-chinese-government-wants-a-data-trading-market-but-it-may-never-happen/.

The goal is to create databases and establish data marketplaces. For now, this has remained in the initial stages. A lack of unified regulatory standards and practices for data validation, transactions, and security still hampers such efforts on a national scale.[45] But testing and scaling up the best practices remain a key approach in China's policymaking, and in early 2024 the State Council and Central Committee released new guidelines to better leverage the trove of public data.[46]

Despite repeated references to fostering "market-driven allocation of data," party-state steering plays a central role, especially regarding regulation of cross-border data transfers and availability of data to different actors. Here concerns over national security and maintaining a competitive edge in leveraging digital technologies are foremost for the party. Plans for improving data sharing are, however, focused on the domestic realm. Transfer abroad of personal and other key data has been significantly restricted. The leadership is especially wary of insights that foreign governments might garner from publicly available data. They have launched national security reviews of targets as diverse as ride-sharing apps and China's leading scientific publishing platform CNKI.[47]

Ensuring state guidance over the private sector and specifically China's tech sector has driven what has been coined China's "private sector crackdown" in international media. Since late 2020, a wide array of rules and guidelines has sought to regulate e-commerce platforms, social media platforms, livestreaming services, and other service providers that form the backbone of China's digital economy. All key ministries and state organs were involved in this mission to tame the private sector. They have targeted monopolistic behaviors, false advertising, and other deceptive practices detrimental to privacy of personal data and consumer rights, in line with new privacy legislation (see p. 229). They have also made efforts to improve workers' rights in the gig economy, as well as to contain financial risks through online financial products and lending platforms.[48]

The confluence of regulatory actions aligns corporate behavior with party-state goals for the broader economy as well as its ambition to

---

[45] Rebecca Arcesati, "China Activates Data in the National Interest," *MERICS: Mercator Institute for China Studies* (July 4, 2022), https://merics.org/en/short-analysis/china-activates-data-national-interest.

[46] *China Daily*, "Public Data Potential Set to Be Unleashed," *China Daily* (October 1, 2024), https://www.chinadaily.com.cn/a/202410/11/WS670878d1a310f1265a1c7008.html.

[47] Stella Chen and David Bandurski, "CNKI's Security Problem," *China Media Project* (July 6, 2022), https://chinamediaproject.org/2022/07/06/cnkis-security-problem/.

[48] Kai von Carnap and Valarie Tan, "Tech Regulation in China Brings in Sweeping Changes," *MERICS: Mercator Institute for China Studies* (November 3, 2021), https://merics.org/de/kurzanalyse/tech-regulation-china-brings-sweeping-changes; "China's Big Tech Crackdown: A Complete Timeline," *The China Project* (August 2, 2021), https://thechinaproject.com/big-tech-crackdown-timeline/.

become a leader in informatization and on its way to a global cyber power by 2035, especially in terms of technology and talent development.[49] The party-state expects companies to channel their resources toward innovation in a manner that supports its political priorities, rather than seeking short-term profits in ways that may spur public discontent, for example, through unsustainable online lending schemes, excessive collection of user data, and unfair labor practices. To this end, the party leadership is willing to accept significant financial pain: between mid 2021 and early 2022, stock market losses amounted to over US$1 trillion, hitting hard many of China's biggest tech companies, from key e-commerce players JD and Alibaba to food-delivery and ride-sharing giants Meituan and Didi.[50]

Generating Support for CPC Rule through Smart Governance

Digitalization and informatization remain key items on China's political agenda, with the explicit goal of using big data to modernize national governance. The Fourteenth Five-Year Plan (2021–2025), adopted by the National People's Congress in March 2021, is supposed to usher in a new chapter of "smart" and modern rule.[51] Building on the "internet+" strategy established in the previous five-year plan, it focuses on leveraging information and communication technologies to improve governance efficiency across sectors.

The CPC's hope is that digital technologies can provide new channels for people to access public goods and lodge complaints about local problems or official corruption, and ultimately bolster the Chinese people's trust in the party and its leadership.[52] Whether in poverty reduction, basic services, or public security, the party-state expects digital technologies to contribute to sustainable economic and social

---

[49] Xinhua, "*Zhongyang wangluo anquan he xinxihua weiyuanhui: 2035 nian jiben jiancheng zhuzi rencai qiangguo*" [Central Commission for Cybersecurity and Informatization: By 2035, a digital talent powerhouse will be basically built], *Xinhua* (November 11, 2021), www.news.cn/fortune/2021-11/05/c_1128036094.htm.

[50] Rebecca Feng and Michelle Chan, "Alibaba, Tencent, Meituan's $1.2 Trillion Selloff Might Not Be the Bottom," *The Wall Street Journal* (online) (August 10, 2022), www.wsj.com/articles/chinese-tech-bulls-load-up-but-doubts-remain-11660124022.

[51] State Council (PRC), "Internet Plus: A Life-Changing Initiative," The State Council (January 21, 2018), http://english.www.gov.cn/premier/news/2018/01/21/content_281476021268046.htm.

[52] Ausma Bernot and Susan Trevaskes, "Smart Governance, Smarter Surveillance," in *China Story Yearbook 2021: Contradiction*, ed. Linda Jaivin and Esther Sunkyung Klein (Canberra: ANU Press, 2022), 17–38. www.thechinastory.org/yearbooks/yearbook-2021-contradiction/chapter-1-smart-governance-smarter-surveillance.

development. The concept of "smart cities" involves designs for sustainable management of urban areas – an urgent topic given the sheer number of large cities in China, all of which use vast amounts of scarce resources such as water and energy and struggle with transport and social infrastructure bottlenecks due to high population density.[53]

While digital infrastructure is catching up quickly in rural areas, literacy still notably lags behind urban areas. The government still plans to expand access to internet services and e-commerce platforms in rural areas, as well as training in the use of digital platforms to promote economic growth and consolidate its poverty-reduction achievements.[54] Indeed, direct sales via online retail and livestreaming sales have become an important new channel for rural producers.[55] Even if rural residents won't all turn into online entrepreneurs overnight, this has already provided faster and cheaper access to goods.[56]

Digitalization also accompanies institutional reforms in the areas of social security and health. For example, the new digital social security card had already been issued to over 715 million citizens by the end of 2022. It allows them easier access to benefits wherever they are in China, with no need to return to their place of household registration. This has helped address a long-standing problem for China's large domestic migrant population of more than 370 million (based on the most recent population census from 2021).[57] But with roughly 200 million gig workers in 2024, many working in food delivery, ride-hailing, e-commerce, or other segments of the new service economy, the digital turn also brings new challenges for comprehensive social security coverage.[58]

---

[53] *Future Cities Advisory Outlook 2020: Urban Technologies in China* (Report, UN Habitat, 2020), https://unhabitat.org/future-cities-advisory-outlook-2020-urban-technologies-in-china.

[54] Xinhua, "14th Five-Year Plan for Economic and Social Development of the People's Republic of China," *Xinhua* (March 13, 2021), www.xinhuanet.com/2021-03/13/c_1127205564.htm.

[55] *China News*, "*Nongcun dian shang mairu xingnong xin jieduan*" [Rural e-commerce ushers in a new stage of promoting agriculture], *China News* (July 8, 2022), www.chinanews.com.cn/cj/2022/07-08/9798369.shtml.

[56] Victor Couture, Benjamin Faber, Yizhen Gu, and Lizhi Liu, "Connecting the Countryside via E-Commerce: Evidence from China," *American Economic Review: Insights* 3(1) (2021): 35–50.

[57] Sohu, "*Zhongguo liudong renkou dadao 3.8 yi, tamen zhuyao liuxiang nali*" [China's floating population has reached 380 million. Where do they mainly go?], *Sohu News* (October 14, 2022), www.sohu.com/a/592678288_121253503.

[58] SCMP, "China's gig workers becoming new normal, but 'inevitable trend' comes with a burden," *SCMP* (July 9, 2024), https://www.scmp.com/economy/economic-indicators/article/3269601/chinas-gig-workers-becoming-new-normal-inevitable-trend-comes-burden.

Under the "Healthy China" strategy of 2016, which aimed among other things to optimize healthcare services and delivery by 2030, the state rolled out a national system for digitizing health information and care.[59] E-services and online consultations are intended to better connect doctors and patients, counteract regional inequalities in medical care, and make healthcare more cost-efficient generally.[60] This task can only become more urgent, as China's population is aging rapidly due to the (now abandoned) one-child policy.

In embracing the digitalization of government services, China has made significant strides. Following policy speeches by Xi Jinping in 2016, the construction of a national e-government system was accelerated. Both the Thirteenth and Fourteenth Five-Year Plans set a series of tasks for the years 2016–2025 that aim to increase governance efficiency through digitalization by simplifying procedures, cutting down administrative red tape, and minimizing opportunities for corruption. A key goal is to ensure that citizens "do not have to appear in person more than once" at a government office to access a wide variety of services online. A number of cities, including Fuzhou, have developed comprehensive local service apps to facilitate everything from buying tickets for local public transport to managing social security accounts, starting a business, or paying for doctor's visits, electricity, and other public services.[61] This provides significant time savings for citizens who previously had to wait in long queues or travel to their hometowns just to access basic services.[62]

Since late 2019, the construction of an ecosystem of public databases is in the works under the label of "internet+ monitoring," which collects diverse data on the behavior of companies, nongovernmental organizations, individuals, and public institutions. The most notable example of the government's endeavors is China's Social Credit System, a broad framework under which different subsystems track the compliance of individuals, companies, and institutions with laws and regulations

---

[59] Central Committee, State Council, "*Jiankang Zhongguo 2030 Guihua Gangyao*" [Healthy China 2030 Planning Outline] (October 25, 2016), www.gov.cn/zhengce/2016-10/25/content_5124174.htm.

[60] Matthias Stepan and Jane Duckett, *Serve the People: Innovation and IT in China's Social Development Agenda* (Report, MERICS: Mercator Institute for China Studies, October 18, 2018), https://merics.org/en/report/serve-people.

[61] Xinhua, "China Eyes Digital Technologies to Cut Red Tape," *Xinhua* (May 3, 2019), www.xinhuanet.com/english/2019-05/03/c_138032017.htm.

[62] Cyberspace Administration of China, "*Liucheng wangmin shiyong xianshang zhengwu banshi, zhengwu xin meiti zhuli zhengwu fuwo zhinenghua*" [Sixty percent of netizens use online government services, and new government media help make government services more intelligent] (January 31, 2018), www.cac.gov.cn/2018-01/31/c_1122341540.htm.

under unified identification numbers.[63] Although there is no unified score, it differs from credit-rating systems in other countries in combining aspects of financial credit and legal compliance under a broader category of trustworthiness.

The party-state sees data, including personal data, primarily as a resource for governance and the promotion of economic development. Despite the massive amounts of data collected, privacy and data security issues have only recently (and some would argue, insufficiently) been addressed. Excessive data collection and leaks by companies and public administrations have angered the public. In a 2019 survey, more than 77 percent of internet users reported being affected by leaks of personal data.[64]

The government is taking steps toward greater regulation. China's first Personal Information Protection Law (PIPL) came into effect in early 2021. New privacy and data security regulations, restrictions on the use of facial recognition, and new requirements placed on companies in 2022 to share AI algorithms for state supervision are framed as key measures to protect citizen and consumer rights.[65] Although data security standards apply equally for state administrations, laws and regulations primarily target data collection and use by the private sector. They provide limited protection from state-led efforts to surveil the population. Instead, China's National Security Law, Cybersecurity Law, and other legislation give the state wide remit to monitor public and online spaces. Corporate privacy statements generally include references that data can be shared with relevant agencies where it concerns public and national security.[66]

Harnessing Digital Technologies for Political Control

Safeguarding national and regime security remains at the top of the CPC's political agenda. The party's all-encompassing understanding of

---

[63] Katja Drinhausen and Vincent Brussee, "China's Social Credit System in 2021: From Fragmentation towards Integration," *MERICS: Mercator Institute for China Studies* (March 3, 2021), https://merics.org/en/report/chinas-social-credit-system-2021-fragmentation-towards-integration.

[64] Xinhua, "*Fang xinxi xielou, ju zuo 'touming ren'*" [Prevent information leakage, refuse to be a "transparent person"], *Xinhua* (December 7, 2020), www.xinhuanet.com/politics/2020-12/07/c_1126828874.htm.

[65] Matt Sheehan and Sharon Du, "What China's Algorithm Registry Reveals about AI Governance," Carnegie Endowment (December 9, 2022), https://carnegieendowment.org/2022/12/09/what-china-s-algorithm-registry-reveals-about-ai-governance-pub-88606.

[66] Jamie P. Horsley, "How Will China's Privacy Law Apply to the Chinese State?" *New America* (January 26, 2021), www.newamerica.org/cybersecurity-initiative/digichina/blog/how-will-chinas-privacy-law-apply-to-the-chinese-state/; Katja Drinhausen, "Privacy," *Decoding China Dictionary* (March 2023), https://decodingchina.eu/privacy/.

national security extends to cleansing China's internet of ideas and information that might be harmful to their hold on power.[67] The party's approach to governing digital technologies and information is based on its belief in "scientific", data-based governance and the importance of maintaining social stability and public order. In recent years, there have been concerted efforts to establish a system of social control, which helps to monitor and contain risks but also detects and prevents challenges to party rule before they occur. This involves integrating online and offline tracking of people's behavior, from monitoring online expression to surveillance of public spaces and transport, as well as using personal information and biometric data to identify individuals.

Platforms are legally required to provide online services only after real-name registration and identity verification. In 2024, the Ministry of Public Security and Cyberspace Administration introduced a draft law proposing a new "national internet ID." Touted as a voluntary, protective measure to anonymize and protect citizens' personal data from unwanted use by third parties, the push for a personal digital ID has been criticized by legal experts and internet users for ultimately being aimed at expanding integrated tracking of individual online behavior.[68]

The CPC's main goal in regulating cyberspace is to build an ideologically secure information space. The party places high priority on the state's capacity to monitor and censor discordant views in order to fend off regime threats. From the mid 2000s, China gradually shut out of its market the major international communication and media platforms, such as YouTube, Twitter, Facebook, and Google, that it could not control. Chinese companies have flourished, developing their own innovative products, such as the "everything app" WeChat, while submitting to a high degree of control by the state over content.

To be economically successful and retain market share, Chinese companies must not only provide the public with content that generates engagement and consumption. It is now equally, if not more, important for them to comply with regulatory demands and institutional supervision including in-house CPC committees, licensing procedures, and content review – even if this is detrimental to commercial interests. They are increasingly required to share content that sings the party's praises, for

---

[67] Katja Drinhausen and Helena Legarda, "'Comprehensive National Security' Unleashed: How Xi's Approach Shapes China's Policies at Home and Abroad," *MERICS: Mercator Institute for China Studies* (September 15, 2022), https://merics.org/en/report/comprehensive-national-security-unleashed-how-xis-approach-shapes-chinas-policies-home-and.

[68] Cindy Carter, "Critics of China's Proposed National Internet ID System Hit with Online Bans, Censorship, Harassment," *China Digital Times* (August 9, 2024), https://chinadigitaltimes.net/2024/08/critics-of-chinas-proposed-national-internet-id-system-hit-with-online-bans-censorship-harassment/.

example through directives and guidelines to select or tweak algorithms to ensure top picks and amplified content. This ensures that platforms self-govern in the desired direction and build products and services that only allow for controlled engagement of users with content.[69] Repeated regulatory crackdowns ensure compliance.

The CPC is particularly concerned about the viral dissemination of information that contradicts the official narrative or reflects badly on the government, including criticism, and the potential for such information to spark protest or political movements offline.[70] A core component of media policy under Xi has therefore been building a "healthy internet" in which negative information is contained and "positive energy" is spread by state actors. In recent years, the state has promulgated a lengthy series of laws and regulations for content control in the digital space.[71]

Regulations from January 2021 specifically targeted social media.[72] Responsibility for their implementation was given to online media and communication platforms. A comprehensive system to detect and contain collective online actions harmful to the party is now in place: a mix of censorship, algorithmic manipulation, and flooding of communications platforms with officially sanctioned content. This was visible in the early information management and containment of criticism surrounding the government's handling of the outbreak of the pandemic.[73] Media regulators place noticeably fewer limitations on outbursts of nationalistic fervor, be it campaigns against critical authors within China or boycott calls against international companies perceived to have offended the Chinese people (as with pledges to avoid sourcing from Xinjiang due to forced labor concerns).[74]

---

[69] Vincent Brussee, "Designed for Censorship," *MERICS: Mercator Institute for China Studies* (July 28, 2020), https://merics.org/en/opinion/designed-censorship.

[70] Francois Godement, Angela Stanzel, Marcin Przychodniak, Katja Drinhausen, Adam Knight, and Elsa B. Kania, "The China Dream Goes Digital: Technology in the Age of Xi," *European Council on Foreign Relations* (October 25, 2018), https://ecfr.eu/publication/the_china_dream_digital_technology_in_the_age_of_xi/.

[71] China Media Project, "Positive Energy," *The CCP Dictionary* (April 16, 2021), https://chinamediaproject.org/the_ccp_dictionary/positive-energy/.

[72] Minghe Hu and Iris Deng, "China Updates Rules on Social Media Accounts, Increasing the Already High Cost of Moderation," *South China Morning Post* (January 25, 2021), www.scmp.com/tech/policy/article/3119134/china-updates-rules-social-media-accounts-increasing-already-high-cost.

[73] Sarah Cook, "Coronavirus Cover-ups, Disinformation, Netizen Pushback (April 2020)," *Freedom House China Media Bulletin* 143 (April 2020), https://freedomhouse.org/report/china-media-bulletin/2020/coronavirus-cover-ups-disinformation-netizen-pushback-april-2020.

[74] Raymond Zhong and Paul Mozur, "How China's Outrage Machine Kicked up a Storm over H&M," *New York Times* (March 29, 2021), www.nytimes.com/2021/03/29/business/china-xinjiang-cotton-hm.html.

The party-state not only wants to monitor, shape, and contain online behavior, but it also aims to monitor and control citizens' offline behavior, too. Over the past decades, it has built a layered system of monitoring and surveillance platforms.[75] A key indicator is the growing number of "safe" cities and residential communities. These reflect an intent to tighten social governance, with a heavy emphasis on ensuring "social stability." In China's political context, "safety" is defined by absence of social disturbances and public protest, which is ensured through tight surveillance and grid policing.

Most public spaces are already covered by cameras – not just streets and train stations, but also buses and taxis, schools and universities, places of religious worship, bars, and restaurants. Train and long-distance bus journeys are only possible with real-name registration and identity checks. Under the banner of creating smart and safe cities and communities, digital monitoring has been vastly expanded at the grass-roots level – spurred on by policies rolled out in relation to pandemic management and containment, most importantly the plethora of health-code apps that tracked movement and contact histories of citizens and regulated access to public spaces. A case in Zhengzhou in 2022, where local authorities used their power to turn health codes red and grounded citizens to prevent protests, caused a public outcry and concerns over state abuse of data.[76]

China now boasts the world's most comprehensive surveillance coverage and a growing private sector that provides surveillance goods and services to the state. The authorities widely apply facial recognition technology as part of the development of smart, AI-driven policing. China's initial success in containing the COVID-19 pandemic has highlighted how comprehensive this coverage is, and the Party used the pandemic to legitimize widespread surveillance domestically. The intensity of control is highest in minority regions such as Xinjiang and Tibet, where the party perceives the greatest latent threats to state security. Measures in Xinjiang include the forced installation of spyware on phones and continuous monitoring of mobile devices of ethnic minority members. It also entails the use of apps through which cadres and other public

---

[75] Jessica Batke and Mareike Ohlberg, "State of Surveillance: Government Documents Reveal New Evidence on China's Efforts to Monitor Its People," *ChinaFile* (October 30, 2020), www.chinafile.com/state-surveillance-china; Dahlia Peterson, *Designing Alternatives to China's Repressive Surveillance State* (CSET Policy Brief, October 2020), https://cset.georgetown.edu/research/designing-alternatives-to-chinas-r epressive-surveillance-state/.

[76] Zhanhang Ye, "Henan Bank Depositors Continue to Worry about Red Health Code," *Sixthtone* (July 8, 2022), www.sixthtone.com/news/1010729/henan-bank-depositors-con tinue-to-worry-about-red-health-code.

personnel feed information into databases, most notably the Integrated Joint Operations Platform (IJOP).

The IJOP, built and expanded with support of private Chinese tech companies since 2016, integrates and assesses information about individuals from ethnic and religious minority groups. The public and state security apparatus uses the collected data to identify behavior that deviates from state-defined norms. In the case of the Xinjiang Uyghurs, this could be as simple as refusing to eat pork or drink alcohol. Rooted in highly discriminatory state perceptions of ethnic and religious minorities, the use of such technology has contributed to wide-scale extralegal detention of an estimated more than a million people since 2016 and other significant restrictions on the freedom of movement and expression in Xinjiang and beyond.[77]

A key characteristic of China's growing surveillance state is how it connects with and supports long-established offline capacities in monitoring and policy enforcement. The state has digitized and integrated storage large swaths of personal files to allow accessibility across administrations. The party-state tasks public security personnel, party officials, and residential community workers with maintaining social stability and provides them with digital tools to enter information and help enforce policy, identify risks, resolve issues, and prevent protests. In addition, numerous apps and platforms seek to mobilize citizens, for instance, to alert authorities to suspicious behavior or report ideological failings on the part of others, such as an expressed "incorrect" understanding of the party and its historical contributions.

Hu Jintao established the "grid management system" that divides urban areas into small, discrete units for policing by various local management groups alongside public security officers. In recent years, the system has incorporated broader monitoring and urgent response mechanisms. Smartphones and apps that collect and transmit data are relatively low-tech and require limited digital literacy but provide valuable insights on the ground. Local cadres and volunteers can thus be seen as the foundation of the surveillance state – its eyes and ears – and a key part of what makes it so powerful. Referencing Maoist approaches such as the "Fengqiao Experience" – named after a town in Zhejiang – the party-state encourages self-monitoring among the population through apps and reporting hotlines, to help local cadres detect and "correct" aberrant behavior at the grassroots level.[78]

---

[77] *China's Algorithm of Repression: Reverse Engineering a Xinjiang Police Mass Surveillance App* (Human Rights Watch, May 2019), www.hrw.org/sites/default/files/report_pdf/chi na0519_web5.pdf.

[78] Dominik Mierzejewski, "The Zhejiang Model: Old-New Tools for Managing Contradictions and Creating Win–Win Outcomes in Center–Local Governance,"

Despite the overall push for digitization, within the various surveillance initiatives, especially those commissioned and set up by local governments, automation often remains relatively low. However, China's government is working on joint standards for and better integration of various data sources. The government is striving to eliminate blind spots in monitoring and surveillance. At the same time, it is attempting to make the system less "perceptible" to citizens to avoid pushback, akin to the transformation of online control and censorship, which is most successful when it is most invisible (operating, for example, through algorithms that cause approved social media posts to go viral while suppressing the visibility of unapproved ones, rather than through brute censorship).

Nonetheless, the party-state gets to define what counts as the indicators of compliance or threat by which individual and group behavior is assessed and managed. That there is almost no oversight allows the continued risk of discriminatory actions, high error margins, and government overreach. The ever more stringent zero-COVID controls were a case in point and to some extent made controls visible to the broader population. The outbreak of the White Paper protests in late 2022 showed cracks in the system where public outrage becomes too big to contain – but also the powerful toolbox the party-state has built. The security apparatus was able to quickly locate and disperse gatherings and in the months that followed tracked down leading figures, participants, and supporters (including abroad).[79] To the party, the lesson was likely one of success in containing internal pushback that could derail the country's march to greatness.

Closing Gaps to Achieve a Secure and Controllable Digital Ecosystem

The PRC's technonationalist tradition of seeking independence in key technologies dates from the Mao era, when it focused on strategic weapons.[80] As China opened up and began deeper integration with the global economy from the 1980s onward, the CPC began instituting policies to catch up with advanced economies. These policies sought to foster the indigenous development of technologies that were seen as vital

---

China Brief (October 19, 2022), https://jamestown.org/program/the-zhejiang-model-old-new-tools-for-managing-contradictions-and-creating-win-win-outcomes-in-center-local-governance/.

[79] The Economist, "A Year on from the White-Paper Protests, China Looks Much Different," *The Economist* (November 23, 2023), www.economist.com/china/2023/11/23/a-participant-considers-the-impact-of-the-white-paper-protests.

[80] Evan A. Feigenbaum, *China's Techno-Warriors: National Security and Strategic Competition from the Nuclear to the Information Age* (Stanford, CA: Stanford University Press, 2003).

for economic and military competitiveness, while addressing the global shift in technological innovation from the defense- and state-dominated sectors to civilian industry.[81]

Since coming to power, Xi has stressed that China's "greatest hidden danger lies in core technologies being under the control of others."[82] China's 2016–2020 science and technology innovation plan emphasized growing the nation's capacity for independent innovation, while national policy initiatives like "Made in China 2025" aimed to substitute Chinese-made goods for imports and upgrade the country's industrial capability.[83] The CPC's "Fifth Plenum Proposal" of October 2020, in anticipation of the Fourteenth Five-Year Plan (2021–2025), declared that self-reliance in science and technology was a "strategic support" for national development and gave innovation a "core position" in the national modernization project.[84]

This long-standing awareness of the relationship between technological power, dependency on foreign technology providers, and the party's goal for China to become rich and strong by 2049 sets the context for the party's approach to making China a "cyberspace superpower," able to fully employ digital technology despite the hostility of foreign powers. The CPC's leaders recognize that to secure this vision, China must achieve greater independence in the technologies that constitute the building blocks of cyberspace.

However, they have also grasped that the complexity of new technologies, and the globally connected nature of the digitalized economy, make complete autarky neither realistic nor desirable. China's Fourteenth Five-Year Plan for National Informatization (14th FYPNI) calls for increasing the international openness of China's digital economy, promoting cross-border data flows, and accelerating international trade in data. To this end, the Plan promotes participation in international forums and the development of norms for cyberspace governance, practical cooperation

---

[81] Barry Naughton, *The Rise of China's Industrial Policy, 1978 to 2020* (Mexico City: Universidad Nacional Autónoma de México, 2021).

[82] Xi Jinping, "Speech at the Work Conference for Cybersecurity and Informatization," translated by Rogier Creemers, *China Copyright and Media* (April 19, 2016), https://chinacopyrightandmedia.wordpress.com/2016/04/19/speech-at-the-work-conference-for-cybersecurity-and-informatization/.

[83] State Council, "*Guowuyuan guanyu yinfa 'shisanwu' guojia keji chuangxin guihuade tongzhi*" [Notice of the State Council on issuing the "13th Five-Year Plan" National Science and Technology Innovation Plan], State Council (June 28, 2016), www.gov.cn/zhengce/content/2016-08/08/content_5098072.htm.

[84] "*Zhonggong zhongyang guanyu zhiding guomin jingji he shehui fazhan di shisi ge wunian guihua he erlingsanwu nian yuanjing mubiaode jianyi*" [Proposal of the Central Committee of the Communist Party of China on formulating the fourteenth five-year plan for national economic and social development and the visionary goals for 2035] (November 2020), www.gov.cn/zhengce/2020-11/03/content_5556991.htm.

to facilitate cross-border activity, and efforts to attract foreign capital and business participation in developing China's digital infrastructure and economy.[85] In September 2022, China's senior leaders reiterated that the nation's capacity for breakthroughs in frontier technologies lies in the "dialectical unity of scientific and technological self-reliance with international cooperation in science and technology."[86]

This is not merely rhetoric. Executive agencies, including those mentioned earlier, are translating it into policy. In January 2022, for example, the head of MIIT published a commentary stating that state policies will promote "all-round opening-up in the manufacturing sector," foreign investment in mid- and high-tier manufacturing, and international cooperation on industrial and supply chains.[87] The goal is to remain plugged into global economic and technological systems while increasingly shaping them on China's terms, through improving both domestic technological capabilities and international engagement.

Internally, greater self-reliance is being pursued by stimulating self-contained domestic economic activity (the internal side of a so-called dual-circulation economy, alongside international trade) while requiring foreign technology providers selling to China increasingly to conform to Chinese rules ("secure and controllable"). This addresses the threat of foreign state intervention in China's digital networks. This threat has exercised China's top leaders since 2013, when Edward Snowden revealed the potential vulnerability of corporate technology providers. China's expanding cyberspace governance regime increasingly gives state agencies the tools to police both domestic and foreign providers and operators of ICT infrastructure.

Yet even as the party-state tightens its surveillance and control over China's cyberspace, it is still trying to accommodate the developmental imperative for cross-border flows of information. Trial projects to facilitate international data transfers are being developed in pilot zones around China at the central authorities' direction.[88] China is seeking accession to

---

[85] "'Shisiwu' guojia xinxi guihua" [Fourteenth Five-Year Plan for National Informatization] (December 2021), https://www.gov.cn/xinwen/2021-12/28/5664873/files/1760823a10 3e4d75ac681564fe481af4.pdf.
[86] "Guanyu jianquan shehuizhuyi shichang jingji tiaojian xia guanjian hexin jishu gongguan xinxing juguo tizhide yijian" [Opinions on sounding a new national system for tackling key core technologies under the conditions of socialist market economy] (September 2022), www.china-cer.com.cn/zhengcefagui/2022090821090.html.
[87] Xiao Yaqing, "Chongfen fahui gongyede 'ya cang shi' zuoyong (jingji xingshi lixing kan)" [Give full play to the role of industry as a "ballast" (A rational view of the economic situation)], (people.com.cn) *People's Daily* (20 January 2022), http://theory.people.com.cn/n1/2022/0120/c40531-32335445.html.
[88] Ministry of Commerce, "Shangwubu guanyu yinfa quanmian fuwu maoyi chuanxin fazhan shidian zongti fang'ande tongzhi" [Notice by the Ministry of Commerce on issuing the overall plan for comprehensively deepening the pilot program for the innovation and

regional trade agreements such as the Comprehensive and Progressive Agreement for Trans-Pacific Partnership that address cross-border data exchange and the digital economy. The 14th FYPNI emphasizes promoting the international integration of China's digital economy and infrastructure through diplomatic and technocratic approaches, such as by promoting Chinese tech firms and data-driven governance solutions. It also stresses the need to propagate China's normative ideas and positions globally through international exchanges on cyberspace governance, including cyber sovereignty and the prerogative of states to control content and cross-border data flows.[89]

The CPC's long-standing, pragmatic approach of "crossing the river by feeling the stones" can be expected to inform future efforts to reconcile its seemingly contradictory goals of control and interconnectedness in a digitalized society. These contradictions are unlikely to be resolved by 2035. The party-state has sought to mitigate the risks of continued use of foreign technology by building structural dependence on China into global production chains, as Xi himself has said.[90] The willingness over the last decade of foreign interests to continue investing and, increasingly, to locate research and development (R&D) operations in China, despite the growing intrusiveness of China's cyberspace governance system and the associated risks, has made this approach continue to seem viable. Major European firms have confirmed their plans to increase investment in R&D in China, a 2022 survey found; US firms such as Microsoft have built AI research hubs in China, despite warnings; and the State Council issued a notice in January 2023 to encourage investment in this field.[91]

The risks of continued dependence on foreign technology escalated dramatically in October 2022, when the US government introduced new export controls to restrict China's access to semiconductors and related technologies. Semiconductors are a foundational ICT technology with a complex, knowledge-intensive and globalized supply chain.[92] The

---

development of trade in services] (August 12, 2020), www.gov.cn/zhengce/zhengceku/2020-08/14/content_5534759.htm.

[89] Rogier Creemers, Hunter Dorwart, Kevin Neville, Kendra Schaefer, Johanna Costigan, and Graham Webster, "Translation: 14th Five-Year Plan for National Informatization – Dec. 2021," *DigiChina* (blog), Stanford University (January 24, 2022), https://digichina.stanford.edu/work/translation-14th-five-year-plan-for-national-informatization-dec-2021/.

[90] Xi Jinping, "*Guojia zhongchangqi jingji shehui fazhan zhanle ruogan zhongda wenti*" [Major issues with the national medium and long-term economic and social development strategy] (April 4, 2020), www.qstheory.cn/dukan/qs/2020-10/31/c_1126680390.htm.

[91] www.reuters.com/world/china/china-encourages-foreign-capital-set-up-rd-centres-country-2023-01-18/.

[92] John Lee, *Mapping China's Semiconductor Ecosystem in Global Context: Strategic Dimensions and Conclusions* (MERICS and Stiftung Neue Verantwortung e.V., 2021),

steady increase over the last few years in US export controls selectively cutting off Chinese firms' access to foreign products and services in this field had already reinforced to the party-state the urgency of plugging these supply chain "chokepoints."

As one analyst put it, the October 2022 US controls targeting semiconductors (followed up subsequently by additional measures) amount to "strangling with an intent to kill" China's capacity to meet the party-state's technology goals.[93] These controls were instituted in the acknowledged absence of commitments by US-allied countries to follow suit. The Biden administration clearly saw China's technological development as such a threat that it took unilateral action, in the expectation that this would leave other countries no choice but to align their policies. As US National Security Adviser Jake Sullivan said in September 2022, this represents a shift in US strategic policy, from staying a couple of technology generations ahead of China to maintaining "as large of a lead as possible."[94] Sullivan reportedly said in closed-door meetings with industry executives earlier in 2022 that the goal was to "freeze" Chinese technological progress.[95] The policy framing of these controls, and that of various subsequent technology controls and prohibitions targeting China in fields such as connected vehicle technology, points toward a US strategy for the technological containment of China. The constitute, in effect, a US response to the global implications of the CPC's own strategy for making China a "cyberspace superpower."

Conclusion

China's leadership takes a two-pronged approach to using ICT in domestic governance. To strengthen its legitimacy, the party-state invests in efficient and better services for the population, while building up capacities to safeguard its hold on power. The government has built a solid foundation of digital infrastructure. Despite worries surrounding data

---

https://merics.org/en/report/mapping-chinas-semiconductor-ecosystem-global-context-strategic-dimensions-and-conclusions.

[93] Gregory C. Allen, "Choking Off China's Access to the Future of AI," *CSIS: Center for Strategic & International Studies* (October 11, 2022), www.csis.org/analysis/choking-chinas-access-future-ai.

[94] The White House (US), "Remarks by National Security Advisor Jake Sullivan at the Special Competitive Studies Project Global Emerging Technologies Summit," speech (September 16, 2022), www.whitehouse.gov/briefing-room/speeches-remarks/2022/09/16/remarks-by-national-security-advisor-jake-sullivan-at-the-special-competitive-studies-project-global-emerging-technologies-summit/.

[95] Ana Swanson and Edward Wong, "With New Crackdown, Biden Wages Global Campaign on Chinese Technology," *New York Times* (October 13, 2022), www.nytimes.com/2022/10/13/us/politics/biden-china-technology-semiconductors.html.

privacy and criticism of digital barriers for the elderly, disabled, and poor, China's citizens and private sector have seen tangible gains: a flourishing digital economy, better access to goods and services, and improved public services. Digital solutions will continue to improve governance efficiency in the coming years – including in the application of repressive policies such as censorship and surveillance for preemptive risk prevention.

In Beijing's eyes, China is pioneering the future of governance, based on centrally guided and constant monitoring, surveillance, and risk assessment. China's data- and technology-driven governance model contrasts with what it considers an outdated Western model centered on the separation of powers, press freedom, and civil society, all of which prevent the concentration of power. The government has attempted to frame its initial success at containing the pandemic as a direct result of its systemic advantage – even though that narrative frayed as lockdowns and a hasty reopening in 2023 took a toll on economic development and people's livelihoods that could not be prevented through data-driven, "smart" governance.[96]

Despite Beijing's narrative of China's superior model of governance, the sheer amount of investment in resources needed to detect and contain perceived threats to social stability and the security of the regime – such as protests and public questioning of party-state policies – tells another story. China's growing surveillance infrastructure reflects the party-state's fears about the true level of support it enjoys among its own people and corporate actors. It is a costly undertaking. According to an analysis by the Jamestown Foundation, the Chinese government spent around US$6.6 billion on censorship – most importantly on human monitoring and intervention – in 2020.[97] Building this tight security network swallows public funds that could be spent on addressing root causes of discontent such as regional and economic inequalities, rising living costs, and gaps in the education and welfare system – especially in a time of slowing economic growth and strained public finances.

The leadership's security-focused approach to domestic governance also has international implications. The party-state has identified (in broad terms) data that it sees as important and has taken steps to regulate and guarantee state access. This includes setting strict data localization requirements for all actors, including foreign businesses operating in

---

[96] Mengjie Wang, "China's Governance Model in Response to the Coronavirus Outbreak," *CGTN* (February 20, 2020), https://news.cgtn.com/news/2020-02-20/China-s-governance-model-in-response-to-the-coronavirus-outbreak-OcLTh8x9u0/index.html.

[97] Ryan Fedasiuk, "Buying Silence: The Price of Internet Censorship in China," *Jamestown China Brief* 21(1) (2021), https://jamestown.org/program/buying-silence-the-price-of-internet-censorship-in-china/.

China, and legally mandating access rights for state organs under broad national security exceptions.

Broad "national security exemptions" permitting the state to demand information have also increased suspicion of Chinese companies abroad and fed into political pressure for constraints on their activities. Companies which are known to have taken part in the suppression of dissent or have violated the human rights of ethnic and religious minorities such as in Xinjiang have come under additional scrutiny. Various countries and the European Union have taken steps toward restricting Chinese firms' market access and other activities.[98] As of late 2024 however, such measures remained largely confined to a relatively small group of advanced economies politically aligned with the US, and in some cases (such as EU tariffs on Chinese-made electric vehicles) have been framed in economic rather than political terms.

At home, China is building a resource-intensive but effective system of digitally enabled social control and governance. Abroad, it is building a national profile in the integrated global digital economy, in which Chinese firms have become increasingly competitive. The CPC's leaders have recognized that to realize their 2035 goals, reconciling this model with growing external pressures for digital "decoupling" will be critical. They have understood that in many areas Chinese industry continues to play technological catch-up with more economically advanced countries, and that China therefore should strive to maintain access to key foreign markets and partnerships.

But the contradictions in this strategy increasingly seem irreconcilable. Long-standing concerns about Chinese state-linked industrial cyberespionage, and the restrictive conditions placed on foreign businesses participating in China's digital economy, have been aggravated by tensions stemming from the global COVID-19 pandemic and China's position on Russia's invasion of Ukraine. As the US, European Union, and other jurisdictions increasingly develop and enforce their own cyberspace governance regimes, incompatibilities with that of China will multiply and become impossible to avoid.

The sweeping US export controls of October 2022 and their various follow-up measures reflect the growing irrelevance, at least from a US viewpoint, of a distinction between the military and economic aspects of China's rise. Although these controls were justified in terms of countering Chinese military modernization and human rights abuses, the dual-use

---

[98] Zack Whittaker, "US Towns Are Buying Chinese Surveillance Tech Tied to Uighur Abuses," *TechCrunch* (May 24, 2021), https://techcrunch.com/2021/05/24/united-states-towns-hikvision-dahua-surveillance.

and foundational nature of semiconductors means that the controls are likely to impede development of China's civilian economy across a broad front. In a speech of October 2022, the US Trade Representative said that Chinese industrial policy threatens the survival of free societies, and that open international trade with China can no longer continue in this context.[99]

Even before these controls, China faced significant obstacles to closing the gap with global industry leaders in key digital technologies. Complex inputs and intellectual property rights are often still dominated by US firms or those headquartered in US-allied nations. However, China's domestic economy and innovation system increasingly appears to be capable of relative self-sufficiency and even global competitiveness in many fields. In a worst-case scenario, this means that an autarkic "fortress China" approach would probably be technologically sustainable, allowing the CPC to maintain its authority at home even as China's international connections and global influence withered.

Experience to date suggests that the US-led effort to isolate China technologically is unlikely to succeed in confining Chinese firms to their domestic markets. Much of the growth in the global digital economy is occurring in regions where China's economic influence is relatively strong or is at least not being shut out by local politics. For example, Southeast Asia's digital economy is projected to triple in value to US$300 billion by 2025.[100] And even among the technologically advanced economies, virtually all of which are US allies, the appetite for a technological containment of China remains far from clear.

The coming years will reveal whether China's party-state can navigate these obstacles. Decisions made both in China and abroad will determine whether the world sees China retreat into a technologically fortified isolation or increasingly fractures between countries reducing and growing their ties with China. By 2035, it should be apparent whether the CPC's approach to cyberspace has achieved its goal of cementing the party's authority at home while making China a "cyberspace superpower" on the global stage.

---

[99] "Remarks by Ambassador Katherine Tai at the Roosevelt Institute's Progressive Industrial Policy Conference," speech, Office of the United States Trade Representative (October 2022), https://ustr.gov/about-us/policy-offices/press-office/speeches-and-remarks/2022/october/remarks-ambassador-katherine-tai-roosevelt-institutes-progressive-industrial-policy-conference.

[100] Google, *e-Conomy SEA 2020* (Report, Google, Temasek and Bain & Company, 2020), https://storage.googleapis.com/gweb-economy-sea.appspot.com/assets/pdf/e-Conomy_SEA_2020_Report.pdf.

11 Social Stability through Responsive Social Policy

Bingqin Li

Introduction

Responsive social policy has been crucial to enabling the Chinese Communist Party (CPC) to maintain social stability. After the launch of the economic reforms in 1978, for example, many scholars argued that sustained economic growth was central to the political legitimacy of the CPC.[1] They supposed that if the economy stopped growing and people's living standards dropped, support for the CPC would decline.[2]

The GDP growth rate has been declining since 2007, when it reached a high of 14.2 percent, and has stayed below 10 percent since 2010 – still impressive by world standards. With the sudden hit of COVID-19, the forecast growth rate slipped below 6 percent, reaching its lowest point of 2.3 percent in 2020, and returned to 5.2 in 2023.[3] Contrary to expectations, none of the bad economic news seems to have seriously threatened the party's grip on power. How has this been possible? What alternative sources of legitimacy have stepped in where performance falters? Another line of research has identified nationalism as a source of confidence in national identity and thus the legitimacy of the one-party state.[4] Nationalism feeds into patriotism, which can be manipulated to redirect public discontent toward enemies at home and abroad[5] or to generate the

---

[1] Bruce Gilley and Heike Holbig, "The Debate on Party Legitimacy in China: A Mixed Quantitative/Qualitative Analysis," *Journal of Contemporary China* 18(59) (2009): 339–358.

[2] Yang Zhong, "Legitimacy Crisis and Legitimation in China," *Journal of Contemporary Asia* 26(2) (1996): 201–220.

[3] World Bank (2025), GDP growth (annual %) – China, https://data.worldbank.org/indicator/NY.GDP.MKTP.KD.ZG?locations=CN.

[4] Hieke Holbig and Bruce Gilley, "Reclaiming Legitimacy in China," *Politics & Policy* 38(3) (2010): 395–422.

[5] Christopher Hughes, "Reclassifying Chinese Nationalism: The Geopolitik Turn," *Journal of Contemporary China* 20(71) (2011): 601–620.

illusion that the grass is greener in China than elsewhere.[6] A more enlightened version of nationalism advocates the use of traditional culture to boost cultural confidence.[7]

Within the People's Republic of China (PRC), scholars have focused on the CPC's ability to meet challenges by stressing its capacity to govern (*zhizheng nengli*). Responsive methods of governance have contributed to a high degree of political trust in the party.[8] In recent years, the party's attention to building and maintaining good infrastructure and utilities, including railways, underground rail, roads, and water supplies, as well as sound environmental governance, has increased the people's satisfaction with its rule.[9]

This chapter highlights an equally important yet less well understood dimension of CPC legitimacy – "people's livelihoods policy" (*minsheng zhengce*). This is an important policy focus for the CPC. It occupies the lion's share of each year's "Report on the Work of the Government" (*zhengfu gongzuo baogao*) issued by the State Council. State media widely and intensively publicize the policy to promote the idea that the party-state cares about the challenges faced by the people in their daily lives.

In this chapter, we will examine people's livelihood policy changes over time, providing context to the driving forces behind the changes and unpacking the meaning of responsiveness in Chinese social policy. The following section first introduces the theoretical background on using responsive social policy to address public discontent. It argues that in a society going through rapid development and transformation, unmet needs and social risks lead to discontent, and so a political regime seeking political legitimacy must act promptly to address causes of discontent. However, whether the resulting policies are effective remains ambiguous.

---

[6] Liza G. Steele and Scott M. Lynch, "The Pursuit of Happiness in China: Individualism, Collectivism, and Subjective Well-Being during China's Economic and Social Transformation," *Social Indicators Research* 114(2) (2013): 441–451.

[7] Fei Shen and Zhongshi Steve Guo, "The Last Refuge of Media Persuasion: News Use, National Pride and Political Trust in China," *Asian Journal of Communication* 23(2) (2013): 135–151.

[8] Cary Wu and Rima Wilkes, "Local–National Political Trust Patterns: Why China Is an Exception," *International Political Science Review* 39(4) (2018): 436–454.

[9] Longjin Chen and Yu You, "How Does Environmental Pollution Erode Political Trust in China? A Multilevel Analysis," *Environmental Impact Assessment Review* 88 (2021): 106553; Bingqin Li and Guy Mayraz, "Infrastructure Spending in China Increases Trust in Local Government," *Social Indicators Research* 132(1) (2017): 341–356; Nahui Zhen, "Political Trust in China: Evidence from Water Consumption in Shanghai" (PhD diss., University of Melbourne, 2017).

Responsive Social Policies for Political Stability

Social policy analysts have diverse perspectives on the link between social policies and political outcomes. Li argues that the Chinese government has focused on economic and social stability, and its social policies are designed to support these goals.[10] Huang argues that the Chinese government uses social policies to provide desired social welfare, such as pensions and health insurance.[11] Tillin and Duckett take the view that China is not different from liberal democracies in the developing world in that the government, mindful of the need for economic development, tries to create a social welfare system to achieve long-term development, rather than just formulating policy in response to protests.[12] This contrasts with the idea of a reactive liberal-conservative welfare regime proposed by Ringen and Ngok.[13] Each theory reflects some aspect of how the Chinese social policy system functions. It is a complex behemoth, which the party-state is continuously upgrading and reshaping and expanding into more policy fields at the national level. There are local variations in policy targets and methods of delivery, and numerous pilot programs which are attached loosely to the main frame. In this system, both long-term agendas and responsive strategies are needed.

As discussed by Kang, political instability occurs when groups of people dissatisfied with their status quo attribute their problems to the current political regime.[14] Opportunistic violence breaks out when they have no other means to solve their problems. When social problems are related to unmet social needs and anxiety, as in education, housing, healthcare, and old-age care, social policies can potentially provide the solution. Issues of livelihood (*minsheng wenti*) relate to available resources for human necessities (food, clothing, shelter), income and assets (jobs, housing, land), sanitation and infrastructure (road, water supply), social services (education, healthcare, aged care), and environmental resources (land, water) necessary for survival.[15] Ong and Han find that people usually only participate in protests

---

[10] Bingqin Li, "Social Welfare and Protection for Economic Growth and Social Stability: China's Experience," in *A Changing China: Emerging Governance, Economic and Social Trends* (Singapore: Civil Service College, 2012), 39–60.

[11] Xian Huang, "The Politics of Social Welfare Reform in Urban China: Social Welfare Preferences and Reform Policies," *Journal of Chinese Political Science* 18(1) (2013): 61–85.

[12] Louise Tillin and Jane Duckett, "The Politics of Social Policy: Welfare Expansion in Brazil, China, India and South Africa in Comparative Perspective," *Commonwealth & Comparative Politics* 55(3) (2017): 253–277.

[13] Stein Ringen and Kinglun Ngok, "What Kind of Welfare State is Emerging in China?" in *Towards Universal Health Care in Emerging Economies* ed. Ilcheong Yi (London: Springer, 2017), 213–237.

[14] Kang Xiaoguang, "China: Political Development and Political Stability in the Era of Reform," *Chinese Economy* 35(5) (2002): 6–92.

[15] Peter B. Evans and Patrick Heller, "Chapter 37 Human Development, State Transformation, and the Politics of the Developmental State," in *The Oxford Handbook*

in the PRC when their interests are affected.[16] People worry not only about what they do not have, but also about what they may lose in the foreseeable future due to natural disasters, aging, health issues, lack of access to education, or unemployment. Their level of anxiety accords with how well prepared for or protected they feel against these risks.

Persistent social inequality leading to social injustice can also lead to public outcry. When social media and the internet expose socially unjust situations and events, this can undermine the trust people have in the party-state. However, if the party-state appears to be responsive and handles the situation satisfactorily, public discontent may be calmed down. For example, after the migrant worker Sun Zhigang was beaten to death in Guangzhou's Detention and Eviction Center (where people without appropriate urban resident permits were held) in 2003, the authorities closed all detention and eviction centers and removed legal barriers preventing people from rural areas from working in cities throughout the country.[17] The causes of anxiety and anger can also be subjective, such as depression resulting from long working hours, or worries about social status.[18] Again, the perception that the party-state is acting to address these problems helps shape public opinion in the party's favor.[19]

Given that the CPC came to power by mobilizing the discontented poor in a revolution, it is more than sensitive to the fact that local social problems might escalate to become a nationwide political movement. This can be observed by the fact that each Party Secretary of the CPC since Mao has publicly cited the saying in the *King's Rule* of the Confucian philosopher Xunzi: "The ruler is like a boat and the people like water. Water can support a boat and can also capsize it."[20] This saying reminds the leadership, party members, and government officials

---

of *Transformations of the State*, ed. Stephan Leibfried, Evelyne Huber, Matthew Lange, Jonah D. Levy, Frank Nullmeier, and John D. Stephens (Oxford: Oxford University Press, 2015), 691–713.

[16] Lynette H. Ong, and Donglin Han, "What Drives People to Protest in an Authoritarian Country? Resources and Rewards vs Risks of Protests in Urban and Rural China," *Political Studies* 67(1) (2019): 224–248.

[17] Qianfan Zhang, "A Constitution without Constitutionalism? The Paths of Constitutional Development in China," *International Journal of Constitutional Law* 8(4) (2010): 950–976.

[18] Chenxi Li, "From Involution to Education: A Glance to Chinese Young Generation." Paper presented at the 2021 4th International Conference on Humanities Education and Social Sciences (ICHESS), 2021.

[19] Feng Sun, and Jiang Jian Xiao, "Perceived Social Policy Fairness and Subjective Wellbeing: Evidence from China," *Social Indicators Research* 107(1) (2012): 171–186.

[20] Ernst-Ulrich Petersmann, "Methodology Problems in International Economic Law and Adjudication," *Jindal Global Law Review* 7(2) (2016): 279–332; Bert Quade, "Open Journal of Political Science," *Open Journal of Political Science* 1 (2011): 1–9.

not to be complacent, to listen to people's voices and respond to their needs and concerns. Obviously, not all social problems can be or even need to be addressed by social policy. It is also obvious that social problems cannot be solved all at once. The central or local leadership's perceptions of the levels and prominence of threats to the party will influence which social needs are prioritized and how – by long-term programs or by responsive policies.

How to Tell Whether Policies Are Targeting Political Resentment

This chapter deploys a comprehensive methodology to scrutinize the interplay between social policy and social stability as represented by public resilience or expressions of discontent, such as protests in the PRC. The analysis is grounded in evaluating the extent to which social policies are responsive to public needs and sentiments, particularly those related to public discontent.

The chapter divides the historical context into distinct periods, each characterized by specific sociopolitical environments and policy responses. These include the early reform period from 1978 to 1991, the era of accelerated reforms from 1992 to 2010, and from 2011 to the present. Each period is analyzed in light of the guiding questions and criteria outlined previously. Three questions shape the discussion in each era:

(i) **Long-Term Welfare System Changes:** Has the welfare system evolved over the long term to address the needs of the population?
(ii) **Feedback Integration in Policy Changes:** Are there tangible attempts to address public discontent?
(iii) **Effectiveness of the Responsive Approach**: Has the party won the "hearts and minds" of the Chinese people?

Historical review provides the landscape and the evolution of social policies since the beginning of the economic reform period. Specific policy cases such as housing reform are discussed in depth or as examples to illustrate the roles of the corresponding policies in targeting and mitigating public discontent. Supporting the qualitative assessment, I also referenced data analysis published in existing research.

The discussion of effectiveness is put together in a separate section. This framework facilitates a comprehensive examination of how the CPC's social policies have evolved in response to social challenges and political discontent, thus contributing to the overarching goal of maintaining social stability.

Gradual Reforms That Actively Avoided Conflicts (1978–1991)

The reforms during the period of 1978–1991 aimed to release China from the dysfunctional system of central (top-down) economic planning. They embraced decentralization, market competition, and privatization, as well as "opening up to the world" (*zouxiang shijie*), which involved expanding both international trade and foreign direct investment, including joint ventures and foreign enterprises (100 percent owned by foreign investors). However, conservatives opposed the reforms, claiming they strayed from the path of communism. Deng Xiaoping wanted the party to abandon the Maoist mindset of "politics in command" (*zhengzhi guashuai*) for one of pragmatism, trial, and error. At the same time, there were also concerns that the people would not be able to cope with the shocks of radical economic reforms,[21] such as the privatization of housing and price reform. Mao's radical "Great Leap Forward," intended as a quick fix (*ji yu qiu cheng*) for economic backwardness and a way for China to catch up and even overtake the UK and the US, had resulted in the disastrous famine that killed tens of millions of people between 1958 and 1961. In this sense, maintaining a slower pace of reform – including the gradual dismantling of the *danwei* system (also known as the work unit system, a Mao-era work unit structure that tied individuals to state employers, which controlled jobs, welfare, and daily life) beginning in the 1980s – was an attempt to preempt both public dissatisfaction and disaster. The main reforms in social policy in this era dealt with the following concerns:

(i) Housing was the earliest social policy field that was subjected to marketization. The government started by selling private housing, then encouraging subsidized ownership, and moved on to rental reform.[22]

(ii) The healthcare system also underwent major changes. The government gave urban employers a fixed amount of healthcare funds for each employee, and employers had to match those funds. If the healthcare costs exceeded a threshold amount, employees had to pay out of pocket first and claim the money back afterward.[23] The

---

[21] Hui Wang, *The Gradual Revolution: China's Economic Reform Movement* (New Jersey: Transaction Publishers, 1994).

[22] Bingqin Li, "Housing Welfare Policies in Urban China," in *Handbook of Welfare in China*, ed. Beatriz Carrillo, Johanna Hood, and Paul Kadetz (Cheltenham: Edward Elgar Publishing, 2017), 123–143.

[23] Yanzhong Huang, *Governing Health in Contemporary China* (New York: Routledge, 2015).

rural cooperative healthcare system collapsed, as rural collectives could not pool enough funds to cover rural residents' healthcare.[24]

(iii) A "beacon school" system was established to identify and train primary and secondary school students for university education. Students were selected strictly according to their exam results. As rural areas were less densely populated, some local regions merged schools for efficiency.[25]

While the reforms initiated in this period were intended to be transformative and long-term, they were met with a mix of short-term reactions, adjustments, and challenges, reflecting the complexities of transitioning from a centrally planned economy to a more market-oriented system.

In the early 1980s, the party championed marketization as a great if gradual transition that might cause temporary pain but would bring a better future. People greeted economic changes with optimism. However, when people realized that their welfare entitlements might disappear as the economic reforms progressed, they started to become unhappy. In the more open environment, people were ready and willing to criticize or even resist the reform measures.

The several rounds of housing reform were a good example of such tensions. The first step was selling new houses to urban residents without any subsidy. In 1979, the governments in Xinan and Nanning started to sell apartments. Sixty-square-meter houses were offered for CNY9000; only eighteen out of thirty-seven houses were sold. Plans to build more houses for sale in twenty-three provinces were abandoned due to lack of interest, as people living in public housing were unwilling to buy new apartments in the private market and showed little enthusiasm for purchasing the ones they already occupied. In 1982, the government started to experiment with subsidized home ownership in Siping, Shaishi, Zhengzhou, and Changzhou. But only 2,140 apartments were sold across the four cities by the end of 1984. In 1985, 160 cities and more than 300 counties started to subsidize house purchases. About two million apartments were bought with heavy subsidies. However, employers were unhappy about the high subsidies and were not keen to sell, and the reform was terminated quickly. Local governments then decided to focus on rental reform. They tried varied measures to leave the subsidized housing sector.[26] Tangshan, Yantai, Bengbu, and

---

[24] Yuanli Liu, William C. L. Hsiao, Qing Li, Xingzhu Liu, and Minghui Ren, "Transformation of China's Rural Health Care Financing," *Social Science & Medicine* 41(8) (1995): 1085–1093.

[25] Bingqin Li and David Piachaud, "Urbanization and Social Policy in China," *Asia Pacific Development Journal* 13(1) (2006): 1–26.

[26] Victor N. Shaw, "Urban Housing Reform in China," *Habitat International* 21(2) (1997): 199–212.

Changzhou started rent reforms in 1986. Their initial tactic of aggressively increasing rents led to panic. Rumors about rising inflation added to the panic and led to the hoarding of consumer goods. The government had to pause further reform. As a response, local reformers decided that after the delay, rollback, or termination, it was necessary to let people realize that their low rent was due to government subsidies. The plan was to reveal the true market price of housing to people by raising rents while providing cash subsidies or vouchers to keep expenses close to what they had been.[27] After this, the rent subsidies were gradually reduced.

To further reduce the shock of the reforms, some local governments introduced the New Policies for Newly Built Homes (*xinfang xinzhengce*), which required that all newly built houses be sold on the market (as opposed to being purchased by employers) and barred new school or university graduates from accessing public housing. At the same time, older employees would continue to enjoy their existing arrangements. This compromise acknowledged that it was difficult for people to accept radical policy changes all at once, and that older workers on low salaries who had always relied on their employers for housing should not suffer unduly. The New Policies for Newly Built Homes focused on a smaller group of people who could afford higher rents, had not yet taken welfare housing for granted, and thus would put up less resistance to marketization.[28] This strategy was later applied to pension reform as a way of avoiding conflict.

The 1989 political turmoil – student-led demonstrations which became a prodemocracy movement, put down by the government with lethal force in early June – was triggered by the more visible inequality resulting from the economic reforms. Economic restructuring had led to rising unemployment, and corruption became more serious than at any time since 1949, feeding into growing public discontent. However, the CPC leadership did not see the public protests as a request for better reforms but rather as a demand for regime change. The CPC was very worried about political instability. They suppressed the student-led movement. Almost all reforms toward marketization were put on hold, and they even backtracked in some fields.[29]

---

[27] Tony Dorcey, Achim Steiner, Michael Acreman, and Brett Orlando, *China: Implementation Options for Urban Housing Reform* (Washington, DC: The World Bank, 1992).

[28] Xianghong Wang, "Behavioural Labor Economics," in *Routledge Handbook of Behavioral Economics*, ed. Roger Frantz, Shu-Heng Chen, Kurt Dopfer, Floris Heukelom, and Shabnam Mousavi (New York: Routledge, 2016), 377–390.

[29] Yan Sun, "The Chinese Protests of 1989: The Issue of Corruption," *Asian Survey* 31(8) (1991): 762–782; Dale Swartz, *Jasmine in the Middle Kingdom: Autopsy of China's (Failed) Revolution*, Asian Outlook 1 (Washington, DC: American Enterprise Institute for Public Policy Research, 2011).

Generally speaking, the changing directions in welfare reform policies in this period were in response to the social pressure which arose from economic and political changes. Welfare reform, especially when it permitted state enterprises to reduce their welfare obligations, encountered resistance. Consequently, these reforms were delayed, reduced in scope, or terminated when public discontent intensified. The backlash took the form of widespread stockpiling, a hesitancy to buy homes, and opposition to rent increases.

Maintaining Social Harmony (1992–2010)

The period following Deng Xiaoping's endorsement of economic reforms in 1992 saw a resumption and acceleration of change in China, with significant implications for social policy and public sentiment. This period, leading up to and including the Hu–Wen administration, saw a number of different responses to the reforms.

The reforms got back on track in 1992 after Deng Xiaoping toured the south and made an important speech endorsing them. From 1995, enterprise reform accelerated. Official media used the term *xiagang* ("laid-off") or *daiye* ("waiting to be employed") rather than the politically sensitive *shiye* ("unemployed"). Even when workers were laid off, their *dang'an* (personal files) continued to be held at their former employers, meaning that they were formally still members of the *danwei* where they used to work. Some people successfully negotiated for compensation from their former *danwei* or found ways to continue to live in worker housing.[30] Many work units still provided some aspects of welfare, such as regular health checks, to their laid-off workers. But the availability of such benefits varied according to factors such as whether the work unit was still solvent.[31] However, public sentiment was in favor of continued economic reform. The state media guided public discourse away from the topic of reducing the suffering of laid-off workers in favor of how they should abandon the mindset of lifetime employment and *xiahai*, "jump into the sea," the popular slang for going into the private sector.[32] The state media promoted success stories of those who embraced the transition to

---

[30] Bingqin Li, "Housing Welfare Policies in Urban China," in *Handbook of Welfare in China*, ed. Beatriz Carrillo, Johanna Hood, and Paul Kadetz (Cheltenham: Edward Elgar Publishing, 2017), 123–143.

[31] Thomas B. Gold, Wiliam J. Hurst, Jaeyoun Won, and Li Qiang, *Laid-Off Workers in a Workers' State: Unemployment with Chinese Characteristics* (Cham: Springer, 2009).

[32] Eva P. Hung and Stephen W. K. Chiu, "The Lost Generation: Life Course Dynamics and Xiagang in China," *Modern China* 29(2) (2003): 204–236.

a market economy. Unsuccessful people seemed to have only themselves to blame.[33]

Significant efforts were made to establish a social pension system independent of employers. This system was seen as a crucial buffer against the social conflicts emerging from the privatization of enterprises. Pilot programs commenced in the 1980s amid widespread discontent over corruption, job losses, and growing uncertainty. Following the easing of tensions in 1989, one major policy measure was the national rollout of the social insurance system in 1991, formally implemented in 1992. This was a pivotal move toward creating an alternative system of social protection, aimed at mitigating opposition to enterprise reforms.[34]

Even though the fast-growing private sector absorbed the pressure of unemployment, it wasn't easy to get rich. Inequality increased rapidly. People's concerns about how to make a living, pay for accommodation, and so on, in both cities and rural areas, focused resentment toward the institutional constraints (*zhidu quxian*) of the Chinese political system – where leaders are not elected with one person, one vote.

In 2002–2012, the period directly preceding the ascension of Xi Jinping, the government of Party Secretary-General Hu Jintao and Premier Wen Jiabao picked up on and responded to public discontent. The party's "pro-growth" discourse was modified to stress that economic growth should also lift people from poverty and address income inequality while maintaining social harmony and social stability. The government introduced several types of social policies to sustain social stability. The first offered protection for people trapped in poverty. These mostly involved central government-directed direct cash transfers to poor regions and poor people. Eligibility was defined by local government policies at provincial or city/county level depending on which level of government was in charge of a certain policy at the point of discussion. Poor regions were defined according to GDP per capita, income per capita, and local government revenue per capita. Poor people were defined by income per capita at household level and employability. However, the practice of poverty reduction was often criticized for missing the target: It was not always the poor who benefited from poverty-alleviation measures, which also generated perverse

---

[33] Yueran Zhang, *Welfare Reform and the Mobilization Power of the Displaced Workers in China, 1994–2004* (New York: City University of New York, 2010).

[34] Gordon White, "Social Security Reforms in China: Towards an East Asian Model?" in *The East Asian Welfare Model: Welfare Orientalism and the State*, ed. Roger Goodman, Gordon White, and Huck-ju Kwon (London: Routledge, 1998), 175–197.

incentives, creating the impression that it was easier to stay poor and get handouts than actively work to improve economic opportunity.[35]

The second type of government policy for maintaining social stability involved social insurance schemes funded by personal and employer contributions. These included maternity insurance (1988), a pension (1992), a housing provident fund (1994), unemployment insurance (1999), work injury (2004), and medical insurance (2007). They were gradually simplified into two main subsystems: employment-based social insurance with higher contributions and entitlements, and residence-based social insurance with lower contributions and entitlements.[36] Employees and employers jointly contributed to the employee insurance; resident insurance was paid for by individuals only. Rural social insurance was similarly paid for individually by the farmers themselves or collectively by their villages. The funding for rural social insurance was managed separately from that for urban social insurance. Unlike the urban social insurance schemes, rural social insurance was locally organized.

The third type of social stability maintenance policy was designed to address public anger. New rules introduced in 2003 allowed migrant workers to enter cities to work without jumping over endless administrative hurdles such as impossible-to-obtain legal work status and residence permits. Also that year, rescue and management centers (*jiuzhu guanli zhan*) for homeless people and "wanderers and beggars" (*liulang qitao*) replaced detention and eviction centers (*shourong qiansong zhan*). This implied that the government would stop criminalizing these people and instead would treat them as people in need of temporary help with shelter and food. This was against the backdrop of the public anger at the death of Sun Zhigang, a young man beaten to death in the detention and eviction center in Guangdong.[37] Another series of policies gradually integrated migrant workers into urban society. The state cracked down on late payment or nonpayment of migrant workers' wages and required their employers to contribute to their social

---

[35] Li Xiaoyun and Joe Remenyi, "Towards Sustainable Village Poverty Reduction: The Development of the County Poverty Alleviation Planning (CPAP) Approach," in *Community Participation in China*, ed. Janelle Plummer and John G. Taylor (New York: Routledge, 2013), 294–329.

[36] Qin Gao, Sui Yang, and Shi Li, "Labor Contracts and Social Insurance Participation Among Migrant Workers in China," *China Economic Review* 23(4) (2012): 1195–1205; Bingqin Li, "Social Pension Unification in an Urbanising China: Paths and Constraints," *Public Administration and Development* 34(4) (2014): 281–293; Albert Park, Yaowu Wu, and Yang Du, *Informal Employment in Urban China: Measurement and Implications* (Washington, DC: World Bank, 2012).

[37] Sarah Biddulph, Elisa Nesossi, Flora Sapio, and Susan Trevaskes, "Detention and Its Reforms in the PRC," *China Law and Society Review* 2(1) (2017): 1–62.

insurance.[38] These policies were introduced as migrant farmers increasingly organized protests over local authorities' behavior, and when their complaints were not addressed, traveled to Beijing to deliver complaint letters to the central government.[39]

The signature social policy of the Hu–Wen era was the removal of rural agricultural taxes and surcharges in 2005. This instantly relieved the highly pressurized relations between rural village and county governments. Before that, county governments suffered from serious financial pressures resulting from the 1994 reform of public finance, which allowed the central government to take an incrementally increasing share of revenues. Over time, county governments had to rely on collecting more taxes and surcharges, which caused serious tension between farmers and county officials. The 2005 reform fixed that, even if the loss of rural tax revenues would later shrink rural public services, such as education, and the provision of other basic public services and goods.[40]

A minimum living standard guarantee system (*dibao*) was introduced in urban areas in 1999 for people with no income living in difficult conditions. This was in response to the growing protests of laid-off workers[41] who had lost their means of earning as a result of enterprise reforms.[42] Funding from both central and local governments increased *dibao* coverage in 2001.[43] In 2003, the central government piloted a rural minimum-living-standard guarantee system. The fear of potential instability caused by the growing number of laid-off workers was evident in the state media for some years.[44] Initially, laid-off workers protested about their loss of income; later, about not being able to afford privatized social services. New policies were introduced gradually to catch up with the need for

---

[38] Pun Ngai and Lu Huilin. "A Culture of Violence: The Labor Subcontracting System and Collective Action by Construction Workers in Post-socialist China," *The China Journal* 64 (2010): 143–158.

[39] Xinhua Jian and Huang Kun. "Up-to-Date Investigation Report on Rural Migrant Workers in China," *China Population, Resources and Environment* 17(6) (2007): 1–6.

[40] Xuefeng He, "*Quxiao nongyeshui dui guojia yu nongmin guanxi de yingxiang*" [The impact of the abolition of the agricultural tax on the relationship between the state and farmers], *Gansu shehui kexue* [Gansu social science] 2 (2007): 1–3.

[41] Hong Yung Lee, "Xiagang, the Chinese Style of Laying Off Workers," *Asian Survey* 40(6) (2000): 914–937.

[42] Dorothy. J. Solinger, "Labour Market Reform and the Plight of the Laid-Off Proletariat," *The China Quarterly* 170 (2002): 304–326.

[43] Bjorn A. Gustafsson, and Feng Quheng, "Di Bao Receipt and Its Importance for Combating Poverty in Urban China," *Poverty & Public Policy* 3(1) (2011): 1–32.

[44] Chih-Jou Jay Chen, "Growing Social Unrest and Emergent Protest Groups in China," in *Rise of China: Beijing's Strategies and Implications for the Asia-Pacific*, ed. Hsin-Huang Michael Hsiao and Cheng-Yi Lin (London: Routledge, 2009), 87–106; K. Sen and T. Lee, "The Curse of the Everyday: Politics of Representation and New Social Semiotics in Post-socialist China," in *Political Regimes and the Media in Asia* (London: Routledge, 2008), 45–62.

further inclusion. By the end of 2006, all provincial level regions had agreed to join the scheme. The beneficiaries could also receive other subsidies for fee-based social services, such as healthcare and education.[45]

Cities expanded outward, and within the city centers, governments carried out large-scale demolition of existing neighborhoods to clear the way for new developments. This resulted in personal land and property loss in both urban and rural areas. For much of the 2000s, involuntary resettlement because of urban regeneration was a main cause of urban protests.[46] Rural unrest also erupted in response to forced resettlement where climate change and environmental degradation had made rural areas unlivable, the construction of megadam projects,[47] and poverty-reduction schemes that forced people living in mountainous areas to relocate closer to the city.[48] Endless disputes arose between dispossessed farmers and village authorities or property developers – or village authorities in cahoots with property developers. Land and housing disputes became one of the main reasons for social unrest in the 1990s and beyond.[49] Numerous social policies were introduced to appease dislocated urban residents and farmers. These include cash compensation, housing relocation, employment arrangements and social insurance contributions.[50] Cash compensation and housing relocation were used most frequently up until 2004. However, many farmers did not manage their finances well and were quickly left with nothing. In 2004, the government started to talk about setting up a social security system for landless farmers. In 2006, a practice first trialed in Zhejiang in the 1990s that funneled some of the compensation into social insurance contributions, the "land in exchange for social security" scheme (*tudi huan shebao*), was rolled out nationwide.[51]

---

[45] Liqiu Zhao, Yu Guo, and Ting Shao, "Can the Minimum Living Standard Guarantee Scheme Enable the Poor to Escape the Poverty Trap in Rural China?" *International Journal of Social Welfare* 26(4) (2017): 314–328.
[46] Chih-Jou Jay Chen, "Peasant Protests over Land Seizures in Rural China," *The Journal of Peasant Studies* 47(6) (2020): 1327–1347.
[47] Bingqin Li, Chunlai Chen, and Biliang Hu, "Governing Urbanization and the New Urbanization Plan in China," *Environment and Urbanization* 28(2) (2016): 515–534.
[48] Min Tang, "Inclusive Growth and the New Phase of Poverty Reduction in the People's Republic of China," *Asian Development Review* 25(1/2) (2008): 81–99.
[49] Chen, "Peasant Protests over Land Seizures in Rural China."
[50] Yingui Cao, Martin Dallimer, Lindsay C. Stringer, Zhongke Bai, and Yim Ling Siu, "Land Expropriation Compensation among Multiple Stakeholders in a Mining Area: Explaining 'Skeleton House' Compensation," *Land Use Policy* 74 (2018): 97–110; Maitreesh Ghatak and Dilip Mookherjee, "Land Acquisition for Industrialization and Compensation of Displaced Farmers," *Journal of Development Economics* 110 (2014): 303–312.
[51] Yan-gang Fang, Ke-jian Shi, and Cai-cheng Niu, "A Comparison of the Means and Ends of Rural Construction Land Consolidation: Case Studies of Villagers' Attitudes and Behaviours in Changchun City, Jilin Province, China," *Journal of Rural Studies* 47 (2016): 459–473.

When newly introduced policies became too controversial or led to unrest, the government could decide to terminate them to avoid conflict. For example, some giant enterprises started to introduce industry- (or sectoral-)level pension pooling in 1998. They had large numbers of employees, and their average income was higher than the city average income that was used to calculate pension contributions and entitlement. Local governments, under pressure to set up pensions for all, were not happy about these large enterprises removing themselves from the broader social funding pool. So they decided to terminate the giant-enterprise pension pooling. Another abandoned policy initiative was the Starlight project, which aimed to provide community-based old-age care in urban communities, withdrawn after it became clear that the users were not satisfied with the services.[52] The aggressive policy of merging schools in rural areas was also terminated after it was openly criticized by scholars and in the media for making it even harder for rural children to get an education.

Since the turn of the century, the number of market-oriented reforms in the social policy field has decreased from the previous period. In contrast, there have been growing numbers of social assistance programs for the poor and more types of social insurance emphasizing the combination of personal responsibilities and mutual support. These policy changes reflected a gradual shift toward a more socialist approach, as it was increasingly recognized that economic growth could not eliminate poverty and could even result in greater inequality.[53] People at the bottom became less patient with unfulfilled promises of "getting rich later" (*houfu*) and expressed growing discontent, which was more easily spread with the rapid growth in internet usage.[54]

The overarching theme during this time was the government's effort to manage the social impacts of market-oriented reforms while maintaining social harmony and addressing growing inequality. The prioritization of a "harmonious society" and the stress on the elimination of income inequality at the national level generated the impression that the party-state did care for those left behind.

---

[52] Lijie Fang, Bingqin Li, and Tom Cliff, "Emergent Political Norms in Local State–Private Enterprise Relations during China's Big Push for Poverty Reduction," *American Behavioral Scientist* 66(2) (2021): 00027642211020050.

[53] Sen Gong and Bingqin Li, "Inequality in China: A Case Study," Report for Save the Children (2013), www.savethechildren.org.cn/images/stories/Recource_Center/publication/inequality_in_china_eng.pdf.

[54] Yuntao Zhang and John Tomlinson. "Three Constituencies of Online Dissent in China," *Chinese Journal of Communication* 5(1) (2012): 55–60.

Lifting the Bottom (2011 to the Present)

Politically, China has experienced a sharp left turn since Xi came into power. He considered this shift away from market-driven reform necessary to ensure a future for the CPC. Xi has defined the central task of social policy since 2012 as "lifting the bottom (*doudi*)."[55] The pressure of economic slowdown was looming large, especially with the repercussions of the Global Financial Crises of 2007–2008 still rippling through the world economy. As mentioned earlier (p. 251), it was already becoming obvious in the Hu Jintao–Wen Jiabao administration that it would be necessary to improve policy implementation. There was a popular saying that "policies never left Zhongnanhai [party headquarters]" (*zhengce bu qu Zhongnanhai*). The CPC's local offices in major cities opened specialist units for specific social services, showing that the party was already paying attention to the implementation of social policy before Xi came to power. Since he took office, the party has placed great emphasis on improving people's perception of what they have gained (*huode gan*) from the reforms. No matter how much the economy grows and whatever the government does for the people, if they are not aware of how this has benefited them, political trust and happiness will disappear.

Xi's pet project, Targeted Poverty Alleviation (also known as precise poverty reduction), was introduced in 2013. Social policy played a supporting role: improving housing through relocation and housing repair funds, skills development, healthcare, and help with job searches. The unemployable, such as the old and the frail, would receive cash benefits. Apart from the enormous amount of money devoted to poverty alleviation, implementation on the ground was relentless. Each official in rural areas was given strict targets. Failing to deliver would lead to job loss or public humiliation. Businesses, NGOs and civil servants in wealthier regions were also required to "volunteer" for what became a mass war on absolute poverty. Xi's self-imposed deadline for the elimination of "absolute poverty" was 2020, ten years earlier than the international deadline set by the United Nations Sustainable Development Goals. Elites and the wealthy did not like the style of the poverty alleviation program as they had to devote time to activities outside their professional responsibilities or give money to the poor. Also, it is not at all clear whether the intensive campaign would be able to eradicate poverty permanently. However, many comments posted on social media pointed out that government

---

[55] Zhai Fuhua and Gao Qin, "Strengthening Coordination between Rural and Urban Dibao: Evidence and Implications," *China: An International Journal* 17(1) (2019): 96–108.

officials and wealthier people had finally come to know the hardship of the poor. The program has thus grown political trust overall.[56]

In this period, a large number of left-leaning policies (entailing social redistribution of resources rather than personal contribution) were introduced. The focus went beyond financial arrangements to improving social services, such as providing community-based aged care and healthcare. The local governments now provide telephone hotlines to the general public and digital apps for those receiving various kinds of social services, allowing them to comment on the quality of the services and lodge complaints. The authorities closely monitor how fast service providers (government employees or contracted service providers) solve problems and incentivize timely responses.[57] Such solutions make people feel more empowered in their daily life, and the quick responses enhance their trust in the government's ability to deliver what it promised.[58]

However, it is also important to note that not all social policy-related public discontent can be solved by adjusting social policies. The privatization of healthcare, which has made it unaffordable for many, has forced some people to choose between escaping poverty or preserving their health. There have been frequent attacks on doctors and nurses as people blame them for the failures of the system, including creeping corruption.[59] Some scholars cannot see any way out apart from turning healthcare into a public service again.[60] Others, however, consider this a matter for law enforcement. Local governments eager to maintain social stability have preferred to keep patients happy by forcing hospitals to compensate them for unsatisfactory treatment, which encouraged patients to sue the hospitals. Some lawyers, legal advisors, or even gangsters took advantage of patients' distrust of the system and encouraged patients or their families to escalate minor disputes and go to the courts in a bid for more medical compensation.[61] In 2015, new legislation was introduced to criminalize troublemaking in hospitals. Similar hard-line

---

[56] Cai Zuo, Zhongyuan Wang, and Qingjie Zeng, "From Poverty to Trust: Political Implications of the Anti-Poverty Campaign in China," *International Political Science Review* 44(2) (2021): 01925121211001759.
[57] Zhongyuan Wang and Jianjun Liu, "Representation as Responsiveness in China: Evidence from a City Public Service Hotline," *Asian Survey* 60(2) (2020): 366–390.
[58] Wang and Liu, "Representation as Responsiveness in China."
[59] Jiong Tu, "Yinao: Protest and Violence in China's Medical Sector," *Berkeley Journal of Sociology* 11 (2014): 1-14; Liuyi Zhang, Teresa E. Stone, and Jingping Zhang, "Understanding the Rise of Yinao in China: A Commentary on the Little Known Phenomenon of Healthcare Violence," *Nursing & Health Sciences* 19(2) (2017): 183-187.
[60] Tu, "Yinao."
[61] Tianyang Liu and Xiao Tan, "Troublemaking in Hospitals: Performed Violence against the Healthcare Professions in China," *Health Sociology Review* 30(2) (2021): 157–170.

responses were also adopted in the field of land disputes to overcome the perverse incentives for people to escalate disputes. When compensation cannot persuade people to give up protests, the government cracks down on the demonstrators.[62]

Under Xi, the party-state has improved the social welfare system in a way that could have lasting effects; at the same time, responsive social policies have come with stricter law enforcement. The effectiveness of such a carrot-and-stick approach is not very clear. Patients have continued to attack doctors, and farmers keep protesting. Interestingly, the experience of the COVID-19 response to some extent restored the trust of the public in medical professionals, as people witnessed doctors risking their lives to save their patients.[63] However, trust was quickly eroded as the strict lockdowns stayed in place even as the pandemic became less severe.

The year 2020 marked "the end of absolute poverty," and the country moved on to address relative poverty, even though the impact of COVID and geopolitical conflicts had resulted in a serious economic downturn with more unemployment and lower incomes, even a return to poverty. Public discontent, though not as openly expressed now because of more heavy-handed social control and much stronger digital monitoring, can be observed in other ways, such as increased emigration, in particular of entrepreneurs. It has become urgent for the government to revive the economy and reduce public anxiety. In response to the challenges, China has implemented a series of social policies aimed at stabilizing the economy, safeguarding the well-being of its citizens, and promoting social harmony. Apart from economic recovery and stimulus packages, there has been a wide range of social policies to improve the coverage of social security and assistance, public health system reforms, education and training, community support, and civic participation, as well as mental health and psychological support. These economic stimulus measures are designed to mitigate the impact of the pandemic on the economy, protecting and creating jobs, and thereby maintaining social stability.

In terms of public health, strengthening disease prevention and control systems, as well as investing in basic medical infrastructure, helps to enhance public confidence in the government's crisis-response capabilities. There is also continuing reform of the healthcare system, in particular the regulation of the pricing of prescription drugs and hospital treatments. These measures also came with a heavy-handed anticorruption campaign

---

[62] Chen, "Peasant Protests over Land Seizures in Rural China."
[63] Charles Calisher, Dennis Carroll, Rita Colwell, et al., "Statement in Support of the Scientists, Public Health Professionals, and Medical Professionals of China Combatting COVID-19," *The Lancet* 395(10226) (2020): e42–e43.

in the health sector. Even though this caused concern among elites in hospital and pharmaceutical companies, the general public benefits from more affordable healthcare and drugs.

Furthermore, enhancing community services, encouraging civic participation, and providing mental health services are key measures in maintaining social stability and building a harmonious social environment. To maintain China's economic competitiveness, education and vocational training policies focus on providing new opportunities for human resource development. Social policies have been tailored to attract skilled workers locally.[64]

Overall, these policies, by addressing the economic, social, and psychological issues caused by the pandemic, are designed to alleviate social tensions and dissatisfaction and increase public trust and satisfaction with the government. Effective implementation and continuous adjustment of policies are crucial for achieving social stability. The Chinese government has demonstrated strong organizational capabilities in responding to the pandemic, but the implementation of postpandemic social policies also faces numerous challenges, including uncertain economic recovery, increased pressure on the social security system, and the need for ongoing reforms in the public health system.

Have Responsive Social Policies Maintained Social Stability?

The previous section has shown how the party-state has actively used social policy to respond to social discontent and meet social needs. A follow-up question is whether these social policies worked to win over the hearts and minds of the Chinese people. Some evidence shows that responsive social policies have affected public opinion and achieved temporary social stability. This can be taken in a number of ways.

First, improved social provision may positively influence public opinion on the governments and the Party. For example, in 2018 Li and Wu analyzed the 2010 Chinese General Social Survey (CGSS) for the impact of the New Rural Pension Scheme (NRPS) on political trust and policy expectations among the Chinese populace.[65] The study reveals that individuals in NRPS pilot areas exhibit higher levels of trust in both central and local governments compared to those in non-NRPS areas,

---

[64] Yang Shen and Bingqin Li, "Policy Coordination in the Talent War to Achieve Economic Upgrading: The Case of Four Chinese Cities," *Policy Studies* 43(3) (2022): 443–463.

[65] Zhonglu Li and Xiaogang Wu, "Social Policy and Political Trust: Evidence from the New Rural Pension Scheme in China," *The China Quarterly* 235 (2018): 644–668.

with a more pronounced increase in trust observed for the central government. Additionally, potential beneficiaries of the NRPS demonstrate similarly elevated trust levels in government institutions compared to nonbeneficiaries. However, the results also show that this policy enhanced trust in central government rather than local government. In contrast, Li and Mayraz's 2017 analysis of CHARLS (China Health and Retirement Longitudinal Study) datasets found that by improving local infrastructures such as roads and basic facilities, local governments gained more trust than the central government.[66] Further research also found that political trust in local government has been strongly influenced by the perception that these governments perform well, are responsive to citizens' needs, and were free from corruption.[67]

Second, new government provisions may help to establish that certain services should be government responsibilities, where the supply may generate more demand. Using two waves of Chinese national surveys, Lü[68] found that a policy of abolishing school fees significantly increased citizens' demand for greater government responsibility in financing compulsory education. He argued that policy awareness, rather than policy benefits, drove this demand. Also, policy awareness has enhanced citizens' trust in China's central government, but not local government. Given that citizens' responses are primarily influenced by policy awareness that is promoted by the state media, the use of social policies cannot sustain long-term political support.

Third, more inclusive policies would enhance trust in local government from social groups who would benefit from inclusion. Niu and Zhao compared migrants with urban locals and found that both rural migrants and urban migrants had lower levels of trust in local government. This could be the effect of *hukou*-based social exclusion in cities, where the *hukou* system – a household registration system that ties access to public services to one's registered place of origin – limits migrants' eligibility for urban welfare and social benefits. When it came to trust in the central government, urban migrants had the lowest level of trust, whereas rural migrants had more. The article also examined how these three groups of people (local city residents, rural migrants, and urban migrants) viewed trust in general, inequality, and authority differently, which affected their

---

[66] Li and Mayraz, "Infrastructure Spending in China Increases Trust in Local Government."
[67] Lisheng Dong and Daniel Kübler, "Sources of Local Political Trust in Rural China," *Journal of Contemporary China* 27(110) (2018): 193–207.
[68] Xiaobo Lü, "Social Policy and Regime Legitimacy: The Effects of Education Reform in China," *American Political Science Review* 108(2) (2014): 423–437.

political views. The central findings were that when migrants felt politically excluded, they trusted the government less.[69]

However, other research indicates that using responsive social policy as a means to maintain social harmony can be problematic. Göbel and Ong found that when the government's implementation of these policies falls short of what was promised, it can lead to increased complaints from the public.[70] Greater awareness of problems and inequalities can decrease trust in political institutions.[71] This implies that government efforts to address unmet social needs might inadvertently raise public awareness of these issues, leading to increased expectations for services and, consequently, more dissatisfaction if these expectations are not met. Additionally, the drive to ensure social stability by enhancing social services might prompt service users to demand quicker and better services, with similar results.

In summary, the relationship between social policies and public sentiment is complex. The effectiveness of these policies in winning over the hearts and minds of the people depends on the circumstances. While there is evidence of improved public satisfaction in certain areas,[72] ongoing challenges and the state's approach to governance continue to shape public opinion in diverse ways.

Conclusion

In conclusion, while this analysis emphasizes the role of China's social policy in maintaining social stability and reinforcing the CPC's political legitimacy, it is crucial to add a cautionary note. The intent is not to suggest that China's social policy is designed solely to respond to social needs and instability. It is also instrumental in advancing the CPC's long-term development agenda. The relationship between social policy and the party's broader objectives is complex and multifaceted, with these two aspects being deeply intertwined.

---

[69] Geng Niu, and Guochang Zhao, "Identity and Trust in Government: A Comparison of Locals and Migrants in Urban China," *Cities* 83 (2018): 54–60.

[70] Christian Göbel and Lynette H. Ong, *Social Unrest in China* (London: Europe China Research and Academic Network [ECRAN], 2012).

[71] Yingnan Joseph Zhou and Shuai Jin. "Inequality and Political Trust in China: The Social Volcano Thesis Re-examined," *The China Quarterly* 236 (2018): 1033–1062; Xiaolong Wu, Dali L. Yang, and Lijun Chen, "The Politics of Quality-of-Life Issues: Food Safety and Political Trust in China," *Journal of Contemporary China* 26(106) (2017): 601–615.

[72] Bingqin Li and Guy Mayraz, "Infrastructure Spending in China Increases Trust in Local Government"; Zhonglu Li and Xiaogang Wu, "Social Policy and Political Trust: Evidence from the New Rural Pension Scheme in China," *The China Quarterly* 235 (2018): 644–668.

The evolution of social policy in China, from the economic reforms of 1978 through subsequent administrations, including the era of Xi Jinping, reveals a dynamic interplay between immediate societal needs and longer-term developmental goals. These policies have been not only reactive measures to address discontent and enhance social stability, but also proactive strategies to fulfill the CPC's vision for national development.

However, the effectiveness of these policies in achieving both immediate social stability and long-term political support remains uncertain. Influenced by factors such as policy implementation, public perception, and the sociopolitical context, these strategies have met with varying degrees of success. They have been instrumental in addressing specific societal needs and concerns but have also been subject to heightened public expectations and awareness, which can lead to increased demands and potential dissatisfaction.

In navigating its future path, the PRC's approach to social policy will continue to be a balancing act between addressing short-term societal challenges and achieving long-term developmental objectives. This triple role of social policy, as a tool for one-off response to unmet needs, a mechanism for long-term strategic planning and a temporary reaction to strong discontent, is a key feature of the CPC's social and political governance. It will remain a significant building block in the PRC's social and political landscape.

12   Dealing with Dissent

Anna Hayes

In China, dissent can be anything the Communist Party of China (CPC) decides is a threat to its existence. It follows that a key source of CPC power has been its ability to manage or eliminate any form of dissent, and to weaken, co-opt, or destroy any organization or individual who does not express or demonstrate loyalty to the party. This includes "nonpatriotic" religious organizations or groups, ethnic groups that have shown any tendencies toward "separatism" or divided loyalties (Tibetans' loyalty to the Dalai Lama, for example), nongovernmental organizations (NGOs), rights lawyers, and activists. The party seeks co-option wherever possible, deploying its large and well-resourced United Front Work Department (UFWD) for such purposes. However, the party will not hesitate to use coercive means to subdue dissent or deter anyone deemed to be insufficiently aligned with the party's "socialist core values." It forcefully deploys mechanisms of surveillance and control against all groups and individuals deemed to threaten party legitimacy.

This chapter examines the ways in which the party secures and enforces nationwide loyalty to its political leadership and ruling ideologies, including in the border regions of Xinjiang, Tibet, and, more recently, Hong Kong. It argues that while the massive amount of spending on digital surveillance has attracted considerable scholarly attention, it is necessary to situate such tactics within the historical narrative of how the party has dealt with dissent, including before it came to power. The institutions and practices identified here have played, and continue to play, a significant role in the effort to eradicate or silence dissent within China.

Background

Elizabeth Economy has identified that the kinds of NGOs based in China more likely to fall afoul of the party are those wanting to "change or [represent] those who seek a greater voice in political life, such as women, labour, or legal rights activists."[1] Beijing defines dissent in highly political terms that are governed by the sensitivities of the party at a given time. Although the party seeks wherever possible to co-opt groups – to win their cooperation and fealty through friendly overtures, tangible benefits (for their work or family, for example), and other such means – it does not hesitate to use coercion.

Since the 1990s, the party has built a massive domestic security apparatus consisting of paramilitary, security, policing, and intelligence-gathering personnel as well as high-tech surveillance. By some estimates, the party-state has spent more in recent years on domestic "stability maintenance" (*wending*) than on external defense.[2] Mechanisms of surveillance and control have been deployed especially forcefully against minority nationalities such as Tibetans and Uyghurs, whose restiveness is perceived as a grave threat to national unity, social stability, and the security of sensitive national borders. Much contemporary focus on how the party tries to deal with dissent centers around online activism and censorship. However, many of the party's responses to online activism are simply tech-enhanced versions of the coercive measures long used by the party to monitor and crush dissent. For their part, online activists tend to replicate long-standing strategies of "offline" dissent in China.

Prior to taking power, the CPC tried to weaken and co-opt minor democratic parties which like them opposed or were unhappy with the ruling Kuomintang through united front work (political work). Once in power, and throughout the Mao years, the CPC frequently used terror as their mechanism for dealing with dissent. Across the 1950s, there were many efforts at co-opting the population to stand with the goals of the CPC. Given that these efforts ran against the backdrop of parallel terror tactics, such as executing accused counterrevolutionaries, the motivation for co-option was strengthened, and hence co-option and terror worked in tandem. Today, the CPC tries to weaken and co-opt some groups, while deploying coercion, manipulation, and terror against others. In his book *The Party*, Richard McGregor identified that from the point of view of the CPC, "terror remains essential to the system's survival and is deployed without embarrassment when required."[3] One official, cited by McGregor, explains the CPC's rationale for the continued use of

---

[1] Elizabeth Economy, *The Third Revolution: Xi Jinping and the New Chinese State* (New York: Oxford University Press, 2018), 11.

[2] Adrian Zenz, "China's Domestic Security Spending: An Analysis of Available Data," *China Brief* 18(4) (March 12, 2018), https://jamestown.org/program/chinas-domestic-security-spending-analysis-available-data.

[3] Richard McGregor, *The Party: The Secret World of China's Communist Rulers*, rev. ed. (London: Penguin, 2012), 265.

terror: "People need to fear the government in China, otherwise the country will fall apart."[4] Therefore, when persuasion, influence, weakening, and co-option does not work, the party resorts to manipulation through threats or enticements, harassment, torture, and even killing. To counter dissent, the UFWD and its associated bureaus and units monitor and try to co-opt dissidents and potential dissidents; and it reports directly to the party. The party is responsible for thought work – including coercive campaigns of rectification and forced criticism and self-criticism. The security and judicial organs are responsible for detention, arrest, and punishment (which, of course, may be at the order of the party).

The sociologist Yang Guobin has identified the internet as providing a "new form of civic association" in China where "play is mingled with politics."[5] He also provides a typology of online activism there: cultural, social, political, and nationalistic. Cultural activism is concerned with values, morality, lifestyles, and identities. Social activism includes advocating for the rights of disadvantaged and vulnerable groups and environmental protection as well as speaking out against problems such as corruption. Political activism, which he acknowledges can be present in both cultural and social activism, is defined as acts intentionally oppositional to the government, often involving examinations of how and by whom China is governed. Nationalistic activism encompasses the often-large-scale mobilization of netizens behind a nationalist cause in the defense of China and the party (and sometimes by the party); by redirecting attention and, in many cases, anger to foreign states and other external actors, it distracts people from focusing on any discontent with the party itself.[6] In their examination of online dissent in China, Zhang Yuntao and John Tomlinson identify three basic groups of dissenters: liberal intellectuals, grassroots activists, and young, urban netizens united by their opposition to state censorship and regulation over the internet.[7] Considered part of a "new social class" in China, these groups represent the continuation of preinternet, and indeed pre-1949 movements, ranging from the New Culture and May Fourth Movements of the early twentieth century to the April 5, 1976 Tiananmen Incident by which Beijing youth signaled they wanted an end to the Cultural Revolution;

---

[4] McGregor, *The Party*, 265.

[5] Guobin Yang, "Online Activism," *Journal of Democracy* 20(3) (2009): 33–36, 34.

[6] Tao has argued this strategy is also present within Xi Jinping's "China Dream" and "Great Rejuvenation of the Chinese People" rhetoric. See Yi-feng Tao, "The Political Economy of Xi Jinping's Political Rollback," *Issues & Studies: A Social Science Quarterly on China, Taiwan, and East Asian Affairs* 57(2) (2021): 1–20.

[7] Yuntao Zhang and John Tomlinson, "Three Constituencies of Online Dissent in China," *Chinese Journal of Communication* 5(1) (2012): 55–60, 56.

and the 1989 anticorruption, prodemocracy protests. Hence, there is nothing new about these forms of dissent or types of dissidents. What is new is the amplifying nature of the online space that extends their reach, audience, and impact – and the Chinese government's ability to identify such acts via their pervasive digital surveillance systems.[8]

The internet opened new avenues for faster and more widespread interactions among China's dissidents, with real potential to turbocharge their activism. Reflecting on the early days of internet activism in China, the late dissident and Nobel Peace Laureate Liu Xiaobo stated he believed the civic association and space provided by the internet, for those who could access it, was "God's gift to China."[9] He believed the internet would more easily connect intellectuals with political activists and grassroots protesters, stating that for his own writing "the Internet was like a super engine. It makes my writing burst out like an oil well."[10] Not surprisingly, when the internet came to China in the mid 1990s, the free and unfettered flow of online information and ideas was a source of anxiety for Beijing. Chinese internet users numbered just 40,000 in 1995, but by the end of 2000 there were 22.5 million internet users. In 2005, that number had grown to 111 million, and today, there are nearly a billion users.[11] In response, the CPC worked to develop strong internet controls with the help of Western technology companies such as Cisco and Juniper Networks. Companies such as Yahoo, Google, and Microsoft later complied with the CPC desire to restrict searchable content and shut down sites they deemed unfavorable.[12]

After much time and investment, in 2003 the CPC launched its Golden Shield project, which included what was dubbed by Geremie Barmé and Sang Ye in *Wired* the "Great Firewall." In 2015, the Great Cannon was introduced, adjusting and replacing content, as well as redirecting users to acceptable sites of information rather than blocking them outright.[13] The Golden Shield sets guidelines and polices online information and

---

[8] See Jean-Pierre Cabestan, "The State and Digital Society in China: Big Brother Xi Is Watching You!" in *Political and Social Control in China: The Consolidation of Single-Party Rule*, ed. Ben Hillman and Chien-wen Kou (Canberra: ANU Press, 2024), 159–191.
[9] Cited in Zhang and Tomlinson, "Three Constituencies of Online Dissent," 57.
[10] Cited in Zhang and Tomlinson, "Three Constituencies of Online Dissent," 57.
[11] Graham Webster, "A Brief History of the Chinese Internet," *Logic* (May 1, 2019), https://logicmag.io/china/a-brief-history-of-the-chinese-internet; Palash Ghosh, "China Now Has Almost 1 Billion Internet Users," *Forbes* (February 4, 2021), www.forbes.com/sites/palashghosh/2021/02/04/china-now-has-almost-1-billion-internet-users/?sh=23ee75e26d91.
[12] Economy, *The Third Revolution*; Robert McMahon and Isabella Bennett, "US Internet Providers and the 'Great Firewall of China'," *Council on Foreign Relations* (February 23, 2011), www.cfr.org/backgrounder/us-internet-providers-and-great-firewall-china.
[13] Economy, *The Third Revolution*.

public opinion in China, employing more than two million people, their work aided and reinforced by digital tools such as internet filtering, tracking applications, rerouting, and denial of service blocks.[14] Described by computer science academics at the New York Institute of Technology, Nanjing University, as "not only a powerful political tool but also an exquisitely designed network security program," the Golden Shield has meant that on the Chinese internet, information does not flow as freely as it does elsewhere.[15] The Golden Shield has always had a primarily domestic focus, with the party recognizing early on its value in facilitating control over the domestic population.[16]

China's state-level information control has achieved ever greater heights via Safe Cities and Skynet.[17] Safe Cities involves remote sensing and surveillance technology enabling citywide, real-time surveillance of all people and activity within its target range. Skynet, which derives its name from chapter 73 of Laozi's *Tao Te Ching*, "*Tianwang huihui, shu er bu lou*" (The nets of Heaven are wide, but nothing escapes its grasp), involves a dedicated urban surveillance program which tracks individuals in real time, enabling their every move to be surveilled and punished by the state (Heaven). With echoes of the Cultural Revolution slogan "Father is dear, Mother is dear, but neither are as dear as Chairman Mao" (*Die qin niang qin buru mao zhuxi qin*), a Beijing subway advertisement seen by the author described the Safe Cities and Skynet applications as "more dear than mummy or daddy."[18] Safe Cities and Skynet combined ensure that everything and everyone can be surveilled via an integrated grid of cameras employing facial recognition algorithms. The Golden Shield, Safe Cities, and Skynet represent the pinnacle of surveillance and control for which the CPC had long yearned and strived for; as the systems that undergird what Western commentators call China's digital totalitarianism – or as *The Economist* put it, "Big Data, meet Big Brother" – they are indeed "God's gifts" to the party.[19]

---

[14] Economy, *The Third Revolution*; Jonathan E. Hillman, *The Digital Silk Road: China's Quest to Wire the World and Win the Future* (London: Profile Books, 2021); Sonali Chandel, Jingji Zang, Yunnan Yu, Jingyao Sun, and Zhipeng Zhang, "The Golden Shield Project of China: A Decade Later An In-Depth Study of the Great Firewall," in *International Conference on Cyber-Enabled Distributed Computing and Knowledge Discovery* (Institute of Electrical and Electronics Engineers, 2019), https://ieeexplore.ieee.org/document/8945933.

[15] Chandel et al., "The Golden Shield Project of China," 111.

[16] Hillman, *The Digital Silk Road*. [17] Hillman, *The Digital Silk Road*.

[18] Special thanks to Linda Jaivin for pointing out this important comparison and the previous reference to Laozi and Skynet.

[19] For more information, see Hillman, *The Digital Silk Road*; *The Economist*, "China Invents the Digital Totalitarian State" (December 17, 2016), www.economist.com/briefing/2016/12/17/china-invents-the-digital-totalitarian-state.

Perhaps tolerance of such intrusive control stems from decades of conditioning by the CPC. Since taking power in 1949, the CPC has worked tirelessly to control, monitor, and censor information and eradicate dissent. Many of the seemingly new tactics of control in contemporary China simply replicate long patterns of control over information, movement, and individuals' lives. The contemporary surveillance state has its grounding in entities such as residents' committees and the "work unit" (*danwei*). At its core, the *danwei* provided a social space within factories, education institutions, and government agencies and was responsible for the lives of their employees. One's *danwei* served both formal and social/community functions – and kept files on all members (*dang'an*, or dossier). Examinations of how the CPC deals with dissent today must consider the types of practices enacted since 1949, because in China, everything old is new again, with many of the current mechanisms for dealing with dissent simply tech-enhanced versions of existing forms. While its defenders may describe China's contemporary surveillance state as enhancing productive efficiency, increasing public safety, and improving people's behavior – all part of state rationale in the past – the intrusion into people's lives is more pronounced than ever before, and the CPC is pushing boundaries via digital totalitarianism.[20]

Community-Based Surveillance, Instilling Loyalty, and a Network of Spies/Informants

Neighborhood Communities

In 1954, the CPC established Residents' Committees (*juweihui*), sometimes called Neighborhood Committees in English, in all Chinese cities with a population of 50,000 or over.[21] Originally, they were staffed on a voluntary basis by members of the community, usually retirees, who wanted to uphold moral and political order within their neighborhood.[22] Prior to reorganization in the 1990s, while the volunteers sometimes mediated neighborhood disputes, a critical focus of the Residents' Committees was enforcing political control and instilling loyalty to the party via the door-to-door distribution of party propaganda to residents. They noted comings and goings in the neighborhood and asked about

---

[20] Economy, *The Third Revolution*; Hillman, *The Digital Silk Road*.
[21] Joe Leung, "The Community-Based Welfare System in China," *Community Development Journal* 25(3) (1990): 195–205.
[22] Judith Audin, "Governing through the Neighbourhood Community (*shequ*) in China: An Ethnography of the Participative Bureaucratisation of Residents' Committees in Beijing" (trans. Katharine Throssell), *Revue française de science politique* 65(1) (2015): 85–110.

visitors who were strangers, always looking out for suspicious people and suspicious acts, as well as anyone who contravened or challenged the rules set by the party. They achieved this through personal contact, getting to know residents, engaging in conversations, convening meetings, and in their mediation work. They played a multifaceted role, one of which was political control, making these volunteer cadres one part of the cogs in China's early surveillance state.

Initially a peripheral institution within the socialist-authoritarian regime, the Residents' Committees played a vitally important monitoring role. They focused on women of childbearing age, the elderly, the unemployed, the disabled, and the poor.[23] Prior to recent changes to China's population policy, Residents' Committees were on the front line in policing the bodies of urban Chinese women, tracking their fertility and menstruation cycles, identifying "unauthorized" pregnancies, and targeting women for contraception.[24] It was the Residents' Committees that reported unmarried cohabitation, residency law violations, birth control regulation breaches, and public security issues – reflecting their importance in the public security system.[25] The Residents' Committees were particularly entrusted with monitoring those residents who did not come under a *danwei* and the regularized surveillance, monitoring, and control the work units carried out on behalf of the state.[26] However, given that the roles were voluntary and staffed primarily by retirees, their efficiency and fervor in carrying out their duties varied depending on location, the political atmosphere at the time, and individual levels of ability and enthusiasm. While they were formally constituted and regulated, there was much informality and variation within the Residents' Committees prior to their reorganization in the 1990s, a point we will address shortly.

The *danwei*, by contrast, was a more structured element within the early surveillance state, one also focused on social control. As mentioned previously, the *danwei* kept dossiers (*dang'an*) on all its members. Their powers included granting permission to marry or have a child, dealing with life from cradle to grave, resulting in the everyday life of the people becoming governmentalized.[27] While social scientist Lu Feng argues that

---

[23] Audin, "Governing through the Neighbourhood Community."
[24] Susan Greenhalgh, "The Peasantization of the One-Child Policy in Shaanxi," in *Chinese Families in the Post-Mao Era*, ed. Deborah Davis and Stevan Harrell (Berkeley: University of California Press, 1993), 219–250.
[25] Thomas Heberer and Christian Gobel, *The Politics of Community Building in Urban China* (Abingdon: Routledge, 2011).
[26] Audin, "Governing through the Neighbourhood Community."
[27] David Bray, *Social Space and Governance in Urban China: The Danwei System from Origins to Reform* (Stanford, CA: Stanford University Press, 2005); Robert Gamer, "Chinese Politics," in *Understanding Contemporary China*, ed. Robert Gamer, 4th ed. (Boulder,

the *danwei* system was undergirded by, and fostered, "an ethical order based on an internal code of conduct,"[28] the cultural anthropologist Frank Pieke characterizes *danwei* decision-making as "highly personalised and often wanton,"[29] making them, in some ways, closer to the Residents' Committees than may generally be imagined. Decisions over promotions, work assignments, and other critical issues were at the sole discretion of the work unit leader – personalized leadership structures that could become inconsistent, cruel, and corrupt. The system was thus sustained via carrots and sticks, sometimes violent ones. Not having a *danwei* was highly problematic, though, because it implied a person was not contributing to the state and was therefore inherently suspicious.[30]

The economic changes brought about during Reform and Opening in the 1980s and the 1990s greatly weakened the *danwei* as a mechanism for organizational and social control. *Danwei* were not designed to compete in a market economy. No longer fit for purpose, they were allowed to fail.[31] Many *danwei* disbanded due to factory closures or bankruptcy, and those that survived scaled down, no longer taking responsibility for the housing, health, education, and entertainment of their workers, and no longer guaranteeing both employment and retirement pensions. This was a traumatic experience for those who lost their "iron rice bowl" and their sense of community and belonging.[32] The dismantling of the *danwei* system, which led to a sharp rise in unemployment, saw the emergence of a new underclass within China, along with an increase in street crime, protests, and unrest. Some of the newly unemployed took this opportunity to become individual entrepreneurs or became involved in newly established collective enterprises, while others found it harder to adjust, turning to petty theft and crime or entering the ranks of the long-term

---

CO: Lynne Rienner Publishers, 2012), 71–122; He Xinghan, "People of the Work Unit," in *Streetlife China*, ed. Michael Dutton (Cambridge: Cambridge University Press, [1993] 1998), 42–53.

[28] Lu Feng, "The Work Unit: A Unique Form of Social Organisation," in *Streetlife China*, ed. Michael Dutton (Cambridge, Cambridge University Press, [1989] 1998), 53–58, 57.

[29] Frank N. Pieke, *Knowing China: A Twenty-First Century Guide* (Cambridge: Cambridge University Press, 2016), 18.

[30] Zhongtian Yi, "The Work Unit: 'Face' and Place," in *Streetlife China*, ed. Michael Dutton (Cambridge: Cambridge University Press, [1996] 1998), 58–61, 59.

[31] Kevin Lin, "Work Unit," in *Afterlives of Chinese Communism: Political Concepts from Mao to Xi*, ed. Christian Sorace, Ivan Franceschini, and Nicholas Loubere (Canberra: ANU Press, 2019), 331–334.

[32] Known as the "iron rice bowl," state-owned enterprises provided their employees with a job for life, followed by an old-age pension upon retirement. With the closure of many state-owned enterprises, the end of the iron rice bowl was an intense shock for those who were relying upon it, thereby compounding the trauma of the loss of their job and *danwei* connections. Lin, "Work Unit," 331.

unemployed. This signaled to the party the vital role the *danwei* had played in maintaining social stability and order.

Following the contraction of the *danwei*, the Residents' Committees emerged as the core of urban self-governance. The 1989 Law Governing the Organizing of the Residents' Committees was a critical element within the process of "neighborhood construction" (*shequ jianshe*) and elevated the status of the Residents' Committees. Under this law, their role was first, to support the government by ensuring social stability within their district and, second, to continue their role in providing both social and community services to their resident members.[33] They also underwent meaningful change. The introduction of paid positions, the professionalization of their ranks, and greater capacities to carry out their duties via higher entry qualifications, better training, access to telecommunications devices, and computers strengthened the power of the Residents' Committees within the system.[34] In addition, the committees have continued to serve as a communication and propaganda tool for the party, and the employees of the Residents' Committees continue to operate as police informants. To this day, they remain the CPC's reliable, human, critical eye over the people, making sure outsiders, agitators, or (for whatever reason) suspicious characters come to the attention of relevant authorities.

Local Spies and Informants

The CPC also uses the knowledge that there are formal and informal spies and other informants among the people to prompt the Chinese population to conform to party rules and regulations. Such knowledge fosters a climate of self-censorship and self-restraint, and where that does not suppress dissent or disobedience, the local informants and spies quickly identify the troublemakers, whom the authorities can then detain and punish. In minority regions across China, such as Xinjiang, community-based spying within ethnic groups has long been used to gather information on individuals and groups, creating what Hamut Gokturk, former general secretary of the Istanbul-based East Turkistan Foundation, calls "a class of 'local traitors.'"[35] In 2007, social anthropologist Joanne Smith made similar observations, writing:

---

[33] Heberer and Gobel, *The Politics of Community Building in Urban China*.
[34] Audin, "Governing through the Neighbourhood Community."
[35] Cited in Kurban Niyaz and Richard Finney, "Uyghur Villagers Forced by 'Contract' to Spy on Neighbors," RefWorld (April 29, 2016), https://www.rfa.org/english/news/uyghur/contract-04292016154541.html.

In a 1996 interview, Dilsat [a Uyghur informant who worked in tourism] told me that some Uyghurs were supplying information to the Chinese authorities in the hope of bettering their personal circumstances: People are really scared in Kashgar. And what they're most scared of is other Uyghurs ... spies. These fears had multiplied by the time of my return to Xinjiang in 2002. Some said that the arrest of Rabiya Qadir[36] (popularly known as Xinjiang's millionaire businesswoman) in 1999 has been made on the basis of information leaked to the Chinese authorities by precisely such inside spies. They deemed such behaviour widespread and attributed it to petty jealousy and a reluctance to see others achieve.[37]

The CPC uses both intraethnic and interethnic spies in Xinjiang. In August 2014, the Peyziwat county government in Kashgar prefecture mandated that villagers had to spy on their neighbors, forcing them to sign a "Joint Responsibility Contract."[38] The Uyghur villagers were threatened with collective punishment if they failed to spy on other Uyghurs. Interethnic spying is also common in Xinjiang. An open letter cosigned by Liu Huijun, the party secretary of Kizilsu Kyrgyz Autonomous Prefecture, and the prefecture governor, Dilshat Kidirhan, and published on the government's news portal, noted that Kyrgyz herdsmen, another minority nationality in the region, had been urged to spy on their Uyghur neighbors and could earn an additional 500 yuan above their monthly salary for doing so.[39] This kind of strategy seeks to divide vulnerable communities, increase levels of mutual distrust, and weaken them from within.

The CPC also seeks out spies within the expatriate Uyghur community to spy on other Uyghurs living outside of China.[40] Attempts at recruiting

---

[36] Also spelled Rebiya Kadeer.
[37] Joanne N. Smith, "The Quest for National Unity in Uyghur Popular Song: Barren Chickens, Stray Dogs, Fake Immortals and Thieves," in *Music, National Identity and the Politics of Location: Between the Global and the Local*, ed. Ian Biddle and Vanessa Knights (Farnham: Ashgate, 2007), 115–142, 131.
[38] Niyaz and Finney, "China." In 2018, *The China Story* published a table identifying the "48 suspicious signs of extremist tendencies" being used by the CPC in the mass detention of Uyghurs in concentration camps. They included signs such as "owning a tent," "praying," "fasting," "owning extra food," traveling abroad or speaking to someone about traveling abroad, "abstaining from alcohol," or just being related to someone who has one of the forty-eight signs. The full list can be accessed at: www.thechinastory.org/yearbooks/yearbook-2018-power/chapter-4-internment-and-indoctrination-xis-new-era-in-xinjiang/forty-eight-suspicious-signs-of-extremist-tendencies.
[39] Eset Sulaiman, "Authorities Urge Kyrgyz Herdsmen to Spy on Uyghurs in China's Xinjiang," *Radio Free Asia* (April 12, 2017), www.rfa.org/english/news/uyghur/authorities-urge-kyrgyz-herdsmen-to-spy-on-uyghurs-in-chinas-xinjiang-04122017153521.html.
[40] Paul Mooney and David Lague, "The Price of Dissent: Holding the Fate of Families in Its Hands, China Controls Refugees Abroad," *Reuters* (December 30, 2015), www.reuters.com/investigates/special-report/china-uighur.

Uyghurs internationally are consistent with attempts to recruit Uyghur spies domestically. First, authorities identify a trustworthy and credible potential Uyghur informant and approach them through security or police officers, often still in China, to request they act as a spy on the Uyghur expatriate community where they live. If the selected target refuses, authorities harass, threaten, intimidate, or detain them during return visits to Xinjiang. It is exceedingly difficult to refuse such requests, as family members in Xinjiang are frequently used as bargaining chips. Threats of retribution for family members still in China are also used against vocal members of the dissident community.

There is growing evidence of a global web of intelligence-gathering on expatriate citizens of China of all ethnicities, including Uyghurs and Tibetans as well as Falun Gong practitioners, democracy activists, and critics of the party.[41] The spying network includes both coerced community-based spies/informants as well as trained intelligence operatives employed to spy for the state on expatriate communities and foreign actors.[42] In 2009, German authorities searched the homes of four suspected Chinese intelligence operatives in Munich, and there were allegations that the Chinese general consulate in Munich had become a front for a spy operation focused on Munich's Uyghur community.[43] Throughout the 2000s, Chinese spying efforts in Germany had become a contentious issue within the China–German bilateral relationship. In 2008, Germany's Federal Prosecutor's Office established a new procedure to collate evidence of such spying activities. It has been alleged that Beijing's actions were triggered by its concern over the growing alliance between the World Uyghur Congress and the Falun Gong in Munich[44] – two of what the CPC calls the "five poisons" (the other three being Tibetan separatists, Hong Kong democracy activists, and advocates of Taiwan independence).

As in China itself, the actual or perceived presence of informants/spies within an expatriate community works to silence voices through self-censorship. This self-censorship was observable inside the Uyghur diasporic community prior to the mass detention of Uyghurs in Xinjiang.

---

[41] Roger Faligot, *Chinese Spies: From Chairman Mao to Xi Jinping*, trans. Natasha Lehrer (London: Hurst & Company, 2019).

[42] Clive Hamilton, *Silent Invasion: China's Influence in Australia* (Richmond: Hardie Grant Books, 2018); Clive Hamilton and Mareike Ohlberg, *Hidden Hand: Exposing How the Chinese Communist Party Is Reshaping the World* (Richmond: Hardie Grant Books, 2020).

[43] Holger Stark, "Police Raid in Munich: Germany Suspects China of Spying on Uighur Expatriates," *Spiegel Online* (November 24, 2009), www.spiegel.de/international/germany/police-raid-in-munich-germany-suspects-china-of-spying-on-uighur-expatriates-a-663090.html.

[44] Faligot, *Chinese Spies*.

However, once its members realized the extent of the mass detention, this silence gave way to a trickle, then a flood, of accounts of persecution and disappearances of relatives, friends, and associates. Uyghur groups abroad have joined other persecuted groups such as Tibetans, Falun Gong, and Hong Kong democracy activists to raise awareness overseas of the nature of CPC coercion and control. In the end, the CPC's actions in Xinjiang caused their fears in Munich to become a self-fulfilling prophecy.

The CPC also mishandled the Rebiya Kadeer incident, unintentionally elevating her plight and status. While still living in Xinjiang, the authorities arrested and imprisoned Kadeer, who had once been a successful businesswoman and delegate to the National People's Congress, for disclosing state secrets while she was en route to meet and pass on information to members of the US Congressional Research Service. In 2005, she was released from prison on medical grounds. Following international pressure, she was permitted to leave China for the US, where she was reunited with her husband and, like him, granted asylum.[45] However, her children in Xinjiang have been repeatedly arrested and jailed, denied employment, and prevented from leaving Xinjiang.[46] The authorities intended the treatment of Kadeer's children to send a chilling message to other diasporic Uyghurs to stay silent and not attack the party. This tactic worked for many years.

The CPC's harassment of Kadeer extended beyond China's borders. In 2009, and reminiscent of past attempts to disrupt international speaking engagements by the Dalai Lama, the Chinese state tried to prevent Kadeer from being granted travel visas to Australia, New Zealand, and Taiwan.[47] In the case of Australia, where she was due to show her documentary *The 10 Conditions of Love* at a film festival in Melbourne, Beijing hinted at retaliation should Australia grant Kadeer a visa. These events were debated in the Australian parliament. However, the Labor government held steadfast and granted Kadeer her visa, refusing China's

---

[45] Nick Holdstock, *China's Forgotten People: Xinjiang, Terror and the Chinese State* (London: I. B. Tauris, 2015).

[46] Mooney and Lague, "The Price of Dissent."

[47] Beijing has applied pressure on countries and leaders to deny the Dalai Lama a visa or for leaders not to meet with him while in their countries. See, for example: news24, "Dalai Lama Denied Visa to SA for a Third Time" (September 4, 2014), www.news24.com/News24/Dalai-Lama-denied-visa-to-SA-for-a-third-time-20140904; and *Sydney Morning Herald*, "Howard Stands Firm on Dalai Lama Meeting" (May 17, 2002), www.smh.com.au/national/howard-stands-firm-on-dalai-lama-meeting-20020517-gdface.html.

attempt at interference in Australian domestic affairs.[48] The media attention around these incidents created a far larger-than-anticipated audience for the documentary and created greater awareness in Australia of the Uyghurs' plight. Subsequently, Beijing canceled a high-level visit to Australia, further politicizing the incident and demonstrating their willingness to use coercion in the Australia–China bilateral relationship.[49] Like Australia, New Zealand held out against Beijing's attempts at interference and granted Kadeer a visa. During her New Zealand stay, Kadeer discussed Beijing's efforts to silence her.[50] The Taiwanese government buckled under the pressure, however, and did not grant Kadeer a visa, although they did permit the screening of her documentary.[51] Just months later, Taiwan and China signed an economic agreement, signaling that Beijing's threat of economic punishment – or the offer of sweeteners – was likely to be a factor in Taiwan's visa decision.[52]

Australian authorities have long been aware of attempts to control and monitor groups in Australia that may be critical of the CPC and its policies. In June 2006, Australia's Department of Foreign Affairs and Trade warned it was highly likely the Chinese authorities were monitoring Uyghur groups in Australia and might harass individuals and family members upon their return to China, or those still residing in China.[53] The international reach of the CPC's global surveillance and intelligence-gathering on Chinese nationals targets all Chinese, not just minority nationalities. In a sworn statement to Australian immigration authorities, a Chinese university student studying in Australia stated that three agents met with his parents in China, warning them of his involvement in prodemocracy activities. He stated: "[The agents] pressed the point that my parents must ask me to stop what I am taking part in and keep a low

---

[48] Anna Hayes, "Legacies of the Uyghur Homeland and Uyghur-Australians," in *Legacies of Violence: Rendering the Unspeakable Past in Modern Australia*, ed. Robert Mason (New York: Berghahn Books, 2017), 89–123.
[49] Sabra Lane, "Smith Confirms: China Cancelled High-Level Visit," *PM: ABC News*, aired August 18, 2009, www.abc.net.au/pm/content/2008/s2659742.htm.
[50] Carolyn Meers, "Rebiya Kadeer Visits NZ, Discusses Her Cause," *Scoop News* (October 15, 2009), www.scoop.co.nz/stories/HL0910/S00144/rebiya-kadeer-visits-nz-discusses-her-cause.htm.
[51] *Taipei Times*, "Editorial: Kadeer Is Entitled to a Visa" (September 24, 2009), www.taipeitimes.com/News/editorials/archives/2009/09/24/2003454302.
[52] Agence France-Presse "China to Sign Taiwan Pact after Rebiya Kadeer Ban: Report," *Taiwan News* (October 2, 2009), www.taiwannews.com.tw/en/news/1071673.
[53] DIAC Country Information Service, cited in Refugee Review Tribunal, "RRT Research Response: CHN31854" (May 29, 2007), https://web.archive.org/web/20230622222826/https://www.ecoi.net/en/file/local/1079563/2107_1310371298_chn31854.pdf.

profile."[54] Australian authorities later issued the man a protection visa allowing him to stay in Australia. This kind of interference across state borders, aimed at controlling and monitoring what Chinese nationals say abroad about the CPC, further demonstrates the lengths to which Beijing is prepared to go in dealing with dissent. Many of these efforts are carried out by the international umbrella of the UFWD.

Co-opt, Coerce, Weaken, or Destroy: United Front Work

United front work can be defined as political work that seeks to influence and co-opt targets. China's united front work draws on Lenin's ideas about forming strategic alliances to advance one's goals.[55] During China's civil war, the CPC began to formulate its ideas and practices around the United Front (*tongzhan*). It also began perfecting methods for politicizing everyday life via political campaigns and meetings, which later included an often-violent process of land reform to redistribute privately held land to the poor and "middle" peasants while publicly punishing the landholder class. This served not just to change the structure of economic relations in the countryside, but also to embed the notions of political participation under the direction of the party in mass campaigns to vanquish and control the "enemies of the people."

Between 1942 and 1944, the CPC underwent a period of self-strengthening via its Rectification Movement (*zhengfeng yundong*). It demanded that those who had joined the communists at their base in Yan'an, many of whom were young intellectuals – including writers and actors – like the communists themselves, undergo a process of rigorous criticism and self-criticism to eliminate independent thought. The most famous targets of the campaign, Wang Shiwei, was punished for speaking out on the gap between the theory and practice of egalitarianism in Yan'an itself.[56] Thus, the Rectification Movement set a model for the CPC's later campaigns aimed at tightening control and constraint over the thoughts and ideas of its members and others, stressing trust and loyalty. This occurred during the similarly named, but distinct in meaning, "united front" between the Communists and the Nationalists as they attempted to repel Imperial Japanese occupiers during the Second World

---

[54] Tony Chang, cited in Nick McKenzie, Richard Baker, Sashka Koloff, and Chris Uhlmann, "The Chinese Communist Party's Power and Influence in Australia," *ABC News* (June 5, 2017), www.abc.net.au/news/2017-06-04/the-chinese-communist-partys-power-and-influence-in-australia/8584270.
[55] Vladimir Lenin, *"Left-Wing" Communism, An Infantile Disorder* (Moscow: Foreign Languages Publishing House, 1950).
[56] Michael Dillon, *China: A Modern History* (London: I. B. Tauris, 2010).

War. Throughout this campaign, Mao Zedong also institutionalized united front work under the CPC to increase its chances of continuing its challenge against the Nationalists once peace was secured.[57]

The development of the UFWD enabled the CPC to reach out to potential sympathizers, including prominent intellectuals and cultural figures as well as advocates of representative democracy, inviting them to take part in a Preparatory Committee for an advisory group, the Chinese People's Political Consultative Conference (CPPCC). The CPC promised influential leaders, including religious figures, intellectuals, minority nationality representatives, overseas Chinese, and non-communist political parties, a participatory voice in the running of the Chinese state once the CPC won the civil war. Under the guidance of the CPC, the CPPCC drafted the "Common Program." It stated that the future of China would be a "dictatorship of people's democracy" and that the CPC was prepared to use force (which is not defined) against imperialism, feudalism, bureaucratic capitalism, and counterrevolutionaries.[58] By co-opting these various elites as allies, the UFWD helped the CPC to secure broader public support in its struggle to defeat the KMT (Kuomintang) government.

Following their victory in the Chinese civil war, the CPC continued united front work, including via the CPPCC, to assist China's transition to socialism. Led by the party, the UFWD denounced and categorized groups inside of China, identifying "hidden enemies" and traitors within the civilian population. They supported the party as it carried out a number of mass campaigns aimed at cementing its political control over the population.[59] Some people who had united with the CPC under the United Front, including many former KMT officials and soldiers, became targets when the party no longer needed them to achieve victory; others, including liberal intellectuals, were forced to undergo intense periods of criticism and self-criticism on the Yan'an model.[60] In his book *The Tragedy of Liberation*, Frank Dikötter labeled this period the "Great Terror."[61] According to Dikötter, "ideological education now became the norm, as sessions of self-criticism, self-condemnation and

---

[57] Ray Wang and Gerry Groot, "Who Represents? Xi Jinping's Grand United Front Work, Legitimation, Participation and Consultative Democracy," *Journal of Contemporary China* 27(112) (2018): 569–583.
[58] Dillon, *China: A Modern History*, 263.
[59] Initial campaigns included Land Reform, the Movement for the Suppression of Counter-Revolutionaries, the Three-Anti and Five-Anti Campaigns, and later, the Hundred Flowers Movement; however, mass campaigns remained a feature of the Mao Years.
[60] Wang and Groot, "Who Represents?"
[61] Frank Dikötter, *The Tragedy of Liberation: A History of the Chinese Revolution 1945–1957* (London: Bloomsbury, 2013), 92.

self-exposure followed one another, day in, day out, until all resistance was crushed and the individual was broken, ready to serve the collective."[62] The public nature and violence of the campaigns, which included struggle sessions where people confessed to their "crimes," beatings, public trials, executions, and public parades of the accused, had a chilling effect on the populace. This resulted in a high degree of self-censorship, restraint, and compliance.

Beginning with the Anti-Rightist campaign of 1958–1959, which targeted many of those whom the UFWD had previously sought to co-opt, Mao's preference for "class struggle," which saw its fullest expression during the turbulent years of the Cultural Revolution, led to a sidelining of the UFWD.[63] After the death of Mao, however, the UFWD slowly revived to become a crucial cog in the party's ongoing campaign to draw people back to it after the violence of the Cultural Revolution, as well as to appeal to overseas Chinese to help with the economic reforms and to win hearts and minds in Hong Kong and Taiwan.

Dealing with Dissent in the "New Era"

Across the 1980s, united front work grew in significance as the party sought to win diverse, typically victimized groups and individuals back to its side through a consultative democracy model. This approach also sought to legitimize the party and its decisions by demonstrating that it governed via an inclusive and responsive process. The party was especially interested in the recently rehabilitated victims of the Anti-Rightist campaign, for their foreign contacts and their needed skills and knowledge.[64] The UFWD helped Rightists and targets of Mao's campaigns to clear their names, seek compensation, recover confiscated property, and even regain party membership. They also sought to woo traditional united front targets, including those with business or professional qualifications who would be particularly useful to the economic reforms. United front work continued to bring together diverse and potentially discontented groups under the watchful eye of the party, helping them to build loyalty to the party while monitoring their activities.

In the early years of reform, the UFWD cooperated with the State Ethnic Affairs Commission (SEAC) on issues related to ethnic minorities. The SEAC, established in 1949 and shuttered during the Cultural

---

[62] Dikötter, *The Tragedy of Liberation*, 181.
[63] Taotao Zhao and James Leibold, "Ethnic Governance under Xi Jinping: The Centrality of the United Front Work Department and Its Implications," *Journal of Contemporary China* 29(124) (2020): 487–502; Wang and Groot, "Who Represents?"
[64] Wang and Groot, "Who Represents?"

Revolution, was also revived in the 1980s, boosted by Hu Yaobang's attempts to increase minority nationality rights within the central leadership of the CPC.[65] For a time, the SEAC and the UFWD were of equal bureaucratic status. The UFWD originally had eight bureaus, with Bureau Two concerned with religious and ethnic affairs. In 2017, it added a ninth, to oversee Xinjiang affairs; this marks the point at which the repression of the Uyghurs and other Muslim minorities in the region radically intensified, most notably in the mass detention of reportedly upwards of one million people, mostly Uyghurs.[66] By then, the UFWD had gained more control over ethnic and religious policy and affairs than the SEAC.

Xi Jinping has championed and strengthened the work of the UFWD, identifying it as one of China's "magic weapons" – drawing on Mao's original concept and terminology from 1938. According to one report, he has elevated the UFWD to "a level of significance not seen in China since the years before 1949, when the [CPC] was in opposition."[67] The first major UFWD conference for many years was held in 2015, during which Xi Jinping stressed that united front work was important to the work of the party and was the responsibility of all party members.[68] Also in 2015, the Politburo passed the Chinese Communist Party's United Front Regulations, which prioritized united front work for all cadres, including setting goals and targets and meeting them, and reinstating the UFWD's role in ensuring the loyalty of party cadres and maintaining the party's ideological purity.[69] The UFWD's focus on regions such as Xinjiang

---

[65] Zhao and Leibold, "Ethnic Governance under Xi Jinping."
[66] Zhao and Leibold, "Ethnic Governance under Xi Jinping"; Wang and Groot, "Who Represents?"; Sean Roberts, *The War on the Uyghurs: China's Campaign against Xinjiang's Muslims* (Manchester: Manchester University Press, 2020); Anna Hayes, "'Arab Revitalisation' and the Uyghur Crisis: The Problematic Nature of Sino-Arabic Cooperation in the 'Silk Road Spirit' Era," in *Between Scylla and Charybdis: Is There a Middle Path for Middle Powers in the Indo-Pacific Region?*, Proceedings of the U.S. Naval War College and East Asia Security Centre Conference, October 3–5, 2019, Bond University, Gold Coast (East Asia Security Centre, 2020), https://easc.scholasticahq.com/article/14489-arab-revitalisation-and-the-uyghur-crisis-the-problematic-nature-of-sino-arabic-cooperation-in-the-silk-road-spirit-era; Anna Hayes, "The Kashgar Dangerous House Reform Program: Social Engineering, 'a Rebirth of the Nation' and a Significant Building Block in China's Creeping Genocide," in *The Xinjiang Emergency: Exploring the Causes and Consequences of China's Mass Detention of Uyghurs*, ed. Michael Clarke (Manchester: Manchester University Press, 2022), 61–89.
[67] Anne-Marie Brady, "Magic Weapons: China's Political Influence Activities under Xi Jinping," 7. Conference paper presented at "The Corrosion of Democracy under China's Global Influence," supported by the Taiwan Foundation for Democracy, Arlington, Virginia, USA, September 16–17, 2017, www.wilsoncenter.org/article/magic-weapons-chinas-political-influence-activities-under-xi-jinping.
[68] Zhao and Leibold, "Ethnic Governance under Xi Jinping."
[69] Wang and Groot, "Who Represents?" 582.

reflected the shift in party policy away from the accommodation of minority nationality cultural, religious, and other identity, toward national integration, with assimilation the party's overriding goal in minority regions.[70] Since then, control over these regions and peoples has intensified.

The Falun Gong Crackdown: The Bridging Period between Old and New

The crackdown on Falun Gong that began in the 1990s continues into the present. For then-leader Jiang Zemin, the approximately 10,000 Falun Gong practitioners who surrounded Zhongnanhai in a surprise demonstration on 24–25 April 1999 were the Chinese equivalent of Poland's Solidarity Movement, directly threatening the party and their hold on power.[71] Following this incident, the party established the 610 (June 10) Office to counter that threat; it is the implementation arm of the Central Leading Group on Dealing with Heretical Religions. One of their tasks was to disseminate propaganda condemning Falun Gong and its leader as a dangerous cult.[72]

From the start of its crackdown on Falun Gong, the CPC used all means of control at its disposal, including the Residents' Committees. According to Judith Audin, "during the campaign against the Falun Gong movement in 1999, the Residents' Committees were mobilised as investigators and informers."[73] At this time, Beijing banned Falun Gong, claiming it was an evil cult, harmful to people, criminal, hypocritical, superstitious and antiscientific, treasonous, seditious, and disruptive to institutions and social order.[74] Henceforth, those accused of practicing Falun Gong were sent to labor camps for thought reform. Richard McGregor described Beijing's actions against Falun Gong, like those in Tibet and Xinjiang, as "political campaigns which come with the imprimatur of the very top ... implemented with zeal." However, the crackdown on Falun Gong became a centripetal force for other groups dissenting against the party.

---

[70] Zhao and Leibold, "Ethnic Governance under Xi Jinping."
[71] Faligot, *Chinese Spies*; Dillon, *China: A Modern History*.
[72] Sarah Cook and Leeshai Lemish, "The 610 Office: Policing the Chinese Spirit," *China Brief* 11(17) (September 16, 2011), https://jamestown.org/program/the-610-office-policing-the-chinese-spirit.
[73] Audin, "Governing through the Neighbourhood Community," 16fn.5.
[74] Maria Hsia Chang, *Falun Gong: The End of Days* (Carlton North: Scribe, 2004), 97; Ministry of Foreign Affairs of the People's Republic of China, "The Ban of Falun Gong Is at People's Will," Embassy of the People's Republic of China in the United States (2003), www.mfa.gov.cn/ce/ceus//eng/zt/ppflg/t36589.htm.

During the 2000s, Falun Gong was active in Hong Kong promoting awareness of the campaign against it in mainland China. Hong Kong was already a site of activism and advocacy for democracy, its bookstores offered scathing critiques of the party and party members, and every year it held a commemoration for those killed in the military crackdown on democracy protesters in Beijing in 1989. Political scientist Maria Hsia Chang writes that "Falun Gong also became a test of Hong Kong's promised autonomy from mainland China," further politicizing the issue and testing the boundaries of Beijing's tolerance.[75] When internet keyword censorship became possible under Golden Shield, 20 percent of the first batch of "sensitive words" pertained to Falun Gong, more than any associated with the other sensitive issues of the day; Xinjiang and Tibet were ranked next at 15 percent combined.[76] While the crackdown on Falun Gong began prior to widespread internet access in China, the threat it posed to the party saw the CPC explore all possible internet and technological advances that were springing up alongside of it to ultimately control and eradicate it inside of China. Falun Gong, then, occurred during the bridging period between old (analog) and new (digital) methods of surveillance and control, and it challenged the CPC to stay abreast of the possibilities for tech-enhanced surveillance and control becoming increasingly available in the digital age, which the CPC has now perfected.

The Xinjiang Crisis: The Rise and Rise of Digital Totalitarianism

Xinjiang is where the CPC's digital totalitarianism is most fully realized, and it has become the pinnacle for tech-enhanced surveillance and control in China. The incarceration of more than one million Uyghurs and other Muslim minorities into political reeducation camps, along with the practice of forced labor and labor transfer to the eastern provinces; the removal of minority nationality children from their parents, and hence their culture; the disappearance of many cultural elites into mass detention; the implementation of mass surveillance across the region, transforming it into a police state; and a rapidly growing cultural genocide within the region, evidences the resolve of the party. These measures demonstrate how the CPC is determined to crush not just dissent, for many of those who have been targeted in Xinjiang would not fit most definitions of dissenters or antiparty activists, but even simple difference.

---

[75] Chang, *Falun Gong*, 22.   [76] Faligot, *Chinese Spies*.

Surveillance of Uyghurs across Xinjiang employs high-tech tools including face and voice recognition, iris scanners, DNA sampling, and 3D identification imaging. Thousands of police stations have been built across the region, and from 2017 there was a massive increase in surveillance spending to install the cameras, equipment, and systems necessary to implement the CPC's digital "stability maintenance" of Xinjiang.[77] Across the region, tens of thousands of cameras now monitor mosques, schools, businesses, buildings, and streets, and preemptive policing has become the norm.[78] By conflating Uyghur culture and Islamic identity (difference) with separatism and terrorism, the CPC sees Uyghurs as an acute threat to the party. The still-unfolding Uyghur crisis in Xinjiang provides further evidence of the extreme nature of the CPC's anxiety over its hold on power.

The Slow Death of Autonomous Hong Kong

After the handover of Hong Kong to the People's Republic of China (PRC) in 1997, the potential threats posed by democracy activism inside Hong Kong and the unique autonomy afforded Hong Kong citizens under the "one country, two systems" model were a source of anxiety for the CPC. In the intervening years, there were multiple attempts to restrict freedoms inside of Hong Kong bringing it more in line with any other mainland city. In 2003, attempts to introduce the National Security (Legislative Provisions) Bill were met with widespread demonstrations, with Hongkongers protesting the threats the bill posed to their freedom of speech, and it was eventually shelved.[79] Across the same period, "patriotic education" was introduced into Hong Kong schools to foster loyalty to the CPC and increase its legitimacy inside of Hong Kong.[80] However, the patriotic education curriculum fell well short of its aims largely due to

---

[77] Emily Feng, "Security Spending Ramped Up in China's Restive Xinjiang Region," *Financial Times* (March 13, 2018), www.ft.com/content/aa4465aa-2349-11e8-ae48-60 d3531b7d11; Josh Chin and Clement Burge, "Twelve Days in Xinjiang: How China's Surveillance State Overwhelms Daily Life," *Wall Street Journal* (December 19, 2017), www.wsj.com/articles/twelve-days-in-xinjiang-how-chinas-surveillance-state-over whelms-daily-life-1513700355; Zenz, "China's Domestic Security Spending."

[78] Joanne Smith Finley, "The Wang Lixiong Prophecy: 'Palestinization' in Xinjiang and the Consequences of Chinese State Securitization of Religion," *Central Asian Survey* 38(1) (2018): 81–101.

[79] Kurata Toru, "Development of the Hong Kong Pro-Democracy Protest into a 'New Cold War': Shift from Opposing the Hong Kong National Security Law," *Asia-Pacific Review* 27(2) (2020): 94–108.

[80] Edward Vickers, "The Motherland's Suffocating Embrace: Schooling and Public Discourse on Hong Kong Identity under the National Security Law," *Comparative Education* (2023): 138–158, https://doi.org/10.1080/03050068.2023.2212351.

Hong Kong's free and open media and wider education and cultural institutions that continued to be critical of the CPC.

In 2009, Beijing's anxieties resulted in the introduction of a liberal studies subject into the curriculum, which Beijing hoped would reeducate the younger generations of Hongkongers to love the party and the motherland and instill loyalty to the CPC. However, the subject involved instruction about the societies and political and constitutional systems of both Hong Kong and the PRC, thereby limiting Beijing's ability to Sinicize young Hongkongers. Not satisfied with the compromise subject, in 2012, attempts were made to introduce a more PRC- and party-focused compulsory subject titled "moral and national education" into the curriculum. The bid failed, signaling Hongkongers' continued rejection of Beijing's overt attempts at political reeducation and Sinicization.[81]

In 2014, Hongkongers again took to the streets under the Umbrella Movement, opposing Beijing's attempts to install "Chinese-style" elections in Hong Kong, whereby candidates running for election were preselected by the CPC.[82] While the months-long protest movement ended without any concessions, Beijing's attempts to chip away at Hong Kong's important freedoms saw Hongkongers become ever more vigilant. Then, in 2019, the Carrie Lam government attempted to revise the Fugitive Law, which would henceforth allow Hong Kong citizens to be extradited to any part of the PRC. Given the earlier abductions into China of Hong Kong booksellers critical of the CPC – acts that attracted significant international attention and condemnation – the proposed change sparked concern.[83] It would mean that henceforth, Hong Kong "dissidents," or those critical of the party and its leaders, could simply be charged and extradited to the PRC, with the legal changes providing a degree of "legitimacy" to the process. In June 2019, more than one million protestors took to the streets, and over subsequent months violence spiraled as both police and protestors intensified their force and resistance.[84] More than three million people voted in the district council elections later that year, securing a landslide victory for the prodemocracy camp, further alarming Beijing.

With the outbreak of COVID-19, demonstrations became more difficult, with tensions easing temporarily.[85] However, protests did not stop entirely, and the focus of the prodemocracy camp turned to ensuring they

---

[81] Vickers, "The Motherland's Suffocating Embrace."
[82] Toru, "Development of the Hong Kong Pro-Democracy Protest."
[83] Elizabeth Economy, *The World according to China* (Cambridge: Polity Press, 2022).
[84] Toru, "Development of the Hong Kong Pro-Democracy Protest," and Frank Dikötter, *China after Mao: The Rise of a Superpower* (London: Bloomsbury, 2022).
[85] Dikötter, *China After Mao*.

secured more seats in the September 2020 election. Fearful over the potential seats the prodemocracy camp could secure, and the continued protest actions by Hongkongers, Beijing quickly resumed deliberations on the National Security Law for Hong Kong, which had been shelved in 2003 following the aforementioned demonstrations. Fearing the looming September deadline and the growing prodemocracy camp inside of Hong Kong, the National Security Law on Hong Kong was passed on June 30, 2020, with enforcement of the law starting the same day.[86]

The National Security Law created four new offences in Hong Kong: subversion, succession, terrorism, and colluding with foreign forces.[87] Moreover, the law was extraterritorial in nature – meaning people anywhere in the world could be accused of these crimes – allowing authorities to issue international arrest warrants for the accused.[88] According to Antony Dapiran, inside of Hong Kong, the new law had an immediate and chilling effect. Activists deleted their social media posts and accounts; prodemocracy political parties and activist NGOs disbanded; the Lennon Wall with prodemocracy messages was stripped bare;[89] some movement leaders fled into exile; libraries removed books from their shelves; prodemocracy slogans and protest banners became illegal; within hours, the arrests began, and by November more than 10,000 Hong Kong citizens had been detained.[90] Moreover, the September elections were postponed, with COVID-19 cited as the reason.[91]

With the passage of the National Security Law, not only did the CPC criminalize most forms of protest inside of Hong Kong, it also killed the "one country, two systems" model that was intended to attract Taiwan to peacefully unify with the PRC, and leaders inside of Taiwan publicly disavowed the model.[92] International reactions included condemnation of the National Security Law, visa restrictions, and sanctions; and the

---

[86] Toru, "Development of the Hong Kong Pro-Democracy Protest," and Dikötter, *China after Mao*.

[87] Antony Dapiran, "Hong Kong's National Security Law," in *Crisis*, ed. Jane Golley, Linda Jaivin, and Susan Strange (Canberra: Australian National University Press, 2021), 59–65.

[88] Dapiran, "Hong Kong's National Security Law."

[89] The Lennon Wall in Hong Kong was modeled on the memorial wall in Prague which emerged after the murder of John Lennon. While initially it was a memorial to the singer, it soon also became a site for free expression through graffiti in communist Czechoslovakia, with some using it to voice criticisms and concerns over the regime's policies. The Prague Lennon Wall remains a site for free expression over issues of global concern. Rather than graffiti, the Hong Kong Lennon Wall comprised of thousands of colourful Post-It notes.

[90] Dapiran, "Hong Kong's National Security Law" and Economy, *The World*.

[91] Economy, *The World*.

[92] Kevin Rudd, *The Avoidable War: The Dangers of a Catastrophic Conflict between the US and Xi Jinping's China* (Sydney: Hatchette, 2022).

United States withdrew Hong Kong's special regulatory treatment, making it the same as any other mainland city.[93] Internet censorship has also been imposed, making Hong Kong less desirable as a hub for international trade and business.[94]

Ultimately, the National Security Law allowed Chinese laws to infiltrate Hong Kong's legal system, providing what Han Zhu describes as "a tunnel that connects the two legal systems ... import[ing] a large number of Chinese legal norms and elements into the Hong Kong legal system."[95] This has integrated Hong Kong into the PRC party-state, ending its autonomous status, making it the same as any other mainland city, as well as neutralizing the democracy protest movement inside of Hong Kong.[96]

The Problematic "New Social Class"

The CPC also views what Jiang Zemin identified as a "new social class" (*xin jieceng*) as a potential threat to its power. This group has emerged from the economic transitions brought about by Reform and Opening and has been a difficult group for the party to monitor and control.[97] Their ranks include much of China's middle class, including managerial and technical personnel in both domestic and international private enterprises, self-employed individuals, private business owners, employees of intermediary organizations such as lawyers, accountants, and private nonenterprise units, and new media practitioners who use new media platforms for finance, investment, and research and development.[98] In 2018, Yang Weimin, deputy inspector of the UFWD of the Zhejiang Provincial Committee of the CPC, wrote that the "new era" and "new order" of China would depend on how well the party engaged this "new social class." Estimated to number seventy-two million people, the majority of whom are not party members, the new social class is expected to grow over the coming decades.[99]

---

[93] Dikötter, *China After Mao*. [94] Hillman, *The Digital Silk Road*.
[95] Han Zhu, "A Chinese Law Wedge into the Hong Kong Common Law System: A Legal Appraisal of the Hong Kong National Security Law," *Northwestern Journal of Human Rights* 21(1) (2023): 43–108.
[96] Economy, *The World*.
[97] United Front News, "Further Interpretation of the New Social Class," *The Paper* (May 21, 2021), https://m.thepaper.cn/baijiahao_12795548.
[98] Yang Weimin, "Yang Weimin: On the Responsibility and Value Leadership of the New Class in the New Era," *China Social Science Network*, United Front Work Department of CPC Central Committee (September 29, 2018), https://web.archive.org/web/20201123210143/http:/www.zytzb.gov.cn/llyds/296334.jhtml; United Front News, "Further interpretation."
[99] Yang, "Yang Weimin."

The party attempts to co-opt members of the business sector and prominent nonparty individuals via the strategy of "make friends" (*jiao pengyou*), a deliberate pairing system whereby party cadres are provided a target individual whom they are required to befriend.[100] Guidelines for such friendships identify the minimum number of contacts cadres must have with their friend each year, suggesting both formal and informal chats as well as joint research. This is a clientelist state corporatist model, centered upon the deliberate forging of patron–client relationships to further the goals of the party by co-opting all targets under the political umbrella of the party. The strategy has internal problems, however, because both cadres and nonparty targets hold suspicions and fears related to the party. Targets are fearful of how open they can truly be with their party "friend," knowing full well they may be punished by deliberately or accidentally talking out of turn, and party cadres are fearful that they may be caught on the wrong side of Xi Jinping's Eight-Point Regulations (*ba xiang guiding*), which in seeking to eradicate official corruption have forbidden close relationships between government officials and businesspeople. Nonetheless, via this personalized model, the CPC aims to co-opt business elites, aligning their personal and enterprise goals with those of the party, thereby ensuring their loyalty to the party.

For members of the new social class who are considered more threatening to party interests, such as intellectuals outside of the party's grasp and returning overseas students, UFWD Deputy Inspector Yang warned that united front work needs to co-opt such people from being critical of the party and its goals to embracing them within their own personal goals.[101] Yang also warned that social organizations such as social groups, academic societies, industry associations, or community activity teams comprised of the new social class needed to be vigilant against foreign influence from NGOs and to resist attempts by domestic rights lawyers and dissidents to subvert their thoughts and actions.[102] Hence, for the UFWD, the new social class presents both promise and threat, similar to the overseas Chinese: capable of great contributions to the motherland and yet inherently suspect on account of their material or intellectual independence.

---

[100] Liao Xingmiu and Tsai Wen-Hsuan, "Clientelistic State Corporatism: The United Front Model of 'Pairing-Up' in the Xi Jinping Era," *The China Review* 19(1) (2019): 31–56.
[101] Yang, "Yang Weimin."
[102] See also State Council of the People's Republic of China 2019, "Regulations of the People's Republic of China on the Disclosure of Government Information," State Decree No. 711, www.gov.cn/zhengce/content/2019-04/15/content_5382991.htm.

(Non)Governmental Organizations and Rights Lawyers

From 2008, the CPC severely curtailed the number of NGOs in China and limited their scope of operation.[103] The work of NGOs typically involves advocating for the rule of law, transparency in decision-making, and official accountability, all of which present challenges to the CPC's ability to wield absolute power. The first stage of the crackdown on NGOs involved categorizing them as friendly or nonfriendly, co-opting friendly ones into the state apparatus while shutting those deemed unfriendly out of the state apparatus and excluding them from funding. The next stage involved eliminating the more radical "unfriendly" NGOs by criminalizing their work and forcing them to close. For those that remained, the CPC strengthened efforts to starve them of funding by introducing new foreign exchange regulations, and later the 2017 Overseas Foreign NGOs Law, which cut off all avenues for international funding. The final stage was infiltration via the expansion of the party into the friendly NGOs (making the term a misnomer), whereby the co-opted NGO "mirrors" party rhetoric and slogans, "catering to the government's needs" while adopting a "safe agenda."[104] Although this process began prior to Xi's ascension to power, it became systematized under Xi. It has had a significant impact, resulting in far fewer international NGOs operating in China and an operating environment whereby NGOs avoid sensitive areas in their work and outreach.[105] By categorizing, marginalizing, starving of funds, co-opting, and infiltrating NGOs, the party has gone to extraordinary lengths to control civil society, removing the risk that rights-based advocacy could foment discontent.

Similarly, the party has also targeted the practice of rights law. A nationwide campaign against Chinese human rights lawyers began on July 9, 2015. In just that month, police detained and interrogated over 300 human rights lawyers, their assistants, and other citizen activists across China, warning them to curb their activities.[106] Some faced secret trials and lengthy jail sentences. Some were forcibly disappeared for a time without charge. There was ongoing harassment, and some were made to perform televised confessions (scripted struggle sessions) of their crimes and links to forces hostile to China.[107] Law professor Fu Hualing has argued that the crackdown on rights lawyers stems from the CPC's

---

[103] Han Zhu and Lu Jun, "The Crackdown on Rights-Advocacy NGOs in Xi's China: Politicizing the Law and Legalizing the Repression," *Journal of Contemporary China* 31(136) (2021): 518–538, https://doi.org/10.1080/10670564.2021.1985829.
[104] Han and Lu, "The Crackdown on Rights-Advocacy NGOs," 10.
[105] Economy, *The Third Revolution*. [106] Economy, *The Third Revolution*.
[107] Economy, *The Third Revolution*; Han and Lu, "The Crackdown on Rights-Advocacy NGOs."

fears that because rights lawyering is fundamentally about politics, and may shed light on how the CPC governs, it is inherently dangerous and poses a direct challenge to the primacy and legitimacy of the party.[108] So chilling was the effect of the July 9 crackdown that it raised questions about whether rights law had a future in China.[109]

Combined, these measures demonstrate how in the Xi era, the CPC is increasing the coercive power of the state and it is deliberately targeting those who can challenge such power through the law, the media, and advocacy. The experiences of human rights lawyers, advocacy NGOs, and even individuals such as feminists and journalists illuminate the paradigm shift that has taken place during the Xi era, from the party's previous efforts at stability maintenance to their new focus on consolidating state power.[110] What has already occurred in the minority nationality regions of China is fast becoming mainstreamed across the rest of China. As witnessed across the history of the CPC, and recently, most acutely, in Xinjiang and Hong Kong, when dealing with dissent or difference, the party does not hesitate to rely on tactics of terror and violence to secure its aims.

Conclusion

Dissent is a source of acute anxiety for the party because of the threat it poses to the CPC's legitimacy. A key source of CPC power has been its ability to manage or eliminate dissent, and to weaken, co-opt, or destroy any organization that it suspects of disloyalty. The party tailors its approach to dealing with dissent based on how serious a threat they consider it. In some cases, co-option and infiltration is enough to transform the source (or potential source) of dissent into a tool of the party. By co-opting individuals or groups, through the organs of the UFWD, the party can then use them to legitimize its hold on power, claiming to be responsive to, and inclusive of, the people. Where it deems the potential threat more serious, the party may use coercion, manipulation, and violence against individuals or groups. The consolidation of power by the party during the Mao years was particularly violent, with terror commonly used to force loyalty and to secure power. During the early years of Reform and Opening, the party employed terror less frequently but did not abandon it. Groups including Uyghur rights activists, Falun

---

[108] Fu Hualing, "The July 9th (709) Crackdown on Human Rights Lawyers: Legal Advocacy in an Authoritarian State," *Journal of Contemporary China* 27(112) (2018): 554–568.
[109] Fu, "The July 9th (709) Crackdown on Human Rights Lawyers."
[110] Han and Lu, "The Crackdown on Rights-Advocacy NGOs."

Gong practitioners, human rights lawyers, and democracy activists who are regarded as severe threats to the party have experienced terror-based methods of control by the CPC. The UFWD extends the reach of the party overseas through monitoring, surveillance, and the application of pressure on Chinese living overseas. Holding hostage family members back in China is one of the party's most insidious and callous forms of dealing with dissent. However, it also illuminates the fact that the CPC is nervous about its hold on power. How the party deals with dissent reveals its ongoing fear of how the Chinese people might think, act, and behave if left to their own devices.

While tech-enhanced ways of dealing with dissent all attract considerable, warranted attention within contemporary analysis, they represent a continuation of analog strategies the party has long used even prior to coming to power. The CPC has spent decades perfecting them and conditioning the population to accept them. The party eagerly embraced technologically enhanced versions of their existing measures that extended their means of surveillance, monitoring, and control. The cameras, screening checkpoints, and monitoring applications are a constant reminder that the party is watching. However, for those who have not consented to live under what has increasingly become digital totalitarianism, the increased visibility of the mechanisms of surveillance and control may itself inspire discontent. As Jonathan Hillman put it, "China's digital dream looks increasingly like a nightmare."[111] Like its self-fulfilling prophecy about dissident groups in the Munich example, Beijing's turbo-charged, anxious insistence on pervasive control could itself become a potent source of dissent.

---

[111] Hillman, *The Digital Silk Road*, 243–244.

13 The Party and the Army

Ji You

The resilience of the Communist Party of China (CPC) has been a hot topic for China scholars since its post-Mao revival and is still a puzzle to be deciphered: Under increasingly tough internal and external challenges, the party seems to have further consolidated its domestic support amid economic prosperity.[1] Far less academic attention has gone to studying the special relationship between the party and the People's Liberation Army (PLA) than to the relations of the party with other government institutions. Yet no other organization has contributed more to CPC survival and resilience – or been so solidly identified with the party – than the PLA. As Mao Zedong famously said: "Political power grows out of the barrel of a gun." Significantly, he continued: "Our principle is that the Party commands the gun, and the gun must never be allowed to command the Party."[2] The intimate ties between the party and the army it commands constitute the foundation of CPC rule – and the PLA's special status within the People's Republic of China (PRC).

Throughout 2021, the CPC celebrated the party's centennial. A mass campaign was launched to study the CPC's history, focusing substantially on its long years of hard struggle to win national power. This retelling of contemporary history has relied heavily on PLA history. It was through recounting the PLA's battlefield success that the party portrayed its own glory to the masses. Will the party still frame its history in the same way via the PLA when it celebrates the centennial of the nation in 2049? If so, it will be due to the shape of the CPC/PLA special relationship.

The success of this relationship may lie in how firmly the party commands the gun. Despite PLA disobedience being very rare, the CPC's

---

[1] Edward Cunningham, Tony Saich, and Jesse Turiel, *Understanding CCP Resilience: Surveying Chinese Public Opinion through Time*, Ash Center for Democratic Governance, Harvard Kennedy School (July 2020); Cheng Li, "The End of the CCP's Resilient Authoritarianism? A Tripartite Assessment of Shifting Power in China," *The China Quarterly* 211 (September 2012): 595–623.

[2] *Mao Zedong Junshi Zhenyan* [Mao Zedong's Military Mottos], Zhonggong zhongyang dangshi wenxian yanjiushi [The History and Literature Research Department of the CCP Central Committee] (Shenyang: Liaoning People's Publishing House, 2017), 42.

relationship with its army was not always smooth, especially in their formative years in the 1920s and 1930s. Mao's assertion that the gun must never be allowed to command the party hints at the existence of challenges to party control. Mao also once said that nothing was absolute in this world. Since Xi Jinping took over the command of the gun as CPC general secretary in 2012, he has greatly tightened party leadership over the PLA by emphasizing the Central Military Commission's Chairman Responsibility System (CMCCRS), which is anchored in the history of personalized power and authority exercised by Mao over both party and army in wartime and continued after the PRC was established. With the one-man-rule mechanism in the CMCCRS, it has become tradition for the party leader to command the generals, since theoretically the position of Central Military Commission (CMC) chairman is part of a civilian institution of control over the military. However, the efficiency and effectiveness of this kind of personal control vary among CMC chairmen, as the level of the CMC chairman's authority is determined by many factors. Xi has probably been the most powerful CMC leader since the departure of Mao.

Conceptualizing the CPC/PLA Special Relationship in Transition

In the West's literature of PLA studies the notion of symbiosis has long been used to define the CPC/PLA relationship. It describes a state of mutual survival in the twenty-eight years of bloody civil war when the demise of one would lead to the elimination of the other. Further, it also indicates the degree of CPC/PLA organizational integration, where party cells were inserted into PLA units and the PLA became the military arm of the party. This phenomenon of the party in uniform informs the nature of communist civil–military relations.[3]

The political foundation for the paradigm of symbiosis was traditionally built on four pillars:

(i) Identical goals: political (seize state power), ideological (disseminate communism), and revolutionary (promote socioeconomic change through armed struggle);
(ii) An overlapping personnel structure reflecting an integrated civil–military decision-making process at the apex of power;

---

[3] Amos Perlmutter and William LeoGrande, "The Party in Uniform: Toward a Theory of Civil–Military Relations in Communist Political Systems," *American Political Science Review* 76(4) (1982): 778–789.

(iii) A near equal political/social status;
(iv) A shared mentality and vested interests in governance.[4]

Even after the founding of the PRC, this tight integration has continued and guarantees the CPC's ability to stay in power.

Conceptually, symbiosis constitutes the PLA's ultimate defense line for the party, typically seen in a major political crisis like the one in 1989. Predictably, Chinese dynastic cycles still cycle on and make such special relationships persistently relevant. Symbiosis, though, is a rare type of civil/military relationship worldwide and is built upon unique sociopolitical conditions. China's conditions today are so different to those of the 1920s that it is natural to question whether symbiosis can still serve as a tangible conceptual description of Chinese civil/military integration. For instance, the PLA is no longer a sole parallel power with the CPC, as it coexists with other political and state institutions in China's hierarchical polity, such as the State Council, which is above the CMC in official ranking. The peacetime evolution of the CCP/PLA relationship has given rise to functional differentiation and divergent institutional interests of the two organizations, constituting a source of fragmented authoritarianism in China.[5]

Changes have taken place in all the four areas just mentioned since 1949. First, the PLA has defined itself as a revolutionary professional army, an inherently contradictory depiction. So far the PLA has reconciled *revolutionary* and *professional* by redefining the original goals of revolution, just as the CPC has transformed itself from a revolutionary party to a ruling party.[6] The PLA keeps the description "revolutionary" still in order to express two things: subordination to the party, and protection of party domination, both of which are somewhat abstract and rhetorical in practice unless there is a crisis. In contrast, military professionalism is a concrete and daily concern of soldiers. They join the organization to fulfill specific occupational tasks.

Secondly, long gone are the days when party and PLA leaders took holding simultaneous positions in both bodies for granted. Today, no civilians hold military rank. Membership from the PLA in the Politburo has been minimal – two CMC vice-chairmen in the last two decades – and their role remains largely functional. Thirdly, despite its pivotal position in PRC politics, the PLA is under codified rules when pursuing

---

[4] Ji You, *China's Military Transformation: Politics and War Preparation* (Cambridge: Polity Press, 2016).
[5] Kjek Erik Brodsgaard (ed.), *Chinese Politics as Fragmented Authoritarianism* (London: Routledge, 2017), 204–222.
[6] In 2000, Jiang Zemin called on the CPC to transform itself from a revolutionary party into a catch-all ruling party. This was meant to enlarge the party's social base by welcoming members of the nonproletarian classes to join.

nonprofessional activities. For instance, its role in determining leadership succession has been substantially curbed. Generals wield political influence through their support for the CMC chair's exercise of power, especially by way of helping to forge elite consensus amid controversies. Last but not least, PLA status has been deprivileged in the party/state apparatus and in society. Partly this was by design: CPC leaders wanted to reduce the weight of the military's role in domestic affairs, learning the lessons of the Cultural Revolution (CR). It was also the PLA's own choice to ease its involvement in nonprofessional affairs, as seen by its push to renounce its once-vast business empire in exchange for guaranteed growth in the defense budget. Deprivileging the PLA is in line with global trends in sociopolitical change: Military roles are gradually narrowed as a society becomes more modernized and the middle-class population is more influential.[7]

The changes in the fourth category are subtler. The PLA shares CPC core interests (*hexin liyi*) to maintain China's political system and makes itself available to the CPC to act against organized opposition. The party rewards military compliance by respecting the PLA voice in major national issues and by supporting PLA transformation. Their converged vested interests are embodied in Xi's China dream of national rejuvenation under the century-old slogan of "a rich nation and a powerful military." The special Xi/PLA relationship is part of Xi's political leadership, reflected by his willingness to use the PLA as his primary power base if necessary. Shared civil–military national goals and political agenda have created a CPC/PLA "community of common destiny" (*mingyun gongtongti*): The PLA has little incentive or need to disobey the party when it remains a privileged body in PRC politics. Each benefits from supporting the other. Barring a domestic crisis, the current pattern of mutual support will continue: PLA generals buttress Xi's political line and authority as the CPC core. In return, Xi and party elites guarantee the generals a special sociopolitical status and a handsome budget.

Yet a special CPC/PLA relationship is not strictly symbiotic. The deepening of CPC/PLA functional differentiation and their divergent interests have reshaped the texture of civil–military politics in a more complex manner than the paradigm can describe adequately. In any country, the military's search for operational autonomy puts military pressure on civilian leaders. The clash between the military's assertion of its own interests and "absolute civilian control" supports a hypothesis that symbiosis is a phenomenon normally found in transitional regimes. It

---

[7] Muthiah Alagappa, *Coercion and Governance: The Decline Political Role of the Military in Asia* (Stanford, CA: Stanford University Press, 2001).

evolves through stages of weakened military influence in the course of political change. Prior to transformation in an authoritarian regime, the ties between the state leader and the generals seem to be symbiotic. Once a regime-threatening crisis erupts and puts their common survival at stake, each party may tend to place its own interests above those they used to share.[8] The cases of the USSR, Indonesia, and Korea, for instance, showed empirically that the military was better able to survive than the existentially challenged political regime. A symbiotic civil–military relationship was neither a given nor unshakable. The desymbiotic process begins with a military embracing professionalism, deemphasizing ideology, and protecting its own prestige in keeping with general social change.

Likewise, although in a more complex context, the CPC/PLA "community of common destiny" may also evolve under a similar logic that represents a logical direction of political transformation. The differentiated civil–military interests may widen the fault lines of civilian control over the gun, while shared CPC/PLA interests continue to guarantee party domination. The long-term and strategic challenge lies on the domestic front: how the PLA positions itself in the tripartite relationship with the party and society. The generals face a conundrum if grassroots protests grow to the point of challenging party rule. In a symbiotic relationship, PLA support for the party in a crisis would be automatic, but in a relationship of interest-sharing, this support may be conditional, with the generals calculating the stakes. The CPC and the PLA have not faced such a crisis since 1989. Yet Chinese history has recorded no permanent symbiotic civil–military relationship.

The Deliberate Civil–Military Division of Power at the Apex of Power

Mao Zedong established that the Politburo would take charge of political affairs in the country and the CMC would handle military affairs (*zhengzhiju yi zheng, junwei yi jun*). Over time the Politburo–CMC functional divide has evolved into an institutional divide, creating traditions and norms guiding civilian–soldier interaction.[9] This institutional separation of civil–military power is further evidenced by total absence of civilian Politburo members at key PLA events, particularly since Xi came to power. For instance, few media reports of the meetings where Xi

---

[8] Muthiah Alagappa, *Coercion and Governance*.
[9] Mao reiterated this formula in a Politburo meeting in December 1972. As the chaos of the Cultural Revolution continued, Mao added that the PLA should also involve itself in political affairs. *The PLA Life* (August 20, 2009).

announced the giant PLA reforms mentioned the word "Politburo," suggesting that it played no role in the decision-making process. The Overall Program to Deepen National Defense and Military Reforms (*Shenhua guofang he jundui gaige zongti fang'an*) was endorsed by the CMC's Deepening Reform Leadership Group in its third plenary session on July 14, 2015, and tabled to the CMC weekly meeting on July 22. This reform package was officially approved by the Politburo Standing Committee (PSC) meeting on July 29.[10] This tight timetable showed that the PSC had only a week to assess a very complicated and comprehensive reform program. One has to wonder whether this rushed schedule indicates that Xi's PSC colleagues simply rubber-stamped the program. In fact, however, this practice has been the norm since the Mao era. Consequently, PLA personnel would see the PSC as the highest party organ and the CMC as the highest military authority and their ultimate boss.[11]

Mao's formula grants the CMC chairman unparalleled personal control over the military vis-à-vis his Politburo colleagues. Jiang Zemin employed his civilian institutional posts to command the PLA, which compensated for his power deficits vis-à-vis the top soldiers. When he disagreed with certain points in CMC policy proposals presented to him, he would require the CMC to submit them to the Politburo for discussion, giving him a chance to reshape the policy. When he did not want the Politburo to get involved, he would end the policymaking process at the CMC level.[12] This legitimate but tactical use of institutional power helped him interact with Politburo colleagues from a position of strength.

In practice the Politburo/CMC separation of power results in no civilian Politburo members charged with military affairs, causing a vacuum in the CPC leadership chain over the PLA. This renders party supremacy over the military less than substantial, as the Politburo and the CMC function on their own initiatives.[13] Nowhere is the autonomous status of the CMC more clearly demonstrated than its decision-making role in national security matters. The CMC has been the sole initiator of all wars China has fought since 1949, with

---

[10] The Military General Political Affairs Department [Zhongyang Junwei Zhengzhi Gongzuobu], "Jiang gaige jinxing daodi" [Carry the Reforms to the End], *CCTV Documentary Series 7* (November 2017).

[11] Hu Guanzheng, *Dangdai junshi tizhi biange yanjiu* [Research on Restructuring Contemporary Military System] (Beijing: The PLA Academy of Military Science [Junshi kexue chubanshe], 2007), 470.

[12] Interview information from Jiang's former staffers, Beijing 2022.

[13] Wang Yong and Chen Senlin, *Research on National Security Crisis Management* (Beijing: the PLA National Defense University Press, 2011), 194.

the only exception the Korean War, when Mao convened full Politburo meetings to debate his decision to join the war. Admiral Liu Huaqing revealed in his autobiography that the PLA operation to take six islets in the Spratlys in the South China Sea in 1988 arose from a decision exclusively made by the CMC and approved by Deng with no Politburo involvement. He also revealed that China's nuclear submarine program was a naval initiative with CMC support. If the civilian government played no role in strategic matters such as war, PLA autonomy in decision-making of national significance can be said to be unparalleled in the world.[14]

Military Influence, Civil–Military Culture, and Leadership Politics

Mao's formula was intended to erect organizational and psychological barriers to nonauthorized fraternization among senior CPC cadres and PLA officers.[15] The CPC and the CMC both have set highly restrictive regulations in this regard. Even Politburo members have to apply to the PSC for permission to visit PLA units, with approved visits arranged by the CMC. Likewise, without CMC approval no general is permitted to engage in national or regional civilian affairs. For instance, in 1974 Mao's widow Jiang Qing paid a personal visit to the Twentieth Army to propagate the anti-Confucianism campaign. She had neither a PSC permit for the trip nor any CMC arrangement. This incident is still mentioned today as a negative educational case to warn anyone against crossing the red line (civil–military organizational boundaries). The visit in February 2012 to the Fourteenth Group Army (GA), founded by Bo Yibo in the late 1930s, by his son Bo Xilai allegedly also violated the proper procedures and was seen as revealing the younger Bo's political ambitions. Months later, he was accused of corruption and imprisoned for life.

China's time-honored civil–military culture denounces military involvement in court politics. The rise of warlordism at the end of each dynasty typically involved the military usurpation of regional government with the support of segments of civilian elites. The PLA holds the balance of power in China's elite politics, a fact long recognized by the party. As Mao once said in reference to his rival Zhang Guotao's attempt to seize party leadership through splitting the Red Army, "the Party can create an

---

[14] Liu Huaqing, *The Memoirs of Liu Huaqing* (Beijing: PLA Publishing House, 2004), 324–345.
[15] *The PLA Life* (August 20, 2009).

army but an army can also create a Party."¹⁶ A popular saying in CPC studies captures the nature of this reality: who controls the army controls the party. The CPC's vigilance is constant against any potential PLA attempts to intervene in elite politics and state governance, but these most likely occur at the invitation of senior party cadres.

The cause for concern is real, often based on organic linkages between CPC and PLA leaders, leading to faction formation. In 1992, Yang Shangkun (president of the PRC, and previously vice-chairman and secretary-general of the CMC) and his younger half-brother Yang Baibing (his successor as CMC secretary-general as well as director of the PLA General Political Department), issued a call for the PLA to protect Deng's reform process through safeguarding him on his "southern tour" (*baojia huhang*). They did this without formal approval from the party center or CMC chair Jiang Zemin. It is natural that the incumbent and retired party leaders should entertain different visions of reform. However, the Yang brothers' unauthorized interference on behalf of the armed forces with civilian leadership exposed the danger of generals overstepping the civil/military disciplinary limits and showed the ease with which this could be done. Both were relieved of their hold on military power. It was a serious lesson for both civilian and PLA Politburo members.

Deng's departure inflicted structural changes on CPC/PLA relations, with significant impact on the CPC's control of the gun. Jiang had limited authority over the PLA, which led him to behave dialectically with the generals: personal arbitrariness as the commander-in-chief coupled with a consultative leadership style. The fact that he had to rely on the Politburo mechanism to solicit CMC support opened a new era of institutionalized power-sharing with CMC members until Xi came to power.

One reason the PLA accepted Jiang Zemin was his inability to dominate the PLA as his predecessors did. It was easy to give positive support, but the test of authority came when the two sides encountered sharp disagreement. While Mao and Deng easily triumphed in such situations, Jiang always tried to avoid them. For the first time in decades, the PLA was free from the strongman control that had damaged its key corporate interests.¹⁷ Moreover, the essence of power-sharing was a give-and-take approach by a weak commander-in-chief, which was harmful to a normal civil–military relationship. For instance, in order to win personal support from CMC

---

¹⁶ Gao Minzheng, *Chinese Politico-military Theory: The Communists' Thought on Civil–Military Relations* (Beijing: Current Affairs Publishing House, 2011), 200.
¹⁷ This can be vividly seen by Mao's involvement of the PLA in the CR, which politicized and split the military thoroughly, and by Deng's order to the PLA not to demand more military budget in the 1980s, which substantially disrupted the PLA's modernization momentum.

members to contain factional rivalry in the Politburo, Jiang, and later Hu, chose to tolerate this abuse of power to the point where corruption became structural. The lasting impact is still felt today, as seen in the corruption case of CMC member Li Shangfu (national defense minister), disgraced in August 2023. Li's embezzlement could be traced to the Hu Jintao era.

The Shifting CPC–PLA Balance of Power

Post-Deng CPC leaders have realized that institutionalized civil–military relations can be achieved only when party leaders and generals strike a balance between effective party control and sufficient military autonomy. Without the former, the generals may be tempted to maximize their personal influence over politics. Without the latter, party cadres may be tempted to intrude on PLA daily management and forge irregular personal ties with senior officers. Either would be destabilizing. A related point is that the PLA has its own (separate) system of personnel management. In August 1950, Mao ordered the party's Central Organizational Department (COD) to formally transfer its responsibility for PLA cadre management to the PLA General Cadre Department.[18] This severed the party's organizational oversight over PLA personnel matters. The party and CMC personnel systems have remained separate ever since. The PLA submits its senior appointment lists to the COD for their records, not for approval. According to the "PLA Active Duty Officer Appointment Regulations and Procedures," with the CMC chairman's signature, the CMC can by itself appoint commanders up to the level of heads of the *Dadanwei*: headquarters departments, war zone commands, the Four Services (Army, Navy, Air Force, Rocket Force), and the People's Armed Police. There is no mention of the role of the party center (the Politburo).[19] Traditionally, CMC chairmen are given the privilege in personnel appointments of not needing to seek the opinion of fellow Politburo members, still less their approval.[20]

Even the selection of CMC candidates is exclusively based on CMC recommendations on behalf of the CMC chairman, although the PSC acts as a nominal filter by rubber-stamping the list.[21] With little personal contact, PSC members are generally not familiar with PLA generals and are thus not likely to have strong preferences about appointments. This

---

[18] Mu Song, "Mao Zedong and the Creation of the PLA General Cadre Department," *The PLA Daily* (September 14, 2009).
[19] The General Political Affairs Department, "The Officer Appointment Regulations and Procedures of the PLA," promulgated and implemented on January 14, 2002.
[20] Cadre Department of the GPAD, *The PLA Institutions of Cadre Management* (Beijing: The PLA Academy of Military Science Press, 1988), 158.
[21] "How Many Generals Did Jiang and Hu Promote during Their Term in Office," *people'sdailynet* (November 19, 2012).

The Party and the Army

has been especially true since Xi took the party's helm in 2012, since Xi has further maximized the CMC chairman's authority over personnel affairs under the CMCCRS.

The CPC exercises leadership over PLA affairs in the form of ideological guidance and ensuring the party line is followed.[22] Without an effective mechanism of organizational oversight, the top generals have enjoyed a free ride in abusing power, as evidenced by CMC vice-chairmen Guo Boxiong (also a Politburo member from 2002 to 2012), who was handed a life sentence for bribery in 2016, and Xu Caihou, who sat on the Politburo from 2007 to 2012 and died of cancer in 2015 before he could be tried for corruption. If the commander-in-chief takes no action, CMC members are virtually untouchable. Additionally, the PLA's own legal and discipline authorities entertain full autonomy in handling criminal cases within the PLA. However, the corruption cases of Guo and Xu showed that when the PLA's legal and discipline system are under the control of senior, corrupt CMC officials, the system breaks down. This resulted in an appalling rise of corruption in the PLA in the Hu era (2002–2012): Four senior CMC members and over 150 serving officers of the rank of major general or above were persecuted for serious violations of law and discipline in the last decade, which is unprecedented in PLA history.

Xi Jinping's Core-Building through Personalizing CMC Power

Xi's first task on assuming CMC chairmanship was to establish his absolute personal authority through tackling the negative legacy of his predecessor Hu in leading CMC affairs. Anticorruption measures were an early means to achieve such an objective. However, what Xi has done more strategically is to rectify Hu's hands-off approach in exercising CMCCRS power, which had substantially diminished the personal authority of the CMC chairman.[23] Moreover, a new balance has now been set in regard to PLA autonomy.

Dealing with Hu Jintao's Legacy

Guo and Xu were accused of hollowing out the CMCCRS through their manipulation of Hu. They adopted various tactics to sideline Hu by concealing top information, selectively reporting key issues, and monopolizing the personnel appointment process. Xi made it clear that corruption was not

---

[22] PLA National Defense University, *Guidance for enhancing the PLA's political and ideological work in the new era*, Beijing: The National Defense University, 2000, p. 307.
[23] Xu Qiliang, "Uphold and Improve the Party's Absolute Leadership System over the PLA," *People's Daily* (November 23, 2019).

the most serious crime for Guo and Xu but rather the deliberate violation of the CMCCRS.[24] Moreover, Guo and Xu also marginalized Xi as the heir apparent and first deputy CMC chairman. Xi court-martialed Guo and Xu once in full control of the CMC, but as far as he was concerned, it was Hu's loose exercise of CMCCRS power that had induced Guo and Xu to sideline Hu in the first place.[25] One example of Hu's hands-off management of the PLA is that Hu missed a large proportion of CMC weekly meetings and let Guo chair them, following a provision in the Party Charter of 2004 that "when the CMC is absent from a CMC weekly meeting, he can entrust his deputy to preside over it." One of the first things Xi did as CMC chairman was to remove this clause in the Party Charter.

Hu's CMC chairmanship could be best defined as reign without rule (*tong er buzhi*), issuing only broad policy guidance rather than detailed instructions. As such, Hu's control over the PLA was minimized: The top brass supported Hu's CPC leadership in exchange for maintaining their autonomy in PLA administration and operations. It is alleged that Hu made the final decision to purge Bo Xilai after he received firm backing from Guo and Xu.[26] Hu's hands-off style was particularly reflected in the way he handled PLA corruption. He mainly responded to the CMC reported concrete cases to him in a passive manner.

Ultimately Hu's weak leadership was rooted in his technocrat approach. Xi rightly pointed out that authority building had to be based on the leader's courage to confront challenges head-on. In contrast, Hu's basic principle was *buzheteng* ("not to rock the boat") in dealing with elite strife. For instance, he did not punish Guo and Xu before their retirement for the sake of maintaining "CMC unity," even though he clearly knew how corrupt the two were. He could have reshuffled CMC membership and replaced Guo with his own man, which was very much within his legitimate authority rooted in the CMCCRS.[27] He did not because CMC stability was more important to Hu than anything else.[28] His eight years as CMC chairman were largely uneventful but his tenure seriously distorted civil–military relations.

[24] The CMC Political Affairs Department (ed.), *Key Speeches of Xi Jinping on National Defence and PLA Force Building* (Beijing, PLA Publishing House, 2016), 7.
[25] Xi had little respect for Hu and the CPC elites of the Tuanpai, a faction with origins in the Youth League. Many of my interviewees made similar comments on Xi's attitudes toward Youth League cadres.
[26] Oral sources from the PLA researchers in Beijing in March 2013.
[27] This does not mean that Hu failed to employ the PLA for the exercise of his personal power. He mobilized CMC support when he moved on Politburo members Chen Liangyu and Bo Xilai.
[28] Ji You, "Hu Jintao's Succession and Power Consolidation Strategy," in *China's Political and Social Change in Hu Jintao Era*, ed. John Wong and Lai Hongyi (Singapore: World Scientific, 2006), 33–60.

Therefore, from his first day at the apex of power, Xi started to reshape the unbalanced relations between the CMC chairman and the top brass by consolidating and personalizing the power of the former in the name of reinforcing party leadership over the PLA. Xi's hands-on approach has led him deep into running PLA administration and operations, arguably in a more detailed manner than all his predecessors. This includes purging top generals and reshuffling CMC membership, taking the appointment of senior officers into his own hands, and requiring that top brass submit personal work reports to him. Xi has reinforced the lines of separation between the Politburo and the CMC. Since, like his predecessors, he is the only civilian leader of the armed forces, the party's organizational grip on the PLA is still structurally thin. This raises the question of whether the enhanced CMCCRS means stronger party control of the military more generally.

Shaping Elite Acquiescence to Xi's Core-Building

The granting of unprecedented personal power to Xi has been on the basis of an expedient consensus by the CPC–PLA that this was necessary to deal with structural problems in the CPC, including resistance to systematic reforms that hurt powerful interest groups and deeply rooted military arrogance and conservatism. This process of power personalization has been labeled as establishing the "core" (*hexin*) of central party leadership, essential for the CPC to consolidate and sustain its rule. In this view, Xi's assertive claim on CMC dominance is compensation for the eroded power of the top leader in the post-Deng era of collective leadership, most exemplified by Hu Jintao.

The elites of the CPC and PLA now share a common belief that collective leadership without a firm core encourages zero-sum factional competition at the center of politics. The history of the CPC suggests that whenever the top leader is weak, party cohesion and unity is at risk, which is why CPC elites repeatedly welcome strongmen to the top job, despite other risks associated with strongman rule (see the final chapter in this volume on the pitfalls of strongman rule). Indeed, they are not insensitive to the perils of grooming a strongman they cannot control. However, they consider the threat of fragmentation and disunity to be more dangerous. The absence of an effective central authority inevitably accelerates party decay. This has been the bitter lesson that Xi has taken from Hu's weak CMC chairmanship, and he has instilled his view among party and PLA elites.

More generally, China's elites accept the institutional logic of corebuilding. The CPC–CMC *nomenklatura* structure necessitates a strong core. Without it, the CPC and the Chinese polity become immobilist, profoundly resistant to change. This is ironic considering that the post-Mao reform has been premised on the institutionalization of CPC power to avoid overt concentration of power in a strongman, who would govern excessively arbitrarily. The pendulum has now moved to the other direction. The party and military elites seem to have agreed that in choosing between two evils – a strong leader who might make policy blunders due to his assertiveness and a weak leader unable to maintain political stability, thus facilitating the party's atrophy – the former is a lesser evil at this moment.[29]

On the other hand, worries about the rebirth of strongman politics in the CPC have never ceased. In Xi's first term in office, voices saying that the party center should avoid enshrining one particular leader in media portrayals were occasionally heard from Politburo members.[30] Such advocacy gradually disappeared after the Nineteenth Congress. However, this does not mean the disappearance of elite concern about the possibility of the reemergence of a CR-type disaster brought about by strongman politics. Here, an interesting question arises – whether Xi's power consolidation has facilitated this acquiescence, or the acquiescence has facilitated Xi's core-building. The answer may be a dialectical combination of both: The imperative to allow the top leader enough personal power to prevent excessive factional and policy rivalry in the Politburo creates a logic of power grab of its own. This can be seen from the fact that Xi largely followed the party norm of factional balance in forging the Eighteenth CMC which was composed of generals from different PLA factional origins. In contrast there is only the Xi faction in the membership of the Twentieth CMC, largely composed of generals from GA 31, deployed in Fujian where Xi was party secretary at the time.[31]

Core-building in the CPC reached a new height with the abolition of the state presidency's two-term limit at the Thirteenth National People's Congress in March 2018. Deng advocated a trinity of powers – CPC general secretary, the PRC president, and the CMC chairman (the

---

[29] General Jin Yinan justified support for Xi's assertiveness by saying that strong leadership may cause policy errors, but the gravity of such errors is less than that of party disunity as a result of weak leadership. Jin's speech to a public seminar of the Zhejiang Business Association, Hangzhou, October 18, 2018, accessed on YouTube, June 23, 2019.

[30] Li Keqiang, for instance, insisted that sentences dealing with opposition to personality cults and vigilance against leftist practices should be put into the communiqués of the plenary sessions of the Eighteenth Central Committee. He was successful in the first few years but chose to remain silent later when he realized he was out of step with the party's efforts in core-making. Talk with Li's former staffers in Beijing in 2021.

[31] Ji You, "How Xi Jinping Dominates Elite Party Politics: A Case Study of Civil–Military Leadership Formation," *The China Journal* 84 (2020): 1–28.

current party boss) – as a leadership core.[32] However, Deng also imposed an unwritten restriction on the top leader's party and CMC tenure by setting a presidential term limit. For instance, the two-term state presidency mitigates the tenured chairmanship of the State Military Commission (SMC). Since the position of party general secretary is institutionally linked to the chairmanship of the SMC, this gray-area term limit for the SMC chairman indirectly affects the tenure of the CMC chairman. The objective of Deng's formula was clear: When in office, the party leader should be powerful enough to handle party, state, and military affairs, but with a nominal limit on their office-holding. Hu Jintao followed Deng's formula faithfully, but the formula remained institutionally inconsistent: Only the presidency has a term limit, not the leadership of the CPC and CMC. Here, the party's search for power institutionalization is at the mercy of an individual leader's personal choice. In this respect, the constitutional revision in March 2018 may have bridged the discrepancy between the terms of the state presidency and CMC chairmanship, but it also removed the gray area that could be used against the top leader's attempt to stay in office beyond the two terms.[33] Thus the revision has cast a cloud over the core of the CPC's post-Mao reforms – institutionalization of China's political system. It has sparked concern among many about the potential repetition of CPC history: Political and policy disasters are inherently connected to a lifetime tenure system.

Xi has got his third term in office. However, he will be seventy-four by the end of his third term, which will dictate the need eventually to select a successor. Xi probably is not seeking life tenure, and he made it clear in 2021 to the party's National Organization Conference that orderly succession is a CPC norm that cannot be violated.[34] The cycle of orderly succession has always been a vulnerable issue for the CPC. It will be interesting to see if Xi can do better than his predecessors. The PLA's role will be crucial in determining whether it will be a smooth transfer of power or otherwise.

If Xi were to pursue a fourth term after 2027, he would still be younger than US President Biden when he commenced his first term. The CPC's decision not to stick strictly to a two-term limit may be sensible in the face of grave internal and external challenges, including the slowed economic

---

[32] Robert Kuhn, *The Man Who Changed China: Life and Legacy of Jiang Zeming* (New York, Crown, 2003), 123.
[33] Zheng Yongnian, "The Constitutional Revision Furthered the Integration of the Party and the State," *Lianhezaobao* (Singapore) (March 12, 2018), 1.
[34] Xi Jinping's speech on the CPC's work on the People's Congress system, *The PLA Daily* (October 14, 2021).

growth at home and worsening Sino-US relations abroad. In the two-term formula, as in Hu's case, the top leader has to focus on consolidating power in the first term and cultivating a successor in the second as he gradually becomes a lame duck. Casualties include the opportunity to enact major but controversial reform initiatives – without which the party atrophies. When Xi wrote in an article commemorating the CPC centennial birthday that the party had achieved an orderly transfer of power, he might have been hinting at a middle-ground solution: The future succession plan would be neither an arrangement for life tenure nor a restrictive two-term limit. Xi's exit may be determined not solely by his willingness to quit but also by whether a suitably qualified successor can be located or whether the domestic/international environment warrants it.

If this analysis of the CPC political succession contains a level of speculation, the role of the PLA in supporting Xi's extended tenure is certain and essential. In CPC–PLA relations, the generals are not kingmakers, but they do oversee the transfer of power. Their backing for Mao was the key to his rise to the top in Zunyi in 1935, during the Long March, and they backed Deng in 1978. More recently, the CMC insisted on Jiang Zemin's continued CMC chairmanship after he resigned from all his other party and state positions.[35] As mentioned earlier (p. 293), the PLA, as the primary power base for the CPC's leader, has served whoever heads both the party and the CMC well. Yet the PLA retains an institutional role in key matters such as the selection and tenure of the party's general secretary, who is the leader of not only the party but also the armed forces, affecting vital vested institutional interests of the military. The CPC's history has shown that the party would be in grave crisis if the civilian and military choice for the top leader was not in accord. Fortunately for both, such a crisis has been averted in the post-Deng era.

Xi's Domination of Military Affairs through PLA Reforms

In 2015, Xi launched the most thorough and sweeping package of military reforms since 1949. Politically, this has reinforced the party/PLA consensus on building a powerful military as a legitimacy statement. The reform's expressed goals have been to modernize the PLA into a superpower fighting force along the lines of the US theory and practice of a "Revolution of Military Affairs," which set the highest standard of

---

[35] Benjamin Yang, "The Zunyi Conference as One Step in Mao's Rise to Power: A Survey of Historical Studies of the Chinese Communist Party," *The China Quarterly* 211 (1986): 235–271.

military transformation in the high-tech IT era.[36] An unspoken but more fundamental objective has been to accelerate the consolidation, centralization, and personalization of Xi's power. The consolidation of the CMCCRS allows him to handle CPC and PLA affairs with unparalleled power. The military reforms are politically motivated as well, as part of the CPC's own deep structural and functional changes.

Enhancing the CMC Chairman Responsibility System

The key to Xi's centralization of power is the reinforcement of the supreme authority of the CMC chairman, which had been weakened in Hu Jintao's reign. Since Xi came to power, the Politburo has repeatedly issued directives stressing the inviolability of the CMCCRS and equating it with the party's absolute control of the PLA. Former executive deputy CMC chairman Fan Changlong has reinforced the notion that "firmly safeguarding and implementing the system of one-man rule by the CMC chairman is the crux and primary mission of the PLA reforms. It gives concrete criteria to measure PLA loyalty to the Party and the embodiment of the PLA's iron discipline."[37]

Enhancing the personal authority of the CMC chairman has always been a political act, and Mao and Deng emphasized the CMCCRS each time they perceived an internal challenge to their leadership. Xi's reiteration of this control mechanism is not new and is similarly more politically than militarily or managerially oriented. It empowers him further to control both the party's agenda and CPC factions, especially when there is disagreement among the elite over his political line, choice of successor, and strategic policies.

Combined Political and Operational Power

One specific move to personalize Xi's PLA leadership has been to let him take practical charge of PLA operational command, which is the ultimate form of personal authority any leader can receive. Traditionally in China, all effective emperors enjoyed operational command of their military forces, appointing field commanders, approving battlefield deployment, and sometimes participating in campaigns. Mao's unchallengeable power could be traced to his direct and successful command of major campaigns in wartime that laid the foundation of his leadership legitimacy in the

---

[36] Joel Wuthnow and Phillip C. Saunders (eds.), *Chairman Xi Remakes the PLA: Assessing Chinese Military Reforms* (Washington, DC: National Defense University Press, 2019).
[37] "Plenary Session of the PLA Delegation to the 16th NPC Conference," *The PLA Daily* (March 8, 2016), 1.

party and the PLA. Deng too personally commanded field armies that allowed him later to call on the support of senior officers in his efforts to dominate party and PLA politics. That only the CMC chairman has the final say in matters of war declaration, troop deployment, and senior officer appointment has been written into the PRC Constitution. Nobody and no other organization can interfere with the chairman's military command.[38]

In peacetime, CMC chairmen normally delegate operational aspects of PLA management to trusted deputies, while they spend more time on other pressing political issues. Mao and Deng seldom chaired routine CMC meetings in their last years in office. Hu Jintao was the same. Their hands-off style relied on a trusted executive vice-chairman to manage day-to-day PLA affairs. Top CPC leaders from Mao to Jiang took great pains to select their CMC deputies. It didn't always work out: The chairman's trust may allow their deputies the opportunity to become overly powerful. Eventually, the deputies pose a potential threat to their bosses, especially when they do not agree with the boss politically. Peng Dehuai and Lin Biao are typical examples. Xi has learned this lesson. He attends CMC meetings regularly, reads the periodic work reports by senior commanders carefully, inspects troops frequently, and appoints senior officers personally. His command of the PLA is more like that of Mao's in wartime than any of his predecessors.

One typical example of Xi's hands-on style is how he made himself chief of the CMC Supreme Joint Command Center, the establishment of which was personally ordered by Xi in the latest round of PLA reforms. Xi's role in the center effectively puts the PLA's operational command in his hands. This is the equivalent of taking on the duties of both commander-in-chief and chairman of the Joint Chiefs of Staff in the American system. It requires Xi to engage in detailed combat command of troops and battle designs, even in peacetime. Such a position of operational command further substantiates Xi's personal authority as CMC chairman. Since 2015, Xi has repeatedly inspected the Supreme Joint Command Center to familiarize himself with the concrete procedures of combat execution, including troop deployment, computerized war-gaming, weapons prepositioning in various war theaters, and monitoring real-time, campaign-level, joint war drills. As a result, Xi has set a much longer list of PLA tasks that need his personal oversight than most of his predecessors ever did. While this concretely enhances the CMCCRS and Xi's personal grip on strategic PLA activities, it adds to Xi's already extremely busy agenda,

---

[38] The PLA Research Center of Xi Jinping Thought, "Firmly Carrying Out CMCCRS," Red Flag Manuscript 14 (2023).

including chairing China's State Security Council and most CPC central leadership groups.[39]

This round of PLA reform also overhauled the structure of daily administration and operational command within the CMC. Before November 2015, for nearly seven decades, the General Staff Department (GSD), the General Political Affairs Department, the General Logistical Department, and the General Armaments Department administered the PLA's daily and strategic affairs. Although the CMC was the ultimate locus of policy approval, the four departments were entrusted with major decision-making power in managing their portfolios. They routinely issued policies and orders to PLA units in the CMC's name and on its behalf.

The 2015 round of reform stripped their powers in recognition that, although all their major decisions still bore the CMC name, they could stand between the CMC chairman and leading PLA agencies, such as the commands of the services and military regions. Often, and especially under a hands-off CMC chairman, the CMC's ultimate authority could be circumvented when the four departments took over policy initiatives and selectively reported these to the CMC chairman. This was particularly true in the case of the General Staff Department (GSD), which oversaw daily operational command. The line distinguishing authorization by the CMC per se or by the GSD on behalf of the CMC was thin and often confusing, and this led to power struggles among some of China's top professional soldiers.

Xi's decision to downgrade the four headquarters departments from being virtually autonomous power-holders to functional CMC offices was one of the most far-reaching reforms in this round of PLA restructuring. It kills two birds with one stone. With the CMC as the sole authority to make strategic decisions, it's easier to achieve the centralization of power. Restricting the power of generals to mainly functional and administrative duties also restricts the space for their abuse of power; the PLA's legal and disciplinary organs are now directly responsible to the CMC chairman. Second, the CMC's chairman runs the fifteen central departments institutionally and personally, and they are directly answerable to him. More than 200 central agencies at or above the divisional level were disbanded or absorbed into other units, with one-third of their personnel made redundant.[40] This much smaller body politic has made it easier for the CMC chairman to handle than it was to control the four powerful central departments.

There are many other measures designed to serve the sweeping reforms' politicized objectives. Among them is the reform of the

---

[39] Ji You, "China's National Security Council: Evolution, Rationality and Operations," *Journal of Contemporary China* 25(98) (2016): 178–196.
[40] CPC Publicity Department and the CMC Political Affairs Department: "Carry the Reforms to the End," Series Number 7, CCTV-1, November 2017.

command-and-control system of the People's Armed Police (PAP), a final front on which civilian Politburo members had a say in the past, specifically the premier and the general secretary of the CPC Political and Legal Affairs Commission. The premier used to have administrative responsibility over the PAP, which the PRC constitution placed under the dual leadership of the State Council and the CMC. In 2018, the reforms stripped the premier's authority over the PAP. Xi's reasoning was that there can be no fragmentation in control of the military. Now the PAP has only one master: the CMC, whose master is the general secretary of the party.

Conclusion

CPC–PLA relations are complicated and sensitive. There have been enormous changes as both the party and the military have hugely revised their organizational objectives, personnel structures, functional imperatives, and policymaking mechanisms. For instance, the concept of the CPC being a ruling party is identical to that of a catch-all party (a standard political science term to describe a party that absorbs different classes of people). For the PLA, its professionalization and the fact that it serves national interests as its organizational goal parallels the party in its evolution, as it gradually becomes middle-classized (*zhongchan jieji hua*), embracing more broadly defined national interests than the narrow class interests for which it was created in the first place.

There is a constant process of bargaining between party and PLA elites when the latter try to maximize PLA corporate interests and organizational autonomy. They regard a level of autonomy to be crucial to upholding their decision-making power over administrative and operational management, budgetary allocation, formulation of national defense strategy, and officers' promotion. This is also essential for the PLA to deepen professionalization and achieve a shift of focus from internal politics to external military threats. Yet a question arises here: how much the PLA's search for autonomy might erode the party's political and ideological control. Clearly, if the CMC chairman takes a hands-off approach, the balance may be upset.

This is the background of Xi's assertive leadership, intended to reassert party control to prevent people like Guo and Xu from reemerging in the CMC. This demonstrates his style of political leadership in comparison to Hu Jintao's technocratic style.[41] But if Xi has successfully tightened his personal grip on the PLA, he has not necessarily strengthened the Party's

---

[41] Xi has substantiated the one-man-rule mechanism of CMC chairmanship with more detailed institutional powers. See an unprecedented central document on enhancing CMC chairman authority, *The People's Daily* (January 31, 2015).

broader organizational oversight over the military, especially if the only Politburo member involved in CMC affairs is the general secretary himself.

But does the PLA prefer a strong civilian commander-in-chief overseeing its top solders and routine management or a weak one who facilitates the PLA's pursuit of institutional autonomy and corporate interests? For the first time in many years, the PLA has returned to the strict control of a party leader. The PLA might bristle under a Xi, Deng, or Mao. On the other hand, the problems caused by weak leadership such as that of Hu Jintao seem to have prompted support from within the PLA for a hands-on leader to ensure the force's integrity and unity. The PLA's unprecedented support for Xi, and his support for the PLA's transformation into a professional fighting force, indicates a subtle balance between firm leadership and the Chinese military's ability to remake itself into a modern, battle-ready, capable, and professional organization.

14 After Xi

Richard McGregor and Jude Blanchette

> In any personal dictatorship or tyranny, one thing is certain: someday there will be a succession crisis. That dread day casts a long shadow before, influencing the period of dictatorial rule by anticipation.
>
> Myron Rush, *The Khrushchev Succession Problem*

At the Twentieth Congress of the Communist Party of China (CPC) in October 2022, Xi solidified his position as the overwhelmingly dominant figure in China's political system. He has gained command of the military, the Communist Party of China (CPC) apparatus, and diplomatic and economic policymaking, all while sidelining or locking up rivals to his leadership. His drive for power, however, has destabilized elite political consensus and dismantled power-sharing norms that have evolved since the 1980s.

By removing de jure term limits on the office of the presidency – and thus far refusing to nominate his successor for this and his other leadership positions – Xi has solidified his own authority at the expense of the most important political reform of the last four decades: the regular and peaceful transfer of power. In doing so, he has pushed China toward a potentially destabilizing succession crisis, one with profound implications for the international order and global commerce.

This chapter assesses possible scenarios for leadership succession in the coming years and decades. Is Xi akin to Stalin after the purges of the 1930s – a leader who has so thoroughly eliminated rivals and cowed the system that he will remain in power until he can no longer perform the duties of office, leaving a succession battle in his wake? Or will the system produce a Newtonian reaction against his all-encompassing power, either forcing him out of office prematurely or at least pushing him to set a timetable for his departure? Alternatively, what are Xi's options for a middle path between these scenarios, an orderly succession in the next five to ten years?

Introduction

The peaceful, orderly, and regular transfer of power, while largely taken for granted in modern democracies, remains a source of conflict and instability around the world. As the efforts by former president Donald Trump to discredit the electoral victory of President Joe Biden demonstrate, even in democratic systems with robust legal procedures and long-standing conventions governing the peaceful transfer of power, succession can be precarious. From Malaysia to North Korea, Burundi to Russia, insufficient or impotent legal and political constraints allow incumbents to remain in power for indeterminate time periods, often indefinitely. Where legal processes are more robust, leaders intent on remaining in office often preemptively sideline or even jail political opponents. While some autocrats are able to remain in office for life, efforts to hold power indefinitely can also trigger succession crises, formal leadership challenges, or even military coups.

China, under the rule of the CPC, is not immune to these realities. Scholar Bruce Dickson described leadership succession as "the central drama of Chinese politics almost since the beginning of the People's Republic in 1949."[1] During the Mao Zedong era, which lasted until his death in 1976, leadership battles were frequent and fierce, from the "Gao Gang Affair" in the early 1950s to the violent and mysterious demise of Mao's one-time chosen heir Lin Biao, who perished in a plane crash while fleeing China in 1971, allegedly following a failed assassination attempt on Mao himself.[2] Mao had already sidelined another potential successor, Liu Shaoqi, at the start of the Cultural Revolution; Liu was beaten by Red Guards before dying in captivity in 1969. In late 1976, the "Gang of Four" was arrested just months after Mao's death. Deng Xiaoping and his allies then sidelined Mao's handpicked successor, Hua Guofeng, in the late 1970s. The two leaders chosen by Deng to take charge of the CPC, Hu Yaobang and Zhao Ziyang, were both unseated from power in the late 1980s amid intense political turmoil and elite infighting. Such leadership crises are dangerous for the party on many levels, not least because they threaten to magnify instability by exposing divisions within the ruling elite to the public.

---

[1] Bruce J. Dickson, "Unsettled Succession: China's Critical Moment," *National Interest* (September 1, 1997), https://nationalinterest.org/article/unsettled-succession-chinas-critical-moment-785.

[2] Michael Sheng, "Mao and Chinese Elite Politics in the 1950s: The Gao Gang Affair Revisited," *Twentieth-Century China* 36(1) (2011): 67–96, https://doi.org/10.1179/1521 53810X12925963452826; and Frederick C. Teiwes and Warren Sun, *The Tragedy of Lin Biao: Riding the Tiger during the Cultural Revolution 1966–1971* (Honolulu: University of Hawaii Press, 1996).

Looking back in history, instability and volatility have long been features of Chinese politics. According to Harvard University's Wang Yuhua, of the 282 emperors ruling across 49 dynasties, roughly half were deposed by being "murdered, overthrown, forced to abdicate, or forced to commit suicide."[3] Less than half designated a successor, and the majority of those only did so in the final years of their reign. These successors were themselves regularly murdered by rival members of the political elite or members of their own families.

While the fallout from previous Chinese dynastic power struggles was largely domestic, the global impact of a twenty-first-century succession crisis would be immense. Under Xi Jinping, the likelihood of such a crisis grows daily, as he continues to concentrate political power and personalize his rule in contravention of decades of evolving (albeit imperfect and limited) political norms. Since coming to power in late 2012, he has eviscerated the few formal constraints and de facto conventions that were implemented to curtail leadership struggles in the post-Mao era. As he began his norm-breaking third term in office, Xi and the rest of the senior leadership in Beijing – all of whom, following the personnel changes at the Twentieth Congress, are considered Xi loyalists – have remained silent on how long he plans to remain in power. Only a small handful of senior party officials are likely to have any idea of Xi's longer-term plans.

Xi is the single most important political figure in the country with the world's largest population, second-largest economy, and second-largest active-duty military force, as well as a growing arsenal of nuclear and conventional weapons. From global economic volatility to the ripple effects on the fourteen countries that share a land border with China, to say nothing of concerns over China's significant offensive capabilities and territorial claims, the risks flowing from domestic instability are enormous.

This chapter surveys possible leadership succession scenarios, ranging from the sudden death or incapacitation of Xi Jinping to an overt leadership challenge or coup. We do not claim to be able to predict the future. Our main argument is that it is imperative for governments and their militaries as well as global institutions and businesses to be prepared for future political volatility in China, including a leadership that devolves into infighting, instability, and intrigue. If Xi clings to power well into old age, the political system will likely calcify into structures of rigid

---

[3] Wang Yuhua, "Can the Chinese Communist Party Learn from Chinese Emperors?," LARB China Channel (March 22, 2018), https://chinachannel.org/2018/03/22/chinese-emperors/.

repression, creating their own set of challenges. The implications for the rest of the world from either scenario are immense, as are the costs of ignoring the reality of China's current political trajectory.

We begin with a historical overview of post-Mao efforts to normalize leadership succession in China, followed by a brief discussion of how Xi Jinping has worked to undo many of these recent constraints. We then turn to an analysis of four possible succession scenarios and what they would mean for Chinese politics and the rest of the world.

From Deng to Jiang: A Partial, Imperfect Solution

In the shorthand of news reports, Xi Jinping's abolition of presidential term limits in early 2018 overturned the most important legal constraint put in place a quarter of a century earlier by Deng Xiaoping to prevent a repeat of Mao Zedong's dictatorial rule-for-life. More precisely, the two-term limit for the presidency – formalized in the constitution of the People's Republic of China (PRC) in 1982 – was the beginning of the incremental, imperfect, and, as it turned out, fragile process of institutionalizing elite politics.[4] Although regular and orderly transitions of top leadership came to be considered the cornerstone of this process, this in fact only took place once in a fully fledged manner, when Xi himself took office in 2012, succeeding Hu Jintao.[5]

Deng's imposition of term limits for the office of the presidency had limited applicability when it was introduced in 1982. For starters, it did not restrict Deng himself, whose real power was wielded informally, as well as through his sole high official position as chairman of the Central Military Commission (CMC), which he relinquished in 1989. Even after his formal "retirement," Deng continued to be the dominant figure in China's political system. The position of president was, and remains, relatively weak when compared to the roles of CPC general secretary and CMC chair.

The introduction of de jure term limits was nonetheless meaningful, for it signaled that the CPC wanted to avoid a return to the one-man rule that had predominated since the beginning of the Mao period. (Only the

---

[4] Some scholars argue that too much credit is given to Deng for political reform and modernization, especially in the realm of reforming the leadership system. See Joseph Torigian, "The Shadow of Deng Xiaoping on Chinese Elite Politics," War on the Rocks (January 30, 2017), https://warontherocks.com/2017/01/the-shadow-of-deng-xiaoping-on-chinese-elite-politics.

[5] While some point to the leadership handover from Jiang Zemin to Hu Jintao at the Sixteenth Party Congress as an example of a successful transition, in fact Jiang Zemin remained head of the Central Military Commission for another two years, thus giving Hu only a partial hold on power.

"one" was a problem, not the "man" – no woman has ever sat on the highest leadership council, the Politburo Standing Committee.) Modernizers within the political system were very concerned to end – or at least limit – the unpredictability of succession politics that had typified the Mao era. As Yan Jiaqi, the former director of the Institute of Political Research of the Chinese Academy of Social Sciences, wrote in late 1979:

> The history of socialism in the past sixty years makes it plain that whenever there is a system of life-tenure for the highest Party and state leaders, [a cult of personality] commonly occurs. Although it begins with an emphasis on collective leadership and the promotion of democracy, it culminates in an arbitrary rule that destroys collective leadership while safeguarding the power of the individual.[6]

The orderly transition of power at the executive level – covering the presidency and, by extension, the position of CPC general secretary and chair of the CMC – became the centerpiece of elite political reform over time. But it was just one of many formal and informal reforms that began in the early 1980s to limit the ability of party officials at any level to build political fiefdoms and independent centers of power that could frustrate or contravene policy emanating from Beijing. The central leadership appointed senior provincial leaders, for example, from outside the province itself. An "up-or-out" system of age limits was put in place for both the Central Committee (no older than sixty-three) and the Politburo (no older than sixty-eight). These party rules inevitably applied to government positions as well. By capping the age at which one could join the Central Committee, the party stopped anyone older than sixty-three from becoming a provincial party secretary, governor, or member of the State Council.

As in any political system, short-term considerations molded the rules. In 1997, then-general secretary Jiang Zemin pushed out a Politburo rival, Qiao Shi, by declaring that anyone over seventy had to retire, even though Jiang himself was seventy-one at the time.[7] He successfully pulled off a similar maneuver in 2002, this time lowering the age limit to join the Politburo to sixty-eight, thus ending the career of another rival, Li Ruihuan. Despite the circumstances of their creation, these rule changes have had an enduring impact.

While the position of CPC general secretary is not constrained by de jure term limits, by fusing the job with that of president and military

---

[6] Yan Jiaqi, *Toward a Democratic China: The Intellectual Autobiography of Yan Jiaqi* (Honolulu: University of Hawaii Press, 1989), 52.
[7] Seth Faison, "China President Ousts Rival from High Party Positions," *New York Times* (September 17, 1997), www.nytimes.com/1997/09/19/world/china-s-president-ousts-rival-from-high-party-positions.html.

leader beginning in early 1993, the CPC effectively, if informally, set the general secretary's tenure at two five-year terms. It also created a new expectation that the three top titles (CPC general secretary, CMC chair, and PRC president) would be held concurrently by one individual. Short-term considerations drove Deng Xiaoping's decision to grant Jiang Zemin all three top jobs, as he was trying to insulate him from potential challengers.[8] The trade-off for making the leader supremely powerful was the implicit understanding that he would step aside after two terms.

The person who benefited most from the emerging norms of elite politics was Xi himself. He was formally anointed as Hu Jintao's successor at the Seventeenth Party Congress in 2007 and prepared for taking the top job five years later. At the Eighteenth Party Congress in 2012, Xi assumed the country's two most important offices, CPC general secretary and CMC chairman, and became PRC president the following March at the subsequent session of the National People's Congress (which, like the presidency, is part of the state, as opposed to party, apparatus). Jiang Zemin had handed over the first two titles to Hu Jintao in late 2002 and early 2003 but, straining under the conventions of term limits himself, delayed handing over the military chair for two years. Hu, on the other hand, relinquished all three titles to Xi at once, a move that can either be explained by his lack of political authority within the system or by his intention to give Xi more room to pursue his own agenda. Hu himself had to contend with constant maneuvering from Jiang and his allies during his ten years in office.

The clean handover of power to Xi in 2012 was seen by respected and credentialed observers as a historic turning point in Chinese elite politics. The party, media, and scholars depicted the formal and orderly process of transition as something which had evolved into a permanent feature of the system. "Succession itself has become a Party institution," wrote two scholars, reflecting what was becoming conventional wisdom.[9] Ding Yijiang argued, "the five-year term of office for a maximum of two consecutive terms has been further established and become a primary

---

[8] This is also why Deng declared Jiang the "core" of the third generation of leaders in a June 16, 1989, speech entitled "Urgent Tasks of China's Third Generation of Collective Leadership." As Deng said to members of the Central Committee, "You should make an effort to maintain the core – Comrade Jiang Zemin, as you have agreed. From the very first day it starts to work, the new Standing Committee should make a point of establishing and maintaining this collective leadership and its core." Full text available via people.com.cn, "Urgent tasks of China's third generation of collective leadership," China Daily.com.cn (October 26, 2010), http://www.chinadaily.com.cn/china/19thcpcnationalcongress/2010-10/26/content_29714412.htm.

[9] Wang Zhengxu and Anastas Vangeli, "The Rules and Norms of Leadership Succession in China: From Deng Xiaoping to Xi Jinping and Beyond," *The China Journal* 76 (July 2016), https://doi.org/10.1086/686141.

feature of China's leadership system."[10] Before Xi's abolishment of presidential term limits in 2018, CPC scholars and officials had proudly highlighted the 1982 constitutional limits on power as a bedrock constraint on the lifelong tenure of senior leaders.[11] Han Dayuan, dean of Renmin University's law school – a position with vice-ministerial status in the party-state – argued in a 2018 article that the constitutional term limits provided an "effective constraint on life-long tenure, a fairly good prevention of personal power concentration and the emergence of a personality cult."[12]

Xi Consolidates Control

The new norms of succession were widely accepted within the party until early 2018, when articles in state media appeared, arguing that the three titles of CPC general secretary, CMC chair, and PRC president needed to remain unified (*sanwei yiti*). The Chinese-language version of the *Global Times* published an editorial in February that year, later reposted by Xinhua, which stated, "the removal of the term limit through constitutional amendment is helpful in protecting unity in the three offices and improving the leadership system of the Party and the country."[13] To achieve this policy outcome, Xi could have added term limits on the party and military positions to bring them into line with the presidency. Instead, he focused on removing the two-term limit on the office of the presidency – the option that paved the way for him to remain in power after the Twentieth Party Congress in 2022. There were already signs in late 2017 that Xi was clearing the way to indefinite tenure. Two up-and-coming officials whose career tracks had positioned them as his potential successors – Hu Chunhua and Sun Zhengcai – were both eliminated from the running. Sun was detained for alleged corruption in August that year; two months later, Hu failed to win promotion to the Politburo inner circle, the Standing Committee, at the Nineteenth Party Congress, removing him from immediate consideration for the top job.

But if the groundwork was being laid for a constitutional amendment to remove the term limit at the annual session of the National People's

---

[10] Ding Yijiang, "Consolidation of the PRC's Leadership Succession System from Hu Jintao to Xi Jinping," *China Report* 51(1) (2015): 49–65, https://doi.org/10.1177/0009445514557389.

[11] "1982," cpc.people.cn (September 29, 2015), http://cpc.people.com.cn/n/2015/0929/c69120-27648073.html.

[12] Han Dayuan, "Remembering the 1982 Constitution 35 Years On," calaw.cn (January 20, 2018), www.calaw.cn/article/default.asp?id=12543.

[13] Xinhua (February 26, 2018), www.xinhuanet.com/comments/2018-02/26/c_1122456995.htm.

Congress in March 2018, not everyone had noticed.[14] The announcement that Xi could now become, in effect, leader in perpetuity caused shock, anger, and dismay among some party elites. As late as May 2020, a former professor at the Central Party School in Beijing, Cai Xia, complained bitterly that the constitutional change had been sprung on the Central Committee. "He forced everyone at the [Plenum] to swallow the revision like he was stuffing dogshit down their throats," she said in a widely circulated speech. "So many Central Committee members were at the session, yet not one dared to raise this issue."[15] The official press, perhaps because of the seismic implications of the change, played it down.

It is notable that Xi's suggestion to abolish presidential term limits – but not, it should be pointed out, the age restrictions or term limits for any other high office – came less than one month before the Nineteenth Party Congress in late 2017. The congress also enshrined "Xi Jinping Thought on Socialism with Chinese Characteristics for a New Era" in the CPC constitution as a "beacon" for the party's work. Xi dominated the meeting, cementing his position at the center of the party and proving himself to be an unrivaled political tactician and bureaucratic infighter.[16] His forcing through of the constitutional amendment was the culmination of efforts to consolidate his power that began almost as soon as he took office in 2012. The anticorruption campaign Xi launched in 2013 was key to establishing his authority over the system and served as an important tool for boosting his own position. The campaign allowed him to increase his

---

[14] Some scholars have made light of the 2018 constitutional amendment, with Ling Li of the University of Vienna going so far as to argue, "the only legal consequence of lifting the term limit ... is that Xi Jinping is allowed, if re-elected, to continue to be the face of the PRC when addressing dinner guests at diplomatic events that he hosts and to continue to enjoy the diplomatic privileges accorded to the Head of State during his state visits to other countries." Ling Li, "Xi Jinping's Succession: What Did the West Get Wrong?," *Made in China Journal* (May 23, 2019), https://madeinchinajournal.com/2019/05/23/xi-jinpings-succession-what-did-the-west-get-wrong/.

[15] "Former Party Professor Calls CPC a 'Political Zombie,'" *China Digital Times* (June 12, 2020), https://chinadigitaltimes.net/2020/06/translation-former-party-professor-calls-CPC-a-political-zombie/.

[16] A detailed exploration of how Xi consolidated power is beyond the scope of this short chapter. For more thorough accounts of Xi's political machinations, see Dimitar D. Gueorguiev, "Dictator's Shadow: Chinese Elite Politics under Xi Jinping," *China Perspectives* 1–2 (2018), https://doi.org/10.4000/chinaperspectives.7569; Michał Bogusz and Jakub Jakóbowski, *The Chinese Communist Party and Its State: Xi Jinping's Conservative Turn* (Warsaw: Centre for Eastern Studies, September 9, 2019), www.osw.waw.pl/en/publikacje/osw-report/2019-09-18/chinese-communist-party-and-its-state; Sangkuk Lee, "An Institutional Analysis of Xi Jinping's Centralization of Power," *Journal of Contemporary China* 26(105) (2017), https://doi.org/10.1080/10670564.2016.1245505; Ji You, "How Xi Jinping Dominates Elite Party Politics: A Case Study of Civil–Military Leadership Formation," *China Journal* 84 (July 2020), https://doi.org/10.1086/708647; and Richard McGregor, *Xi Jinping: The Backlash* (Sydney: Lowy Institute Penguin Specials, 2019), www.lowyinstitute.org/publications/xi-jinping-backlash.

popular appeal by combating the universally reviled scourge of official graft and political privilege while also sidelining rivals and instilling fear up and down the bureaucratic hierarchy. At the same time, Xi utilized ideological campaigns to enforce tighter political boundaries over speech, thought, expression, and debate, thus squeezing space for permissible disagreement and dissent over policy choices. His major efforts toward "governance modernization" have significantly eroded the responsibilities and authority of the PRC State Council (i.e., the government) in favor of increased de facto and de jure power for the CPC. Gone are the days when the general secretary of the CPC and the State Council premier acted as a political and governing team.[17] Under Xi, the division between the party and the government has disappeared, with the former subsuming the latter. Premier Li Keqiang was sixty-seven by the time of the Twentieth Party Congress. Although not technically disqualified by virtue of his age, he lacked standing with the military and state security, and Xi had provided him no leeway in recent years to develop these connections. As a result, Premier Li Keqiang was largely relegated to second-tier status in policy formulation during his time in office and was effectively retired in 2022, when he didn't even retain a seat on the party's Central Committee.

While the CPC constitution bans personality cults, Xi has actively used individual propaganda campaigns to solidify his own power.[18] While far less extreme than the deification of Mao Zedong during the height of the Cultural Revolution in the mid to late 1960s, Xi has done more than recent leaders to elevate his status both among the general public and within the CPC, ranging from his self-designation as the "core" of the CPC Central Committee in 2016 to the promulgation of the related "two safeguards" (*liangge weihu*) in early 2019, which called for all party members to "safeguard" both Xi's status as the core and the unrivaled leadership of the party's Central Committee.[19] Since the announcement of the "two safeguards," the phrase has become standard political

---

[17] See Nis Grünberg and Katja Drinhausen, *The Party Leads on Everything: China's Changing Governance in Xi Jinping's New Era* (Berlin: Mercator Institute for China Studies, September 2019), https://merics.org/en/report/party-leads-everything; and Neil Thomas, "Party All The Time: Xi Jinping's Governance Reform Agenda after the Fourth Plenum," Macro Polo (November 14, 2019), https://macropolo.org/analysis/xi-jinping-CPC-china-governance-reforms-the-fourth-plenum/.

[18] Article 10, section 6 of the CPC constitution reads "The Party proscribes all forms of personality cult." Full text of the constitution can be found at www.xinhuanet.com//english/download/Constitution_of_the_Communist_Party_of_China.pdf.

[19] See "*Zhonggong zhongyang guanyu jiaqiang dangde zhengzhi jianshede yijian*" [Opinions of the central committee of the CPC on strengthening the party's political construction], Xinhua (January 31, 2019), www.xinhuanet.com/politics/2019-02/27/c_1124171974.htm.

language in key government and CPC documents and was written into the Party Constitution in 2022.

Hardening demands for political conformity under Xi, combined with the more banal realities of bureaucratic politics, have led to numerous officials publicly declaring fealty to Xi, either out of an instinct for political survival or owing to their own ambition.[20] In November 2019, Politburo member and Xi chief of staff Ding Xuexiang argued:

> The "two safeguards" are essentially one body. To maintain the core position of General Secretary Xi Jinping is to maintain the authority of the Party Central Committee and its centralized, unified leadership; to maintain the authority of the CPC Central Committee and its centralized, unified leadership means, at its foundation, to maintain the core position of General Secretary Xi Jinping.[21]

At the Twentieth Party Congress, Ding was promoted to the Politburo Standing Committee.

Tianjin Municipal party secretary Li Hongzhong spoke to cadres at a municipal Party Committee work meeting in October 2016, where he declared, "[all cadres] must be highly aligned with the Party Center and with Xi Jinping as the General Secretary. If the loyalty is not absolute, it is [equivalent to] absolute disloyalty."[22] Xi thus attempted to transform himself into the very embodiment of the party, sending a message that any future without him (or his direct blessing) would put the CPC – and therefore the PRC itself – at risk of instability.

Three Possible Scenarios

Xi's consolidation of power and the absence of any designated successor, combined with the dismantling of China's existing – if weak – term limits on executive power, have profound implications for China's future trajectory. The number of variables, not to mention the sheer opacity of China's political system, significantly complicates speculation on when the "post-Xi" era will begin and what it will look like. Will he retire at the upcoming Twenty-First Party Congress in 2027, or will he cling to power

---

[20] For more on how political incentives impact party cadres, see Victor Shih, "Nauseating Displays of Loyalty: Monitoring the Factional Bargain through Ideological Campaigns in China," *Journal of Politics* 70(4) (October 2008): 1177–1192, https://doi.org/10.1017/S0022381608081139.
[21] *People's Daily*, cpc.people.com.cn (November 18, 2019), http://cpc.people.com.cn/n1/2019/1118/c64094-31459391.html.
[22] China News Service, Sohu (October 22, 2016), http://news.sohu.com/20161022/n470979031.shtml.

for life? If he dies suddenly in office, as Stalin did in 1953, how would the succession process unfold? Would external observers be able to pick up on signs of emerging discord?

Even before the Twentieth Party Congress, there was a conspicuous absence of official commentary about his political future.[23] In order to help contemplate China's political futures and impacts, this study examines what happened in 2022 when Xi was reappointed for a third term and outlines three possible scenarios for the future.

This is not a prediction, or a judgment on which scenarios are more or less likely. The number of variables with potential impact on the probability of a given outcome are innumerable, as are the factors that would shape how these scenarios play out in. Rather, the below analysis is designed to provoke discussion about what is *possible*, given that Xi is leading China's political system – and all countries that have a stake in China's future trajectory – into uncharted territory.

Scenario One: Xi Prepares a Succession Plan to Retire at Twenty-First Party Congress in 2027 or the Twenty-Second Party Congress in 2032

Xi Jinping is clearly aware of the importance of a well-functioning leadership succession process. At the 2014 National People's Congress, he declared: "The best way to evaluate whether a country's political system is democratic and efficient is to observe whether the succession of its leaders is orderly and in line."[24] Assuming this sentiment is sincere, a delay in retirement might not signal the *complete* breakdown of cumulative efforts to normalize succession. Rather, Xi may have decided to delay retirement until he feels that he can both safely retire and be assured that his chosen successor will preserve his domestic and international legacy. Xi might also have believed that 2022 was too early to hand over power to an individual who has not had sufficient time to prepare for higher office. It is worth noting that any potential successor would almost certainly have to have been appointed to the leadership's inner sanctum at the Twentieth Party Congress in 2022 and be under sixty-three years of age: Li Qiang was exactly sixty-three and Ding Xuexiang sixty; the others were all older.

---

[23] *Global Times*, Xinhua (February 26, 2018), www.xinhuanet.com/comments/2018-02/26/c_1122456995.htm.

[24] qstheory.cn (January 1, 2021), www.qstheory.cn/dukan/qs/2020-01/01/c_1125402833.htm.

The question of how to ensure a safe and prosperous political afterlife ranks high on the list of concerns for any autocratic leader.[25] In most modern democracies, outgoing leaders are confident that once out of power, they will remain at liberty and free to engage (or not) in political life as they see fit.[26] Authoritarian leaders, by contrast, have no such security and must do deals to protect their own safety, and that of their family and their financial assets, once they step down. For example, in late 2020, the Russian Duma began considering a bill that would grant legal immunity for former presidents and their families. This was a clear sign that Vladimir Putin is worried about legal and other kinds of retribution for actions taken in office once he retires. Research by Alexandre Debs and H. E. Goemans has found that 41 percent of autocrats experience either exile, imprisonment, or death within one year of leaving office, compared to 7 percent of democratic leaders.

The authors conclude, "nondemocratic leaders ... can and indeed do anticipate significant punishment when they lose office."[27] In the case of Mikhail Gorbachev, the exception proves the rule. As a Russian paper quipped on the former Soviet leader's ninetieth birthday in March 2021: "He's the first leader in Russia's thousand-year history who voluntarily stepped down, stayed alive and at liberty."[28]

In China, all of Mao's potential successors died or were brutally ousted. Deng's two handpicked successors (Hu Yaobang and Zhao Ziyang) were both toppled and removed from public life, with Zhao spending decades under house arrest. By contrast, the Chinese leaders who relinquished power voluntarily, Jiang Zemin and Hu Jintao, enjoyed a safe retirement and kept their immediate family members out of jail. This is why the norm on term limits was widely considered to have become entrenched and indeed institutionalized – it worked well in keeping the system stable while the economy grew. Political stability and economic growth seemed to reinforce each other.

What, then, could give Xi the confidence to retire in 2027 or 2032? If Xi stayed on as PRC president, he would retain one important de jure title

---

[25] For more on this, see Ludger Helms, "Leadership Succession in Politics: The Democracy/Autocracy Divide Revisited," *British Journal of Politics and International Relations* 22(2) (May 2020): 328–346, https://doi.org/10.1177/1369148120908528.

[26] There are exceptions, such as South Korea, where most presidents have either been jailed while in office, or after their term has finished.

[27] Alexandre Debs and H. E. Goemans, "Regime Type, the Fate of Leaders, and War," *American Political Science Review* 104(3) (2010): 430–445, https://doi.org/10.1017/S0003055410000195.

[28] "As Mikhail Gorbachev turns 90, one Russian paper says 'he's the first leader in Russia's thousand-year history who voluntarily stepped down, stayed alive and at liberty.'" Steve Rosenberg, Twitter post (March 2, 2021), 9:22 a.m., https://twitter.com/BBCSteveR/status/1366680400173674500?s=20.

from which he could maintain an element of control and oversight. Granted, the office of the presidency comes with little actual power when compared with the title of CPC general secretary or CMC chairperson. Yet President Xi would keep some control over personnel appointments and officially represent China on state visits. In effect, he would retain a diplomatic and public role as the face of China, even if a great deal of power is shifted to his successor, and especially if there is no change to the status of Xi Jinping Thought as a core ideology. Alternatively, he could keep his position as head of the CMC, a position much more powerful than that of president, albeit without the same ceremonial role or visibility. Deng Xiaoping held the position from 1981 to 1989, and, as mentioned, Jiang Zemin kept this position from 1989 to 2004, in a power play which trimmed the power of his successor, Hu Jintao, who would otherwise have taken over when he became head of the party in 2002.

Xi could spend the period between 2022 and 2027 (or 2032) broadening the anticorruption campaign to fully and finally clean out any actual or would-be political opponents, using their dismissal as an opportunity to install a new generation's worth of cadres loyal to him. While this would not completely remove the possibility of a postretirement purge, it would mitigate it to a significant degree and allow Xi to "rule from behind the curtain," much as Deng Xiaoping played kingmaker well after giving up his final remaining leadership title in 1989.

Xi's cult of personality, small by Mao's standards, could reach new heights, as he looks to elevate his status within the CPC's political and organizational DNA to equal that of Mao. In late 2021, Xi oversaw a new historical resolution, only the third since the CPC's founding a century earlier, praising his "decisive significance" in China's rejuvenation. As Yale University's Milan Svolik writes, "Under established autocracy, the dictator's outward appearance of invincibility is as important as his actual power."[29] While such facades of power can and do collapse, Xi has increased the cost of a potential leadership challenge by imprinting his name and persona on the party's ideological and organizational structure.[30] Just as Xi has insisted on protecting the legacy of Mao Zedong, his successors might be bound to protect him, lest they unravel the foundations of the CPC's power.

---

[29] Milan W. Svolik, *The Politics of Authoritarian Rule* (Cambridge: Cambridge University Press, 2012).

[30] For a good overview of Xi's early efforts on this front, see Susan Shirk, "China in Xi's 'New Era': The Return to Personalistic Rule," *Journal of Democracy* 29(2) (April 2018): 22–36, www.journalofdemocracy.org/articles/china-in-xis-new-era-the-return-to-personalistic-rule/.

But even assuming Xi does retire in 2027 or 2032 – in part or in full – it stands to reason that he would continue to exercise enormous power, as did Deng Xiaoping after 1989. All-powerful leaders do not often voluntarily and fully relinquish power. In the rare case of leaders willingly abdicating, they often play the role of kingmaker, formally or informally.

Scenario Two: Leadership Challenge or Coup

Senior Chinese officials, including Xi himself, have widely spoken of plots to overthrow him and his administration. Many of these plots allegedly date back to the early months of 2012, suggesting that Xi believed that rivals wanted to prevent him from taking over the leadership of the CPC later that year. There are also vague accusations of unnamed "plots" by anonymous "traitors" that appear to justify Xi's shake-up of the party bureaucracy and his wide-reaching intraparty discipline campaigns. In an internal speech published in 2016, Xi spoke of "political plot activities" designed to "wreck and split the Party."[31] That same year, the then-head of the China Securities Regulatory Commission, Liu Shiyu, accused disgraced officials, including Sun Zhengcai and Zhou Yongkang, both of whom lost their positions in Xi-initiated purges, of "[plotting] to usurp the party's leadership and seize state power."[32] Vice President Wang Qishan echoed Liu's remarks, warning that "some [senior officials] even sought to ... seize party and state power."[33]

Of course, fears of political plots and coups are the norm for most authoritarian leaders, just as worries over election challenges are the natural and inevitable concern of politicians in democratic systems. According to Milan Svolik, "an overwhelming majority of dictators lose power to those inside the gates of the presidential palace rather than to the masses. The predominant political conflict in dictatorships appears to be not between the ruling elite and the masses but rather one *among* regime insiders."[34] While coups in one-party communist regimes are infrequent, the fate of authoritarian leaders who are overthrown is typically grim, with 73 percent consigned to death, imprisonment, or exile.[35]

---

[31] Didi Kirsten Tatlow, "In Book, Xi Jinping Taints Ousted Rivals with Talk of Plots," *New York Times* (January 27, 2016), www.nytimes.com/2016/01/28/world/asia/china-xi-jinping-plot.html.

[32] Wendy Wu and Choi Chi-yuk, "Coup Plotters Foiled: Xi Jinping Fended Off Threat to 'Save Communist Party'," *South China Morning Post* (October 19, 2017), www.scmp.com/news/china/policies-politics/article/2116176/coup-plotters-foiled-xi-jinping-fended-threat-save.

[33] Ibid. [34] Svolik, *The Politics of Authoritarian Rule.*

[35] Erica Frantz and Elizabeth A. Stein, "Countering Coups: Leadership Succession Rules in Dictatorships," *Comparative Political Studies* 50(7): 935–962.

Even the most powerful of leaders retain office owing to the support of a coalition of actors and interests. Their backing is conditional and based on shifting domestic and international variables. While the precise conditions of the deals Xi has made with members of the political, economic, and military elite are unknown, a dramatic economic slowdown (such as began in 2022) or the repeated mishandling of international crises would likely make their support more tenuous. Every coalition has a breaking point. This, of course, is why attempted coups are dealt with so severely, to frighten off would-be challengers. As Gambian president Yahya Jammeh warned after a failed coup attempt in 2014: "Anybody who plans to attack this country, be ready, because you are going to die."[36]

That said, successfully organizing a coup against an incumbent leader – especially one in a Leninist one-party state – is a daunting challenge.[37] A would-be coup leader faces numerous barriers. In the first place, they need to gather support from key members of the military and security forces without alerting the incumbent leader and their personal security apparatus. The chances of a coup being mounted against Xi, absent a systemic crisis, are exceedingly small. Given the technological capabilities of the CPC security services, which Xi controls, such an endeavor would be fraught with the risk of detection and the possible defection of early plotters who change their mind. It is true that Xi has a host of enemies in the party. It is equally true that the barriers to organizing against him are nearly insurmountable.

Yale University political scientist Dan Mattingly points to another important reality: Chinese leaders are well aware of possible coup threats and explicitly act to mitigate against such efforts. Utilizing a dataset of more than 10,000 People's Liberation Army (PLA) appointments, Mattingly finds that Xi has overseen personnel rotations within China's military that favor awarding high-level command positions to "officers whose ethnic, class, and ideological backgrounds make them unlikely to back anti-regime protesters."[38] Given that the military would play an outsized role in any coup, Xi's control of official placements in the military would go a long way to stopping a coup attempt before it could even begin.

A continued economic slowdown or the repeated mishandling of international crises – including in the Taiwan Strait – would likely make Xi's

---

[36] Ibid.
[37] Brett Allen Casper and Scott A. Tyson, "Popular Protest and Elite Coordination in a Coup d'État," *Journal of Politics* 76(2) (2014): 548–564, https://doi.org/10.1017/s0022381613001485.
[38] Dan Mattingly, "How the Party Commands the Gun: Coups, Revolts, and the Military in China," *American Journal of Political Science* 68(1) (2024): 227–242.

job of managing his coalition of supporters within the various categories of elites more difficult.

A conventional leadership challenge, which would proceed according to formal legalistic processes, would face similar obstacles to that of a coup. Xi's increasing grip over the domestic security apparatus would make communication among would-be challengers about logistics next to impossible. Despite their enormous power, even senior members of the CPC and the PLA are under constant surveillance.

A challenge could occur seemingly spontaneously at a formal meeting of the Politburo or the full Central Committee. But that would require several officials to be confident that any such move would trigger a cascade of support. Yet until a colleague raises their hand to register their dissent, for all the reasons just listed, it would be impossible to know how many would join the effort to unseat Xi – especially given how no one made an effort to intervene when Hu Jintao was being removed from the Party Congress, and in front of the world's media, in 2022.

Scenario Three: Unexpected Death or Incapacitation

> No one dared bid him prepare for death; none dared to try on the crown in his presence.
>
> Bertram Wolfe, *The Struggle for Soviet Succession*

Even if the CPC's claim that Xi Jinping has no designs to remain in office for life is true, his evisceration of succession norms leaves the country ill prepared in the event of his sudden death or incapacitation. Xi Jinping was sixty-nine years old in 2022. He has been a smoker, is overweight, has a high-stress job, and, according to state media, "finds joy in exhaustion."[39] The year 2035 marks the midway point between the two "hundred-year goals" of achieving moderate prosperity in 2021 (the hundredth anniversary of the founding of the CPC) and becoming a "strong, democratic, civilized, harmonious and modern socialist country" by 2049 (the hundredth anniversary of the founding of the PRC). It is also the year by which a number of Xi's signature programs are due to be completed. He will be eighty-two that year, coincidentally about the same age as Joe Biden was at the end of his first term in the White House.[40]

Rumors about Xi's ill health have swirled for several years, sparked by video footage appearing to show his unsteady gait while meeting foreign

---

[39] David Bandurski, "Busy Bee President Xi," *China Media Project* (October 27, 2014), https://chinamediaproject.org/2014/10/27/busy-busy-president-xi/.

[40] Katsuji Nakazawa, "Xi Jinping Sends Shock Waves with His 2035 Manifesto," *Nikkei Asia* (August 6, 2020), https://asia.nikkei.com/Editor-s-Picks/China-up-close/Xi-Jinping-sends-shock-waves-with-his-2035-manifesto.

leaders.[41] While much about his health is unknown, any severe or terminal illness would initially be treated as a state secret. Yet it wouldn't stay secret for long, given the visibility and demands on a modern leader as opposed to in the time of Mao or Franklin D. Roosevelt. Nonetheless, the authorities tightly control reporting about Xi's health within China and have threatened foreign journalists who write about the issue with the cancellation of their visas.[42] For Xi, projecting vim and vigor are important, as much to keep any potential political challengers at bay as anything else.[43] During the 1991 "August Coup" against Soviet president Mikhail Gorbachev, coup plotters made a public announcement over state radio that Gorbachev was "unable to perform his presidential duty for health reasons," an accusation that Gorbachev would later describe as a "monstrous deception."[44] In the end, of course, the coup failed, but the connection between an autocrat's health and his political security are well established.

Owing to the lack of detail on Xi's health, this chapter will refrain from speculating on any likely cause of death or incapacitation. Likewise, the exact circumstances of a sudden health event, including where Xi might be when it occurs, are too numerous to consider. For the sake of simplicity, this chapter will assume that Xi's death is sudden and unexpected.

What steps would be taken once Xi's death has occurred or is imminent? On paper, at least, the process is straightforward. According to the CPC constitution, only a plenary session of the Central Committee can "elect" the party's general secretary, and only from among the current members of the Politburo Standing Committee. Similarly, the constitution simply states: "Members of the Central Military Commission of the Party are decided on by the Central Committee." For the office of the presidency, the PRC constitution stipulates that the president and vice president are "elected by the National People's Congress."

Thus, assuming the process and institutions work according to plan, in the event of Xi's death, the full CPC Central Committee would be summoned to decide who, among the remaining members of the Politburo Standing Committee, should be elevated to take Xi's position as general secretary and CMC chairman. It is unclear if the National

---

[41] Chun Han Wong, "Xi's Unsteady Steps Revive Worries over Lack of Succession Plan in China," *Wall Street Journal* (April 23, 2019), www.wsj.com/articles/xis-unsteady-steps-revive-worries-over-lack-of-succession-plan-in-china-11556011802-succession-plan-in-china-11556011802.

[42] Private communication from the Beijing bureau chief of a major US newspaper.

[43] Bruce Bueno de Mesquita and Alastair Smith, *The Dictator's Handbook: Why Bad Behaviour Is Almost Always Good Politics* (New York: Public Affairs, 2016), 26.

[44] Mikhail Gorbachev, *The August Coup: The Truth and the Lessons* (New York: HarperPerennial, 1991), 35.

People's Congress would need to convene to formalize the elevation of the vice president, as per the PRC constitution, or if the power would automatically be transferred once the leader's death was certified.

This brief description in the PRC and CPC constitutions are almost certainly inadequate to describe what would happen in reality. In practice, a process of informal consultation and horse trading would determine the choice of a new leader, after which the Central Committee would give its approval. As discussed above, Xi's tenure in office has been enabled by a relatively coherent and stable group of governing and supporting elites; these have a vested interest in maintaining the status quo once he passes away. While Xi's anticorruption campaign has swept aside hundreds of senior officials in both the civil and military establishments, the stability at the top of Xi's government has been striking. His chief ideologue, Wang Huning, moved up to fourth from fifth place in the Politburo Standing Committee. Of his two top foreign policy officials, Yang Jiechi and Foreign Minister Wang Yi, Yang retired from the Politburo in 2022, but Wang was promoted to it. The organizational apparatus of the CPC itself acts as a buffer against instability, with (albeit imperfect) internal mechanisms and procedures in place for managing some of the immediate post-Xi volatility.

In a power vacuum, however, the Politburo could devolve into infighting, a nightmare scenario for the CPC as an institution. Members of Xi's coalition might splinter into different groups backing rival potential successors. Those who had been punished or marginalized by Xi's coalition, meanwhile, might well see his death as a rare opportunity to reassert or even grab power, and thus they too could be vying for control.

As it is impossible to predict how the process would unfold given all the variables, a more practicable undertaking would be to ask: what are externally observable signs of a succession process going smoothly, and what are signs of an emergent leadership split? Signs of irregularity might include:

> The absence of the premier or the vice president from regularly scheduled meetings;
> Changes to the scheduling of state-run TV news broadcasts, radio programs, and the morning editions of the major national and metropolitan newspapers;
> Sudden internet outages and disruptions to social media. Owing to its popularity, WeChat in particular might experience "technical difficulties" or, conversely, be an important channel for the opposition if a power struggle breaks out;

- Inexplicable disruptions of flight and rail schedules at major Chinese airports and train stations; and
- Competing or contrasting narratives emerging from various organs of the central government, in the official media, or on the internet – and remaining there.

There is another important scenario to consider: that of health-related incapacitation (e.g., stroke, heart attack). Unlike a leader's death, incapacitation forces the system into a political purgatory of indeterminate length. In such unpredictable circumstances, regime supporters and detractors alike may have to hedge between the recovery of the leader, or his or her expiry, which in turn produces further instability.

In the case of Stalin, it took nearly five full days for him to finally succumb to the debilitating stroke he suffered on March 1, 1953. In the intervening days, various groupings of high-ranking Soviet officials plotted against one another as they contemplated the potential shape of a post-Stalin era. As Khrushchev later recalled, Lavrentiy Beria, the feared head of the secret police, cursed Stalin as his condition worsened, but when signs of recovery emerged, "Beria threw himself on his knees, seized Stalin's hand, and started kissing it."[45] It is worth remembering that the comedy movie inspired by the former Soviet leader's passing, *The Death of Stalin*, was only funny because the actual events surrounding his death were so farcical.[46]

But what would happen if Xi died "in installments," as someone remarked about Stalin, and was incapacitated while in office? According to the PRC constitution, the vice president can assume the powers of the president "when so entrusted by the president." Obviously, this creates a dilemma if the president is suddenly stricken and unable or unwilling to assent to such a move. Nonetheless, at least for the office of the presidency, it can be assumed that the vice president would be the natural choice to temporarily assume these powers. Similarly, Article 84 of the constitution stipulates: "In the event that the office of president of the People's Republic of China becomes vacant the vice president shall succeed to the office of president."

But there are, of course, degrees of incapacitation. While Stalin took only a few days to die, Leonard Brezhnev atrophied for years before passing away, dragging down the capacity of the government with him. The same applies to Mao Zedong, who was seriously ill for years

---

[45] Quoted in Joshua Rubenstein, *The Last Days of Stalin* (New Haven, CT: Yale University Press, 2016).

[46] *The Death of Stalin*, directed by Armando Iannucci (2018; Quad Productions).

before his death. In the case of a lengthy illness in China, the problem is what constitutes the presidency being "vacant." Does this only pertain to a full and final departure from office? Or would a temporary incapacitation render the president "vacant" from their office?

And what of the more consequential offices of general secretary and CMC chairperson? Here there is far less certainty. There exist no publicly known procedures or legal regulations governing such a situation. Even more than an untimely death, incapacitation – in the absence of a clear and empowered successor – would be dangerous for the party, as it would slowly unravel the status quo and allow for new factional jostling, alignments, and splits. Top party leaders who owe their positions directly to Xi, such as Cai Qi, currently the top party official in Beijing and, as of 2022, the fifth-ranked member of the Politburo Standing Committee, would be vulnerable. This was a problem for both Hua Guofeng and Jiang Qing ("Madame Mao"); outside of their connection to Mao Zedong, neither had an independent support base in the party or the military. Without Mao, they were exposed. At the same time, the positions within the CPC hierarchy that hold enormous power, such as head of the party's personnel and anticorruption departments, could come into play. Without an active CMC chair, the military itself could take on a more independent political role. In the case of Mao, the Central Bodyguard Bureau played a pivotal role in the arrest by the reformist faction of Jiang Qing and the three other members of the "Gang of Four." It is hard to imagine such drama inside the walls of Zhongnanhai in the twenty-first century. Nonetheless, there is no road map for the ruling party should Xi fall seriously ill.

Conclusion

The three scenarios above are not offered as precise or exhaustive blueprints for China's future. Many other scenarios are possible, including Xi's voluntary retirement in 2035. Instead, this study's aim is to point to genuine problems in China's political trajectory under Xi Jinping, most notably the likelihood of a peaceful and predictable transfer of power. For decades after Mao's death in 1976, the country's political system seemed increasingly stable, the occasional outbreak of top-level turmoil notwithstanding. Today, however, China's political path is shrouded in great uncertainty. While the topic of leadership succession is not something Chinese officials are willing to discuss in public, the world has a huge stake in how China deals with this increasingly pressing challenge. Much commentary now focuses on the instability triggered by Xi's assertive leadership. A sudden or prolonged power vacuum in China could be equally destabilizing, for China and, given the country's size, much of the rest of the world as well.

Index

A4 protests. *See* white paper protests
ACG subculture (Animation, Cartoons, and Games)
   and online patriotism, 124
activism
   cultural, 265
   nationalistic, 265
   online, 265, 266
   political, 265
Adaptive State Capitalism, 17
Ai Siqi (Li Shengxuan), 51
Alibaba Group, 16, 192, 224, 226
   and party study app, 14
All-China Federation of Industry and Commerce (ACFIC), 179, 191
   and United Front, 179, 180
   composition of, 180
All-China Women's Federation, 134
April Huawen Syndicate, 109
April Media, 109
Arab Spring, 126
Asian Infrastructure Investment Bank, 202

Barmé, Geremie, 69, 266
Beijing Olympics, 108, 126
Belt and Road Initiative (BRI), 165, 195
Beria, Lavrentiy, 328
Biden administration
   attacks on autocracy, 39
Bo Xilai, 296
Bo Yibo, 296
Brief History of the CPC, A, 161
business associations, 180, 190

Cai Qi, 329
Cai Xia, 317
Caixin, 122
campaigns
   Anti-Confucianism Campaign, 296
   Anti-Rightist Campaign, 58, 278
   Hundred Flowers Campaign, 58
   Patriotic Education Campaign, 104
   Sweep Away Black and Eliminate Evil, Campaign to (2018–2020), 6
censorship, 122, 265
   methods for avoiding, 118
   whitelist scheme, 122
Central Academy of Fine Arts, 65
Central Commission for Comprehensive Deepening of Reform, 11
Central Commission for Cybersecurity and Informatization (CCCI), 216
   membership and heads, 216
Central Commission for Disciplinary Inspection (CCDI), 141
   Xi Jinping's 2013 address to, 148
Central Commission for Discipline Inspection (CCDI), 212
Central Committee, 10
   General Office of, 10
Central Discipline Inspection Commission, 12
Central Discipline Inspection Committee, 11
Central Military Commission (CMC), 21, 216, 313
Central Military Commission's Chairman Responsibility System (CMCCRS), 291, 299, 301, 305
   and Deng Xiaoping, 305
   enhancement of, 305
   Supreme Joint Command Center, 306
Central Organization Department, 210
Central Party School, 6, 167
Central Political-Legal Commission, 216
Central Propaganda Department, 216
Cheek, Timothy, 49, 54, 70
Chen Boda (Chen Jianxiang), 51
Chen Duxiu, 52
Chen Jiangxiang. *See* Chen Boda
Chen Kaige, 104
Chen Ping, 112
Chen Yun, 169

Index

Chen, Jie, 186
Chengwei Capital, 108, 109, 111, 112
Chenxiaotao (manga artist)
  depictions of Wuhan and Tianjin, 135–136
Cheung Kong Graduate School of Business, 188
China Academy for Information and Communication Technologies (CAICT), 219
China Association for Promoting Democracy, 183
China Association of Promoting Democracy (CAPD), 182
China Central Television (CCTV), 114, 121, 124, 132, 135, 295, 307
China Democratic Construction Association (CDCA), 182, 183, 184
  member expectations, 184
China Democratic League (CDL), 182, 183
China Dream, 24, 26, 34, 40, 86, 157, 158
China Europe International Business School, 188
China Federation of Literary and Art Circles, 106
China Film Association, 102
China Huarong Asset Management, 199
China Information Technology Security Evaluation Center (CNITSEC), 218
China Mobile, 209
China Red, 95
China Women's News, 134
China Zhi Gong Party (CZGP), 182
Chinese General Social Survey, 259
Chinese nation
  definition, 28
  pan-Chinese nature of, 28
  three-tiered formation of, 28
Chinese Peasants' and Workers' Democratic Party (CPWDP), 182
Chinese People's Political Consultative Committee. *See* National People's Congress
citizen journalists, 117
class struggle, 24, 37
  end of, 4
  language of, 5
classes, 28–30
  and ideological consistency, 30
  post-1956 reclassification of, 29
  shift from working class to middle class, 29
  two-class scheme, current, 29
coercion, 18–21

Comintern, 47
Commission for Disciplinary Inspection (CDIs), local, 141
  targeting of local officials, 144
Communist Manifesto, 26, 160
Communist Party of China
  administrative capabilities and policy responsiveness, 17–18
  and "spiritual genealogy", 13
  and 2008–2009 Global Financial Crisis, 17
  and central inspections, 165
  and dissent, 21, 263, 264
  and extrajudicial detention, 12
  and Key Opinion Leaders (KOLs), 9, 87, 113, 115, 123, 124
  and minor political parties, 183
  and monopoly on political power, 2
  and PLA, 21–22
  and public discourse, 5
  and three periods of party history, 3
  and traditional Chinese culture, 7
  antagonism toward the West, 166
  as revolutionary party, 2
  cadre education, 14
  ceremonies and ritual, 162
  class-based or nationalist, 24–41
  cohesion and unity, efforts to maintain, 14, 140, 158
  disciplinary measures, history of, 141
  discipline of party members, 12, 140
  ideology, 3
  intraparty democracy, 148
  legitimacy, 4, 24, 39, 171
  longevity, 1, 2, 115
  noneconomic achievements, 165
  official party history, 3
  organization, 9–16
  three key departments. *See* Publicity Department, Organization Department, United Front Work Department
  transition to communism, 3
Communist Party of the Soviet Union (CPSU), 148
  and *Glasnost*, 140
  in late 1980s, 140
Communist Youth League, 11, 110, 134, 162, 182
Confucius, 72
  and language, 5
Constitution of the People's Republic of China (1954), 27, 28
  post 1988 amendments, 28

Index

Constitution of the People's Republic of China (1982), 31, 177
  1999 amendment, 177
co-optation, 15–16
Corporate Social Credit System, 222
corruption, 12–13
Covid-19
  and censorship, 137–138
  and lab leak theory, 132, 167
  and State Council White Paper, 116, 128
Cultural Revolution
  and definition of, 29
  and exegetical bonding, 55
  and extreme leftism, 25
  and Maoism, 60
  and United Front Work Department, 278
  Mao Zedong, popularity during, 59
  Maoist personality cult during, 318
  party discipline during, 169
  private ownership after, 177
  slogans, 267
Cybersecurity Law (CSL), 221
cyberspace, 215. *See also* Golden Shield project
  and "new productive forces", 224
  institutional control, 217, 266
  National Cybersecurity Strategy, 220
  Strategy for International Cooperation in Cyberspace, 220
Cyberspace Administration of China (CAC), 122, 217
  and Ministry of Public Security, 218
  Provisions on Promoting and Regulating Cross-Border Data Flows, 221
  regulatory role, 217

Dalai Lama, 274
danwei system, 270
  and Reform and Opening-up, 270
Dapiran, Antony, 284
Data Security Law (DSL), 221
  and state agencies, 222
  extraterritorial juristriction, 222
Davies, Gloria, 56
Debs, Alexandre, 321
democracy
  and economic liberalization, 174
  classical theories of, 174
Deng Liqun, 149
Deng Xiaoping, 82, 200
  and class structure, 30
  and leadership succession, 311, 315
  and Mao Zedong Thought, 44, 51
  and World Bank, 207
  as CMC chairperson, 322
  as kingmaker, 322
  criticisms of, 158
  departure from Mao's ideology, 6, 158
  politics in command, opposition to, 247
  post-1989 power, 323
  reform and opening-up, 24, 201
  southern tour, 25, 202, 250
  term limits, 313
Deng Xiaoping Theory, 86
Diary of Fang Fang, The, 116
Dickson, Bruce, 186, 311
Didi, 193, 226
digital surveillance, 21
Dikötter, Frank
  Tragedy of Liberation, The, 277
Ding Ling, 54
Ding Xuexiang, 319, 320
Ding Yijiang, 315
Dirlik, Arif, 49
dissenters
  types, 265
dissidents
  types, 266
dossiers, 12
Douyin, 9
Du Qiang, 110

East Turkistan Foundation, 271
economic development, 1, 24, 175
  and performance based legitimacy, 159
  and private entrepreneurs, 176
  and relation between party and private sector, 176
economy, planned
  during Mao era, 30
Engels, Friedrich
  and "three laws of dialectics", 36–37
  and Maoism, 36

Falun Gong, 19, 20, 273, 274
  and Residents' Committees, 280
  crackdown (1999), 280
  Hong Kong, activities in, 280
  surveillance, 273, 281
Fan Changlong, 305
Fang Fang
  perceived threat to state authority, 129
  Wuheqilin's statirical image of, 130
Fang Fang, The Diary of, 129
  accusations of antigovernment stance, 129
  and official media account use of the term "diary", 134–135
  censorship of, 129
  Global Time criticism of, 131

Index

Fang Fang, The Diary of (cont.)
   translation and publication, 130
   Wuhan Covid lockdown, 129
Federation of Commerce and Industry, 11
Federation of Industry and Commerce, 181
Feng Bo, 112
fifty-cent army, 9, 118, 123, 127
first stage of socialism, 42
Fort Detrick, 132
Fortune Global 500 ranking
   Chinese state-owned companies, 17
Foster, Kenneth W., 180
Fu Hualing, 287

Glasnost
   contemporary views of, 6
   Xi Jinping's views on, 140
Global Times, 109, 131, 316
   petition for WHO investigation of US Fort Derick military base, 132
Goemans, H. E., 321
Gokturk, Hamut, 271
Golden Shield project, 266
   and Falun Gong, 281
Gorbachev, Mikhail, 326
   August Coup (1991), 326
Gourevitch, Peter, 200
Great Cannon, 266
Great Leap Forward, 3, 23, 69
Guancha Syndicate, 131
Guo Boxiong, 299

Han Dayuan, 316
harmonious society, 255
Harpre Ke, 111
Heberer, Thomas, 190
Heilmann, Sebastian, 197
Hong Kong, 263
   Fugitive Law (2019), 283
   integration with, 26
   National Security Law (2020), 284
   National Security Legislative Provisions Bill (2003), 282
   patriotic education in, 282, 283
   protests, 167
Hsia Chang, Maria, 281
Hu Chunhua, 316
Hu Jintao, 167
   "grid management system", 233
   and harmonious society, 26
   and leadership succession, 315
   and nationalism, 26
   and scientific outlook on development, 32
Hu Xijin, 109, 112

Hu Yaobang, 57, 311, 321
Hua Chunying, 128
Hua Guofeng, 82, 155, 200, 329
   and leadership succession, 311
   Deng Xiaoping's criticisms of, 154
Huang Daoxuan, 54
Huawei, 95
human rights lawyers, 287

information and communication technology (ICT), 214
   14th Five-Year Plan for National Informatization (14th FYPNI), 235, 237
   and "smart governance", 226
   and economic growth, 214
   and political control, 230
   and public databases, 228
   and social security, 227
   and surveillance, 267
   export controls, US government, 237, 238, 240, 241
   semiconductors, 237
   surveillance, 232, 234
Integrated Joint Operations Platform (IJOP), 233
internet. *See* media and social media; *see also* information and communication technology (ICT); cyberspace
Internet News Management Office, 117

Ji, Yingying, 190
Jiang Bingzhi. *See* Jiang Bingzhi
Jiang Qing, 60, 82, 150, 155, 296, 329
   theatrical works, 103
Jiang Wen, 104
Jiang Zemin, 6, 33, 202
   and "new social class" concept, 285
   and change of party identity, 26
   and class structure, 30, 31, 32
   and Falun Gong, 280
   and leadership succession, 315
   party identity under, 31
   SEO policies, 209
Jiangxi Soviet, 48
Jin Canrong, 110
Jiusan Society (JS), 182
Journey to the West, The, 5

Kadeer, Rebiya, 274
   media attention), 275
   The 10 Conditions of Love (film), 274
Kang Sheng, 51
Kokolevskiy, Vladislav Yuryevich, 113
Korean War, 296

Index

Lai Xiaomin, 199
Land Reform movement (1946–1952), 28
language
    and party ideology, 6
    and linguistic engineering, 6
    and party ideology, 6
    Confucian concepts of, 5
    in the Mao era, 5
Leading Small Group on Comprehensively Deepening Reform, 146
Leninism
    democratic centralism, Leninist principle of, 10
    power and social institutions, notion of, 15
Li Hongzhong, 319
Li Keqiang, 216, 318
Li Lisan, 52
Li Qiang, 320
Li Rongrong, 210, 211
Li Ruihuan, 314
Li Shangfu, 298
Li Shengxuan. *See* Ai Siqi
Li Shulei, 170
Li Su, 110
Li Wenliang
    Covid, punishment as whistleblower, 136
    Weibo account and commemoration, 137
Li Xuezheng, 107
Li Yi, 110
Li, Eric X., 107, 108, 111, 112
Liberation Army Daily, 62
Lin Biao, 68, 81, 155, 306
    and leadership succession, 311
    and Mao Zedong Thought, 62
    and Maoism, 60
    and symbolic capital, 59
    as Minister of Defense, 59
Lin Chao
    and *Year Hare Affair*, 124
linguistic engineering, 5
    in Imperial China, 72–76
    in Mao Era, 76–81
    in Reform Era, 82–90
little pinks. *See* patriotism, online
Little Red Book, 61–64. *See Quotations from Chairman Mao*
Liu Chunhua, 66
    Chairman Mao Goes to Anyuan (1967 oil painting), 66, 67
Liu Huaqing, 296
Liu Huijun, 272
Liu Shaoqi, 59, 67
    as potential successor to Mao, 311
Liu Xiaobo, 266
Long March, 304
Luo Gongliu, 61, 65
    Chairman Mao Making a Report on the Rectification Movement (1951 oil painting), 66

Ma Ning, 111
Ma, Jack, 192
Macau
    integration with, 26
MacFarquhar, Roderick, 56
Madame Mao. *See* Jiang Qing
mandate of heaven, 18
Mao Daolin, 108
Mao Zedong. *See also Quotation from Chairman Mao*
    "On Contradiction" (1937), 49
    "Analysis of the Classes in Chinese Society" (1926), 48
    "On New Domocracy" (1940), 49
    "On Practice" (1937), 49
    "On Protracted War" (1938), 49
    "On the New Stage" (1938), 50
    "Report on an Investigation of the Peasant Movement in Hunan" (1927), 49
    "Xingguo Investigation" (1930), 48
    and Bolshevism, 5, 47
    and class struggle, 4
    and party discipline, 141
    and the "four olds", 7
    and United Front Work Department, 277
    as editor, 53
    as icon, 59
    Marxism, early readings, 47
    modern significance, 5
    mythic aspects, 4
    portrait in Tiananmen Square, 4
    Sinification of Marxism, 50, 51
Mao Zedong Thought, 43, 44, 45, 46, 50, 55, 56, 59, 70, 86, 177
    adaptability, 51
    and mass mobilization, 103
    and praxis, 45–46, 49–52
    and Wang Ming, 52
    as irrefutable wisdom, 59
    contemporary relevance, 4, 71
    origins, 44, 46–50
    reevaluation under Deng Xiaoping, 154
    Sinification of Marxism, 50–51
    Xi Jinping's definition of, 42
Marx, Karl, 40
Marxism
    and class conflict, 40

Marxism (cont.)
  as "empty signifier", 4
Marxism-Leninism, 177
Marxist-Leninist ideology, 4
  party interpretation of, 4
McGregor, Richard, 264, 280
media and social media, 9
  and manufacturing consent, 115
  commercial and professional, 117
Meituan, 226
Mencius, 97
Meng Wanzhou, 95, 167
Ministry for Industry and Information Technology (MIIT), 218, 221
Ministry of Finance, 210, 216, 222
Ministry of Foreign Affairs, 219
Ministry of Industry and Information Technology, 216
Ministry of Public Security (MPS), 216, 218, 230
  and social media, 134
Ministry of Science and Technology, 216
Ministry of State Security, 19, 218
Moore, Barrington, 174
Moravia, Alberto
  Red Book and the Great Wall An Impression of Mao's China, The (1967), 64
Museum of the Communist Party of China, 163

National Development and Reform Commission, 217
National Flag Act (1990), 31
National Information Security Standardization Technical Committee (TC260), 219
National People's Congress, 11, 15, 181
  official reports, rise in since 2012, 151
National Radio and Television Administration, 101
National Security Commission, 11
National Security Law, 229
National Stadium, 163
National State-Owned Assets Administration Bureau, 206
nationalism, 4, 28, *See also* red nationalism
  and "the people", 27–33
  and Chinese terms for nation, 27
  and class, 25–41
  and party doctrines, 4
  and traditional Chinese culture, 34–36
  cultural nationalism, 8, 37
nationalists, cultural
  and Confucianism, 37–38

  criticisms of Marxism, 38
Naughton, Barry, 199
Neighborhood Committees. *See* Residents' Committees
New Houses New Policy, 249
New Rural Pension Scheme, 259
new social class
  and United Front Work Department, 286
  definition, 285
Non-Governmental Organizations (NGOs), 263
  crackdown on, post-2008, 287
Notice on an Enhanced Response to Public Discourse on Governance Affairs in Transparent Governance Work, 119

"Office 610", 19
Ōkita Saburo, 201
On Promoting the Sound and Orderly Development of Government New Media, 122
Organization Department, 9, 11, 183

Party Research Office, 6
patriotism
  and China's cultural heritage, 8
patriotism, online
  and ACG subculture, 125
  and fan club culture, 126
  and Key Opinion Leaders (KOLs), 133, 139
  and new patriotism, 126
  and participatory cencorship, 133
  little pinks, 9, 126
  symbiotic relationships between online groups, 127
Pei, Minxin, 175, 178, 199
Peking University, 147
Peng Dehuai, 23, 59, 306
People's Armed Police, 18, 298, 308
people's commune movement
  economic failure, 3
People's Congresses, 190, 191
People's Daily, 109, 121, 132, 135, 138, 155, 167, 168
People's Liberation Army, 18, 60
  and Central Military Commission, 295
  and Politburo, 294
  as professional army, 292
  Central Organizational Department (COD), 298
  corruption, 298, 299
  Deng Xiaoping, control under, 297
  divergent interests with party, 293
  domestic affairs, reduced role in, 293

Index

General Armaments Department, 307
General Cadre Department, 298
General Logistical Department, 307
General Political Affairs Department, 307
General Staff Department, 307
  Jiang Zemin, control under, 295, 297
  Overall Program to Deepen National Defense and Military Reforms (2015), 295
  reforms under Xi, 304, 305
  relationship with party, 21–22, 290, 291
  Xi Jinping, tightened control under, 291
People's Political Consultative Conferences, 190, 191
Perry, Elizabeth J., 197
Personal Information Protection Law (PIPL), 221, 229
Policy Research Office, 11
Politburo, 10, 314
Politburo Standing Committee, 10, 22, 146, 216, 295, 314, 319, 326, 327, 329
  member's annual work report, 146
Political and Legal Affairs Commission, 308
primary stage of socialism, 26
private enterprise
  and Jiang Zemin's three represents, 178
  and minor political parties, 182, 183
  and Party School system, 178
  as advanced productive force, 178
  concerns with party presence, 185
  democracy, attitudes to, 187
  ideological barriers to, 177
  party cells in, 184
  party membership, 182
  policy influence, 189
  political partiicipation, 184
  reliance on the state, 178
  support for party, 185–186
Private Enterprises Association (PEA), 179
private ownership
  reintroduction of, 177
propaganda
  digital, 115
Propaganda Department. *See* Publicity Department
Publicity Department, 6, 9, 11
  evolution of, 9
Putin, Vladimir
  and leadership succession, 321

Qiao Shi, 314
Qu Qiubai, 52
Quotations from Chairman Mao, 61

Rao Jin, 107, 108, 112
Rectification Movement, 276
Rectification of Names, 72–73
red culture, 43
Red Guards, 64, 65
  destruction of cultural artifacts, 7
red nationalism, 8
reeducation camps, 20
reform and opening-up, 3, 24, 29, 34, 175
Regulations on Disciplinary Actions
  2015 and 2018 revisions to, 148
Regulations on the Selection of Party and Government Leading Cadres
  2014 and 2019 revisions of, 151
Residents' Committees
  and surveillance, 268, 269
  Law Governing the Organizing of the Residents' Committees, 271
Resolution on Certain Issues in the History of Our Party (1945), 153, 155
Resolution on Certain Questions in the History of Our Party since the Founding of the People's Republic of China (1981), 68, 152, 154
  and legitimizing Deng's reforms, 154
  and Mao's errors, 155
  neo-Maoist post-1990 questioning of, 154
Resolution on the Major Achievements and Historical Experience of the Party over the Past Century (2021), 154–157, 166, 167
  and Dengist period, 3
  and Maoist period, 3
  and post-1957 errors, 161
  and Western bullying, 167
  and Xi Jinping era, 3
  overview, 3
  praise of Xi's leadership, 155
  reform and opening up, view of, 3
  villains, lack of specific, 155
Revolutionary Committee of the Chinese Kuomingtang (RCCK), 182
Revolutionary Symbolic Capital, 44–45, 52–55, 60–61
  and legitimation of the party in Reform Era, 68–71
  and Little Red Book, 61–62
  and performative loyalty, 62–64
  Mythologizing Mao, 65–69
  Reform Era, 64

Revolutionary Symbolic Capital (cont.)
  revived by Lin Biao, 59–65
  the Maoist legacy in the Reform Era, 65
revolutions, color, 8

Safe Cities, 267
Saich, Tony, 47, 52, 53, 54
Sakisaka Masao, 201
Sang Ye, 266
Schram, Stuart, 50
Schubert, Gunter, 190
Schumpeter, Joseph, 174
Self-Employed Laborers Association (SELA), 179
  and local government, 180
Shanghai Academy of Social Sciences, 112
Shanghai Massacre, 47
Shanghai Municipal People's Government Weibo account, 120
Sichuan earthquake, 117
Sima Nan, 110
Sitong Bridge incident, 19
Skynet, 267
Sneevliet, Henk, 47
Social Credit System, 228
social media
  and China as Hare meme, 124–125
  and collective memory, 128
  and state control of narrative, 117
social media platforms. *See also* WeChat, Weibo, Douyin
  Bilibili, 113, 114, 124
  Sina, 117
  Sohu, 117
social policy, 242
  and political legitimacy, 242
  and political outcomes, 244
  and political resentment, 246
  education, 248
  healthcare, 248
  housing, 247
  minimum living standard guarantee system, 253
  people's livelihood policy, 243
  reform era (1978–1991), 247
socialism with Chinese characteristics, 3, 4, 34, 43
Socialist Education Movement, 55
Southern Weekly, 110
Stalin, Joseph, 153
  History of the Communist Party of the Soviet Union (Bolsheviks) a Short Course, 153
Stalinist period
  horrors of, 6

Standing Committee. *See* Politburo Standing Committee
State Council, 18, 145
State Emblem Act (1991), 31
State Ethnic Affairs Commission (SEAC)
  and United Front Work Department, 278
state media
  and corrective collective memory, 133
State Military Commission (SMC), 303
State-owned Assets Supervision and Administration Commission (SASAC), 210
state-owned enterprises (SOEs), 11, 145, 169
  2015 reforms, 147
  and Chinese economy, 194
  and corruption, 199
  and Special Economic Zones, 201
  and state capitalism, 197
  and World Bank, 207–208
  and WTO, 208
  capital investment, 195
  international role, 195, 201, 204
  Japanese influence on, 205
  profitability, 195
  reform, 205
  reforms to, 200
  Singapore's Temasek model, 211–212
  transfer of SOE executives to government positions under Xi Jinping, 152
  Xi Jinping, changes under, 203
Sun Zhengcai, 316
  punishment for violation of discipline, 143
surveillance state
  and Residents' Committees, 269
  informants, 271
  overseas surveillance, 273
surveillance state
  and *danwei*, 269–270
  history, 268
  monitoring of groups in Australia, 275–276
  Xinjiang, 282
Sustainable Development Goals, 256
Svolik, Milan, 322

Taiwan Democratic Self-Government League (TDWGL), 182
Taiwan independence, 273
Taiwan, reunification with, 26
Targeted Poverty Alleviation, 256
Tencent, 224
terminology. *See* language
Three Represents, The, 6, 32, 159, 177

Index

and private enterprise, 182
Tiananmen Incident (1976), 265
Tiananmen Square protests, 18
  aftermath of, 25
  and rise of neoconservatives, 201
  and subsequent focus on nationalism, 157
  effects on diplomacy, 201
Tianjin explosion, 117
Tibet, 263, 264, 273, 280
TikTok. *See* Douyin
Tomlinson, John, 265
Trade Unions, 182
Tsai, Kellee S., 175, 186

Ukraine, Russian invasion of, 133
Umbrella Movement, 283
United Front Work Department, 10, 11, 15–16, 183, 263, 264, 265
  and elites, 277
  and minor political parties, 184
  and party loyalty, 279
  and private enterprise, 15–16
  Chinese Communist Party's United Front Regulations (2015), 279
  history, 276
  Rightists, rehabilitation of, 278
  strengtheningduring Xi era, 279
United Front, First, 47
universities
  party oversight of, 147
Uyghurs. *See* Xinjiang

Voitinsky, Grigori, 47

Wagner, Martin, 55
Wang Fang. *See* Fang Fang
Wang Huning, 158, 161, 327
Wang Ming, 52, 53, 153, 155
  as rightist, 53
Wang Qishan, 151, 323, 329
Wang Shiwei, 54, 276
Wang Sidao. *See* Wang Shiwei
Wang Yi, 327
Wang Yuhua, 312
Weber, Isabella, 196
WeChat, 9, 122, 230
Weibo, 9
  algorithm adjustment in 2022, 134
  and Covid-related topics, 133
  and *Guideline on Developing a More Civilized and Well-Regulated Cyberspace*, 134
  and patriotic individuals, 115
  and whitelist scheme, 122

and Xinhua News Agency matrix, 121
  government accounts, 118, 120
  Weibo Trending Topics account, 134
Wenzhou high-speed train collision, 117
white paper protests, 19, 234
Wolf Warrior, 8
Wolf Warriors, 65
Women's Federation, 11, 181, 182
World Bank, 17
World Health Organization (WHO), 132
World Trade Organization (WTO), 17, 196, 202
World Uyghur Congress, 273
World War II, 25
Wu Jinglian, 199
Wuheqilin, vii, 137, 138
  and Australian soldier and Afghan child image, 125
  and Fang Fang, 130
  and *Guancha Syndicate*, 131
  and influence on youth culture, 125
  and social media following, 125

Xi Jinping, 26, 42
  "Advancing research on the history of Chinese civilization, and developing a keener awareness of history while building up cultural confidence" (2022), 7
  2013 speech "Carry on the Enduring Spirit of Mao Zedong Thought", 42
  2018 address, 165
  address to the CPC Central Committee (2014), 13, 142
  and, 140
  and "Internet Army", 118
  and "people-centered philosophy of development", 33
  and "top-level design", 11
  and focus on "struggle", 167–168
  and historical revisionism, 161
  and Mao Zedong Thought, 43, 45–46, 52
  and national rejuvenation, 7, 141, 157, 168
  and nationalism, 26
  and the "Two Establishes", 161
  and the propaganda matrix, 116
  and traditional Chinese culture, 34, 35
  anticorruption campaigns, 13, 22, 142, 157, 317, 322, 327
  centralized personnel control under, 151
  discipline system, 8
  discourse system, 7
  dissenting views, crackdowns on, 143
  Eight-point Regulations, 286
  eliminating political rivals, 157

Xi Jinping (cont.)
   first term (2012–17), 140, 141
   focus on "struggle", 167
   Governance of China, The (2014), 64
   intraparty democracy, criticisms of, 150
   intraparty elections, diminishing dissent in under, 152
   Leading Small Group for Comprehensively Deepening Reform, 120
   leading small groups, 11
   mass line campaign, 119
   motivational spirits of the party, 166
   Neo-Maoist Strategy for Party Cohesion, 173
   party discipline, changing views of, 141
   party discipline, crackdowns on, 144
   personal loyalty to, 22
   personalization of power, 10, 22
   personnel management initiatives under, 152
   Politburo, changing roles under Xi, 147
   Putin, friendship with, 173
   strengthening of institutional practices, 145
   successorship issues. *See* Xi Jinping leadership succession scenarios
   third term (2022–27), 23
Xi Jinping leadership succession scenarios, 310
   Brezhnev, comparisons to, 328
   constitutional stipulations in case of presidential vacancy, 328
   coup, 312, 323–325
   death or incapacitation, sudden, 320, 325–329
   death or Xi Jinping leadership succession scenarios, sudden, 312
   domestic instability, 312
   dynastic power struggles, historical incidence of, 312
   health issues, Xi's, 325
   incapacitation, 312
   leadership challenge, 312, 323–325
   leadership consolidation under Xi, historical overview of, 316–319
   leadership succession, historical overview of pre-Xi period, 313–316
   Mao, comparisons to, 329
   retirement, 320–323
   Stalin, comparisons to, 320, 328
   succession crisis, global impacts of, 312
   term limits, historical background, 313
   Xi loyalists, current leadership as, 312
Xi Jinping Thought, 64, 146

   research centers dedicated to, 8
Xiao Yang, 149
Xiao Yi, 144
Xiaomi, 185
Xiaomi Corporation
   party committees in, 184
Xinhua News Agency
   editorial on ceremonies, 163
Xinjiang, 263, 280
   and United Front Work Department, 279
   detention camps, 20
   digital surveillance, 233
   party disciplinary enforcement in, 144
   protests, 19
   surveillance, 271, 272
   terrorist attacks, 19–20
   Urumqi Railway Station bombing, 20
   Uyghur expatriate community, 273
Xu Caihou, 299
Xu Jizhou, 105
Xunzi, 18, 245

Yan Jiaqi, 314
Yan'an Rectification, 52
   and exegetical bonding, 53–55
   and revolutionary symbolic capital, 52–55
   Mao's ideological campaign during, 153
Yang Baibing, 297
Yang Guobin, 265
Yang Jiechi, 327
Yang Shangkun, 297
Yang Weimin, 285, 286
Yang, Mayfair, 188
Yao Zengke, 151
Yin Hong, 102, 103, 106
YouKu, 108
Young Pioneers, 162
Yu Fei, 105

zero-Covid policy, 173
   and censorship, 116
   and collective memories, 136
   protests, 19
Zhang Chunqiao, 56
Zhang Guotao, 296
Zhang Tiesheng, 149
Zhang Weiwei, 112
Zhang Wentian, 51
Zhang Yimou, 104
Zhang Yuntao, 265
Zhang Zhehan, 106, 107
Zhao Ziyang, 311, 321
Zheng Wang, 98
Zhu Jiamu, 169
Zhu Rongji, 198

For EU product safety concerns, contact us at Calle de José Abascal, 56–1°, 28003 Madrid, Spain or eugpsr@cambridge.org.

www.ingramcontent.com/pod-product-compliance
Ingram Content Group UK Ltd.
Pitfield, Milton Keynes, MK11 3LW, UK
UKHW020355260326
469371UK00021B/658